Oracle

For Beginners

Second Edition

Oracle

For Beginners

Second Edition

Sharanam Shah
Vaishali Shah

THE X TEAM

SHROFF PUBLISHERS & DISTRIBUTORS PVT. LTD.
Navi Mumbai

Oracle For Beginners, Second Edition
by Sharanam Shah and Vaishali Shah

Second Edition: March 2025

ISBN : 978-93-5542-715-1

Printed at Gapmeta Ventures Pvt. Ltd., Navi Mumbai • Published by Shroff Publishers and Distributors Pvt. Ltd. B-103, Railway Commercial Complex, Sector 3, Sanpada (E), Navi Mumbai 400705 • Tel: (91 22) 4158 4158 WhatsApp +91 7304487700 4158 4141 • E-mail: spdorders@shroffpublishers.com • URL: www.shroffpublishers.com

Preface

Welcome to **Oracle For Beginners**! Thank you for picking up this practical book focused squarely on Oracle's version of SQL. This edition has been significantly updated to cover the latest advancements, including Oracle 23 AI.

I dedicate this book to:

- My wife [also a co-author to this book] who has always encouraged me whenever I thought that I'd never get a manuscript ready for publishing. Vaishali has supported me every step of the way through my career in the world of software, and I thank her deeply.
- My kids, Janya and Dhrish, for tolerating so well the diversion of my attention from them to writing books.

About This Book

Many people entering the world of commercial application development prefer using a tried and tested, robust, production-strength database. Oracle is one such database and is considered the world's largest selling RDBMS product.

Oracle is constantly undergoing change and evolving. This book covers Oracle 9i, 10g, 11g, 12c, and now, significantly expands into the realm of Oracle 23 AI, including most of its latest enhancements.

The motivation behind writing this book comes from our own experiences of learning how to use the Oracle database and Oracle's implementation of the SQL language. We've tried to use our extensive application development experience in Oracle to produce this book that should cover most of the areas that seem to puzzle developers and database users from time to time in their application development career.

This book provides everything you need to know to become a master in Oracle, SQL, and PL/SQL [**P**rocedural **L**anguage**/SQL -** a superset of SQL] with a wealth of practical examples.

What You'll Learn?

In this book, we not only cover the most important and useful Oracle's SQL features, but we show ways to apply them to solve specific problems.

It covers:

- **Introduction to the world's largest selling RDBMS product Oracle:**
  - Introduction To Database
  - Installation Of Oracle 23 AI
  - SQL*Plus
  - Tablespace
- **The natural language of Oracle i.e. SQL:**
  - Entity Relationship Diagram, which holds the Entity Relationship diagrams of all the database tables used throughout this book:
    1. Customer, Employee And Order Management
    2. Subscriber Management
    3. Movie Rentals Management
    4. Student Management
    5. Bank Accounts and Transaction Management
    6. Books, Publishers and Author Management
    7. Audit Trails
    8. Assorted Tables
  - Data Types
  - Working With Database Tables
  - Inserting records in multiple tables
  - Merging rows
  - Alterations to the existing table structures
  - Synonyms
  - Working with external database tables
  - Applying data constraints
- **Working With Data:**
  - Operators
  - Character/String Functions
  - Numeric Functions
  - Date Functions
  - Group Data
  - Subqueries
  - Join multiple tables and retrieve data from them
  - Union, Intersect and Minus
  - Search the desired data using regular expressions
  - Use Pseudo columns provided by Oracle
- **Performance Tuning:**
  - Create a series of numbers and indexes very similar to an index found in a book which allows quick access to table rows.
  - Create views, which are predefined queries on one or more tables. Views allow achieving data abstraction, data integrity, security, privacy and source code protection.
  - Clusters
  - Sequences
- **Introduces Procedural Language/SQL a superset of SQL:**
  - Introduction To PL/SQL
  - Transactions
  - Cursors
  - Procedures

- o Functions
- o Triggers
- o Packages

- ❑ **Chat with your Database using SELECT AI:**
  - o Diving into Oracle Autonomous Database
  - o Setting up Autonomous Database Instance
  - o Integrating GenAI with Autonomous Database
  - o Using Select AI for Natural Language Interaction with the Database
  - o Managing AI Profiles and Credentials

Platform and Version

When we wrote this book, Oracle 12c was released, and we managed to cover some of the interesting and new features in that release of the database. This edition significantly expands into Oracle 23 AI, covering the latest advancements in natural language interaction with the database. Most of the concepts, syntax, and examples apply to earlier releases of Oracle as well. We specifically point out the new Oracle Database 23 AI features.

Who Is This Book For?

- ❑ **Absolute Beginners:** This book assumes the reader with no prior knowledge of the Oracle database, SQL, or PL/SQL. Thus, if you have never used Oracle before, you can use this book.
- ❑ This book is suitable for developers, business users [to write SQL queries to fetch the required information from the company database], technical managers, or consultants.
- ❑ This book would appeal to those who want a hands-on practical book demonstrating examples for almost every topic in this book.

We think that you will get the most out of this book if you go through each chapter in the order in which it is laid out.

How Is This Book Organized

This book presents evenly paced lessons in which each section builds upon the previous one. It contains several chapters held in sections, each discussing an aspect of Oracle. This book includes several special elements that reinforce what you are learning.

Programs In This Book

We've worked carefully together as a team to ensure that all examples in this book are drawn from a single data set. You'll be able to download that data set from **www.sharanamshah.com/books/oracleforbeginners/bookcodesAI.zip**. You can then use it to follow along with our examples.

In a step-by-step, easy-to-follow manner, concepts are built using simple language. Examples chosen have easily understood logic.

The sections that follow present a rundown of what the book delivers as you work through its content.

If you are using an earlier version of Oracle, then you will still be able to use this book, but you won't be able to run the scripts that use the new features added by Oracle Database 23 AI.

Acknowledgments

Writing this book has been one of the most challenging endeavors we've taken on and it would not have been possible without the help and support from several people.

Our sincere thanks go to:

- Our publisher Mr. Aziz Shroff for bringing up the X-Team concept that has brought enormous changes in our lives.
- Our family for their patience, support, and love.
- The many developers who read this book. We welcome both your brickbats and bouquets.
- All those who helped through their comments, feedback, and suggestions.

If you have any questions, comments, or just feel like communicating, please contact us at **enquiries@sharanamshah.com**.

We are now also available on Facebook [http://facebook.sharanamshah.com]. You can Sign up to connect with both of us.

We hope that you will enjoy reading and working through the examples in this book as much as we enjoyed documenting and developing it.

For additional information on this book visit http://www.sharanamshah.com.

Sharanam & Vaishali Shah

Table Of Contents

SECTION IV: SQL PERFORMANCE TUNING

SECTION VI: CHAT WITH YOUR DATABASE USING SELECT AI

Chapter

1

SECTION I: OVERVIEW OF ORACLE DATABASE

Introduction To Database

A **database** is a systematically organized collection of logical and meaningful data stored within a computer system. For instance, an employee's record would typically include details such as the employee's name, department, salary, address and the immediate supervisor to whom the employee reports. When such data of multiple employees is gathered in one place, it constitutes a logical and meaningful collection of information.

The primary purpose of a database is to structure the information in a way that ensures easy access, management and updating. Databases maintained within a computer system, often referred to as **D**ata**B**ase **M**anagement **S**ystems (DBMS), typically include aggregates of data such as:

- Sales transactions
- Inventories
- Product catalogs
- Customer profiles

Database Management Systems

A **D**ata**B**ase **M**anagement **S**ystem (DBMS) is software that enables users to create and access data in a database. It manages, organizes and provides methods for data modification or extraction by users or other programs.

Key functions of a DBMS include:

- ***Data Integrity:*** Ensures consistent and accessible data.
- ***Security:*** Restricts access to authorized users.

The DBMS acts like a file manager but for databases. Examples of DBMS include dBase, FoxPro, ***Oracle***, MySQL, PostgreSQL, Microsoft SQL Server and Sybase.

Creating and managing a database with a DBMS involves:

- Identifying the information to be managed.
- Designing a structure (data table) to store data.
- Inserting data into the structure.
- Updating and deleting data as needed.
- Viewing the data when required.

ANSI SQL - The Standard Language Of The DBMS

Initially, every DBMS had a proprietary language, requiring programmers to learn multiple DBMS languages. This led to **redundant** data since information held by one DBMS couldn't be shared with another.

To address this issue, the **A**merican **N**ational **S**tandards **I**nstitute (ANSI) defined a common DBMS language called **S**tructured **Q**uery **L**anguage (SQL), known as ANSI-SQL. For a product to qualify as a DBMS by ANSI standards, it must conform to ANSI-SQL. This standardization allows programmers to learn only ANSI-SQL and facilitates seamless data sharing across multiple DBMS.

SQL's core consists of commands for:

- Retrieving data
- Inserting data
- Modifying data
- Managing administrative functions
- Deleting data

Benefits of DBMS

- ***Organization:*** Helps in collecting and manipulating information.

- *Structure:* Provides structured fields and tables for data entry.
- *Centralization:* Allows sharing data within an organization.
- *Current Information:* Ensures data is up-to-date, improving communication.
- *Consistency:* Minimizes mistakes by structuring data entry.
- *Reduces Redundancy:* Eliminates duplicate data.
- *Data Integrity:* Ensures only accurate data is stored.
- *Security:* Grants data access only to authorized users.
- *Data Independence:* Separates data from the programs that manipulate it.

What Is Relational Database Management System?

A **R**elational **D**ata**B**ase **M**anagement **S**ystem (RDBMS) is software that enables creating, updating and managing a relational database. It is based on Dr. Edgar F. Codd's relational model, which consists of 13 rules (numbered from zero to twelve) that define what is required for a database management system to be considered relational.

Key Features of RDBMS:

- Data is structured in tables, fields and records.
- Each table consists of rows (records) and columns (fields).
- Tables are related through common fields (columns).

Why Relational?

To understand when a DBMS qualifies itself as Relational, let's analyze the following tables:

Employees Table: Column Description

Column Name	Description
EmployeeName	The name of the employee.
Designation	The designation of the employee.
EmpUserName	The user name of the employee.
EmpPassword	The password for the username of the employee.
Salary	The salary of the employee.
DepartmentName	The department to which the employee belongs.

Departments Table: Column Description

Column Name	Description
DepartmentName	The name of the department.
City	The city in which the department exists.
Capacity	The capacity of that department.

Diagrammatically, the above tables will appear as:

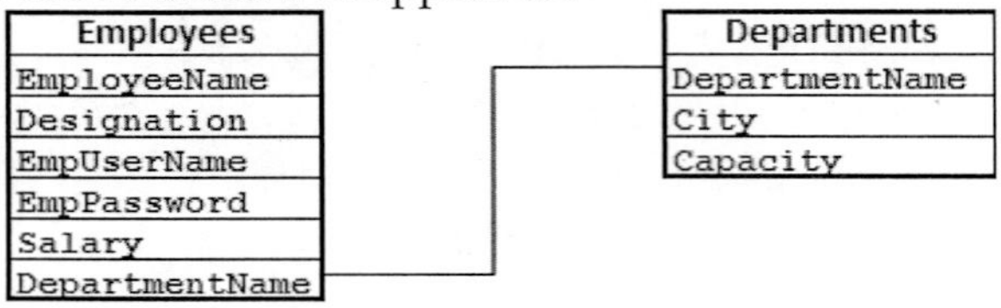

Sample Data

Employees

EmployeeName	Designation	EmpUserName	EmpPassword	Salary	DepartmentName
Sharanam Shah	Technical Author	sharanam	shah	100000	Mahim
Vaishali Shah	Technical Writer	vaishali	vshah	50000	Andheri
Kanchan Toprani	Travel Consultant	kanchan	toprani	50000	Bandra
Narendra Dodhia	Programmer	narendra	dodhia	90000	Andheri
Meenal Joshi	Tester	meenal	joshi	35000	Mahim
Manali Angle	Designer	manali	angle	45000	M.G. Road
Vijay Shukla	HTML	vijay	shukla	35000	Race Course

Departments

DepartmentName	City	Capacity
Mahim	Mumbai	20
Andheri	Mumbai	30
Bandra	Mumbai	50
M.G. Road	Banglore	35
Race Course	Pune	45

In the above defined tables, the Employees table lists departments belonging to several cities and the Departments table depicts that each city has more than one department.

To determine in which city a particular department exist? The Departments table will act as a lookup reference.

DepartmentName	City
Mahim	Mumbai

In the **Employees** table, for a department named *Mahim*,

1. Glance through the data available in the **Departments** table.
2. Identify the value in the **DepartmentName** column.
3. Have a look in the **City** column of the same row and note the City's name.

DepartmentName	City
Mahim	Mumbai

These are two completely separate and independent tables. Each contains its own information in form of rows and within rows, columns. Both these tables have one significant entity in common that is the **DepartmentName** column. For each department in the Employees table, there is an identical department name in the Departments table.

To determine the EmployeeName, Designation, EmpUserName, EmpPassword and Salary of all employees in the Mumbai departments?

1. Glance through the **Departments** table data.
2. Identify the department names under the city Mumbai.

Departments Found

DepartmentName	City
Mahim	Mumbai
Andheri	Mumbai
Bandra	Mumbai

3. Glance though the **Employees** table data.
4. Identify the desired employee details such as EmployeeName, Designation, EmpUserName, EmpPassword and Salary for all the three department names identified earlier.

Employees Found

EmployeeName	Designation	EmpUserName	EmpPassword	Salary	DepartmentName
Sharanam Shah	Technical Author	sharanam	shah	100000	Mahim
Vaishali Shah	Technical Writer	vaishali	vshah	50000	Andheri
Kanchan Toprani	Travel Consultant	kanchan	toprani	50000	Bandra
Narendra Dodhia	Programmer	narendra	dodhia	90000	Andheri
Meenal Joshi	Tester	meenal	joshi	35000	Mahim

Even though both these tables are independent, they are related. DepartmentName column of the Departments table is related to the DepartmentName column of the Employees table.

This relationship is the basis for the name **Relational database.**

From the above example, the following is clear:

- Data is stored in tables.
- Tables have:
  - Columns
  - Rows
  - Values
- Tables can be related to each other if each table has a column with common type of information [in this case DepartmentName].

RDBMS Terminology

- ***Database:*** A collection of **tables.**
- ***Table:*** Contains records (horizontal rows), also called **tuples.**
- ***Record:*** Contains fields (vertical columns), also called **attributes**. For example, an employee record.
- ***Field:*** Classified into different **data types**, which can be standard or specific to each DBMS (like Oracle, MySQL).

Common Data Types

- *Character:* For textual data (e.g., Employee Name).
- *Numeric:* For numerical data (e.g., Employee Salary).
- *Date:* For date data (e.g., Employee Birthdate).

Additional Concepts

- *Domain:* Specifies the possible values for a field (e.g., a field named "Sex" might be limited to values "Male" and "Female").
- *Key:* A logical way to access a record in a table. A key that uniquely identifies a record is called a **Primary Key**. Example: In the Employees table, the EmployeeCode or the EmpUserName field.
- *Foreign Keys:* Used to relate tables to each other.

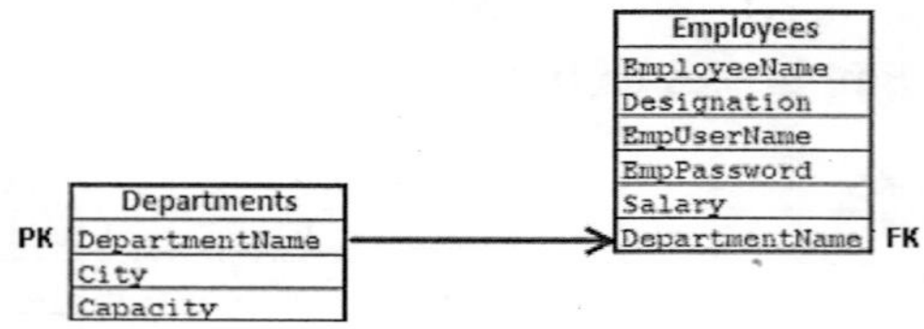

Relationships in RDBMS

- *One-to-One (1:1):* Each instance of Table A is related to only one instance of Table B and vice-versa (e.g., each employee's username is associated with only one employee).
- *One-to-Many (1:m):* Each instance of Table A can be related to many instances of Table B, but each instance of Table B is related to only one instance of Table A (e.g., each department can have many employees, but each employee belongs to one department).
- *Many-to-Many (m:m):* Each instance of Table A can be related to many instances of Table B and vice-versa (e.g., a book can have many authors, and each author can write many books).

Normalization

When designing a relational database, **normalization** is recommended to organize the data efficiently. The goal is to minimize redundancy and ensure data integrity. Typically, databases are normalized to the **Third Normal Form**.

Basic Principle of Normalization: Normalization ensures that the attributes in each table depend only on the primary key, the entire primary key and nothing but the primary key.

A de-normalized database table would look like:

Orders
Order Number
Order Date
Product Number 1
Product Code 1
Product Description 1
Product Number 2
Product Code 2
Product Description 2

The above table will never allow more than two products per order.

To normalize this table to the Second Normal Form:
Move the repeating groups of attributes to a separate database table.

Orders
Order Number
Order Date

Order Products
Order Product Number
Order Number
Product Code
Product Description

A single order can now support any number of products. The **P**rimary **K**ey [PK] of the **Order Products** table is the **Order Product Number**. The **Order Number** is the **F**oreign **K**ey [FK] that has relationship with the **Order Number** [PK] of the **Orders** table.

The **Order Number** [PK] has a <u>one-to-many relationship</u> with the **Order Number** [FK]. This means for <u>each instance</u> of the **Orders** table, <u>many instances</u> of the **Order Products** table exist, but for <u>each instance</u> of **Order Products** table, <u>only one instance</u> of **Orders** table exists.

The **Product Description** field is dependent on the **Product Code** and not on the unique identifier of the Order Products table [i.e. Order Product Number].

To further normalize these tables to Third Normal Form:
Create a master lookup table. New product codes can be added in this table. The Product Description field for a given product code can be altered, if required, which will affect all the products ordered till date.

Orders
Order Number
Order Date

Order Products
Order Product Number
Order Number
Product Code

Product Master
Product Code
Product Description

Oracle Database

The **Oracle Database** is the flagship RDBMS from Oracle Corporation. It was introduced in the late 1970s and became the first database product to run on a variety of platforms, from microcomputers to mainframes.

Here's a brief history of its evolution:

- *Oracle V2 (1979):* The first commercially available SQL-based RDBMS.
- *Oracle V3 (1983):* Introduced concurrency control, data distribution and scalability.
- *Oracle V4 (1984):* Added multi-version read consistency.
- *Oracle V5 (1985):* Supported client/server computing and distributed database systems.
- *Oracle 6 (1988):* Introduced row-level locking, online backup and recovery, PL/SQL and Oracle Parallel Server.
- *Oracle 7 (1992):* Added PL/SQL stored procedures, triggers, shared cursors and the Cost-Based Optimizer.
- *Oracle 8 (1997):* Brought Recovery Manager, partitioning, Dataguard and native internet protocols.
- *Oracle 9i (2001):* Introduced Real Application Clusters (RAC), Oracle XML DB and data mining.
- *Oracle 10g (2003):* Added grid infrastructure, Oracle ASM and Flashback Database.
- *Oracle 11g (2007):* Introduced Active Data Guard, Secure Files and Exadata.
- *Oracle 12c (2013):* Brought multitenant architecture and in-memory column store.
- *Oracle 18c (2018):* Introduced Autonomous Database and Data Guard Multi-Instance Redo Apply.
- *Oracle 19c (2019):* Enhanced features and stability improvements.
- *Oracle 23ai (2023):* Added AI capabilities, JSON relational duality and transactional microservices support.

The Oracle Database runs on over 80 platforms, showcasing its adaptability and wide-reaching impact. Over the years, it has introduced many innovative features that have significantly enhanced data management capabilities.

Introduction to Oracle Database 23ai Free

This book focuses on Oracle 23ai Free. Before we begin, here's an overview of Oracle 23ai Free and the steps to download and install it.

Oracle Database 23ai Free Overview

Oracle Database 23ai Free offers the essential capabilities of Oracle's leading database technologies, designed for small-scale applications, development, and educational purposes. It provides a simplified, cost-free way to learn and test Oracle Database features.

Downloading Oracle Database 23ai Free

1. ***Visit the Oracle website:*** Go to the **Oracle Database Free** download page on the official Oracle website.
2. ***Download the Installer:*** Download the **Oracle Database 23ai Free installer** for Windows (look for the .zip file).
3. ***Extract the Files:*** Extract the downloaded .zip file to a folder on your computer, such as C:\app\oracle\db_home.

Installing Oracle Database 23ai Free

1. ***Run the Installer:*** Open the **setup.exe** file from the extracted folder as an administrator.
2. ***Choose Installation Type:*** Select the **Desktop Class** option and create a new Windows user for the Oracle home user account.
3. ***Configure Installation:*** Choose the typical install configuration and set the password for the global database name (starter database).
4. ***Complete Installation:*** Follow the on-screen instructions to complete the installation process.

Chapter

2

SECTION I: OVERVIEW OF ORACLE DATABASE

Using SQL Plus

SQL*Plus, often pronounced as **Sequel Plus**, is a tool from Oracle that lets you work with databases through a command line interface. It is included with Oracle's Database Client and Server software.

With SQL*Plus, you can:

- Write, edit, save, retrieve and execute SQL commands and PL/SQL code.
- Format, perform calculations, store and print query results in report form.
- Inspect table and object definitions.
- Develop and execute batch scripts.
- Conduct various database administration tasks.

Data**B**ase **A**dministrator**s** (DBAs) and developers commonly use SQL*Plus for managing databases.

How Does SQL Plus Function?

Users input SQL statements at the SQL prompt within the SQL*Plus tool. These statements are then sent to the Oracle database server for processing.

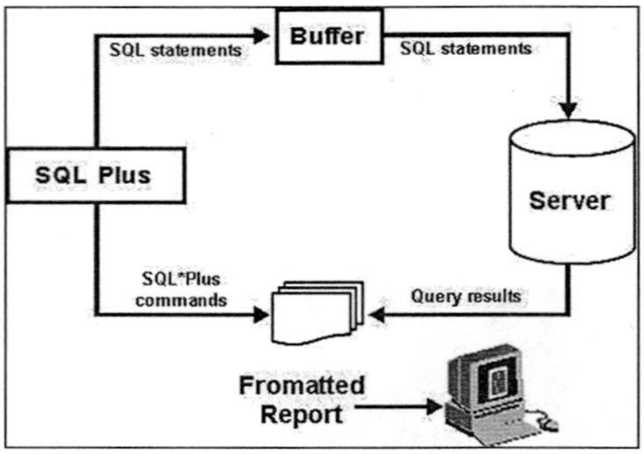

The Oracle database server validates and executes the received SQL statements, returning the results to SQL*Plus, where they are displayed to the end user.

In addition to sending SQL statements to the server, SQL*Plus also saves these statements into a local buffer, allowing users to review and modify them.

The accompanying diagram illustrates how SQL*Plus functions.

Working With SQL Plus Command Line

To invoke the SQL*Plus command line, open the Command Prompt window and type the following command:

```
sqlplus
```

Output:

```
Command Prompt - sqlplus

C:\>sqlplus

SQL*Plus: Release 23.0.0.0.0 - Production on Fri Nov 29 13:33:54 2024
Version 23.6.0.24.10

Copyright (c) 1982, 2024, Oracle.  All rights reserved.

Enter user-name: SYSTEM
Enter password:
Last Successful login time: Thu Nov 28 2024 14:24:17 +05:30

Connected to:
Oracle Database 23ai Free Release 23.0.0.0.0 - Develop, Learn, and Run for Free
Version 23.6.0.24.10

SQL>
```

When you open the SQL Plus command line interface, it will prompt you for a username and password. Enter 'SYSTEM' or 'SYS' as the username, along with the password you set during the Oracle installation in the **Typical Install Configuration** step. Upon successful login, the command prompt will change to **SQL>**, as shown in the diagram. This prompt is where you can enter SQL queries and PL/SQL code blocks to interact with the Oracle database.

Using The Username And Password As Parameters

If the command window is used to invoke SQL Plus, then username and password can be passed as parameters to the **sqlplus** command:

```
sqlplus SYSTEM/<Password>
```

Output:

```
C:\>sqlplus SYSTEM/ <PASSWORD>

SQL*Plus: Release 23.0.0.0.0 - Production on Fri Nov 29 13:41:48 2024
Version 23.6.0.24.10

Copyright (c) 1982, 2024, Oracle.  All rights reserved.

Last Successful login time: Fri Nov 29 2024 13:34:11 +05:30

Connected to:
Oracle Database 23ai Free Release 23.0.0.0.0 - Develop, Learn, and Run for Free
Version 23.6.0.24.10

SQL> |
```

This method of invocation poses significant security risks, as the password is exposed and can be easily seen by anyone nearby.

Using The nolog Parameter

If the command window is used to invoke SQL Plus, then the **nolog** parameter can be used to inform the SQL Plus, that the interface should not attempt to login. This is done manually:

```
sqlplus /nolog
```

Output:

```
C:\>sqlplus /nolog

SQL*Plus: Release 23.0.0.0.0 - Production on Fri Nov 29 13:47:34 2024
Version 23.6.0.24.10

Copyright (c) 1982, 2024, Oracle.  All rights reserved.

SQL> |
```

This brings up the SQL> prompt. Key in the following command, to login as the user SYSTEM:

```
connect SYSTEM/<Password>
```

Output:

```
SQL> connect SYSTEM/ <Password>
Connected.
SQL> |
```

Key in the following command just to ensure, that the login was successful:

```
SELECT * FROM TAB;
```

Key in the following command to logout:

```
disconnect
```

Output:

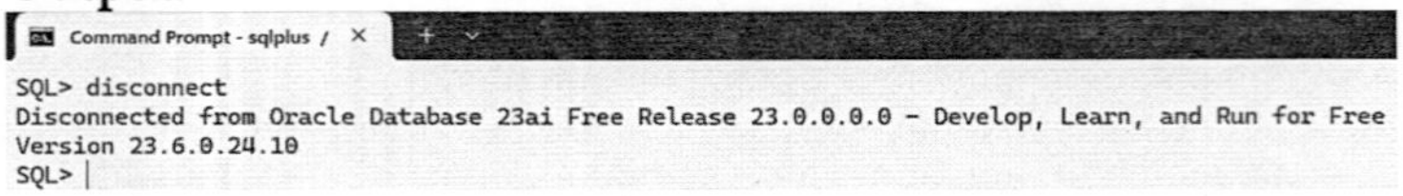

```
SQL> disconnect
Disconnected from Oracle Database 23ai Free Release 23.0.0.0.0 - Develop, Learn, and Run for Free
Version 23.6.0.24.10
SQL> |
```

Quitting SQL Plus Command Line

To quit the SQL Plus command line interface, key in the following command at the SQL prompt:

```
exit
```

Output:

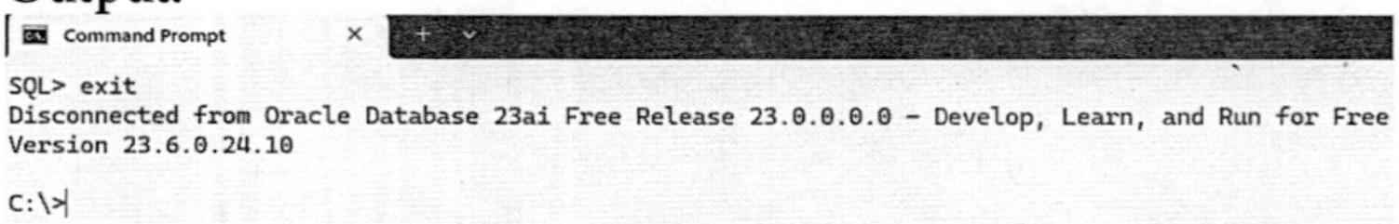

```
SQL> exit
Disconnected from Oracle Database 23ai Free Release 23.0.0.0.0 - Develop, Learn, and Run for Free
Version 23.6.0.24.10

C:\>
```

OR

```
quit
```

Output:

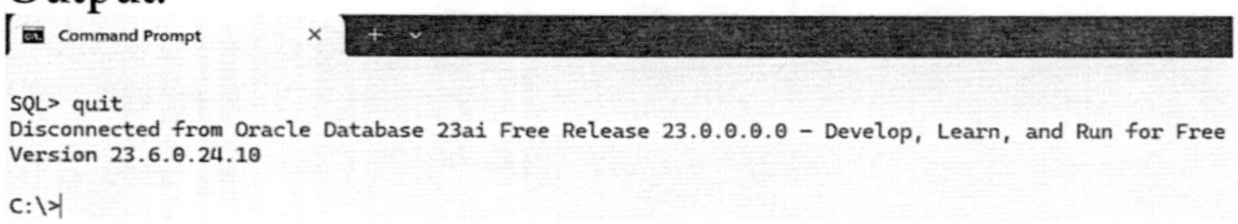

```
SQL> quit
Disconnected from Oracle Database 23ai Free Release 23.0.0.0.0 - Develop, Learn, and Run for Free
Version 23.6.0.24.10

C:\>
```

Executing Commands

To instruct SQL*Plus, type your desired command, ensuring each word is separated by a space.

The following are a few sample commands that can be entered and executed at the SQL prompt:

- SQL commands for working with information in the database:

```
SELECT * FROM TAB;
```

- SQL Plus commands, for formatting query results, setting options and editing and storing SQL commands and PL/SQL blocks:

```
CLEAR SCREEN
SHOW USER
SET PAGESIZE 100
START myscript.sql
```

Let's take an example of Customers and type the following command at the SQL prompt:

```
SQL> SELECT * FROM
  2  CUSTOMERS WHERE CUSTNAME = 'Sharanam';
```

Output:

```
    CUSTNO CUSTNAME ADDRESS
---------- -------- ---------------------------
         1 Sharanam Krihna Kunj, Mumbai
```

After entering the first line at the prompt, press enter, this changes the prompt to **2** to indicate line 2 being entered.

As shown above, the SQL commands can be divided across separate lines at any point as long as individual words are not split between lines:

```
SQL> SELECT * FR
  2  OM CUSTOMERS WHERE CUSTNAME = 'Sharanam';
```

In this command, the **FROM** clause is divided between two lines and hence is not acceptable. SQL Plus displays an error:

```
select * fr
         *
ERROR at line 1:
ORA-00923: FROM keyword not found where expected
```

> Use the BACKSPACE key to correct any mistakes in the line. Once you've rectified the command, press the Enter key to move to the next line.

The semicolon (;) indicates that the command in SQL Plus has ended and is ready to be executed. After typing the semicolon, press the Enter key. SQL Plus will then process the command and display the results on the screen.

After displaying the results and the number of rows retrieved, SQL Plus displays the SQL prompt, indicating readiness for the next command:

```
SQL>
```

An SQL command can be terminated in the following ways:

- A ***semicolon (;)*** signals SQL Plus to execute the command. SQL Plus processes the command and stores it in the SQL buffer.
- A ***forward slash (/)*** on a line by itself also signals SQL Plus to execute the command. SQL Plus processes the command and stores it in the SQL buffer.

- A ***blank line*** signifies that the user has finished entering the command but does not wish to execute it immediately. Pressing ***Enter*** after the last line of the command advances the SQL Plus prompt to the next line number in sequence. Pressing ***Enter*** again changes the prompt to ***SQL>***, indicating readiness for the next command. SQL Plus stores the unexecuted command in the buffer. If a new SQL command is subsequently entered and executed with a semicolon (;) or a forward slash (/), SQL*Plus overwrites the previous unexecuted command in the buffer.

> The SQL buffer stores the most recently entered SQL command or PL/SQL block. However, the SQL Plus commands are not stored. The command or block remains in the buffer until replaced by the next SQL command or PL/SQL block.

Chapter

3

SECTION II: BASICS OF SQL

Entity Relationship Diagram

The examples in this book are based on the following sets of database tables:

1. Subscriber Management
2. Movie Rentals Management
3. Student Management
4. Audit Trails
5. Books, Publishers and Author Management
6. Assorted Tables
7. Customer, Employee And Order Management
8. Bank Accounts and Transaction Management

Each set of database tables is represented diagrammatically using an Entity Relationship Diagram. To create these tables with sample data, you can use the SQL script file named **SQLOracleForBeginners.sql**, available at:
www.sharanamshah.com/books/oracleforbeginners/bookcodesAI.zip.

Customer, Employee and Order Management

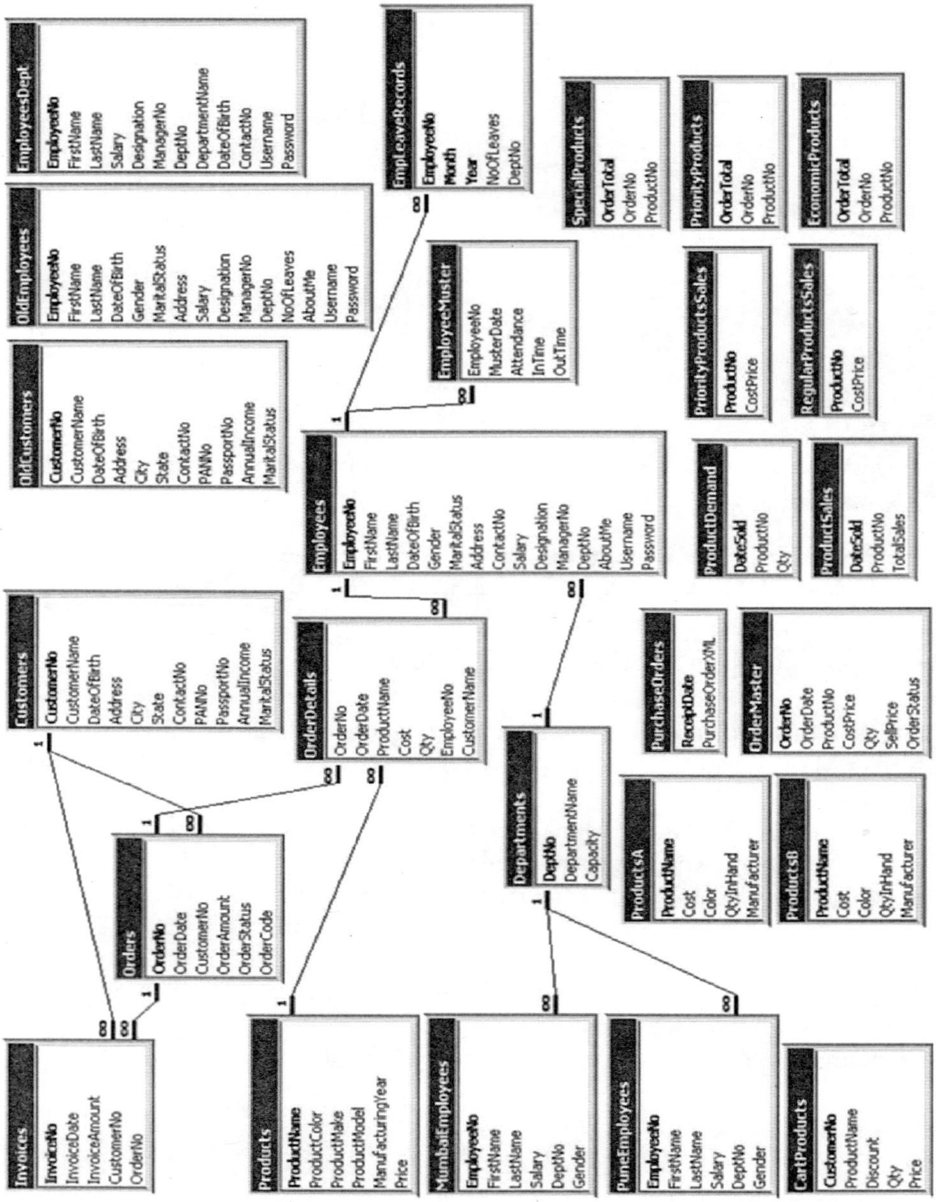

Subscriber Management

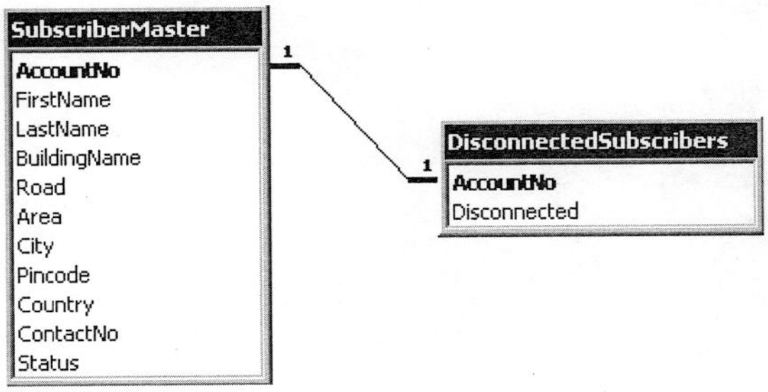

Student Management

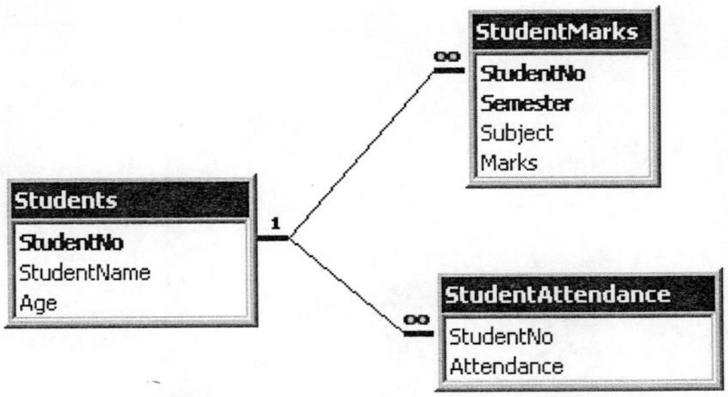

Movie Rentals Management

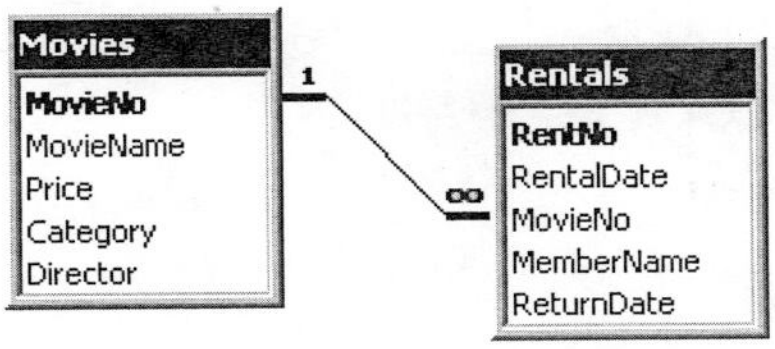

Audit Trails

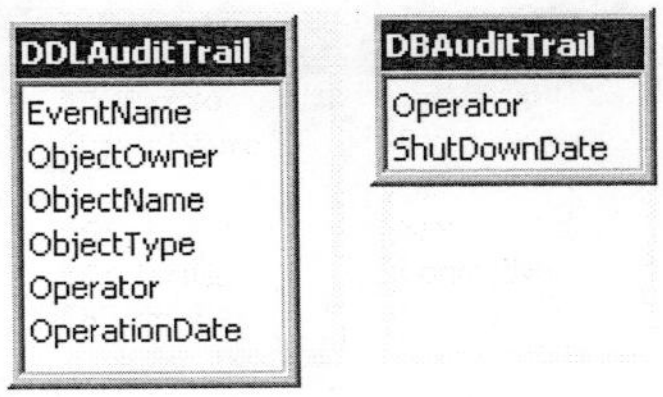

Bank Accounts and Transaction Management

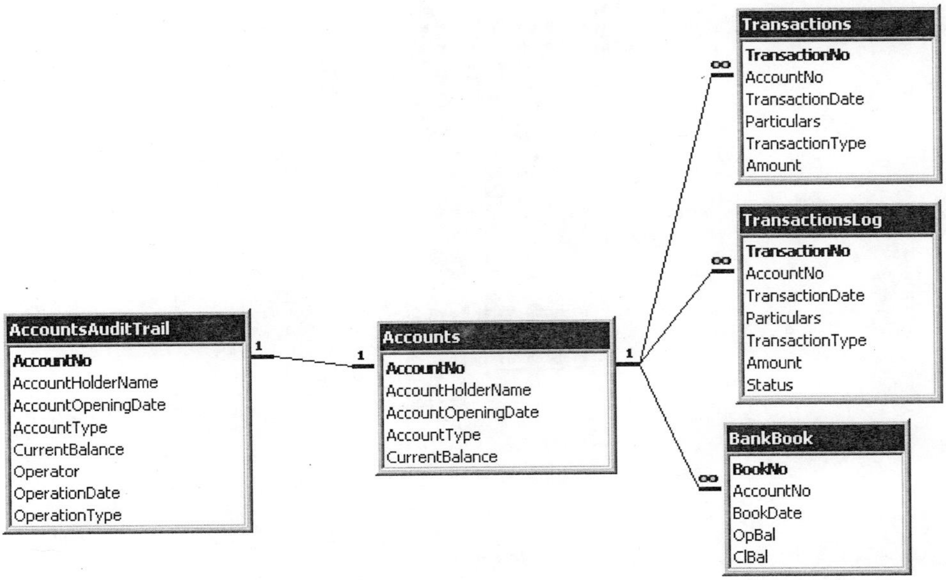

Books, Publishers and Author Management

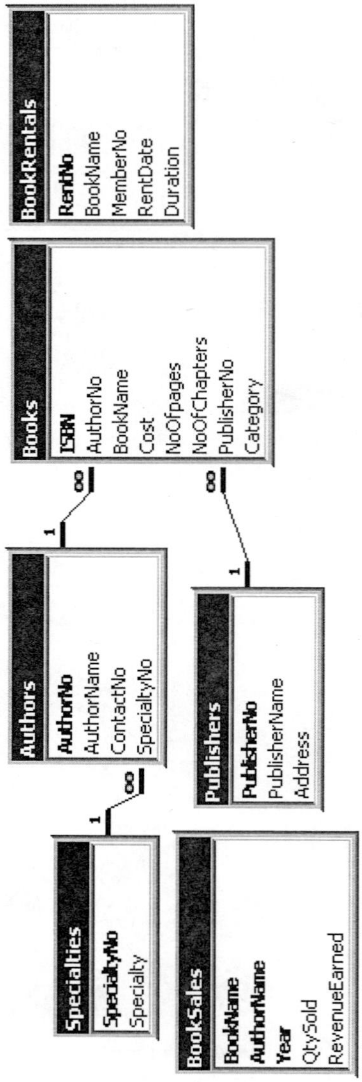

Assorted Tables

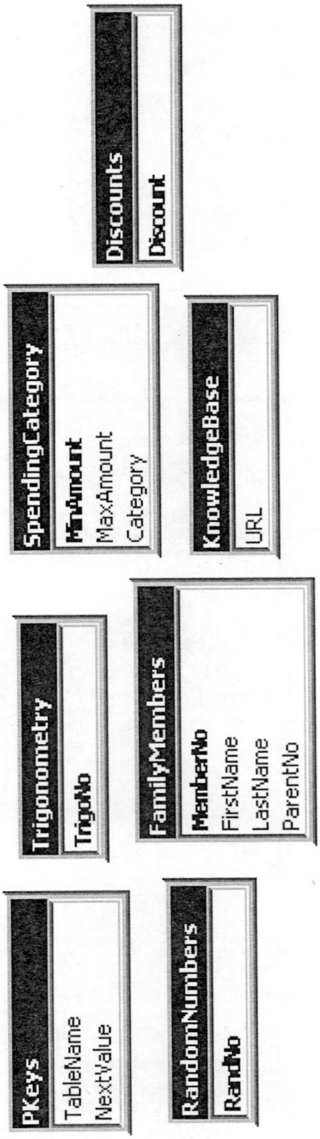

Running SQL Script

Before running the SQL script (SQLOracleForBeginners.sql), follow these steps:

1. Login in to Oracle:

```
SYS/<Password> AS SYSDBA
```

2. Create a tablespace named **OracleForBeginners:**

```
CREATE TABLESPACE OracleForBeginners
  DATAFILE 'MyBooks_OracleForBeginners.dat'
  SIZE 50M
  AUTOEXTEND on
  NEXT 10M
  MAXSIZE 1000M
  ONLINE;
```

> For more information on Tablespace, refer to ***Tablespaces in Oracle*** section of this chapter.

3. Run the script:

```
@<FilePath>\SQLOracleForBeginners.sql
```

Contents of **SQLOracleForBeginners.sql script:**

a. Drops the user named **Vaishali** [if it already exists, which will be the case if this script is re-run]:

```
DROP USER Vaishali CASCADE;
```

b. Creates a user named **Vaishali** [with password set to **vaishali]** and binds this user to the tablespace **OracleForBeginners:**

```
CREATE USER Vaishali
  PROFILE DEFAULT
  IDENTIFIED BY vaishali
  DEFAULT TABLESPACE OracleForBeginners
  TEMPORARY TABLESPACE TEMP
  ACCOUNT UNLOCK;
```

Special Instructions for Oracle 12c and later:

Oracle 12c and later is specifically designed for the cloud, featuring container databases and pluggable databases to manage multiple database instances. Due to these new features, you might encounter the following error when creating users:

```
SQL Error: ORA-65096: invalid common user or role name
```

This error occurs because common user and role names must start with C## or c## and consist only of ASCII characters.

To avoid modifying scripts for different Oracle versions, you can make Oracle 12c or later behave like Oracle 11g by setting the _ORACLE_SCRIPT parameter to true for the session:

```
ALTER SESSION SET "_ORACLE_SCRIPT"=true;
```

Now, run the CREATE USER command again and it works without any error.

c. Grants the following privileges to the user Vaishali:

```
GRANT CONNECT TO Vaishali WITH ADMIN OPTION;
GRANT DBA TO Vaishali WITH ADMIN OPTION;
```

d. Connects as the user Vaishali:

```
connect Vaishali/<Password>
```

e. Executes **DDL** and **DML** commands to **create tables** and **insert data**

Tablespaces in Oracle

A tablespace is a logical grouping of related data. In Oracle, user data is **logically** stored in tablespaces which is **physically** stored in **data files**.

Relationship between Database, Tablespaces and Data files:

- A database can hold multiple tablespaces.
- Each tablespace can span multiple data files.
- The size of a tablespace is the sum of the sizes of all its data files.
- The total size of all the tablespaces represents the storage capacity of the database.

In Oracle, a typical database usually contains at least one tablespace. Conceptually, a tablespace is similar to a folder on a hard disk drive. Tablespaces are used to map logical objects such as tables, indexes and views to a specific data file. Essentially, they group different logical database objects together and manage disk space allocation for database data.

Database administrators use tablespaces to assign specific hard disk space [quota] for specific database users. Tablespaces control the availability of data by allowing individual tablespaces to be set **ONLINE** or **OFFLINE**. They also facilitate partial database backup or recovery operations. Performance can be significantly improved by allocating data storage across multiple devices using tablespaces.

Oracle **strongly recommends** creating a separate tablespace within the database and binding users to it. This ensures that Oracle objects are kept isolated from user objects. A **separate tablespace** can be created using Oracle Enterprise Manager Express or SQL syntax.

The SYSTEM Tablespace

The **SYSTEM tablespace** is used by the Oracle Database Engine to store system information such as:

- ***Data dictionary:*** Stores the metadata, which is data about data, including information such as table access permissions, and details about keys.
- Names and locations of:
  - Tablespaces
  - Tables
  - Indexes
  - Clusters

When installing Oracle for the very first time, a SYSTEM tablespace is automatically created within the new database schema.

Although a small database can fit within the SYSTEM tablespace, it is recommended to create a separate tablespace for user data.

If no other tablespace exists within the database, all the **user objects** such as tables, views and indexes are stored in the **SYSTEM** tablespace. When a user is created and no other tablespace is available, the user is automatically bound to the SYSTEM tablespace.

Creating Tablespace

The following command is used to create a new tablespace with one or more initial data files. This command also allows specifying default storage parameters.

```
CREATE TABLESPACE <Tablespace Name>
  DATAFILE/TEMPFILE '<Path and Filename>'
  SIZE <SIZE>
  AUTOEXTEND [<ON>/<OFF>] NEXT <SIZE> MAXSIZE <SIZE>
  [ONLINE/OFFLINE]
```

It is advisable to name the datafile using:

- The database name that holds the tablespace to which this datafile is associated.
- The tablespace name.
- A number that makes this datafile unique.

For example, for a tablespace called **OracleForBeginners** assigned to a database called **MyBooks**, the datafile can be named **MyBooks_OracleForBeginners**.

```
CREATE TABLESPACE OracleForBeginners
  DATAFILE 'MyBooks_OracleForBeginners.dat'
  SIZE 50M
  AUTOEXTEND on
  NEXT 10M
  MAXSIZE 1000M
  ONLINE;
```

Explanation:

- *Datafile:* Makes up the permanent tablespace.
- By default, an Oracle tablespace does not grow if it runs out of space. This means if all the available space (in this case, 50 MB) is used up, it is a dangerous situation unless the *AUTOEXTEND* keyword is used with the CREATE TABLESPACE command to specify that the tablespace should grow dynamically. Here, the tablespace automatically extends in increments of 10 MB, until it reaches a maximum size of 1000 MB.
- *Next:* Specifies disk space to allocate to the data file when more extents are required.
- *Maxsize:* Specifies the maximum disk space allowed for allocation to the data file.
- *Online:* Makes the tablespace available immediately after creation to users who have been granted access to the tablespace.

TIP: It is recommended to use **AUTOEXTEND** on all tablespaces for production databases.

Dropping A Tablespace

Dropping a tablespace is a structural change to the database that requires a backup.

Example:

```
DROP TABLESPACE OracleForBeginners;
```

Output:

```
Tablespace dropped.
```

Chapter 4

SECTION II: BASICS OF SQL

Data Types

SQL (**S**tructured **Q**uery **L**anguage) is an ANSI (**A**merican **N**ational **S**tandards **I**nstitute) standard computer language designed for accessing and manipulating data in database systems. SQL can be used with a variety of database management systems such as Microsoft Access, Microsoft SQL Server, MySQL, Informix, Oracle and others.

Table fundamentals

A **database** consists of one or more tables, which are objects that hold user data. Each table is identified by a name and is composed of **rows** and **columns**, similar to a spreadsheet.

In a spreadsheet, a row contains multiple cells. These cells are equivalent to the columns of a table, each having a specific data type. If a spreadsheet cell is set to a number data type, storing letters in that cell is not allowed. This principle also applies to a table's column; each column in a table has a specific data type.

A database table named Students:

RollNo	FirstName	LastName	Division	Marks
1	Sharanam	Shah	A	98
2	Vaishali	Shah	B	90
3	Kanchan	Toprani	C	80

This table is structured as:

Column Name	Data Type
RollNo	Number
FirstName	Varchar2
LastName	Varchar2
Division	Varchar2
Marks	Number

The Students table consists of:

- **Three records (rows)**, representing **individual students**
- **Five columns**, each holding specific data about the students.

The Students table holds data for three students across five columns. The columns **RollNo** and **Marks** are of the Number data type, so they will not accept characters.

Oracle ensures that only data matching the column's data type will be stored within the column.

Data Types

A **data type** is an attribute of the data stored in a database that indicates the kind of data being dealt with. Data types allow developers to structure and design tables to suit the scope of the application. Therefore, it's essential to have a detailed understanding of data types to make intelligent decisions when choosing the right data types for columns.

Oracle supports several data types for handling data in an Oracle database. Here are some of the most commonly used data types:

Char(size)

Stores fixed-length character string values. The **size** parameter specifies the string length, with a maximum of 2000 bytes or characters. If a shorter string is stored, it is right-padded with spaces.

Example:

```
FirstName CHAR(50)
```

If "Sharanam" (8 characters) is stored in FirstName, it will be right-padded with 42 spaces. These spaces are removed when the value is retrieved.

NChar[(size)]

A Unicode-only data type. When created with NCHAR, the column length is defined in characters based on the national character set defined at database creation. The maximum length is determined by this character set, with a maximum of 2000 bytes.

Varchar2(size)

Stores variable-length alphanumeric data. The **size** parameter specifies the maximum length, up to 4000 bytes or characters. Unlike Char, Varchar2 values are not padded with spaces.

Example:

```
FirstName VARCHAR2(50)
```

If "Sharanam" is stored, it **won't be** padded with spaces.

> Varchar2 is generally preferred over Char for its flexible length, but Char can be faster, sometimes up to **50%**.

Oracle uses two comparison semantics for string values:

- ***Blank-Padded Comparison Semantics:*** If values differ in length, Oracle pads the shorter one with spaces to make the lengths equal before comparison. This means values differing only in trailing spaces are considered equal. This comparison is used only when both values are Char or text literals.
- ***Non-Padded Comparison Semantics:*** Oracle compares values character by character. If the values differ, the longer one is considered greater. This comparison is used when one or both values are Varchar2.

> TIP
>
> **Example:**
>
> In case of **Blank Padded comparison** semantics,
>
> `'Sharanam ' = 'Sharanam'`
>
> In case of **Non-Padded comparison** semantics,
>
> `'Sharanam ' > 'Sharanam'`

NVarchar2(size)

A Unicode-only data type. When created with NVARCHAR2, specify the maximum characters it can hold. Oracle stores each value as specified, up to 4000 bytes, based on the national character set.

Number (Precision, Scale)

Stores numbers with absolute values from 1.0 x 10^{-130} to almost 1.0 x 10^{126}, with up to 39-40 digits of precision. Precision is the maximum number of digits, and scale is the number of digits to the right of the decimal point. Without specification, it defaults to a precision of 38 digits. Numbers exceeding the precision are **rejected**.

Float

A subtype of Number, specified with or without precision (1 to 126). It uses from 1 to 22 bytes. Conversion from binary to decimal precision is done by multiplying by 0.30103 and vice versa by multiplying by 3.32193. Float is equivalent to 38 digits of decimal precision.

> TIP Oracle recommends using Binary_Float and Binary_Double data types instead of Float, as they are more robust.

BINARY_FLOAT

Introduced in Oracle Database 10g, BINARY_FLOAT is a 32-bit, single-precision floating-point data type, requiring 4 bytes.

BINARY_DOUBLE

Also introduced in Oracle Database 10g, BINARY_DOUBLE is a 64-bit, double-precision floating-point data type, requiring 8 bytes. Binary precision is used instead of decimal precision in BINARY_FLOAT and BINARY_DOUBLE columns.

Long

Stores variable-length character strings up to 2 GB. Use LOB (CLOB, NCLOB, BLOB) instead. Long values can't be used in sub-queries, functions, expressions, WHERE clauses, or indexes, and only one Long value per table is allowed.

Date

Represents date and time. The default format is DD-MON-YY (e.g., 03-Jan-81), with time defaulting to 12:00:00 am if unspecified. Dates and times can be stored between January 1, 4712 B.C. and December 31, 9999 A.D.

The DATE type stores:

- The century
- All four digits of a year
- The month
- The day
- The second
- The minute
- The hour (in 24-hour format)

Timestamp

The Timestamp data type improves on Date by storing fractional seconds, useful for determining intervals between events happening within the same second.

A Timestamp column holds data in the following format:

```
YYYY-MM-DD HH24:MI:SS.SSSSSSSSS
```

Where,

- *YYYY* is the year
- *MM* is the month
- *DD* is the day
- *HH24* is the hour
- *MI* is the minutes
- *SS.SSSSSSSSS* is the seconds and its fraction

Time Intervals

Before Oracle 9i, there was no data type for time intervals. Intervals were converted to raw seconds and stored in Number columns, making calculations complex.

Oracle introduced these interval data types to simplify tasks:

- *Interval Year To Month:* Stores a time interval in years and months.

```
INTERVAL '[+|-] [y] [m]' YEAR (<YearPreceision>) TO MONTH
```

Where,

  - The **+** or **–** indicates the time interval's sign (default is positive)
  - **y** is the optional number of years
  - **m** is the optional number of months. **To Month** is included in instances where the years and months are included in the literal
  - **YearsPrecision** is the optional precision for the year (default is 2)

- *Interval Day To Second:* Stores a time interval in days and seconds.

```
INTERVAL '[+|-] [d] [h[:m[:s]]]' DAY (<DaysPreceision>)
  [TO HOURS | MINUTE | SECOND[(<SecondsPrecision>)]]
```

Where,

  - The **+** or **–** indicates the time interval's sign (default is positive)

- **d** is the optional number of days
- **h** is the optional number of hours. **To Hour** is included in instances where the days and hours are included in the literal
- **m** is the optional number of minutes. **To Minutes** is included in instances where the days and minutes are included in the literal
- **s** is the optional number of seconds. **To Second** is included in instances where the days and seconds are included in the literal
- **DaysPrecision** is the optional precision for the days (default is 2)
- **SecondsPrecision** is the optional precision for the fractional seconds (default is 6)

Raw/ Long Raw

Stores binary data such as digitized images. Data loaded into columns of this type is stored without conversion. The Raw data type has a maximum length of 255 bytes. Long Raw can contain up to 2 GB of binary data. Values in Long Raw columns **cannot be indexed**. Oracle strongly recommends converting LONG RAW to Binary LOB (BLOB).

Large OBject (LOB)

LOB data types (BLOB, CLOB, NCLOB, and BFILE) store large and unstructured data like text, images, video and spatial data. Here's a brief overview:

- BLOB stores unstructured binary large objects.
- NCLOB stores Unicode data.
- CLOB stores single-byte and multibyte character data.
- BFILE allows access to binary file LOBs stored outside Oracle Database. BFILE data can be up to 264-1 bytes, although the operating system may impose restrictions.

The size of BLOB, CLOB, and NCLOB data can be up to (232-1 bytes) * (the value of the CHUNK parameter of LOB storage).

Extended Data Types

Starting with Oracle Database 12c, the maximum size for Varchar2, NVarchar2, and RAW data types is 32,767 bytes. The default size limits are:

- 4,000 bytes for Varchar2 and NVarchar2.
- 2,000 bytes for RAW.

Columns with Varchar2 or NVarchar2 sizes greater than 4,000 bytes, or RAW sizes greater than 2,000 bytes, are considered Extended Data Types. These columns are stored out-of-line using Oracle's LOB technology, which aligns the LOB storage with the table.

Now that we are familiar with the most commonly used data types, let's proceed with table creation. Oracle stores the table structure information, as specified in the CREATE TABLE command, within its Data Dictionary.

Boolean Data Type In Oracle 23

Oracle 23 introduces the SQL **boolean** data type, expanding its functionality. This data type supports three truth values**:** **TRUE** and **FALSE**. Additionally, if there is no NOT NULL constraint, it supports the third truth value **UNKNOWN** (representing null). Case sensitivity is not enforced for the boolean values; you can use **TRUE**, **FALSE**, **true**, **false**, or any combination of upper and lower case letters.

Chapter

5

SECTION II: BASICS OF SQL

Working With Database Tables

Creating Table

The **CREATE TABLE** command uniquely defines each column of the table. A column has the following three attributes:

- A column name
- The data type
- Column size

The table creation command is structured as:

```
CREATE TABLE <TableName>(
  <ColumnName1> <DataType>(<Size>),
  <ColumnName2> <DataType>(<Size>),
  . . .);
```

Each column defined in a table must have a data type. Each column definition is a single clause in the CREATE TABLE syntax, separated by commas. Finally, the SQL statement is terminated with a semicolon.

Rules For Creating Tables

1. A table name can have up to 30 characters.
2. Alphabets (A-Z, a-z) and numbers (0-9) are allowed.
3. A name should begin with an alphabet.
4. The use of the special character like _ is allowed and recommended. Special characters such as $, # are allowed **only in Oracle**.
5. SQL reserved words are **not** allowed (e.g., CREATE, SELECT)

Answer The Following Questions Before Creating A Table

- What are the columns of the rows to be stored?
- What are the data types of the columns and their respective sizes?
- Which column will be the record identifier (usually called primary key)?
- Which columns do/do not allow null values?
- Which columns do/do not allow duplicates?
- Are there default values for certain columns?

Let's take an example. Create a table that allows storing information of all the subscribers of a cable TV operator. A subscriber would have:

- Unique Account Number
- First Name
- LastName
- Address
  1. Building Name
  2. Road
  3. Area
  4. City
  5. Pincode
  6. Country
- Contact Number
- Status [Active or Inactive]

Begin the table creation by answering the above questions:

- What are the columns of the rows to be stored?
  1. AccountNo
  2. FirstName
  3. LastName
  4. BuildingName
  5. Road
  6. Area
  7. City
  8. Pincode
  9. Country
  10. ContactNo
  11. Status
- What are the data types of the columns and their respective sizes?

Column Name	Data Type	Size
AccountNo	Number	10
FirstName	Varchar2	25
LastName	Varchar2	25
BuildingName	Varchar2	25
Road	Varchar2	25

Column Name	Data Type	Size
Area	Varchar2	25
City	Varchar2	25
Pincode	Number	10
Country	Varchar2	25
ContactNo	Number	15
Status	Char	1

- Which column will be the record identifier (usually called primary key)?

Column Name	Primary Key
AccountNo	Yes

- Which columns do/do not allow null values?

Column Name	Allow Null
AccountNo	No
FirstName	No
LastName	No
BuildingName	Yes
Road	Yes
Area	Yes
City	Yes
Pincode	Yes
Country	No
ContactNo	No
Status	No

- Which columns do/do not allow duplicates?

Column Name	Allow Duplicates
AccountNo	No

- Are there default values for certain columns that also allow null values?

Column Name	Default Values
Country	India
Status	A

Based on the above answers, the table can be created using the following command:

```
CREATE TABLE SubscriberMaster(
   AccountNo Number(10) PRIMARY KEY,
   FirstName Varchar2(25) NOT NULL,
   LastName Varchar2(25) NOT NULL,
   BuildingName Varchar2(25),
   Road Varchar2(25),
   Area Varchar2(25),
   City Varchar2(25),
   Pincode Number(10),
```

```
    Country Varchar2(25) DEFAULT 'India',
    ContactNo Number(15) NOT NULL,
    Status Char(1) DEFAULT 'A');
```

In the above code spec, all the columns of the table pertain to a single record. Therefore, the column definitions are enclosed within parentheses.

Output:

```
Table created.
```

Using IF [NOT] EXISTS

Oracle 23 introduces the **IF [NOT] EXISTS** clause for the CREATE TABLE statement. This clause allows you to create a table only if it doesn't already exist. This prevents errors if you try to create a table that's already there, and it's particularly useful in scripting and automated deployments.

The syntax with the new clause is:

```
CREATE TABLE IF NOT EXISTS <TableName>(
    <ColumnName1> <DataType>(<Size>),
    <ColumnName2> <DataType>(<Size>),
    . . .);
```

If the table ***<TableName>*** already exists, the statement will simply do nothing and not raise an error.

Let's recreate the SubscriberMaster table using the IF NOT EXISTS clause:

```
CREATE TABLE IF NOT EXISTS SubscriberMaster(
    AccountNo Number(10) PRIMARY KEY,
    FirstName Varchar2(25) NOT NULL,
    LastName Varchar2(25) NOT NULL,
    BuildingName Varchar2(25),
    Road Varchar2(25),
    Area Varchar2(25),
    City Varchar2(25),
    Pincode Number(10),
    Country Varchar2(25) DEFAULT 'India',
    ContactNo Number(15) NOT NULL,
    Status Char(1) DEFAULT 'A');
```

The IF NOT EXISTS clause ensures that the script will continue to run without error even if the table has been previously created.

Creating Temporary Tables

In complex data processes that can't be completed all in one go, temporary data stores often come to the rescue. These temporary tables significantly boost the performance of intricate and resource-intensive queries by caching their results. Subsequent SQL queries can then reference these cached results, leading to a noticeable improvement in performance.

Imagine a web-based shopping cart where a customer selects multiple products. Each of these selections is stored as a row in a temporary table. The application updates these rows to reflect any changes made to the selected products. Once the customer decides to complete the purchase, the application transfers these rows from the temporary table to a permanent table for processing.

Oracle supports the creation of temporary data stores through **Global Temporary Tables**. Here's a closer look at some key features and behavior:

- ***Indexing:*** Indexes can be created on temporary tables to enhance query performance.
- ***Segment Allocation:*** Unlike regular tables, segments are not allocated upon the creation of a temporary table. Instead, segments are allocated when the first INSERT operation is executed.
- ***Data Lifespan:*** Data in these tables is automatically deleted at the end of the transaction or session, depending on the type of temporary table.
- ***Data Privacy:*** Data in a Global Temporary Table is private. Data inserted by one session is accessible only within that session.

Syntax:

```
CREATE GLOBAL TEMPORARY TABLE <TableName> (
  <ColumnName1> <DataType>,
  <ColumnNameN> <DataType>) ON COMMIT DELETE ROWS;
```

The **ON COMMIT DELETE ROWS** clause indicates that the data should be deleted at the end of the transaction.

Syntax:

```
CREATE GLOBAL TEMPORARY TABLE <TableName> (
  <ColumnName1> <DataType>,
  <ColumnNameN> <DataType>) ON COMMIT PRESERVE ROWS;
```

The **ON COMMIT PRESERVE ROWS** clause indicates that rows should be preserved until the end of the session.

On a temporary table:

- Views can be created.
- Triggers can be associated.
- Indexes can be created.

Let's create a table to hold the product details of items being purchased by a customer using a shopping cart:

```
CREATE GLOBAL TEMPORARY TABLE CartProducts(
   CustomerNo Number(10),
   ProductName Varchar2(25),
   Discount Number(10),
   Qty Number(10),
   Price Number(10)) ON COMMIT DELETE ROWS;
```

Output:

```
Table created.
```

> **TIP** When a TRUNCATE statement is issued against a temporary table, only the session-specific data is truncated. This action has no effect on the data of other sessions.

Inserting Data Into Tables

Once a table is created successfully, it can be loaded with data using the **INSERT INTO** statement. This operation starts by creating a new, empty row in the table and then populating it with the specified values.

The INSERT INTO statement consists of two main parts:

- ***Table and Column Specification:*** This section identifies the table where data will be inserted and lists the columns to be populated with values.
- ***Data Values:*** This section provides the actual data values to be inserted into the specified columns.

Syntax:

```
INSERT INTO <TableName> (<ColumnName1>, <ColumnName2>)
   VALUES (<Expression1>, <Expression2>);
```

For example, let's add new subscribers to the SubscriberMaster table:

AccountNo	FirstName	LastName	BuildingName	Road
1	Sharanam	Shah	Flora Deccan	M. G. Road

AccountNo	Area	City	Pincode	Country	ContactNo	Status
1	Andheri	Mumbai	400058	India	28822883	A

Here's how you can add the new subscribers to the SubscriberMaster table using the INSERT INTO command:

```
INSERT INTO SubscriberMaster (AccountNo, FirstName, LastName, BuildingName,
   Road, Area, City, Pincode, Country, ContactNo, Status)
      VALUES (1, 'Sharanam', 'Shah', 'Flora Deccan', 'M. G. Road', 'Andheri', 'Mumbai',
         400058, 'India', 28822883, 'A');
```

Output:

```
1 row created.
```

TIP: Character expressions within the **INSERT INTO** statement must be enclosed in **single quotes** ['].

In the INSERT INTO statement, each column and value pair follow a **one-to-one** relationship. For example, the first value [1] is inserted into the first column [AccountNo], the second value [Sharanam] is inserted into the second column [FirstName], and so on. If the number of values matches the number of columns and the values are in the same sequence as the table columns' data types, indicating the column names is **unnecessary**.

The above INSERT INTO can be re-written as follows:

```
INSERT INTO SubscriberMaster VALUES (1, 'Sharanam', 'Shah', 'Flora Deccan',
   'M. G. Road', 'Andheri', 'Mumbai', 400058, 'India', 28822883, 'A');
```

Output:

```
1 row created.
```

Insert Data In Specific Columns

When the number of values specified is fewer than the number of columns in the table, you must specify both the column names and their corresponding values in the INSERT INTO statement.

To insert only the following values, the INSERT INTO statement would be:

AccountNo	FirstName	LastName	ContactNo	Status
2	Vaishali	Shah	26822883	A

Solution:

```
INSERT INTO SubscriberMaster (AccountNo, FirstName, LastName, ContactNo,
   Status) VALUES (2, 'Vaishali', 'Shah', 26822883, 'A');
```

Output:

```
1 row created.
```

If the INSERT INTO statement does not specify the mapping between table columns and their respective values, Oracle will be unable to determine which columns the data should be inserted into. This often leads to a loss of data integrity, rendering the data within the table largely useless.

Viewing Data In The Tables

After populating the table with the desired data, you can view it using the **SELECT** SQL command. SELECT is one of the most frequently used SQL commands, allowing you to retrieve data from one or more database tables.

Viewing All Rows And All Columns

To view all records - all rows and all columns - use the following syntax:

```
SELECT * FROM <TableName>;
SELECT <ColumnName1> TO <ColumnNameN> FROM <TableName>;
```

Where,

- The ***Meta character asterisk [*]*** indicates all table rows and columns.
- ***ColumnName1*** to ***ColumnNameN*** represents the names of the table column.

For example, to display the names and contact numbers of all the subscribers, you can use:

```
SELECT FirstName, LastName, ContactNo FROM SubscriberMaster;
```

The SQL statement begins with the SELECT keyword, followed by a list of table columns. This list specifies which columns are to be retrieved from the table. The list of columns is then followed by the SQL keyword **FROM** and the table name from which the data is being retrieved. Oracle parses and compiles the SQL query, executes it, and retrieves data from all rows and columns, or selected rows and columns, from the table.

Output:

```
FIRSTNAME                 LASTNAME                   CONTACTNO
------------------------- ------------------------- ----------
Sharanam                  Shah                        28822883
Vaishali                  Shah                        26128736
Kanchan                   Toprani                     24157362
Anil                      Naik                        24058723
Nikhil                    Arora                       24768788
Stuti                     Shah                        27364812
Anuraddha                 Iyer                        24563567
Mital                     Gandhi                      22356754
Chaitanya                 Malhotra                    25437689
Narendra                  Dodhia                      27865679

10 rows selected.
```

Here's an example to display all the information for all available subscribers:

```
SELECT * FROM SubscriberMaster;
```

Output:

```
ACCOUNTNO FIRSTNAME  LASTNAME BUILDINGNAME   ROAD                 AREA
CITY      ZIPCODE COUNTRY                        CONTACTNO S
--------- ---------- -------- -------------- -------------------- -----------
--------- ------ -------------------------------- --------- -
        1 Sharanam   Shah     Flora Deccan   M. G. Road           Andheri
Mumbai    400058 India                            28822883 A
        2 Vaishali   Shah     Blue Queens    S. V. Road           Bandra
Pune      400050 India                            26128736 A
        3 Kanchan    Toprani  Shankar Apts   L. J. Road           Wadala
Delhi     400031 India                            24157362 N
        4 Anil       Naik     Makanji Kunj   Savarkar Road        Matunga
Bangalore 400025 India                            24058723 A
        5 Nikhil     Arora    Krishna Kunj   Edenwala Road        King Circle
Mumbai    400024 India                            24768788 A
        6 Stuti      Shah     Aashirwad      Gadhakari Road       Colaba
Mumbai    400012 India                            27364812 N
        7 Anuraddha Iyer      Raj Bldg       Navy Road            Khar
Pune      400087 India                            24563567 A
        8 Mital      Gandhi   Prakash Towers Cadell Road          Borivali
Delhi     400045 India                            22356754 N
        9 Chaitanya Malhotra Advani Bldg     Bal., Govinddas, Road Dahisar
Mumbai    400090 India                            25437689 A
       10 Narendra   Dodhia   Pheonix Towers Phoenix Road         Sewree
Delhi     400021 India                            27865679 N

10 rows selected.
```

The above statements help in retrieving all the data from the table. However, this is usually not the case. There are times when specific data needs to be retrieved. The SELECT statement allows the following:

- Retrieve selected columns and all rows.
- Retrieve selected rows and all columns.
- Retrieve selected columns and selected rows.

Retrieve Selected Columns And All Rows

To retrieve specific columns while including all rows from a table, use the following SQL syntax. Specify the desired column names after the SELECT keyword:

```
SELECT <ColumnName1>, <ColumnName2> FROM <TableName>;
```

For example, to display the names and account numbers of all the subscribers, the query would look like this:

```
SELECT FirstName, LastName, AccountNo FROM SubscriberMaster;
```

Output:

```
FIRSTNAME                 LASTNAME                  ACCOUNTNO
------------------------- ------------------------- ----------
Sharanam                  Shah                               1
Vaishali                  Shah                               2
```

```
Kanchan             Toprani             3
Anil                Naik                4
Nikhil              Arora               5
Stuti               Shah                6
Anuraddha           Iyer                7
Mital               Gandhi              8
Chaitanya           Malhotra            9
Narendra            Dodhia             10

10 rows selected.
```

Retrieve Selected Rows And All Columns

The SELECT statement used earlier displayed all rows because no condition was set to inform Oracle how to choose a specific set of rows [or a specific row] from a table. Oracle allows setting a condition using a **WHERE** Clause in an SQL SELECT query to apply a filter for the rows retrieved.

When a WHERE clause is added to the SQL query, each record in the table is compared with the condition specified in the Where clause. Hence, only those records that satisfy the specified condition are displayed.

For example, this could be useful to obtain:

- All the information of a particular subscriber.
- All the information of subscribers meeting particular criteria.

Syntax:

```
SELECT * FROM <TableName> WHERE <Condition>;
```

Where, ***Condition*** is always defined as ***ColumnName = Value***.

Let's take an example to display the subscriber details of a subscriber whose account number is 1:

```
SELECT * FROM SubscriberMaster WHERE AccountNo = 1;
```

Output:

```
ACCOUNTNO FIRSTNAME  LASTNAME BUILDINGNAME   ROAD                 AREA
CITY      ZIPCODE COUNTRY                        CONTACTNO S
--------- ---------- -------- -------------- -------------------- -----------
--------- ------ ------------------------------- --------- -
        1 Sharanam   Shah     Flora Deccan   M. G. Road           Andheri
Mumbai    400058 India                            28822883 A
```

When specifying a condition in the WHERE clause, the following standard operators can be used:

Operator	Description	Examples
=	Equal to	**SELECT * FROM** SubscriberMaster **WHERE** FirstName = 'Sharanam';
<>	Not equal to	**SELECT * FROM** SubscriberMaster **WHERE** FirstName <> 'Sharanam';
!=		**SELECT * FROM** SubscriberMaster **WHERE** FirstName != 'Sharanam';
>	Greater than	**SELECT * FROM** SubscriberMaster **WHERE** AccountNo > 5;
>=	Greater than or equal to	**SELECT * FROM** SubscriberMaster **WHERE** AccountNo >= 5;
<=	Less than or equal to	**SELECT * FROM** SubscriberMaster **WHERE** AccountNo <= 5;
BETWEEN	Between an inclusive range	**SELECT * FROM** SubscriberMaster **WHERE** AccountNo **BETWEEN** 5 **AND** 10;
LIKE	Search for a pattern	**SELECT * FROM** SubscriberMaster **WHERE** FirstName **LIKE** 'Sha%';
IN	Used if the exact column values to be returned are known	**SELECT * FROM** SubscriberMaster **WHERE** LastName **IN** ('Joshi', 'Shah');

Single quotes are required around conditional values for textual values. Numeric values should not be enclosed in quotes.

- **For textual Values**

Correct SELECT SQL Statement	Wrong SELECT SQL Statement
SELECT * FROM SubscriberMaster **WHERE** FirstName = 'Sharanam';	**SELECT * FROM** SubscriberMaster **WHERE** FirstName = Sharanam;

- **For Numeric Values**

Correct SELECT SQL Statement	Wrong SELECT SQL Statement
SELECT * FROM SubscriberMaster **WHERE** AccountNo > 5;	**SELECT * FROM** SubscriberMaster **WHERE** AccountNo > '5';

Retrieve Selected Columns And Selected Rows

To obtain specific rows and specific columns from a table, a SELECT query is written with specific column names along with a WHERE clause.

```
SELECT <ColumnName1>, <ColumnName2> FROM <TableName>
  WHERE <Condition>;
```

Let's take an example to display names and contact numbers of all active subscribers:

```
SELECT FirstName, LastName, ContactNo FROM SubscriberMaster
```

```
WHERE Status = 'A';
```

Output:

```
FIRSTNAME                 LASTNAME                  CONTACTNO
------------------------- ------------------------- ----------
Sharanam                  Shah                        28822883
Vaishali                  Shah                        26128736
Anil                      Naik                        24058723
Nikhil                    Arora                       24768788
Anuraddha                 Iyer                        24563567
Chaitanya                 Malhotra                    25437689

6 rows selected.
```

Adding Line Feeds While Retrieving Data

Display the Employee Details as:
Employee Name: Sharanam Shah
Designation: Technical Writer
Salary: 82500

Solution:

```
SELECT 'Employee Name: ' || FirstName || ' ' || LastName || CHR(10) ||
  'Designation: ' || Designation || CHR(10) || 'Salary:  ' || Salary "Employee Details"
     FROM Employees;
```

Output:

```
Employee Details
--------------------------------------------
Employee Name: Sharanam Shah
Designation: Technical Writing
Salary:  82500
Employee Name: Vaishali Shah
Designation: Database Management
Salary:  55000
Employee Name: Keyur Kapoor
Designation: Testing
Salary:  22000
Employee Name: Amit Haria
Designation: Programming
Salary:  22660
Employee Name: Abhishek Benegal
Designation: Sales
Salary:  13334.2
Employee Name: Chetan Dedhia
Designation: HR
Salary:  13553.1
Employee Name: Narendra Dodhia
Designation: Accounts
```

```
Salary:  13578.4
Employee Name: Meenal Doshi
Designation: Auditing
Salary:  49500
Employee Name: Anil Mayekar
Designation: Peon
Salary:  31207
Employee Name: Chaitanya Kapoor
Designation: Peon
Salary:  1320
Employee Name: Amit Paul
Designation: Peon
Salary:  31207
11 rows selected.
```

Eliminating Duplicate Rows

In databases, tables may contain duplicate data. While duplicate records cannot always be prevented from being entered, they can be eliminated when viewed using the DISTINCT clause in a SELECT SQL query. When the DISTINCT clause is used with the SELECT keyword, it retrieves only unique data based on the specified columns.

> TIP: The DISTINCT clause can only be used with SELECT statements.

Syntax:

```
SELECT DISTINCT <ColumnName1>, <ColumnName2> FROM <TableName>;
SELECT DISTINCT * FROM <TableName>;
```

The ***SELECT DISTINCT <ColumnName1>, <ColumnName2>*** clause scans the values of the specified columns and displays only unique values. The ***SELECT DISTINCT **** syntax scans entire rows and eliminates those with identical contents in each column.

Let's consider the SubscriberMaster table, which has a column named City. This column may contain duplicate values because multiple subscribers reside in the same city. To find out the unique cities being served cable TV, we can use the DISTINCT clause:

```
SELECT DISTINCT City FROM SubscriberMaster;
```

Output:

```
CITY
--------------------------------
Delhi
Mumbai
Bangalore
```

```
Pune
```

Here's an example of how to display unique last names and cities from the subscriber data:

```
SELECT DISTINCT LastName, City FROM SubscriberMaster;
```

Output:

```
LASTNAME                  CITY
------------------------- -------------------------
Gandhi                    Delhi
Dodhia                    Delhi
Naik                      Bangalore
Arora                     Mumbai
Shah                      Pune
Toprani                   Delhi
Shah                      Mumbai
Iyer                      Pune
Malhotra                  Mumbai

9 rows selected.
```

In the original table, there are two users with the same last name, Shah, who both reside in Mumbai. Because the combination of the LastName and City values for these users **is not unique**, only one row is retrieved when using the DISTINCT keyword.

Let's take an example. Add one more column [Pincode] after the DISTINCT keyword:

```
SELECT DISTINCT LastName, City, Pincode FROM SubscriberMaster;
```

Output:

```
LASTNAME                  CITY                         PINCODE
------------------------- ------------------------- ----------
Shah                      Pune                          400050
Arora                     Mumbai                        400024
Naik                      Bangalore                     400025
Gandhi                    Delhi                         400045
Shah                      Mumbai                        400058
Toprani                   Delhi                         400031
Shah                      Mumbai                        400012
Iyer                      Pune                          400087
Malhotra                  Mumbai                        400090
Dodhia                    Delhi                         400021

10 rows selected.
```

This retrieves both the subscribers with last name Shah because they have different Pincodes, making their entries unique.

For example; There may be times when a subscriber's details are entered twice due to data entry errors. In such cases, entire rows are duplicated. The DISTINCT * clause can be used to retrieve only unique subscribers:

```
SELECT DISTINCT * FROM SubscriberMaster;
```

Output: Shows the entry [if the entire row is duplicate] only once, even though entered twice in the table.

```
ACCOUNTNO FIRSTNAME  LASTNAME BUILDINGNAME   ROAD                 AREA
CITY      ZIPCODE COUNTRY                         CONTACTNO S
--------- ---------- -------- -------------- -------------------- -----------
--------- ------ ------------------------------- --------- -
        1 Sharanam  Shah     Flora Deccan   M. G. Road           Andheri
Mumbai    400058 India                             28822883 A
        2 Vaishali  Shah     Blue Queens    S. V. Road           Bandra
Pune      400050 India                             26128736 A
        3 Kanchan   Toprani  Shankar Apts   L. J. Road           Wadala
Delhi     400031 India                             24157362 N
        4 Anil      Naik     Makanji Kunj   Savarkar Road        Matunga
Bangalore 400025 India                             24058723 A
        5 Nikhil    Arora    Krishna Kunj   Edenwala Road        King Circle
Mumbai    400024 India                             24768788 A
        6 Stuti     Shah     Aashirwad      Gadhakari Road       Colaba
Mumbai    400012 India                             27364812 N
        7 Anuraddha Iyer     Raj Bldg       Navy Road            Khar
Pune      400087 India                             24563567 A
        8 Mital     Gandhi   Prakash Towers Cadell Road          Borivali
Delhi     400045 India                             22356754 N
        9 Chaitanya Malhotra Advani Bldg    Bal., Govinddas, Road Dahisar
Mumbai    400090 India                             25437689 A
       10 Narendra  Dodhia   Pheonix Towers Phoenix Road         Sewree
Delhi     400021 India                             27865679 N

10 rows selected.
```

Data Sorting

Data retrieved from the table can be sorted as desired. The rows retrieved using the SELECT query can be sorted in either **ascending** or **descending** order, depending on the specified condition in the SELECT statement.

Syntax:

```
SELECT * FROM <TableName>
  ORDER BY <ColumnName1>, <ColumnName2> <[Sort Order]>;
```

The SQL ***ORDER BY*** clause is used to sort the retrieved data. The sorting can be based on one or more columns in a table.

The ORDER BY clause can only be used in SELECT statements.

For example, to display the account number and subscriber name of all the available subscribers sorted by their last names:

```
SELECT AccountNo, FirstName, LastName FROM SubscriberMaster
```

```
ORDER BY LastName;
```

Output:

```
ACCOUNTNO  FIRSTNAME                  LASTNAME
---------- -------------------------  ----------------------
         5 Nikhil                     Arora
        10 Narendra                   Dodhia
         8 Mital                      Gandhi
         7 Anuraddha                  Iyer
         9 Chaitanya                  Malhotra
         4 Anil                       Naik
         1 Sharanam                   Shah
         2 Vaishali                   Shah
         6 Stuti                      Shah
         3 Kanchan                    Toprani

10 rows selected.
```

When no sort order is specified, data is sorted in **ascending order by default**. To sort the data in descending order, include the **DESC** keyword **after** the column name in the ORDER BY clause, before the semi colon.

For instance, to display the most recently added subscribers before the older ones, you could use the following example:

```
SELECT AccountNo, FirstName, LastName FROM SubscriberMaster
  ORDER BY AccountNo DESC;
```

Output:

```
 ACCOUNTNO FIRSTNAME                  LASTNAME
---------- -------------------------  ---------------------
        10 Narendra                   Dodhia
         9 Chaitanya                  Malhotra
         8 Mital                      Gandhi
         7 Anuraddha                  Iyer
         6 Stuti                      Shah
         5 Nikhil                     Arora
         4 Anil                       Naik
         3 Kanchan                    Toprani
         2 Vaishali                   Shah
         1 Sharanam                   Shah

10 rows selected.
```

The ORDER BY clause can also be used to sort data by multiple columns. When using ORDER BY with more than one column, separate the column names with commas.

Let's take an example to display the subscribers in the order of their last name and within last name, in the order of city:

```
SELECT AccountNo, FirstName, LastName, City FROM SubscriberMaster
```

```
ORDER BY LastName, City;
```

Output:

```
ACCOUNTNO FIRSTNAME       LASTNAME        CITY
---------- --------------- --------------- ---------------
         5 Nikhil          Arora           Mumbai
        10 Narendra        Dodhia          Delhi
         8 Mital           Gandhi          Delhi
         7 Anuraddha       Iyer            Pune
         9 Chaitanya       Malhotra        Mumbai
         4 Anil            Naik            Bangalore
         1 Sharanam        Shah            Mumbai
         6 Stuti           Shah            Mumbai
         2 Vaishali        Shah            Pune
         3 Kanchan         Toprani         Delhi

10 rows selected.
```

When the order of the columns specified after the ORDER BY statement is reversed, the same records are returned, but their order changes. This is because the ORDER BY clause first sorts the retrieved data based on the first column specified, then by the second column, and so on.

Output:

```
ACCOUNTNO FIRSTNAME       LASTNAME        CITY
---------- --------------- --------------- --------------------
         4 Anil            Naik            Bangalore
        10 Narendra        Dodhia          Delhi
         8 Mital           Gandhi          Delhi
         3 Kanchan         Toprani         Delhi
         5 Nikhil          Arora           Mumbai
         9 Chaitanya       Malhotra        Mumbai
         6 Stuti           Shah            Mumbai
         1 Sharanam        Shah            Mumbai
         7 Anuraddha       Iyer            Pune
         2 Vaishali        Shah            Pune

10 rows selected.
```

When you want specific ordering for each column in a multi-column sort, you need to specify **ASC** (ascending) or **DESC** (descending) after each column:

```
SELECT AccountNo, FirstName, LastName, City FROM SubscriberMaster
  ORDER BY LastName DESC, City ASC;
```

Output:

```
ACCOUNTNO    FIRSTNAME       LASTNAME        CITY
------------ --------------- --------------- -------------
3            Kanchan         Toprani         Delhi
1            Sharanam        Shah            Mumbai
6            Stuti           Shah            Mumbai
2            Vaishali        Shah            Pune
4            Anil            Naik            Bangalore
```

```
9          Chaitanya      Malhotra       Mumbai
7          Anuraddha      Iyer           Pune
8          Mital          Gandhi         Delhi
10         Narendra       Dodhia         Delhi
5          Nikhil         Arora          Mumbai

10 rows selected
```

Creating A Table From A Table

To reorganize an Oracle table or move a table to a different tablespace, you can use the **CREATE TABLE AS SELECT** command. This command allows you to:

- Structure and create a new table.
- Copy data from an existing table to the new table.
- Rename the new table.

Syntax:

```
CREATE TABLE <TableName> (<ColumnName>, <ColumnName>)
  AS SELECT <ColumnName>, <ColumnName> FROM <TableName>
```

In a SELECT query, the table name specified refers to the **Source** table from which the data will be fetched. Meanwhile, the table name in the CREATE TABLE statement refers to the **Target** table, which will be created and populated with the data.

Let's create a new table named MumbaiSubscriberMaster with the following columns from the SubscriberMaster. This new table will only include subscribers who belong to Mumbai:

1. AccountNo
2. FirstName
3. LastName
4. BuildingName
5. Road
6. Area
7. Pincode
8. Country
9. ContactNo
10. Status

Solution:

```
CREATE TABLE MumbaiSubscriberMaster (AccountNo, FirstName, LastName,
  BuildingName, Road, Area, Pincode, Country, ContactNo, Status)
     AS SELECT AccountNo, FirstName, LastName, BuildingName, Road, Area,
        Pincode, Country, ContactNo, Status FROM SubscriberMaster
           WHERE City = 'Mumbai';
```

Output:

```
Table created.
```

It's also possible to create a table without copying any data from the source table - this means only the structure of the table is created. To achieve this, the Select statement must include a **WHERE clause** with a condition that **cannot** be met. This ensures that **no rows are retrieved** from the source table. As a result, the SELECT statement in the CREATE TABLE definition will only copy the table structure, creating an empty target table with the same structure as the source table.

Let's create a new table named SubscriberMasterBackup with the same columns as the SubscriberMaster table, but without any records being populated in SubscriberMasterBackup:

```
CREATE TABLE SubscriberMasterBackup (AccountNo, FirstName, LastName,
  BuildingName, Road, Area, Pincode, City, Country, ContactNo, Status)
      AS SELECT AccountNo, FirstName, LastName, BuildingName, Road, Area,
          Pincode, City, Country, ContactNo, Status FROM SubscriberMaster
              WHERE 1 = 2;
```

Output:

```
Table created.
```

While creating such tables, it's not necessary to strictly follow the same structure or use the same column names. For instance, new columns can be added, or existing columns can be merged into a new column.

Let's take an example. Create a table named SubscriberContactDetails with the following columns:

- AccountNo
- Name
- PhoneNumber

The data should be collected from the SubscriberMaster table. The Name column will hold the FirstName and LastName. PhoneNumber should be picked up from the ContactNo column of the SubscriberMaster table:

```
CREATE TABLE SubscriberContactDetails (AccountNo, Name, PhoneNo)
  AS SELECT AccountNo, FirstName || ' ' || LastName, ContactNo
      FROM SubscriberMaster;
```

This allows for flexibility in structuring the new table while still deriving its data from the original table.

Output:

```
Table created.
```

The new table when queried for data will retrieve the following data:

```
SELECT * FROM SubscriberContactDetails;
```

Output:

```
 ACCOUNTNO NAME                               PHONENO
---------- ------------------------------ ----------
         1 Sharanam Shah                    28822883
         2 Vaishali Shah                    26128736
         3 Kanchan Toprani                  24157362
         4 Anil Naik                        24058723
         5 Nikhil Arora                     24768788
         6 Stuti Shah                       27364812
         7 Anuraddha Iyer                   24563567
         8 Mital Gandhi                     22356754
```

```
         9 Chaitanya Malhotra                   25437689
        10 Narendra Dodhia                      27865679

10 rows selected.
```

Copying All Data From Another Table

Data is typically inserted into a table using an INSERT INTO statement. Besides the standard INSERT INTO statement, it's also possible to populate a table with data that already exists in another table. In other words, you can copy data from one table to another.

Syntax:

```
INSERT INTO <TableName>
  SELECT <ColumnName1>, <ColumnNameN> FROM <TableName>;
```

Suppose we have a table called SubscriberMasterBackup that currently holds no data. We want to copy all subscriber data from an existing table, SubscriberMaster, into SubscriberMasterBackup:

```
INSERT INTO SubscriberMasterBackup
  SELECT AccountNo, FirstName, LastName, BuildingName, Road, Area, Pincode,
      City, Country, ContactNo, Status FROM SubscriberMaster;
```

Output:

```
10 rows created.
```

Copying Specific Data From Another Table

Instead of copying all data from the source table, you can also copy only specific data by using the WHERE clause in the SELECT query:

```
INSERT INTO <TableName> SELECT <ColumnName1>, <ColumnNameN>
  FROM <TableName> WHERE <Condition>;
```

Suppose we need to copy the data of all subscribers from Mumbai, which is available in the SubscriberMaster table, into the SubscriberMasterBackup table:

```
INSERT INTO SubscriberMasterBackup SELECT AccountNo, FirstName, LastName,
  BuildingName, Road, Area, Pincode, City, Country, ContactNo, Status
      FROM SubscriberMaster WHERE City = 'Mumbai';
```

Output:

```
4 rows created.
```

Using Timestamp

Let's go through an example of creating a table named EmployeeMuster to hold attendance details of employees. We'll also include a Timestamp column to record the date and time when each attendance record is created:

```
CREATE TABLE EmployeeMuster(
  EmployeeNo Number(10),
  MusterDate Date,
  Attendance Varchar2(15),
  InTime Timestamp,
  OutTime Timestamp);
```

Output:

```
Table created.
```

Display the table structure of the table EmployeeMuster:

```
DESC EmployeeMuster;
```

Output:

```
Name                      Null?    Type
------------------------- -------- --------------
EMPLOYEENO                         NUMBER(10)
MUSTERDATE                         DATE
ATTENDANCE                         VARCHAR2(15)
INTIME                             TIMESTAMP(6)
OUTTIME                            TIMESTAMP(6)
```

Let's populate the EmployeeMuster table using the following INSERT INTO statements:

```
INSERT INTO EmployeeMuster (EmployeeNo, MusterDate, Attendance, InTime,
  OutTime) VALUES(1, SYSDATE, 'Present', Timestamp '2007-01-23 08:35:55.1245',
     Timestamp '2007-01-23 05:05:15.0');
INSERT INTO EmployeeMuster (EmployeeNo, MusterDate, Attendance, InTime,
  OutTime) VALUES(2, SYSDATE, 'Present', Timestamp '2007-01-23 09:25:15.548',
     Timestamp '2007-01-23 05:45:25.45');
```

Output [For each INSERT statement]:

```
1 row created.
```

Now let's display the data available in the EmployeeMuster table:

```
SELECT * FROM EmployeeMuster;
```

Output:

```
EMPLOYEENO MUSTERDAT ATTENDANCE INTIME                         OUTTIME
---------- --------- ---------- ------------------------------ ----------------------------
         1 29-APR-08 Present    23-JAN-07 08.35.55.124500 AM   23-JAN-07 05.05.15.000000 AM
```

```
        2 29-APR-08 Present    23-JAN-07 09.25.15.548000 AM  23-JAN-07 05.45.25.450000 AM

2 rows selected.
```

Using BINARY_FLOAT And BINARY_DOUBLE

Here's an example of creating a table named BankBook that includes OpBal as BINARY_FLOAT and ClBal as BINARY_DOUBLE:

```
CREATE TABLE BankBook(
  BookNo Number(10) PRIMARY KEY,
  AccountNo Varchar2(10),
  BookDate Date,
  OpBal BINARY_FLOAT,
  ClBal BINARY_DOUBLE);
```

Output:

```
Table created.
```

The following command describes the table named BankBook:

```
DESC BankBook;
```

Output:

```
Name                                      Null?    Type
----------------------------------------- -------- --------------
BOOKNO                                    NOT NULL NUMBER(10)
ACCOUNTNO                                          VARCHAR2(10)
BOOKDATE                                           DATE
OPBAL                                              BINARY_FLOAT
CLBAL                                              BINARY_DOUBLE
```

The following statements populate the table named BankBook:

```
INSERT INTO BankBook (BookNo, AccountNo, BookDate, OpBal, ClBal)
  VALUES(1, 'SB100', '03-Jan-2008', 232.7f, 242.7d);
INSERT INTO BankBook (BookNo, AccountNo, BookDate, OpBal, ClBal)
  VALUES(2, 'SB101', '04-Jan-2008', 432.7f, 642.7d);
```

Output: (For each record inserted)

```
1 row created.
```

In addition to literal values, the following special values can be used with the BINARY_FLOAT and BINARY_DOUBLE data types:

- BINARY_FLOAT_NAN: Not a number
- BINARY_FLOAT_ INFINITY: Infinity
- BINARY_DOUBLE_NAN: Not a number
- BINARY_DOUBLE_INFINITY: Infinity

Solution:

```
INSERT INTO BankBook (BookNo, AccountNo, BookDate, OpBal, ClBal)
  VALUES(3, 'SB102', '05-Jan-2008', BINARY_FLOAT_NAN, BINARY_DOUBLE_NAN);
INSERT INTO BankBook (BookNo, AccountNo, BookDate, OpBal, ClBal)
  VALUES(4, 'SB101', '06-Jan-2008', BINARY_FLOAT_INFINITY,
          BINARY_DOUBLE_INFINITY);
```

Output: (For each record inserted)

```
1 row created.
```

The following command displays the contents of the table:

```
SELECT * FROM BankBook;
```

Output:

```
    BOOKNO ACCOUNTNO  BOOKDATE       OPBAL      CLBAL
---------- ---------- --------- ---------- ----------
         1 SB100      03-JAN-08 2.327E+002 2.427E+002
         2 SB101      04-JAN-08 4.327E+002 6.427E+002
         3 SB102      05-JAN-08        Nan        Nan
         4 SB101      06-JAN-08        Inf        Inf
```

Using INTERVAL

Create a table named BookRentals that contains columns to hold the rental details of book along with a special column to hold the duration of rent:

```
CREATE TABLE BookRentals(
  RentNo Number(10) PRIMARY KEY,
  BookName Varchar2(25),
  MemberNo Number(10),
  RentDate Date,
  Duration INTERVAL YEAR(2) TO MONTH);
```

Output:

```
Table created.
```

The following represents a time interval of One year and three months:

```
INSERT INTO BookRentals (RentNo, BookName, MemberNo, RentDate, Duration)
  VALUES(3, 'Famous Five', 1, '01-Jan-2008', INTERVAL '1-3' YEAR TO MONTH);
```

Output:

```
1 row created.
```

Create a table named BookRentals that contains columns to hold the rental details of book along with a special column to hold the duration of rent:

```
CREATE TABLE BookRentals(
   RentNo Number(10) PRIMARY KEY,
   BookName Varchar2(20),
   MemberNo Number(10),
   RentDate Date,
   Duration INTERVAL DAY(2) TO SECOND(6));
```

Output:

```
Table created.
```

The following represents a time interval of 1 day, 1 hour, 20 minutes and 30.15 seconds:

```
INSERT INTO BookRentals (RentNo, BookName, MemberNo, RentDate, Duration)
   VALUES(3, 'Famous Five', 1, '01-Jan-2008', INTERVAL '1 1:20:30.15' DAY TO SECOND);
```

Output:

```
1 row created.
```

Using Boolean

Oracle 23 introduces a native **BOOLEAN** data type, a significant improvement over previous versions where Booleans were simulated using numeric values (like 1 for true and 0 for false). This change brings clarity and simplicity to SQL code, making it easier to read and understand.

A Boolean value represents **truth**. It can be either **TRUE** or **FALSE**. Think of it like a light switch: it's either on (TRUE) or off (FALSE). This concept is fundamental to programming and now directly supported in Oracle SQL.

Previously, developers had to use numbers (often 1 and 0) or other workarounds to represent true/false values. This could make SQL queries harder to read and prone to errors. With the native BOOLEAN type, you can directly express conditions and store boolean values in your tables, leading to cleaner and more intuitive code.

Let's take an example of creating a table using the BOOLEAN data type:

```
CREATE TABLE SleepDerived (
   Name VARCHAR2(100),
   SleepMode BOOLEAN);
```

This SQL statement creates a table named SleepDerived. It has two columns:

- *Name:* Stores a person's name.
- *SleepMode:* Stores whether the person is sleeping (TRUE or FALSE).

Output:

```
Table created.
```

You can modify the properties of a boolean column after the table is created. For example, you can specify that the column cannot be empty (NOT NULL) and provide a default value:

```
ALTER TABLE SleepDerived MODIFY (SleepMode BOOLEAN NOT NULL);
ALTER TABLE SleepDerived MODIFY (SleepMode DEFAULT FALSE);
```

The first statement ensures that every row in the table must have a value for the SleepMode column. The second statement sets the default value for SleepMode to FALSE. So, if you insert a new row without specifying a value for SleepMode, it will automatically be set to FALSE.

Output: (For each ALTER TABLE statement)

```
Table altered.
```

Inserting data into a table with a boolean column is straightforward:

```
INSERT INTO SleepDerived (Name) VALUES ('Sharanam');
INSERT INTO SleepDerived (Name, SleepMode) VALUES ('Vaishali', FALSE);
INSERT INTO SleepDerived (Name, SleepMode) VALUES ('Shah', TRUE);
```

Notice how you can directly insert TRUE or FALSE values. Oracle also often accepts other representations of true/false, like 1 for true and 0 for false, or even 'YES'/'NO', but using TRUE and FALSE is the recommended and clearest approach.

Output: (For each record inserted)

```
1 row inserted.
```

The real power of the BOOLEAN data type becomes apparent when querying data:

```
SELECT Name FROM SleepDerived WHERE NOT SleepMode;
```

NAME
Sharanam
Vaishali

This query selects the names of all people who are not sleeping. The **NOT** operator directly works with the boolean column, making the query very readable. You no longer need to write something like WHERE SleepMode = 0 or some other equivalent.

The following statement will display all the data in the table, including the Boolean values in the SleepMode column:

```
SELECT * FROM SleepDerived;
```

NAME	SLEEPMODE
Sharanam	false
Vaishali	false
Shah	true

While you work with TRUE and FALSE, Oracle stores boolean values internally in a compact way. You can use the DUMP function to see how a value is represented:

```
SELECT DUMP(SleepMode) FROM SleepDerived WHERE Name = 'Shah';
```

DUMP(SLEEPMODE)
Typ=252 Len=1: 1

This will show you the internal representation of the boolean value for 'Shah' (which is TRUE).

Understanding the internal representation isn't usually necessary for day-to-day use, but it can be interesting to explore. For more information on DUMP function, refer to ***Examining The Column Content*** section of the ***Chapter 13: Character/String Function***.

Top-N Queries

Oracle 12c introduced an easier way to limit the rows displayed in a query result set through row limiting. This concept, known as **row limiting**, restricts the result set to a specific range of rows. For example, you might query the top three employees with the highest salary or the first 10 employees who recently joined the office.

Before Oracle 12c, implementing Top-N queries required nested sub-queries or the use of the ROWNUM pseudo-column, which could be complex and cumbersome.

Oracle 12c supports the ANSI-standard Row Limiting clause:

```
SELECT * FROM <TableName>
  ORDER BY <ColumnName1>, <ColumnName2> <[Sort Order]>
     [<OFFSET <ROW Number> ROW>
        FETCH <FIRST>/<NEXT> <ROW Number> [<PERCENT> ROWS ONLY
        [WITH TIES]]]
```

This clause makes it easy to retrieve the first N records from a result set or the first N records after skipping a set of records, enabling efficient pagination through the result set.

Let's retrieve the top 10 most expensive movies:

```
SELECT MovieNo, MovieName, Price, Category FROM Movies ORDER BY Price DESC
  FETCH FIRST 10 ROWS ONLY;
```

Output:

```
   MOVIENO MOVIENAME                           PRICE CATEGORY
---------- ------------------------- ---------- -------------------------
        14 U Me Aur Hum                          600 Romance
         7 Speed                                 500 Action
         9 Koi Mil Gaya                          500 Scientific
        11 All about Science                     500 Scientific
         6 Golmaal                               450 Comedy
        12 The Fast and the Furious              450 Action
         1 Titanic                               400 Romance
         2 DDLJ                                  350 Romance
        15 Taare Zameen Par                      320 Scientific
         5 Rush Hour                             300 Comedy

10 rows selected.
```

The above example displays the top 10 rows in order of their cost. There is no need to add the ORDER BY clause, but without it, the first 10 rows may not make a lot of sense.

If you wanted to show the top 10% of movies based on their cost, regardless of how many movies exist, you could write a query like this:

```
SELECT MovieNo, MovieName, Price, Category FROM Movies
  ORDER BY Price DESC FETCH FIRST 10 PERCENT ROWS ONLY;
```

Output:

```
   MOVIENO MOVIENAME                      PRICE CATEGORY
---------- ------------------------- ---------- -------------------------
        14 U Me Aur Hum                     600 Romance
         9 Koi Mil Gaya                     500 Scientific
```

Retrieve the next 5 top movies based on their cost:

```
SELECT MovieNo, MovieName, Price, Category FROM Movies
  ORDER BY Price DESC OFFSET 5 ROWS FETCH NEXT 5 ROWS ONLY;
```

Output:

```
   MOVIENO MOVIENAME                      PRICE CATEGORY
---------- ------------------------- ---------- -------------------------
        12 The Fast and the Furious         450 Action
         1 Titanic                          400 Romance
         2 DDLJ                             350 Romance
        15 Taare Zameen Par                 320 Scientific
         5 Rush Hour                        300 Comedy
```

Deleting Data From Table

The **DELETE** command is used to remove rows from a table. If no condition is specified using the **WHERE** clause, the command will delete all the rows from the table. However, if a condition is specified with the WHERE clause, only the rows that meet the condition will be deleted. Therefore, the DELETE command can be used to remove either all rows from a table or a specific set of rows.

Deleting All Rows

If you want to delete all the subscriber data from the SubscriberMasterBackup table, you can use the following SQL statement:

```
DELETE FROM SubscriberMasterBackup;
```

Output:

```
10 rows deleted.
```

Deleting Specific Row(s)

Syntax:

```
DELETE FROM <TableName> WHERE <Condition>;
```

Let's take an example of deleting only those subscribers that belong to the city Mumbai:

```
DELETE FROM SubscriberMasterBackup WHERE City = 'Mumbai';
```

Output:

```
4 rows deleted.
```

Deleting Specific Row(s) Using Exists Clause

The traditional DELETE command in SQL does not support specifying multiple table names in the FROM clause. Therefore, a JOIN is necessary to delete records from one table based on criteria from another table.

Let's take an example of a table named DisconnectedSubscribers, which contains the account numbers of all disconnected subscribers. Since these subscribers are no longer active, their related data is redundant in the SubscriberMaster table. The structure of the DisconnectedSubscribers table is as follows:

AccountNo	Disconnected
1	Yes
2	Yes
3	No

Delete all those subscribers who are disconnected. To achieve this, the **EXISTS** clause can be used with the DELETE command:

```
DELETE FROM SubscriberMaster
   WHERE EXISTS (SELECT AccountNo FROM DisconnectedSubscribers
        WHERE DisconnectedSubscribers.AccountNo = SubscriberMaster.AccountNo
             AND DisconnectedSubscribers.Disconnected = 'Yes');
```

A SELECT subquery with a JOIN [*explained later in this book*] is used to retrieve all those account numbers that are disconnected using DisconnectedSubscribers.Disconnected = 'Yes' as the condition. All such account numbers that are retrieved are passed to the DELETE command, for the actual deletion.

Output:

```
2 rows deleted.
```

The EXISTS condition is considered to be met if the subquery returns at least one row. The EXISTS condition can be used in any valid SQL statement - SELECT, INSERT, UPDATE or DELETE.

If UPDATE or DELETE statements are run, ensure that the **ROLLBACK** command is executed immediately after running **every** UPDATE or DELETE statement, so that the output data in this chapter matches the actual query results.

Truncating Data In Existing Tables

To clear the data from an existing table, you can use the **TRUNCATE TABLE** command. This command completely empties a table. Functionally, TRUNCATE TABLE is similar to the DELETE statement with no WHERE clause, as both remove all rows in the table. However, TRUNCATE TABLE is faster and uses fewer system resources than DELETE.

The DELETE command removes rows one at a time and logs an entry for each deleted row. In contrast, TRUNCATE TABLE de-allocates the data pages used to store the table's data, logging only the page de-allocations in the transaction log. While TRUNCATE TABLE removes all rows from a table, the table structure, including its columns, constraints, and indexes, remains intact.

Let's take an example of truncating the data in the SubscriberMaster table:

```
TRUNCATE TABLE SubscriberMaster;
```

Output:

```
Table truncated.
```

Modifying Table Data

Over time, the data held in tables may need modifications for various reasons. To modify the data in a table, the **UPDATE** command is used. Similar to the DELETE command, the UPDATE command can be utilized to update either all rows in a table or a specific set of rows.

Modifying All Rows

The UPDATE command updates the column data in the existing table with new values:

```
UPDATE <TableName>
  SET <ColumnName1> = <Expression1>,
      <ColumnName2> = <Expression2>;
```

The **SET** clause specifies which column data should be modified and the new values to assign. The **WHERE** clause, if provided, indicates which rows should be updated. If the WHERE clause is omitted, **all** rows in the table are updated.

Let's update the country of all the subscribers to "India" in the SubscriberMaster table:

```
UPDATE SubscriberMaster SET Country = 'India';
```

Output:

```
10 rows deleted.
```

Modifying Specific Row(s)

To modify specific rows the WHERE clause can be used:

```
UPDATE <TableName>
  SET <ColumnName1> = <Expression1>,
      <ColumnName2> = <Expression2>
     WHERE <Condition>;
```

Let's update the city named "Mumbai" to "Bombay" in the SubscriberMaster table:

```
UPDATE SubscriberMaster SET City = 'Mumbai' WHERE City = 'Bombay';
```

Output:

```
4 rows updated.
```

Destroying Tables

At times, tables within a database become obsolete and need to be discarded. The **DROP TABLE** statement facilitates this process. The DROP TABLE command removes a table definition along with all the data it holds, as well as its indexes, triggers, constraints, and permission specifications.

If any views or stored procedures reference the dropped table, they must be explicitly removed using the DROP VIEW or DROP PROCEDURE statement.

Be aware that if a table is dropped, all records contained within it are permanently lost and cannot be recovered.

Let's take an example to remove the SubscriberMaster table along with its data:

```
DROP TABLE SubscriberMaster;
```

Output:

```
Table dropped.
```

> DROP TABLE cannot be used to drop a table referenced by a FOREIGN KEY constraint. The referencing FOREIGN KEY constraint or the referencing table must first be dropped.

Retrieving Tables Available In The Schema

To find out which tables you can access in Oracle, you can use a specific command. This command will show you all the tables that are created under the current tablespace you are working with. The term "**TAB**" refers to an Oracle-specific views that stands for **USER_TABLES:**

```
SELECT * FROM TAB;
```

Output:

```
TNAME                          TABTYPE CLUSTERID
------------------------------ ------- ----------------------
ACCOUNTS                       TABLE
ACCOUNTSAUDITTRAIL             TABLE
. . .
TRANSACTIONSLOG                TABLE
TRIGONOMETRY                   TABLE

35 rows selected.
```

Describing Table Structures

To find out more about the columns in a table, use the DESCRIBE command. Here's the basic syntax you need:

```
DESCRIBE <TableName>;
```

Key Points:

- ***No semicolon (;)*** is needed at the end.
- This command ***works specifically in SQL*Plus***.
- It ***shows:***
  - Column names
  - Data types (like number, text)
  - Special attributes (if any)

Think of the DESCRIBE command as a way to peek under the hood and see the structure of your table!

Let's take an example to display the table structure of table SubscriberMaster:

```
DESCRIBE SubscriberMaster;
```

Output:

```
Name                            Null     Type
------------------------------- -------- --------------------
ACCOUNTNO                       NOT NULL NUMBER(10)
FIRSTNAME                                VARCHAR2(25)
LASTNAME                                 VARCHAR2(25)
BUILDINGNAME                             VARCHAR2(25)
ROAD                                     VARCHAR2(25)
AREA                                     VARCHAR2(25)
CITY                                     VARCHAR2(25)
PINCODE                                  NUMBER(10)
COUNTRY                                  VARCHAR2(25)
CONTACTNO                                NUMBER(15)
STATUS                                   CHAR(1)
```

Case Sensitivity

In Oracle, object names **CAN BE** case sensitive, however, by default, they are not. Object names can be written using:

- UPPER CASE
- lower case
- Mixed Case

This typically does not matter, as Oracle forces all such names to **UPPER CASE** by default. To override this default behavior, place object names within double quotes ["ObjectName"]. When object names are specified within double quotes, they are stored as-is, preserving the case.

> **TIP** Oracle behaves exactly the same for column names of objects such as tables and views.

For example, by enclosing object names in double quotes, the following names can be assigned to different objects in the same namespace:

- "authoredbooks"
- "AuthoredBooks"
- "AUTHOREDBOOKS"

Solution:

```
CREATE TABLE authoredbooks (BookName Varchar2(25));
```

Output:

```
Table created.
```

Oracle creates a table named authoredbooks.

Solution:

```
CREATE TABLE AuthoredBooks (BookName Varchar2(25));
```

Output:

```
CREATE TABLE AuthoredBooks (BookName Varchar2(25))
             *
ERROR at line 1:
ORA-00955: name is already used by an existing object
```

Oracle fails to create the table. **A**uthored**B**ooks is converted to **AUTHOREDBOOKS** and then stored. The earlier command created a table named **authoredbooks** which was also converted to **AUTHOREDBOOKS** prior storing it.

Now let's create a table that is exactly named **A**uthored**B**ooks enclose the table named within double quotes:

```
CREATE TABLE "AuthoredBooks" (BookName Varchar2(25));
```

Output:

```
Table created.
```

Oracle creates a table named **A**uthored**B**ooks.

Query User_Tables to list both the tables:

```
SELECT Table_Name FROM User_Tables
  WHERE LOWER(Table_Name) = 'authoredbooks';
```

Output:

```
TABLE_NAME
------------------------------
AUTHOREDBOOKS → Was created for authoredbooks
AuthoredBooks → Was created for "AuthoredBooks"
```

Now since both the tables exist with tables named in different case, double quotes will have to be used to reference the required table.

Now let's add a record in the table named AuthoredBooks:

```
INSERT INTO "AuthoredBooks" VALUES ('Oracle For Professionals');
```

Output:

```
1 row created.
```

Now add a record in the table named authoredbooks:

```
INSERT INTO authoredbooks VALUES ('PHP For Professionals');
```

Output:

```
1 row created.
```

Query the table named AuthoredBooks:

```
SELECT * FROM "AuthoredBooks";
```

Output:

```
BOOKNAME
-------------------------
Oracle For Professionals
```

Here, since the table name is enclosed within double quotes, Oracle references the table that is exactly named **A**uthored**B**ooks.

Query the table named authoredbooks:

```
SELECT * FROM AuthoredBooks;
```

OR

```
SELECT * FROM authoredbooks;
```

OR

```
SELECT * FROM AUTHOREDBOOKS;
```

Output:

```
BOOKNAME
-------------------------
PHP For Professionals
```

Here, since the table name is not enclosed within double quotes, Oracle simply converts the table name specified by the user into UPPER CASE and references the table that is exactly named **AUTHOREDBOOKS**.

Chapter

6

SECTION II: BASICS OF SQL

Multi-Table Insert Statements

The **multi-table insert feature** allows the **INSERT . . . SELECT** statement to use multiple tables as targets. It can also distribute data among target tables based on the logical attributes of the new rows. Thus, multi-table insert enables a single scan and transformation of source data to insert data into multiple tables, sharply increasing performance.

The multi-table INSERT statement:

- Allows records to be inserted into multiple tables at the same time.
- Can be used to copy data from one or more tables to a different set of target tables.

The multi-table INSERT statement inserts computed rows derived from the rows returned by a subquery. There are two forms of the multi-table INSERT statement: unconditional and conditional.

Unconditional Form: An INTO clause list is executed once for each row returned by the subquery.

```
INSERT ALL INTO <TableName1> [VALUES(. . .)]
  INTO <TableName1> [VALUES(. . .)] . . . SELECT . . .
```

Conditional Form: An INTO clause lists are guarded by **WHEN** clauses that determine whether the corresponding INTO clause list is executed or not.

```
INSERT {ALL|FIRST}
  WHEN <Expression1> THEN INTO <TableName1> [VALUES(. . .)]
  WHEN <Expression1> THEN INTO <TableName1> [VALUES(. . .)] . . .
     [ ELSE INTO <TableNameN> [VALUES(. . .)]] SELECT . . .
```

An **INTO** clause list consists of one or more INTO clauses. The execution of an INTO clause list causes the insertion of one row for each INTO clause in the list. An INTO clause specifies the target into which a computed row is inserted. The target specified, can be any table expression that is legal for an INSERT... SELECT statement. However, aliases cannot be used. The same table can be specified as the target for more than one INTO clause.

An INTO clause also provides the value of the row to be inserted using a VALUES clause. An expression used in the VALUES clause can be any legal expression, but can only refer to columns returned by the select list of the subquery. If the VALUES clause is omitted, the select list of the subquery provides the values to be inserted. If a column list is given, each column in the list is assigned a corresponding value from the VALUES clause or the subquery. If no column list is given, the computed row must provide values for all columns in the target table.

The following are the clauses used with INSERT statements for multi-table inserts:

- ***ALL ... INSERT INTO Clause:*** Performs an unconditional multi-table insert. Oracle executes each INSERT INTO clause once for each row returned by the subquery.
- ***Conditional INSERT Clause:*** Performs a conditional multi-table insert. Oracle filters each INSERT INTO clause through the corresponding WHEN condition determining whether that INSERT INTO CLAUSE is executed. A single multi-table insert statement can contain up to 127 WHEN clauses.
- ***ALL Clause:*** Oracle evaluates each WHEN clause, regardless of the results of the evaluation of any other WHEN clause. For each WHEN clause whose condition evaluates to true Oracle executes the corresponding INTO clause list.
- ***FIRST Clause:*** Oracle evaluates each WHEN clause in the order in which it appears in the statement. For the first WHEN clause that evaluates to true, Oracle executes the corresponding INTO clause and skips subsequent WHEN clauses for a given row.
- ***ELSE Clause:*** Oracle reaches the ELSE clause, if no WHEN clause evaluates to true. If ELSE clause is specified, Oracle executes the INTO clause list associated with the ELSE clause. If ELSE clause is not specified, Oracle takes no action for that row.
- ***SUBQUERY:*** Acts as a source to data held in the table. It is responsible for returning rows from the desired table. The subquery can refer to any table, view or materialized view including the target tables of the INSERT statement.

Let's take an example of Unconditional INSERT.
The following table structures are used in the example that follow:

Table Name: OrderMaster

Column Name	Data Type	Size
OrderNo	Varchar2	10
OrderDate	Date	
ProductNo	Varchar2	10
CostPrice	Number	12, 2
Qty	Number	5
SellPrice	Number	12, 2
OrderStatus	Char	2

This table holds the following data:

OrderNo	OrderDate	ProductNo	CostPrice	Quantity	SellPrice	OrderStatus
O10001	30-MAY-07	P0003	50	100	75	F
O10002	03-JUN-07	P0002	35	50	80	F
O10003	03-JUN-07	P0001	120	20	150	P
O10004	15-JUN-07	P0005	450	2	700	F
O10005	30-JUN-07	P0005	450	10	700	P
O10006	29-JUN-07	P0004	145	15	200	P
O10007	20-JUN-07	P0004	145	10	200	P
O10008	03-JUL-07	P0002	35	15	80	F
O10009	09-AUG-07	P0002	35	20	80	F
O10010	09-AUG-07	P0001	120	10	150	F
O10011	09-AUG-07	P0005	450	5	700	P

Table Name: ProductDemand

Column Name	Data Type	Size
DateSold	Date	
ProductNo	Varchar2	10
Qty	Number	5

Table Name: ProductSales

Column Name	Data Type	Size
DateSold	Date	
ProductNo	Varchar2	10
TotalSales	Number	12, 2

Insert data into ProductDemand and ProductSales tables from OrderMaster table using Unconditional INSERT Technique:

```
INSERT ALL
   INTO ProductDemand VALUES (DateSold, ProductNo, Qty)
   INTO ProductSales VALUES (DateSold, ProductNo, TotalSales)
   SELECT TRUNC(OrderDate) DateSold, ProductNo,
        SUM(SellPrice * Qty) TotalSales, SUM(Qty) Qty FROM OrderMaster
             GROUP BY TRUNC(OrderDate), ProductNo;
```

Output:

```
22 rows created.
```

Execute the following query:

```
SELECT * FROM ProductDemand;
SELECT * FROM ProductSales;
```

Output: (ProductDemand table)

```
DATESOLD  PRODUCTNO         QTY
--------- ---------- ----------
09-AUG-07 P0002              20
09-AUG-07 P0001              10
30-MAY-07 P0003             100
03-JUN-07 P0002              50
03-JUN-07 P0001              20
30-JUN-07 P0005              10
15-JUN-07 P0005               2
29-JUN-07 P0004              15
20-JUN-07 P0004              10
03-JUL-07 P0002              15
09-AUG-07 P0005               5

11 rows selected.
```

Output: (ProductSales table)

```
DATESOLD  PRODUCTNO  TOTALSALES
--------- ---------- ----------
09-AUG-07 P0002            1600
09-AUG-07 P0001            1500
30-MAY-07 P0003            7500
03-JUN-07 P0002            4000
03-JUN-07 P0001            3000
30-JUN-07 P0005            7000
15-JUN-07 P0005            1400
29-JUN-07 P0004            3000
20-JUN-07 P0004            2000
03-JUL-07 P0002            1200
09-AUG-07 P0005            3500

11 rows selected.
```

Remember the following points:

- The VALUES clause can only contain columns referenced in the SELECT statement in the subquery.
- If the VALUES clause is not included, the SELECT statement in the subquery will define the values to be inserted.
- ALL indicates evaluation of all WHEN clauses. For each WHEN clause that evaluates to true, Oracle processes the corresponding INTO clause.

The above example inserts OrderDate, ProductNo and Qty into the **ProductDemand** table and inserts OrderDate, ProductNo and TotalSales into the **ProductSales** table. The values are obtained through a subquery retrieving the desired data from the **OrderMaster** table.

Let's take an example of Conditional INSERT FIRST.
The following table structures are used in the examples that follow:

Table Name: PriorityProducts

Column Name	Data Type	Size
OrderTotal	Number	12, 2
OrderNo	Varchar2	10
ProductNo	Varchar2	10

Table Name: SpecialProducts

Column Name	Data Type	Size
OrderTotal	Number	12, 2
OrderNo	Varchar2	10
ProductNo	Varchar2	10

Table Name: EconomicProducts

Column Name	Data Type	Size
OrderTotal	Number	12, 2
OrderNo	Varchar2	10
ProductNo	Varchar2	10

Solution:

```
INSERT FIRST
  WHEN OrderTotal < 1500
     THEN INTO EconomicProducts VALUES (OrderTotal, OrderNo, ProductNo)
  WHEN (OrderTotal > 1500 AND OrderTotal < 3000)
     THEN INTO PriorityProducts VALUES (OrderTotal, OrderNo, ProductNo)
  WHEN OrderTotal > 3000
     THEN INTO SpecialProducts VALUES (OrderTotal, OrderNo, ProductNo)
  SELECT (Qty * SellPrice) OrderTotal, OrderNo, ProductNo FROM OrderMaster;
```

Output:

```
8 rows created.
```

Execute the following query:

```
SELECT * FROM EconomicProducts;
SELECT * FROM PriorityProducts;
SELECT * FROM SpecialProducts;
```

Output: (EconomicProducts table)

```
ORDERTOTAL ORDERNO    PRODUCTNO
---------- ---------- ----------
      1400 O10004     P0005
      1200 O10008     P0002
```

Output: (PriorityProducts table)

```
ORDERTOTAL ORDERNO    PRODUCTNO
---------- ---------- ----------
      2000 O10007     P0004
      1600 O10009     P0002
```

Output: (SpecialProducts table)

```
ORDERTOTAL ORDERNO    PRODUCTNO
---------- ---------- ----------
      7500 O10001     P0003
      4000 O10002     P0002
      7000 O10005     P0005
      3500 O10011     P0005
```

This example:

- Inserts OrderTotal, OrderNo, ProductNo into the **EconomicProducts** table
  If OrderTotal is less than 1500
- Inserts OrderTotal, OrderNo, ProductNo into the **PriorityProducts** table
  If OrderTotal is greater than 1500 but is less than 3000
- Inserts OrderTotal, OrderNo, ProductNo into the **SpecialProducts** table
  If OrderTotal is greater than 3000

The values are obtained through a subquery retrieving the desired data from the OrderMaster table. The INSERT FIRST simply indicates that it will execute the FIRST INTO clause that matches on the expression. It will, then, skip all following WHEN clauses.

> The same table can be specified for multiple target INTO clauses. A multi table INSERT statement, can have up to 127 WHEN clauses in the statement.

Let's take an example of Conditional INSERT.
The following table structures are used in the example that follow:

Table Name: PriorityProductsSales

Column Name	Data Type	Size
ProductNo	Number	10
CostPrice	Number	12, 2

Table Name: RegularProductsSales

Column Name	Data Type	Size
ProductNo	Number	10
CostPrice	Number	12, 2

Solution:

```
INSERT ALL
  WHEN ProductNo IN(SELECT ProductNo FROM PriorityProducts) THEN
     INTO PriorityProductsSales VALUES(ProductNo, CostPrice)
  WHEN OrderStatus = 'F' THEN
     INTO RegularProductsSales VALUES (ProductNo, CostPrice)
  SELECT ProductNo, CostPrice, OrderStatus FROM OrderMaster;
```

Output:

```
11 rows created.
```

Execute the following query:

```
SELECT * FROM PriorityProductsSales;
SELECT * FROM RegularProductsSales;
```

Output: (PriorityProductsSales table)

```
PRODUCTNO   COSTPRICE
---------- ----------
P0002              35
P0004             145
P0004             145
P0002              35
P0002              35
```

Output: (RegularProductsSales table)

```
PRODUCTNO   COSTPRICE
---------- ----------
P0003              50
P0002              35
P0005             450
P0002              35
P0002              35
P0001             120

6 rows selected.
```

The above example:

- Inserts ProductNo, CostPrice into the **PriorityProductsSales** table
  If an entry exists in the **PriorityProducts** table
- Inserts ProductNo, CostPrice into the **RegularProductsSales** table
  If the **OrderStatus** column holds the value **F**

The values are obtained through a subquery retrieving the desired data from the OrderMaster table. The INSERT ALL simply indicates evaluation of all WHEN clauses. For each WHEN clause that evaluates to true, Oracle will process the corresponding INTO clause.

There are a few restrictions on using multi-table INSERTS. Multi-table inserts:

- Cannot be used with views and materialized. Only tables are supported.
- Cannot be performed on a remote table.
- Cannot use a collection expression.
- Cannot be parallelized in a Real Application Cluster environment.
- Cannot use plan stability.
- Cannot use a sequence in a subquery.

Insert Data In One Or More Tables

As your database grows, you'll often find yourself needing to insert the same set of data into multiple tables. Doing this with individual INSERT statements can be tedious and inefficient. That's where the INSERT ALL statement comes in handy. It's a powerful tool in Oracle that lets you insert multiple rows into one or more tables with a single command. Think of it as a batch insert operation, saving you time and effort.

Imagine you're adding a new employee to your system. You might need to add their information to Employees table and the department name they belong to in Departments table. Without INSERT ALL, you'd have to write two separate INSERT statements. INSERT ALL lets you do all this in one go, making your code cleaner and potentially faster.

Syntax:

```
INSERT ALL
  INTO <TableName1> (<ColumnName1>, <ColumnName2>)
     VALUES (<Expression1>, <Expression2>)
  . . .
  INTO <TableNameN> (<ColumnName1>, <ColumnName2>)
     VALUES (<Expression1>, <Expression2>)
SELECT * FROM DUAL;
```

Where:

- *INSERT ALL:* This keyword signals the start of the multi-table insert operation.
- *INTO TableName (ColumnName1, ColumnName2):* This specifies the first table you want to insert into and the columns you're targeting. It's crucial to list the columns explicitly.
- *VALUES (Expression1, Expression2):* This provides the values you want to insert into the corresponding columns of TableName1. The order and number of values must match the columns listed in the INTO clause.
- *INTO TableName ... VALUES ...:* This repeats the INTO and VALUES clauses for each additional table you want to insert into.
- *SELECT * FROM DUAL;:* This might seem a bit strange, but it's a required part of the INSERT ALL syntax. DUAL is a dummy table in Oracle, and this SELECT statement acts as a source for the INSERT ALL operation. Even if you're inserting literal values, this SELECT is necessary.

Let's take an example of inserting a new department and a new employee who belongs to that department using INSERT ALL:

```
INSERT ALL
  INTO Departments (DeptNo, DepartmentName, Capacity)
     VALUES (1, 'IT Department', 20)
  INTO Employees (EmployeeNo, FirstName, LastName, DateOfBirth, Gender,
     MaritalStatus, Address, ContactNo, Salary, Designation, DeptNo, Username,
```

```
    Password) VALUES (1, 'Sharanam', 'Shah', '30-JAN-2000', 'M', 'M',
    'Makanji Mansion', '91-022-24440094', 82500, 'Technical Writing', 1, 'amSh1',
    'ShSh00')
SELECT * FROM DUAL;
```

We insert a new department with DeptNo 1, name 'IT Department', and capacity 20. We then insert a new employee, Sharanam Shah, into the Employees table. Notice how the DeptNo for the employee is also 1, linking them to the newly created Department. We've also included other necessary employee details like date of birth, contact number, salary, etc. Remember to adjust the data types and lengths to match your table definitions.

Output:

```
2 rows inserted.
```

Key Points to remember:

- ***Column Matching:*** Ensure the columns listed in the INTO clauses match the order and number of values in the VALUES clauses.
- ***Data Types:*** The data types of the values must be compatible with the data types of the corresponding columns in the tables.
- ***The DUAL Table:*** Don't forget the SELECT * FROM DUAL at the end. It's essential for the INSERT ALL statement to work.

INSERT ALL is a valuable tool for efficiently inserting data into multiple tables. By understanding its structure and usage, you can streamline your database operations and write cleaner, more maintainable code.

Multi-Value Inserts: Insert Multiple Rows At Once

As a database user, you'll often need to add multiple rows of data to a table. Historically, in older versions of Oracle, you had to write a separate INSERT statement for each row. This could be tedious and inefficient, especially when dealing with many rows.

Let's illustrate with an example. Suppose you have a Departments table with columns for department number, its name, and capacity. To insert five new departments, you would have needed five separate INSERT statements:

```
INSERT INTO Departments VALUES (7, 'IT Department', 20);
INSERT INTO Departments VALUES (1,'Sales Department', 15);
INSERT INTO Departments VALUES (2, 'HR Department', 5);
INSERT INTO Departments VALUES (3, 'Technical Department', 25);
INSERT INTO Departments VALUES (4, 'Purchase Department', 15);
```

This works, but it's a lot of repetition. Imagine having to insert hundreds or thousands of rows!

Use the multi-value INSERT statement. This powerful feature, introduced in Oracle 23, lets you insert multiple rows with a single INSERT statement.

Using the same above example, the multi-value INSERT looks like this:

```
INSERT INTO Departments VALUES (7, 'IT Department', 20),
                               (1,'Sales Department', 15),
                               (2, 'HR Department', 5),
                               (3, 'Technical Department', 25),
                               (4, 'Purchase Department', 15);
```

Output:

```
5 rows inserted.
```

See how much cleaner and more concise that is? We've combined all five inserts into one, separated by commas. Each set of values within the parentheses represents a single row to be inserted.

Benefits of Multi-value INSERTs:

- ***Improved Efficiency:*** A single statement is generally faster than multiple individual statements. The database can optimize the entire operation, leading to better performance.
- ***Simplified Code:*** Your SQL code becomes much more readable and easier to maintain. Less repetition means less chance for errors.
- ***Better Compatibility:*** Multi-value INSERT statements are a common feature in other database systems. Using them in Oracle improves compatibility and makes it easier to migrate code between systems.
- ***Maintaining Consistency in Autocommit Mode:*** In certain environments, like some Oracle APEX applications using autocommit mode, multiple individual inserts might lead to inconsistencies if an error occurs midway. The multi-value INSERT ensures all rows are inserted together, maintaining data integrity.

Chapter

7

SECTION II: BASICS OF SQL

Merging Rows

Sometimes, it is required to perform a combination of INSERT and UPDATE operations on a single table based on the data held in another table. Oracle allows this using the **Merge DML command**.

Syntax:

```
MERGE INTO <TableName> USING <TableViewOrQuery> ON (<Condition>)
  WHEN MATCHED THEN <UpdateClause>
     DELETE <WhereClause>
  WHEN NOT MATCHED THEN <InsertClause>;
```

Where,

- ***MERGE INTO clause:*** Specifies the name of the table to merge the rows into.
- ***USING . . . ON clause:*** Specifies a table join.
- ***WHEN MATCHED THEN clause:*** Specifies the action to take when the *USING . . . ON* clause is satisfied for a row.
- ***WHEN NOT MATCHED clause:*** Specifies the action to take when the *USING . . . ON* clause is not satisfied for a row.

Let's take an example. Two companies dealing in computer products have chosen to join hands with each other. The products sold by Company A and Company B will now be sold by the company A, which has taken over Company B.

Both companies maintain their data in an RDBMS and each has a ProductsMaster table that holds the products being sold. Since both companies sell electronic products, there may be some products that are common to both. For example; Company A sells Logitech Keyboards, which are also sold by Company B.

It is required to merge the contents of both tables into one. This means all the data from Company B should be merged with Company A. The merger should happen as follows:

- Products that already exist in Company A will be updated with Company B's products, especially the QtyInHand.
- Products that are not available in Company A but available with Company B will be added to Company A.

Table Name: ProductsA

ProductName	Cost	Color	QtyInHand	Manufacturer
TV	40000	Black	20	LG
Refrigerator	25000	Grey	10	Godrej
DVD Player	10000	Silver Gray	25	Videocon
Microwave	6000	White	30	Electrolux
Juicer	4500	White	5	Nova

Table Name: ProductsB

ProductName	Cost	Color	QtyInHand	Manufacturer
TV	40000	Black	15	LG
AC	11000	White	10	Voltas
VCD	3000	Silver	35	LG
Microwave	6000	White	15	Electrolux
Juicer	4500	White	30	Nova

The following statement performs the merge as defined:

```
MERGE INTO ProductsA A USING ProductsB B ON (A.ProductName = B.ProductName)
WHEN MATCHED THEN UPDATE SET A.QtyInHand = A.QtyInHand + B.QtyInHand
WHEN NOT MATCHED THEN
   INSERT (A.ProductName, A.Cost, A.Color, A.QtyInHand, A.Manufacturer)
        VALUES (B.ProductName, B.Cost, B.Color, B.QtyInHand, B.Manufacturer);
```

Output:

```
5 rows merged.
```

Explanation:

```
MERGE INTO ProductsA A USING ProductsB B
```

Indicates that the contents of the ProductsB table will be merged with the contents of the ProductsA table.

```
ON (A.ProductName = B.ProductName)
```

Indicates that the products will be compared using the ProductName column value from both the tables.

```
WHEN MATCHED THEN UPDATE SET A.QtyInHand = A.QtyInHand + B.QtyInHand
```

Indicates if a product from ProductsA table matches a product from the ProductsB table, the QtyInHand column of ProductsA table will be incremented with the value held in the QtyInHand column of ProductsB table.

```
WHEN NOT MATCHED THEN
  INSERT (A.ProductName, A.Cost, A.Color, A.QtyInHand, A.Manufacturer)
     VALUES (A.ProductName, A.Cost, A.Color, A.QtyInHand, A.Manufacturer);
```

Indicates if a product from ProductsB table does not exist as a product in ProductsA table, then that product's details are added to ProductsA table.

Now since the data has been merged, query the ProductsA table to have a look:

```
SELECT * FROM ProductsA;
```

Output:

```
PRODUCTNAME   COST    COLOR        QTYINHAND MANUFACTURER
------------- ------- ------------ --------- ------------
TV            40000   Black        35        LG
Refrigerator  25000   Grey         10        Godrej
DVD Player    10000   Silver Gray  25        Videocon
Microwave     6000    White        45        Electrolux
Juicer        4500    White        35        Nova
AC            11000   White        10        Voltas
VCD           3000    Silver       35        LG

7 rows selected.
```

Chapter 8

SECTION II: BASICS OF SQL

Altering Table Structures

The **ALTER TABLE** command is used to modify the structure of an existing table. It allows:

- **Adding** or **Deleting** columns
- **Changing the data type** of existing columns
- **Creating** or **Destroying** indexes
- **Renaming columns** and **tables**

Technically, the ALTER TABLE command performs the following steps:

- Creates a temporary copy of the original table
- Deletes the original table
- Alters the copy of the table
- Renames the new table

To use the ALTER TABLE command, you need the following privileges:

- ALTER
- INSERT
- CREATE

> TIP: While the ALTER TABLE command is executing, the original table remains readable by users. **Updates** and **writes** to the table are held until the new table is ready. Once ready, these operations are automatically redirected to the new table **without any data loss**.

Adding New Columns To Existing Tables

When modifying an application and its data entry screens, you may need to add new columns to the database tables. This can be accomplished with the ALTER TABLE command.

```
ALTER TABLE <TableName>
  ADD(<NewColumnName> <Datatype> (<Size>),
      <NewColumnName> <Datatype> (<Size>)...);
```

Let's add a new column named RegistrationDate to the SubscriberMaster table to keep track of the date when the subscriber registered. The data type of the column RegistrationDate will be Date:

```
ALTER TABLE SubscriberMaster ADD (RegistrationDate Date);
```

Output:

```
Table altered.
```

Dropping A Column From An Existing Table

Syntax:

```
ALTER TABLE <TableName> DROP COLUMN <ColumnName>;
```

Let's drop the column named Country from the SubscriberMaster table:

```
ALTER TABLE SubscriberMaster DROP COLUMN Country;
```

Output:

```
Table altered.
```

Logically Dropping A Column From An Existing Table

In Oracle, columns can be logically deleted from a table. Typically, in a production database, table columns are not physically deleted but marked as unused. This process is known as a **Logical Delete**.

Physically removing a column can be extremely time-consuming for large tables. Therefore, a logical delete is often a more efficient choice. To logically delete a column, the ALTER TABLE command is used.

Syntax:

```
ALTER TABLE <TableName>
  SET UNUSED (<ColumnName1>, <ColumnName2>, <ColumnNameN>);
```

Let's logically delete the column named Status in the SubscriberMaster table:

```
ALTER TABLE SubscriberMaster SET UNUSED (Status);
```

Output:

```
Table altered.
```

The column Status will no longer be visible to the user.

Columns that are logically deleted can be physically deleted using the following command:

```
ALTER TABLE <TableName> DROP UNUSED COLUMNS;
```

To view the columns that are unused, issue the following command:

```
SELECT * FROM USER_UNUSED_COL_TABS;
```

Output:

```
TABLE_NAME                          COUNT
------------------------------- ----------
SUBSCRIBERMASTER                         1
```

Modifying Existing Columns Of An Existing Table

Syntax:

```
ALTER TABLE <TableName>
  MODIFY (<ColumnName> <NewDatatype>(<NewSize>));
```

Let's alter SubscriberMaster table, which allows the FirstName column to hold maximum of 50 characters. Currently this column allows only 25 characters:

```
ALTER TABLE SubscriberMaster MODIFY (FirstName Varchar2(50));
```

Output:

```
Table altered.
```

Renaming Tables

Using Alter Table Command

Syntax:

```
ALTER TABLE <TableName> RENAME TO <NewTableName>;
```

Rename the SubscriberMaster table to Subscribers:

```
ALTER TABLE SubscriberMaster RENAME TO Subscribers;
```

Output:

```
Table altered.
```

Using Rename Command

Tables can be renamed using the **RENAME** command. Oracle performs the rename operation **atomically**, which means that **no other thread** can access any of the tables while the rename process is underway.

Syntax:

```
RENAME <TableName> TO <NewTableName>;
```

Change the name of SubscriberMaster table to Subscribers:

```
RENAME SubscriberMaster TO Subscribers;
```

Output:

```
Table renamed.
```

Renaming Columns

Syntax:

```
ALTER TABLE <TableName>
  RENAME COLUMN <OldColumnName> TO <NewColumnName>;
```

Rename the Pincode column in the SubscriberMaster table to Zipcode:

```
ALTER TABLE SubscriberMaster RENAME COLUMN Pincode TO Zipcode;
```

Output:

```
Table altered.
```

Chapter 9

SECTION II: BASICS OF SQL

Synonyms

A **synonym** is an alternative name for database objects such as tables, views, sequences, stored procedures and other objects. The **CREATE SYNONYM** command is used to provide an alternate name for a table or a view that is present in the same schema or another schema. Synonyms can also be created for other synonyms, resulting in nested synonyms.

Once created, a synonym can be used instead of the original qualified table or view name in SELECT, INSERT, UPDATE, DELETE, or LOCK TABLE statements. Synonyms share the same namespace as tables or views. A synonym with the same name as an existing table cannot be created in the same schema. Similarly, a table or view with a name that matches an existing synonym cannot be created.

Creating Synonyms

Syntax:

```
CREATE [OR REPLACE] [PUBLIC] SYNONYM [SCHEMA .] <SynonymName>
  FOR [SCHEMA .] <ObjectName> [@ DBLINK];
```

Where,

- ***OR REPLACE:*** Allows recreating the synonym [if it already exists] without having to issue a DROP synonym command.

- *PUBLIC:* Indicates that the synonym is a public synonym and is accessible to all users. A database administrator can create a public synonym.
- *SCHEMA:* The appropriate schema. If omitted, Oracle assumes that the reference is made to the user's own schema to which they are currently logged in.
- *OBJECT_NAME:* The name of the object for which a synonym is being created. It can hold one of the following objects:
  - Table
  - Stored Procedure
  - View
  - Materialized View
  - Sequence
  - Function
  - User-Defined Object
  - Package
  - Synonym
  - Java Class Schema Object

Create a synonym to a table named SubscriberMaster:

```
CREATE PUBLIC SYNONYM SM FOR SubscriberMaster;
```

Output:

```
Synonym created.
```

Now, users of other schemas can reference the table SubscriberMaster, which is now called as SM without having to prefix the table name:

```
SELECT * FROM SM;
```

Dropping Synonyms

Syntax:

```
DROP [PUBLIC] SYNONYM [SCHEMA.] <SynonymName> [FORCE];
```

Where,

- *PUBLIC:* Allows to drop a public synonym. If public is specified, then there is no need to specify a schema.
- *FORCE:* Forces Oracle to drop the synonym even if it has dependencies. It is not advisable to use force as it can cause invalidation of Oracle objects.

Drop the public synonym named SM:

```
DROP PUBLIC SYNONYM SM;
```

Output:

```
Synonym dropped.
```

Only a DBA can create or drop **public** synonyms. However, a normal database user [need not be a DBA] can create synonyms to existing tables within their schema.

Chapter

10

SECTION II: BASICS OF SQL

External Tables

Oracle has introduced a new suite of features designed to enhance the scalability and efficiency of ETL [Extraction, Transformation, Load] processes for data warehouses and business intelligence systems. One of the standout features in this suite is the External Table feature.

The External Table feature allows the use of flat files that:

- Reside outside the database.
- Can be accessed just like relational tables within the database.

In essence, this means:

- External tables are defined as tables that do not reside within the database and can be in any format for which an access driver is provided.
- An External table can be viewed as a virtual table that allows SQL queries to be run against external data without the need for the data to be loaded into the database.

Advantages:

- Flat-file data can be queried and joined to other tables using standard SQL.
- Data access can be serial or parallel, ensuring maximum scalability.

- External data can be queried and joined directly, in parallel, **without** being loaded into the database.
- This can eliminate the need for staging the data within the database for ETL operations.
- It's useful in environments where external data needs to be integrated with database objects and then transformed.
- It's particularly beneficial when dealing with large external datasets that are infrequently queried.
- External tables can be used for loading data into database tables.

> From a user's perspective, the main difference between an external table and a regular table is that the external table is read-only.

External tables are invaluable in data warehousing scenarios where data is often sourced from external systems. For example, a data warehouse may contain data extracted from an OLTP system or purchased from a third-party data provider. When integrating new data into a data warehouse, the data needs to be transformed. Transformation tasks may include complex filtering, validation against existing warehouse data, and insertion at both detailed and aggregate levels.

Before Oracle 9i, complex data transformations within Oracle required one of two approaches:

- Load the data into Oracle, store it in a staging table, perform transformations, and then delete the staging table. This approach consumed disk space, administrative resources, and processing time for data already available on disk.
- Transform the external data in flat files outside the database. This approach often required flat-file manipulation and database access, followed by loading the transformed data into the data warehouse. It also involved redundant data storage and processing time.

Oracle's external tables address the limitations of these approaches. External tables provide a new model for loading and transforming external data, presenting the external data to the database as a virtual table. This enables full data processing within the database engine. This seamless integration is referred to as **pipelining**, where the continuous data stream increases ETL process performance.

Metadata for the external table must be created using the **CREATE TABLE . . . ORGANIZATION EXTERNAL** statement and stored within a user schema in the database.

> No DML operations are possible and no indexes can be created on external tables.

The CREATE TABLE ... ORGANIZATION EXTERNAL operation involves creating metadata in the Oracle data dictionary. The external data must reside outside the database. Once the metadata is created, users can easily perform parallel data extraction from the specified external source.

> These tables are primarily intended for use in **INSERT . . . AS SELECT** and **DELETE . . . AS SELECT** statements, rather than for ad hoc querying.

Creating an external table involves:

- Creation of Flat Files.
- Creation of a directory object.
- Creation of an external table [Meta Data] within this directory.

Step I - Creation Of Flat Files

Key in some data in a text file using a text editor such as Notepad:

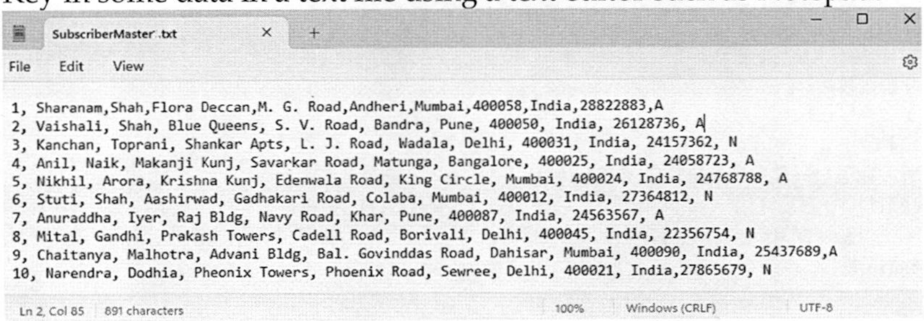

SubscriberMaster.txt

```
1, Sharanam,Shah,Flora Deccan,M. G. Road,Andheri,Mumbai,400058,India,28822883,A
2, Vaishali, Shah, Blue Queens, S. V. Road, Bandra, Pune, 400050, India, 26128736, A
3, Kanchan, Toprani, Shankar Apts, L. J. Road, Wadala, Delhi, 400031, India, 24157362, N
4, Anil, Naik, Makanji Kunj, Savarkar Road, Matunga, Bangalore, 400025, India, 24058723, A
5, Nikhil, Arora, Krishna Kunj, Edenwala Road, King Circle, Mumbai, 400024, India, 24768788, A
6, Stuti, Shah, Aashirwad, Gadhakari Road, Colaba, Mumbai, 400012, India, 27364812, N
7, Anuraddha, Iyer, Raj Bldg, Navy Road, Khar, Pune, 400087, India, 24563567, A
8, Mital, Gandhi, Prakash Towers, Cadell Road, Borivali, Delhi, 400045, India, 22356754, N
9, Chaitanya, Malhotra, Advani Bldg, Bal. Govinddas Road, Dahisar, Mumbai, 400090, India, 25437689,A
10, Narendra, Dodhia, Pheonix Towers, Phoenix Road, Sewree, Delhi, 400021, India,27865679, N
```

Ln 2, Col 85 | 891 characters | 100% | Windows (CRLF) | UTF-8

Step II - Creation of A Directory Object

Solution:

```
CREATE OR REPLACE DIRECTORY ExternalTables AS 'D:\ExternalTables';
```

The directory (in this case **ExtTables**) should physically exist on the HDD. The file (**SubscriberMaster.txt** in this case) should physically exist (in this case under **D:\ExternalTables**) on the HDD.

Output:

```
Directory created.
```

Be informed that this command can only be executed as **SYS** user or by a user who has been granted the CREATE ANY DIRECTORY privilege:

```
GRANT CREATE ANY DIRECTORY TO <Username>;
```

Output:

```
Grant succeeded.
```

Step III - Creation of An External Table [Meta Data] Within This Directory

Solution:

```
CREATE TABLE SubscriberMaster(
   AccountNo Number(10),
   FirstName Varchar2(25),
   LastName Varchar2(25),
   BuildingName Varchar2(25),
   Road Varchar2(25),
   Area Varchar2(25),
   City Varchar2(25),
   Pincode Number(10),
   Country Varchar2(25),
   ContactNo Number(15),
   Status Char(1))
   ORGANIZATION EXTERNAL(
        TYPE ORACLE_LOADER
        DEFAULT DIRECTORY ExtTables
        ACCESS PARAMETERS(RECORDS DELIMITED BY NEWLINE
             FIELDS TERMINATED BY ', ' MISSING FIELD VALUES ARE NULL)
        LOCATION ('SubscriberMaster.txt'))
   REJECT LIMIT UNLIMITED;
```

In this meta data creation:

- *ORACLE_LOADER:* An access driver for loading data from external files into the tables.
- *ACCESS PARAMETERS:* Controls the extraction of data from the flat file using record and file formatting information.
- *RECORDS DELIMITED BY NEWLINE:* Each and every record in the file will appear on a new line.
- *FIELDS TERMINATED BY ',':* Every column will be separated by a comma.
- *MISSING FIELD VALUES ARE NULL:* Columns having no value will be holding NULL.
- *ExternalTables:* A directory where the external flat files reside.
- *Directory:* A non-schema object introduced by Oracle that defines the path to an operating system directory.
- The parameters specified are the same parameters that are used by the SQL*Loader utility.

Output:

```
Table created.
```

Querying External Tables

In the above example, when the external table SubscriberMaster is queried, the data is retrieved from the **external** data files. When the user selects data from the external table, the dataflow goes from the external data source to the Oracle SQL engine, where data is processed. As data is extracted, it is transparently converted by the external agent from its external representation into an equivalent Oracle native representation via the data loader stream.

Query the table SubscriberMaster as:

```
SELECT AccountNo, FirstName, LastName FROM SubscriberMaster;
```

Output:

```
ACCOUNTNO FIRSTNAME  LASTNAME
--------- ---------- --------
        1 Sharanam   Shah
        2 Vaishali   Shah
        3 Kanchan    Toprani
        4 Anil       Naik
        5 Nikhil     Arora
        6 Stuti      Shah
        7 Anuraddha  Iyer
        8 Mital      Gandhi
        9 Chaitanya  Malhotra
       10 Narendra   Dodhia

10 rows selected.
```

The **ORACLE_LOADER** driver allows access to data stored in any format compatible with SQL*Loader. While DML operations cannot be performed on external tables, they can be used for query, join, and sort operations.

Views and synonyms can be created against external tables, making them useful in the ETL process of data warehouses. This is because the data does not need to be staged and can be queried in parallel.

The following are a few limitations bound to the use of external tables:

- An external table does not describe any data that is stored in the database.
- An external table does not describe how data is stored in the external source. This is determined by the access parameters.
- External tables are read-only. Insert operations cannot be performed on them, nor can records be updated.
- These tables are not suitable for frequently queried tables.

Using Multiple Flat Files

Step I - Creation of flat files

SubscriberMaster1.txt

```
1, Sharanam,Shah,Flora Deccan,M. G. Road,Andheri,Mumbai,400058,India,28822883,A
2, Vaishali, Shah, Blue Queens, S. V. Road, Bandra, Pune, 400050, India, 26128736, A
3, Kanchan, Toprani, Shankar Apts, L. J. Road, Wadala, Delhi, 400031, India, 24157362, N
4, Anil, Naik, Makanji Kunj, Savarkar Road, Matunga, Bangalore, 400025, India, 24058723, A
5, Nikhil, Arora, Krishna Kunj, Edenwala Road, King Circle, Mumbai, 400024, India, 24768788, A
```

Ln 2, Col 85 440 characters 100% Windows (CRLF) UTF-8

SubscriberMaster2.txt

```
6, Stuti, Shah, Aashirwad, Gadhakari Road, Colaba, Mumbai, 400012, India, 27364812, N
7, Anuraddha, Iyer, Raj Bldg, Navy Road, Khar, Pune, 400087, India, 24563567, A
8, Mital, Gandhi, Prakash Towers, Cadell Road, Borivali, Delhi, 400045, India, 22356754, N
9, Chaitanya, Malhotra, Advani Bldg, Bal. Govinddas Road, Dahisar, Mumbai, 400090, India, 25437689,A
10, Narendra, Dodhia, Pheonix Towers, Phoenix Road, Sewree, Delhi, 400021, India,27865679, N
```

Ln 1, Col 86 451 characters 100% Windows (CRLF) UTF-8

Step II - Creation of A Directory Object

Solution: [Creating External Tables directory object]

```
CREATE OR REPLACE DIRECTORY ExtTables AS 'D:\ExternalTables';
```

Output:

```
Directory created.
```

Step III - Creation of an external table [Meta Data] within this directory

Solution:

```
CREATE TABLE SubscriberMasterMulti(
   AccountNo Number(10),
   FirstName Varchar2(25),
   LastName Varchar2(25),
   BuildingName Varchar2(25),
   Road Varchar2(25),
   Area Varchar2(25),
   City Varchar2(25),
   Pincode Number(10),
   Country Varchar2(25),
   ContactNo Number(15),
```

```
Status Char(1))
ORGANIZATION EXTERNAL(
    TYPE ORACLE_LOADER
    DEFAULT DIRECTORY ExtTables
    ACCESS PARAMETERS(RECORDS DELIMITED BY NEWLINE
        FIELDS TERMINATED BY ', ' MISSING FIELD VALUES ARE NULL)
    LOCATION ('SubscriberMaster1.txt', 'SubscriberMaster2.txt'))
REJECT LIMIT UNLIMITED;
```

Output:

```
Table created.
```

Querying the table (Multiple Flat Files) created:

```
SELECT AccountNo, FirstName, LastName FROM SubscriberMasterMulti;
```

Output:

```
ACCOUNTNO FIRSTNAME  LASTNAME
--------- ---------- ----------
        1 Sharanam   Shah
        2 Vaishali   Shah
        3 Kanchan    Toprani
        4 Anil       Naik
        5 Nikhil     Arora
        6 Stuti      Shah
        7 Anuraddha  Iyer
        8 Mital      Gandhi
        9 Chaitanya  Malhotra
       10 Narendra   Dodhia

10 rows selected.
```

Creating Views On External Tables

Solution:

```
CREATE VIEW vw_SubscriberMaster
  AS SELECT * FROM SubscriberMaster WHERE LastName = 'Shah';
```

Output:

```
View created.
```

Querying the view created:

```
SELECT AccountNo, FirstName, LastName FROM vw_SubscriberMaster;
```

Output:

```
ACCOUNTNO FIRSTNAME  LASTNAME
--------- ---------- ----------
        1 Sharanam   Shah
        2 Vaishali   Shah
        6 Stuti      Shah
```

Populating Tables Based on Data Held By External Tables

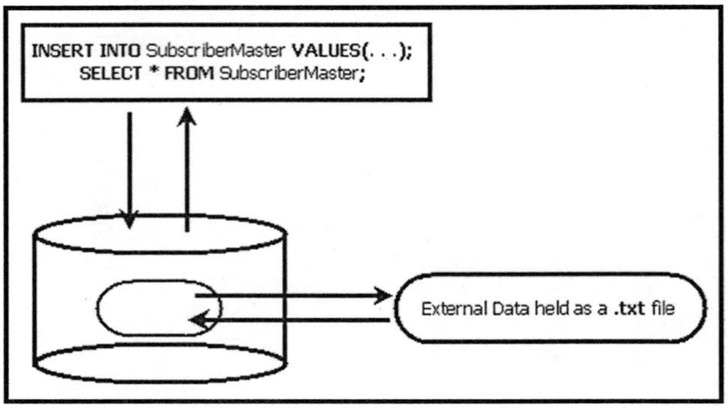

Data from external files can be populated into other tables, using the **INSERT INTO . . . SELECT FROM** statement instead of using SQL*Loader. This method provides very fast data loads.

Consider a table Subscriber which is not external:

```
CREATE TABLE Subscriber(
   AccountNo Number(10),
   FirstName Varchar2(25),
   LastName Varchar2(25));
```

Output:

```
Table created.
```

View the table structure as:

```
DESC Subscriber;
```

Output:

```
Name                 Null?                Type
-------------------- -------------------- --------------------
ACCOUNTNO                                 NUMBER(10)
FIRSTNAME                                 VARCHAR2(25)
LASTNAME                                  VARCHAR2(25)
```

Populate data as:

```
INSERT INTO Subscriber (AccountNo, FirstName, LastName)
   SELECT AccountNo, FirstName, LastName FROM SubscriberMaster;
```

Output:

```
10 rows created.
```

View the data populated as:

```
SELECT * FROM Subscriber;
```

Output:

```
ACCOUNTNO FIRSTNAME  LASTNAME
--------- ---------- --------
        1 Sharanam   Shah
        2 Vaishali   Shah
        3 Kanchan    Toprani
        4 Anil       Naik
        5 Nikhil     Arora
        6 Stuti      Shah
        7 Anuraddha  Iyer
        8 Mital      Gandhi
        9 Chaitanya  Malhotra
       10 Narendra   Dodhia

10 rows selected.
```

Drop The External Table

For an external table, the **DROP TABLE** statement removes only the table metadata in the database. It has no effect on the actual data, which resides outside of the database.

Use the following command to drop the metadata of the table held in the database:

```
DROP TABLE SubscriberMaster;
```

Output:

```
Table dropped.
```

Chapter

11

SECTION II: BASICS OF SQL

Data Constraints

Every business organization needs to gather, store, and analyze data related to their operations. Initially, this data is collected in its raw format. Business managers determine specific rules that must be applied to this raw data before it is stored in the database. Applying these rules ensures **data integrity**.

Each organization's rules are tailored to their unique business model. Consequently, the rules for data gathering and processing can vary significantly between organizations.

Examples of rules include:

- An employee in the Sales Department cannot have a salary exceeding Rs. 10,000.
- A customer's credit card limit cannot be increased until they held the card for at least six months.
- An employee's identification number cannot be assigned to another employee in the same organization.
- The stock in hand cannot fall below the reorder level.

These rules are enforced on the data being stored in the database, ensuring that only data that satisfies these rules is retained. If the data fails to meet these rules, it is rejected, thereby maintaining the validity and integrity of the stored data. In database terminology, a rule that is enforced on data storage is called a **constraint**. Constraints help maintain the integrity of data within the database.

Applying Data Constraints

Data integrity allows defining certain quality requirements that the data in the database needs to meet before storage. If a user tries to insert data that does not meet these requirements, Oracle simply rejects it. Oracle permits data constraints to be attached to table columns using SQL syntax, making these constraints a part of the table column construct.

Once constraints are defined for all required columns in a database table, Oracle checks the data being entered against these constraints. If the data passes this check, it is stored in the table column; otherwise, it is rejected. Oracle rejects the entire record, even if a single column fails a constraint.

Constraints (i.e. Business / System rules) can be attached to table columns using:

- Create Table
- Alter Table

After a constraint is defined for the desired table columns, any SQL INSERT or UPDATE statement automatically applies these constraints to the data before it is inserted into the table column for storage. Constraints can be defined at the column level or table level.

Column Level Constraints

Column-level constraints are defined as attributes of a column definition when creating or altering a table structure. They are applied to the **current column**, which is the column that immediately **precedes** the constraint (i.e., they are local to a specific column). A column-level constraint **cannot** be applied if the data constraint spans **multiple columns** in a table.

Table Level Constraints

Table-level constraints are defined **after specifying all table column attributes** when creating or altering a table structure. These constraints **must** be applied if the data constraint **spans multiple columns** in a table.

Constraints are stored as part of the global table definition by Oracle in its **system tables**. The SQL syntax used to attach the constraint changes depending on whether it is a column-level or table-level constraint.

The Unique Key Constraint

The unique key constraint ensures that all column values within a table do not contain duplicate entries. If the unique constraint is set for two or more columns, no two identical combinations are allowed.

> **TIP** A Unique index is automatically created on the column that holds a unique constraint.

The unique constraint differs from the primary key constraint (*explained later in this chapter*) as:

- A table can have more than one Unique key, which is not possible with a primary key.
- The Unique column constraint allows multiple NULL values, whereas the primary key column does not.

Unique Constraint - At Column Level

Syntax:

```
<ColumnName> <Datatype>(<Size>) UNIQUE
```

Let's create a table named Employees with a Username column that holds only unique values:

```
CREATE TABLE Employees(
   EmployeeNo Number(10),
   FirstName Varchar2(25),
   LastName Varchar2(25),
   DateOfBirth Date,
   Gender Char(1),
   MaritalStatus Char(1),
   Address Varchar2(50),
   ContactNo Number(15),
   Salary Number(12, 2),
   Designation Varchar2(25),
   ManagerNo Number(10),
   DeptNo Number(10),
   AboutMe Varchar2(4000),
   Username Varchar2(25) UNIQUE,
   Password Varchar2(25));
```

Output:

```
Table created.
```

Unique Constraint - At Table Level

Syntax:

```
CREATE TABLE <TableName>(
```

```
<ColumnName1> <Datatype>(<Size>), <ColumnName2> <Datatype>(<Size>),
UNIQUE (<ColumnName1>, <ColumnName2>));
```

If the Employees table already exists, drop it and then create a new Employees table with unique usernames across the entire column:

```
CREATE TABLE Employees(
  EmployeeNo Number(10),
  FirstName Varchar2(25),
  LastName Varchar2(25),
  DateOfBirth Date,
  Gender Char(1),
  MaritalStatus Char(1),
  Address Varchar2(50),
  ContactNo Number(15),
  Salary Number(12, 2),
  Designation Varchar2(25),
  ManagerNo Number(10),
  DeptNo Number(10),
  AboutMe Varchar2(4000),
  Username Varchar2(25),
  Password Varchar2(25),
  UNIQUE(Username));
```

Output:

```
Table created.
```

Run the following INSERT queries to ensure that only unique usernames are accepted:

```
INSERT INTO Employees (EmployeeNo, FirstName, LastName, UserName)
  VALUES(101, 'Sharanam', 'Shah', 'sharanam');
INSERT INTO Employees (EmployeeNo, FirstName, LastName, UserName)
  VALUES(201, 'Vaishali', 'Shah', 'sharanam');
INSERT INTO Employees (EmployeeNo, FirstName, LastName, UserName)
  VALUES(301, 'Vaishali', 'Shah', 'vaishali');
```

The first and the third INSERT INTO statements execute without any errors:

```
1 row created.
```

The second INSERT INTO statement displays an error to indicate the violation of the Unique constraint:

```
INSERT INTO Employees (EmployeeNo, FirstName, LastName, UserName)
*
ERROR at line 1:
ORA-00001: unique constraint (VAISHALI.SYS_C008579) violated on table
VAISHALI.EMPLOYEES columns (USERNAME)
ORA-03301: (ORA-00001 details) row with column values (USERNAME:'sharanam')
already exists
```

```
Help: https://docs.oracle.com/error-help/db/ora-00001/
```

Finally, ensure that the data has been stored by the first and the third INSERT INTO statements, using a SELECT query.

Enforcing Constraints Using Alter Table

Adding Constraints

Integrity constraints can be defined using the **CONSTRAINT** clause of the ALTER TABLE command. Oracle does not permit defining constraints with ALTER TABLE if existing data in the table **violates these constraints**. For example, if a Primary Key constraint is applied to a column with duplicate values, the Primary Key constraint **will not** be set for that column.

To alter the Employees table, add a unique constraint to the Username column as follows:

```
ALTER TABLE Employees ADD CONSTRAINT unq_Employees_UserName
  UNIQUE (Username);
```

Here, the constraint is named **unq_Employees_UserName**. Giving user-defined names to constraint is *explained later in this chapter*.

Output:

```
Table altered.
```

Dropping Constraints

Integrity constraint can be dropped if the rule that it enforces is no longer **true** or if the constraint is no longer **needed**. A constraint can be dropped using the ALTER TABLE command with the **DROP** clause.

Drop the **UNIQUE** constraint named from Employees:

```
ALTER TABLE Employees DROP CONSTRAINT unq_Employees_UserName;
```

Output:

```
Table altered.
```

> Dropping UNIQUE and PRIMARY KEY constraints **also drops all** associated indexes.

The Primary Key Constraint

The primary key constraint uniquely identifies each row in a table. Fields that are part of the primary key cannot contain NULL values. A **primary key** can be a natural attribute of the record, such as an email address, which is unique across all records. Alternatively, it can be an artificial field, such as an auto-incrementing number (e.g., 1, 2, 3), used to identify each record uniquely. A primary key can consist of one or more fields in a table. When **multiple fields** are combined to form a **primary key**, it is known as a **composite key**.

A table can have **only one primary key**. The **primary key column(s)** in a table have special attributes:

- The **NOT NULL** attribute is enabled, making the column mandatory (i.e. it cannot be left blank).
- Duplicate values are not accepted, ensuring that the data in the primary key column is always **UNIQUE**.

For example:

Primary Key				
EmailID	**EmployeeName**	**Salary**		**Reason For Rejection**
rohan@hotmail.com	Rohan	4500	√	
meena@gmail.com	Meena	7500	√	
meena@gmail.com	Tanvi	3500	**X**	Duplicate Value
	Raghu	2800	**X**	Null Value

A primary key with a single column is known as a **simple key**, while one with multiple columns is referred to as a **composite primary key**. Although primary keys are not mandatory, they are highly recommended because they uniquely identify each record in a table.

For example:

Composite Key		
OrderNo	**ProductName**	**Cost**
1	A4 Papers	350
2	Tables	700
3	AC	13000
4	Refrigerator	12000
1	LCD	50000
2	Chairs	500
3	A4 Papers	350
4	Tables	700
5	DVD Player	4000
1	TV	15000

A composite key is typically used when no single column can uniquely identify a record.

The OrderDetails table contains multiple sales order records, with each order consisting of several products. Since both the OrderNo and ProductName fields contain duplicate values, neither can serve as a unique primary key. Therefore, to uniquely identify each record in the table, a composite key composed of both OrderNo and ProductName should be used.

Primary keys can be specified either when a table is created (using CREATE TABLE) or by modifying the existing table structure (using ALTER TABLE). A Unique Index is automatically created when a Primary key is defined.

Primary Key Constraint - At Column Level

Syntax:

```
<ColumnName> <Datatype>(<Size>) PRIMARY KEY
```

Create a table named Employees where each user is assigned a unique username that serves as an identifier for the record. Ensure that no user record is created without a username:

```
CREATE TABLE Employees(
   EmployeeNo Number(10),
   FirstName Varchar2(25),
   DateOfBirth Date,
   LastName Varchar2(25),
   Gender Char(1),
   MaritalStatus Char(1),
   Address Varchar2(50),
   ContactNo Number(15),
   Salary Number(12, 2),
   Designation Varchar2(25),
   ManagerNo Number(10),
   DeptNo Number(10),
   AboutMe Varchar2(4000),
   Username Varchar2(25) PRIMARY KEY,
   Password Varchar2(25));
```

Output:

```
Table created.
```

Primary Key Constraint - At Table Level

Syntax:

```
PRIMARY KEY (<ColumnName>, <ColumnName>)
```

Create a table called OrderDetails. This table holds the following columns:

- ❑ OrderNo
- ❑ OrderDate
- ❑ ProductName
- ❑ Cost
- ❑ Qty
- ❑ EmployeeNo
- ❑ CustomerName

Records will be uniquely identified using a composition of OrderNo and ProductName. Since this constraint spans across columns, **it must be described** at table level:

```
CREATE TABLE OrderDetails(
   OrderNo Number(10),
   OrderDate Date,
   ProductName Varchar2(25),
```

```
Cost Number(12, 2),
Qty Number(5),
EmployeeNo Number(10),
CustomerName Varchar2(25),
PRIMARY KEY(OrderNo, ProductName));
```

Output:

```
Table created.
```

Run the following INSERT INTO statement to add a user to the table:

```
INSERT INTO Employees (EmployeeNo, FirstName, LastName, UserName)
  VALUES(101, 'Sharanam', 'Shah', 'sharanam');
```

Output:

```
1 row created.
```

Verify whether the primary key constraint is enforced by reissuing the same INSERT INTO statement:

```
INSERT INTO Employees (EmployeeNo, FirstName, LastName, UserName)
*
ERROR at line 1:
ORA-00001: unique constraint (VAISHALI.SYS_C008577) violated on table
VAISHALI.EMPLOYEES columns (USERNAME)
ORA-03301: (ORA-00001 details) row with column values (USERNAME:'sharanam')
already exists
Help: https://docs.oracle.com/error-help/db/ora-00001/
```

Run the following INSERT INTO statement to add a user to the table:

```
INSERT INTO Employees (EmployeeNo, FirstName, LastName, UserName)
  VALUES(201, 'Vaishali', 'Shah', 'vaishali');
```

Output:

```
1 row created.
```

Run the following INSERT INTO statement to add the order details to the table:

```
INSERT INTO OrderDetails VALUES(1, '2-Jan-2006', 'TV', 45000, 1, 1, 'Sharanam Shah');
```

Output:

```
1 row created.
```

Verify whether the composite primary key constraint is enforced by issuing the same INSERT INTO statement:

```
INSERT INTO OrderDetails VALUES(1, '2-Jan-2006', 'TV', 45000, 1, 1, 'Sharanam
Shah')
```

```
*
ERROR at line 1:
ORA-00001: unique constraint (VAISHALI.SYS_C008578) violated on table
VAISHALI.ORDERDETAILS columns (ORDERNO, PRODUCTNAME)
ORA-03301: (ORA-00001 details) row with column values (ORDERNO:1,
PRODUCTNAME:'TV') already exists
Help: https://docs.oracle.com/error-help/db/ora-00001/
```

Now, modify the INSERT INTO statement, to allow the record to pass the composite primary key constraint:

```
INSERT INTO OrderDetails VALUES(1, '2-Jan-2006', 'AC', 15000, 1, 1, 'Sharanam Shah');
```

The Foreign Key Constraint

A foreign key constraint links the primary key of one table to another table, establishing a relationship between them. Although this constraint does not uniquely identify rows in its own table, it establishes a connection to matching columns in other tables. The table containing a foreign key is known as the **Foreign or Detail table**, while the table with the primary or **unique key** referenced by the **foreign key** is called the **Primary or Master table**.

The REFERENCES **TableName.ColumnName** clause in the CREATE TABLE command allows a master table to be referenced in the foreign key definition when defining the foreign key's column attributes in the detail table. A foreign key can also be in the same table, which is called **Self-Referencing**.

TIP: A foreign key can only reference a primary key of a master table. Therefore, it is mandatory for the master table to have a column defined as **Unique** or as a **Primary Key**.

The relationship established between tables using foreign keys ensures:

- Records cannot be **inserted** into a **detail table**, if corresponding records in the master table do not exist.
- Records of the master **table** cannot be **deleted**, if corresponding records exist in the detail table.

Insert/Update Operations On The Detail Table

When a foreign key is defined on a detail table, the value being inserted/updated in the foreign key column must already exist in the master table's primary key column to which it is referenced.

For example:

Products Table

Primary Key		
ProductName	**ProductMake**	**ProductModel**
TV	LG	LCD
LCD	LG	XCanvas
Refrigerator	Godrej	350 liters
DVD Player	Philips	XY123
AC	LG	Half Ton
A4 Papers	Canon	Executive Bonds
Tables	Durion	Glass
Chairs	Durion	Foldable

OrderDetails Table

Composite Key		
OrderNo	**ProductName**	**Cost**
1	A4 Papers	350
2	Tables	700
3	AC	13000
4	Refrigerator	12000
1	LCD	50000
2	Chairs	500
3	A4 Papers	350
4	Tables	700
5	DVD Player	4000
1	TV	15000

The **Products** table contains eight products, each uniquely identified by the **ProductName**. The **OrderDetails** table records orders for multiple products, with each order uniquely identified by **OrderNo** and **ProductName**. In the Products table, ProductName serves as the primary key. In the OrderDetails table, ProductName is a foreign key referencing the ProductName column in the Products table.

An order cannot include a product that does not exist in the Products table. Therefore, any ProductName being added/updated in the OrderDetails table **must already be present** in the Products table.

Delete Operation On The Master Table

A record in the master table cannot be deleted if the details table holds child records. If such a delete operation is attempted, Oracle **will display an error message** and **prevent the delete operation** from proceeding.

Example: When a product cannot be deleted from the **Products** table, if it has been ordered and is present in the **OrderDetails** table as a record.

On Delete Cascade

To allow such deletes to proceed, the **ON DELETE CASCADE** option can be used. This option in the foreign key definition ensures that all the corresponding records in the detail table are deleted along with the record being deleted in the master table.

Example: When a product is deleted from the **Products** table, all corresponding records in the **OrderDetails** table are automatically deleted.

On Delete Set Null

Alternatively, the **ON DELETE SET NULL** option can be used while defining the foreign key. This constraint allows the deletion of a record from the master table while preserving the child records in the detail table by setting the values in the foreign key column to null.

Example: When a product is deleted from the **Products** table, all corresponding product names in the **OrderDetails** table are set to NULL.

Self Referencing Foreign Keys

A foreign key can be defined to reference the same table in the CREATE TABLE statement. A foreign key that references another column (i.e., the primary or unique key column) of the same table is called a **self-referencing or recursive foreign key**.

For example: Employees Table

Primary Key		Foreign Key
EmployeeNo	**Name**	**ManagerNo**
1	Sharanam Shah	3
2	Vaishali Shah	1
3	Chaitanya Joshi	

Each employee is identified by a unique EmployeeNo. Every employee has a manager to whom they report, and this manager is also an employee of the company. Therefore, in this table, EmployeeNo serves as the Primary Key, while ManagerNo is a Foreign Key that references the EmployeeNo column within the same table.

Here are some observations from the table data:

- Employee Sharanam Shah reports to manager Chaitanya Joshi.
- Employee Vaishali Shah reports to manager Sharanam Shah.
- Employee Chaitanya Shah does not report to anyone, as they are at the top of the hierarchy.

Foreign Key Constraint - At Column Level

Syntax:

```
<ColumnName> <DataType>(<Size>)
  REFERENCES <TableName> [(<ColumnName>)] [ON DELETE CASCADE]
```

Create a Master table named Employees. This table will include:

- A primary key column to identify unique records within the table.

- A foreign key column, DeptNo, which references the Departments table.
- A self-referencing foreign key column, ManagerNo, that points to the EmployeeNo column within the same Employees table.

```
CREATE TABLE Employees(
   EmployeeNo Number(10) PRIMARY KEY,
   FirstName Varchar2(25),
   LastName Varchar2(25),
   DateOfBirth Date,
   Gender Char(1),
   MaritalStatus Char(1),
   Address Varchar2(50),
   ContactNo Number(15),
   Salary Number(12, 2),
   Designation Varchar2(25),
   ManagerNo Number(10) REFERENCES Employees(EmployeeNo),
   DeptNo Number(10) REFERENCES Departments,
   AboutMe Varchar2(4000),
   Username Varchar2(25),
   Password Varchar2(25));
```

Output:

```
Table created.
```

Defining foreign keys at the column level:

1. **ManagerNo Column:**

```
ManagerNo Number(10) REFERENCES Employees(EmployeeNo),
```

The **REFERENCES** keyword here points to the same table, **Employees**. The **Employees** table contains a column named **EmployeeNo**, which serves as the primary key.

2. **DeptNo Column:**

```
DeptNo Number(10) REFERENCES Departments,
```

The **REFERENCES** keyword here points to the detail table, **Departments**. The **Departments** table holds a column named **DeptNo**, which is the primary key.

An Important Point to note: In the case of DeptNo, no specific column name is mentioned in the foreign key definition. Only the table name, **Departments**, is referenced. In such scenarios, Oracle automatically references the primary key column (DeptNo) of the Departments table.

Foreign Key Constraint - At Table Level

Syntax:

```
FOREIGN KEY (<ColumnName> [,<ColumnName>] )
  REFERENCES <TableName> [(<ColumnName>,<ColumnName>)
```

Create a table named OrderDetails with ProductName as the foreign key referencing column ProductName in the Products table:

```
CREATE TABLE OrderDetails(
   OrderNo Number(10),
   OrderDate Date,
   ProductName Varchar2(25),
   Cost Number(12, 2),
   Qty Number(5),
   EmployeeNo Number(10),
   CustomerName Varchar2(25),
   PRIMARY KEY(OrderNo, ProductName),
   FOREIGN KEY (ProductName) REFERENCES Products(ProductName));
```

Output:

```
Table created.
```

In this example, a foreign key is defined at the table level, appearing after all column definitions are complete:

```
FOREIGN KEY (ProductName) REFERENCES Products(ProductName));
```

The **REFERENCES** keyword points to the detail table **Products,** which contains a column named **ProductName** as the primary key.

Foreign Key Constraint - With ON DELETE CASCADE

Create the Master Table: Products:

- This table will contain a unique record identifier for each product.
- Use ProductName as the unique column in the Products table.

```
CREATE TABLE Products(
   ProductName Varchar(25),
   ProductColor Varchar2(25),
   ProductMake Varchar2(25),
   ProductModel Varchar2(25),
   ManufacturingYear Number(4),
   Price Number(12, 2),
   PRIMARY KEY(ProductName));
```

Create the Table: OrderDetails:

- This table will reference ProductName from the Products table as a foreign key.
- The foreign key should allow deletion of records from the Products table with cascading delete functionality.

```
CREATE TABLE OrderDetails(
   OrderNo Number(10),
   OrderDate Date,
   ProductName Varchar2(25),
```

```
Cost Number(12, 2),
Qty Number(5),
EmployeeNo Number(10),
CustomerName Varchar2(25),
PRIMARY KEY(OrderNo, ProductName),
FOREIGN KEY (ProductName) REFERENCES Products1(ProductName)
    ON DELETE CASCADE);
```

Output: (For each table created)

```
Table created.
```

Insert a few records into both the tables.
Products:

```
INSERT INTO Products VALUES('TV', 'Black', 'LG', 'LCD', 2008, 15000);
INSERT INTO Products VALUES('LCD', 'White', 'LG', 'XCanvas', 2008, 50000);
INSERT INTO Products
  VALUES('Refrigerator', 'Silver gray', 'Godrej', '350 liters', 2006, 12000);
INSERT INTO Products
  VALUES('DVD Player', 'White', 'Philips', 'XYZ123', 2007, 4000);
```

OrderDetails:

```
INSERT INTO OrderDetails
  VALUES(1, '11-Nov-2007', 'Refrigerator', 12000, 4, 3, 'Anil Mayekar');
INSERT INTO OrderDetails
  VALUES(1, '3-Jan-2008', 'LCD', 50000, 10, 3, 'Sharanam Shah');
INSERT INTO OrderDetails
  VALUES(5, '28-Feb-2007', 'DVD Player', 4000, 50, 1, 'Hansel Joshi');
INSERT INTO OrderDetails
  VALUES(1, '3-Jan-2008', 'TV', 15000, 5, 7, 'Sharanam Shah');
INSERT INTO OrderDetails
  VALUES(2, '9-Feb-2008', 'DVD Player', 4000, 1, 4, 'Vaishali Shah');
```

Output: (For each table's records inserted)

```
1 row inserted.
```

Now test the cascade effect, by deleting a record from the Products table as:

```
DELETE FROM Products WHERE ProductName = 'DVD Player';
```

Output:

```
1 row deleted.
```

Query the table OrderDetails table and notice the record deletion:

```
SELECT * FROM OrderDetails;
```

Output:

```
ORDERNO ORDERDATE PRODUCTNAME   COST QTY EMPLOYEENO CUSTOMERNAME
------- --------- ------------ ----- --- ---------- -------------
      1 11-NOV-07 Refrigerator 12000   4          3 Anil Mayekar
      1 03-JAN-08 LCD          50000  10          3 Sharanam Shah
      1 03-JAN-08 TV           15000   5          7 Sharanam Shah
```

When a record is deleted from the Products table, all the corresponding records from the OrderDetails which have the same ProductName are also deleted.

Foreign Key Constraint - With ON DELETE SET NULL

ON DELETE SET NULL is a foreign key constraint that ensures the foreign key fields in the detail table are set to **NULL** whenever a corresponding record is deleted from the master table. Notably, the child records in the detail table remain intact and **are not** deleted.

To illustrate, let's create two tables:

1. **Departments Table:** The master table, where DeptNo serves as the unique identifier:

```
CREATE TABLE Departments(
  DeptNo Number(10),
  DepartmentName Varchar2(25),
  Capacity Number(5),
  PRIMARY KEY(DeptNo));
```

2. **Employees Table:** The detail table, where DeptNo is a foreign key that references the DeptNo column in the Departments table. This reference allows the deletion of records from the master table while preserving the child records in the detail table:

```
CREATE TABLE Employees(
  EmployeeNo Number(10),
  FirstName Varchar2(25),
  LastName Varchar2(25),
  DateOfBirth Date,
  Gender Char(1),
  MaritalStatus Char(1),
  Address Varchar2(50),
  ContactNo Number(15),
  Salary Number(12, 2),
  Designation Varchar2(25),
  ManagerNo Number(10),
  DeptNo Number(10),
  AboutMe Varchar2(4000),
  Username Varchar2(25),
  Password Varchar2(25),
  UNIQUE(EmployeeNo),
  FOREIGN KEY (ManagerNo) REFERENCES Employees(EmployeeNo),
  FOREIGN KEY (DeptNo) REFERENCES Departments(DeptNo)
     ON DELETE SET NULL);
```

Output: (For each table created)

```
Table created.
```

Insert a few records into both the tables.

Departments:

```
INSERT INTO Departments1 VALUES (1, 'Sales Department', 15);
INSERT INTO Departments1 VALUES (2, 'HR Department', 5);
INSERT INTO Departments1 VALUES (3, 'Techinal Department', 25);
INSERT INTO Departments1 VALUES (4, 'Purchase Department', 15);
```

Employees:

```
INSERT INTO Employees VALUES (1, 'Sharanam', 'Shah', '03-Jan-1981', 'M', 'M',
   'Makanji Mansion', '9102224440094', 65000, 'Technical Writing', null, 4, 'I can work
   with PHP, MySQL, Apache, Oracle, JSP. My Contact No is 8121-451969.', null, null);
INSERT INTO Employees VALUES (2, 'Vaishali', 'Shah', '03-Feb-1981', 'F', 'M',
   'Makanji Mansion, Mumbai', '9102231040094', 55000, 'Database Management', 1, 1,
   'I am comfortable working with Word, Powerpoint, Excel. My Phone No is
   7131.461962.', null, null);
INSERT INTO Employees VALUES (3, 'Keyur', 'Kapoor', '14-Oct-1984', 'M', 'U', 'Sita
   Sadan, Delhi', '9102227740094', 48000, 'Testing', 2, 4, 'I am comfortable working
   with only Word. My Phone No is 3131.987344.', null, null);
INSERT INTO Employees VALUES (4, 'Amit', 'Haria', '11-Nov-1972', 'M', 'M', 'Krishna
   Kunj, Mumbai', '9102234340094', 34500, 'Programming', 3, 3, 'Contact me at
   2671.978344.', null, null);
INSERT INTO Employees VALUES (5, 'Abhishek', 'Benegal', '28-Feb-1959', 'M', 'M',
   'Thakur Complex, Mumbai', '9102237640094', 54800, 'Sales', 3, 1, 'Call me at
   3322.554433.', null, null);
INSERT INTO Employees VALUES (6, 'Chetan', 'Dedhia', '02-Sep-1965', 'M', 'U',
   'Upendra Nagar, Mumbai', '9102240940094', 39000, 'HR', 4, 3, 'One year experience
   in Word. Contact No 5544.988765.', null, null);
```

Output: (For each table's records inserted)

```
1 row inserted.
```

Now test the cascade effect, by deleting a record from the ProductMaster table as:

```
DELETE FROM Departments WHERE DeptNo=3;
```

Output:

```
1 row deleted.
```

Query the table Employees table and notice the record deletion:

```
SELECT EmployeeNo, DeptNo, FirstName, LastName FROM Employees;
```

Output:

```
EMPLOYEENO     DEPTNO FIRSTNAME                 LASTNAME
---------- ---------- ------------------------- ------------
         1          4 Sharanam                  Shah
```

```
        2          1 Vaishali              Shah
        3          4 Keyur                 Kapoor
        4            Amit                  Haria
        5          1 Abhishek              Benegal
        6            Chetan                Dedhia

6 rows selected.
```

When a record is deleted from the Departments table, the foreign key DeptNo of all the corresponding records from the Employees which have the same DeptNo are set to **NULL**.

User Defined Constraints Names

Oracle assigns a **unique name** to each constraint it defines. The constraint naming convention used by Oracle is SYS_C**n** where **n** is a numeric value that ensures the constraint name **unique**.

In a production environment, however, it is always recommended to assign user-defined names to constraints. This practice provides developers with complete control over the constraints and simplifies tasks such as dropping a constraint by simply referring to it by its user-defined name.

Syntax:

```
CONSTRAINT <Constraint Name> <Constraint Definition>
```

A constraint can be given a user-defined name by preceding the constraint definition with the reserved word **CONSTRAINT** and a **user-defined name**.

To illustrate, let's create two tables:

1. **Products Table:** The master table, with ProductName as the unique record identifier:

```
CREATE TABLE Products(
  ProductName Varchar(25)
  CONSTRAINT pKey_Products_ProductName PRIMARY KEY,
  ProductColor Varchar2(25),
  ProductMake Varchar2(25),
  ProductModel Varchar2(25),
  ManufacturingYear Number(4),
  Price Number(12, 2));
```

2. **OrderDetails Table:** The detail table, where ProductName is a foreign key referencing the ProductName column in the Products table. User-defined names are given to the constraints being created:

```
CREATE TABLE OrderDetails(
  OrderNo Number(10),
  OrderDate Date,
  ProductName Varchar2(25),
  Cost Number(12, 2),
  Qty Number(5),
```

```
    EmployeeNo Number(10),
    CustomerName Varchar2(25),
    CONSTRAINT cKey_OrderNo_ProductName
        PRIMARY KEY(OrderNo, ProductName),
    CONSTRAINT fKey_OrderDetails_ProductName
        FOREIGN KEY (ProductName) REFERENCES Products(ProductName));
```

Constraints For Data Integrity

Business rules in Oracle can be enforced using the **CHECK** and **NOT NULL** constraints. These constraints can be bound to a **column** or a **table** using the CREATE TABLE or ALTER TABLE command. They are enforced whenever a table **write** operation is carried out. Any insert or update statement triggers the relevant business **constraint**, ensuring the integrity of the data in the tables. For a write operation to succeed, the constraints must be satisfied. This ensures that the data in the tables remains consistent and accurate.

NOT NULL Constraint

The NOT NULL constraint is a column level constraint in Oracle. It ensures that a table column cannot be left empty. When a column is defined as **NOT NULL**, it becomes a **mandatory** column, meaning a value **must be entered** for a record to be stored in the table.

Syntax:

```
<ColumnName> <Datatype>(<Size>) NOT NULL
```

To ensure that the Cost column holds a value every time a record is entered in the OrderDetails table, you can define it as NOT NULL:

```
CREATE TABLE OrderDetails(
    OrderNo Number(10),
    OrderDate Date,
    ProductName Varchar2(25),
    Cost Number(12, 2) NOT NULL,
    Qty Number(5),
    EmployeeNo Number(10),
    CustomerName Varchar2(25),
    CONSTRAINT cKey_Ord_OrderNo_Products
        PRIMARY KEY(OrderNo, ProductName),
    CONSTRAINT fKey_OrderDetails_ProductName
        FOREIGN KEY (ProductName) REFERENCES Products(ProductName));
```

Output:

```
Table created.
```

The **NOT NULL** constraint can only be applied at column level.

Test the NOT NULL behavior by inserting the following record, eliminating the Cost column:

```
INSERT INTO OrderDetails (OrderNo, ProductName) VALUES(100, 'TV');
```

Output:

```
INSERT INTO OrderDetails (OrderNo, ProductName) VALUES(100, 'TV')
*
ERROR at line 1:
ORA-01400: cannot insert NULL into ("VAISHALI"."ORDERDETAILS"."COST")
Help: https://docs.oracle.com/error-help/db/ora-01400/
```

The above **error** message confirms that the NOT NULL constraint is enforced by Oracle.

The **NOT NULL** constraint can also be applied as a **CHECK** constraint. However, Oracle does not recommend this.

The CHECK Constraint

The constraint in Oracle allows the application of logical expressions to a column value that evaluates to either **TRUE** or **FALSE**.

A **CHECK** constraint takes substantially longer to execute compared to NOT NULL, PRIMARY KEY, FOREIGN KEY or UNIQUE. Therefore, it is advisable to avoid using CHECK constraints if the same constraint can be defined using Not Null, Primary key or Foreign key.

Check Constraint - At Column Level

Syntax:

```
<ColumnName> <Datatype>(<Size>) CHECK (<Logical Expression>)
```

To illustrate, let's create a table named **Students** with the following CHECK constraints:

- Values entered in the **StudentNo** column must begin with a capital letter 'S'.
- Values entered in the **Age** column should not be less than 18, as this table is intended to hold students who have registered for a postgraduate course.

```
CREATE TABLE Students(
  StudentNo Varchar2(10) CHECK(StudentNo LIKE 'S%'),
  StudentName Varchar2(25),
  Age Number(3) CHECK (Age > 18));
```

Output:

```
Table created.
```

Check Constraint - At Table Level

Syntax:

```
CHECK (<Logical Expression>)
```

To illustrate, let's create the same **Students** table with the same CHECK constraints at the table level:

```
CREATE TABLE Students(
   StudentNo Varchar2(10),
   StudentName Varchar2(25),
   Age Number(3),
   CHECK(StudentNo LIKE 'S%'),
   CHECK (Age > 18));
```

Output:

```
Table created.
```

Test the constraint enforcement by inserting the following record:

```
INSERT INTO Students VALUES('E14', 'Sharanam Shah', 27);
```

Output:

```
INSERT INTO Students VALUES('E14', 'Sharanam Shah', 27)
*
ERROR at line 1:
ORA-02290: check constraint (VAISHALI.SYS_C008600) violated
Help: https://docs.oracle.com/error-help/db/ora-02290/
```

Test the constraint enforcement by inserting the following record:

```
INSERT INTO Students VALUES('S14', 'Sharanam Shah', 15);
```

Output:

```
INSERT INTO Students VALUES('S14', 'Sharanam Shah', 15)
*
ERROR at line 1:
ORA-02290: check constraint (VAISHALI.SYS_C008601) violated
Help: https://docs.oracle.com/error-help/db/ora-02290/
```

The above **error** messages confirm that the check constraints are enforced successfully.

Check Constraint - With Not Null

A CHECK constraint is useful only if it prevents invalid data from being entered. Hence, the condition/expression used in a CHECK constraint should always return TRUE or FALSE. If the expression in a CHECK constraint does not return **TRUE/FALSE**, the value is considered **Unknown**. Unknown values do not violate a CHECK constraint condition.

Let's take an example: In the OrderDetails table, the Cost column contains a CHECK constraint to ensure that only values greater than 0 are accepted. Additionally, also use a NOT NULL constraint to ensure that the Cost column cannot be left empty:

```
CREATE TABLE OrderDetails(
   OrderNo Number(10),
   OrderDate Date,
   ProductName Varchar2(25),
   Cost Number(12, 2) CHECK (Cost > 0),
   Qty Number(5),
   EmployeeNo Number(10),
   CustomerName Varchar2(25),
   CONSTRAINT cKey_Ord_OrderNo_Products
        PRIMARY KEY(OrderNo, ProductName),
   CONSTRAINT fKey_OrderDetails_ProductName
         FOREIGN KEY (ProductName) REFERENCES Products(ProductName));
```

This rule means that a record will not be inserted if the Cost column in that record holds a value less than 0. However, if a NULL value is inserted, Oracle accepts the record. This is because when a NULL is entered, the check condition is evaluated as unknown, which does not violate the CHECK constraint.

For example:

```
INSERT INTO OrderDetails1 (OrderNo, ProductName) VALUES (100, 'TV');
```

Output:

```
1 row created.
```

This issue can be resolved, by placing the **not null** integrity constraint, along with the check constraint on the **Cost** column:

```
CREATE TABLE OrderDetails(
   OrderNo Number(10),
   OrderDate Date,
   ProductName Varchar2(25),
   Cost Number(12, 2) NOT NULL CHECK (Cost > 0),
   Qty Number(5),
   EmployeeNo Number(10),
   CustomerName Varchar2(25),
   CONSTRAINT cKey_Ord_OrderNo_Products
        PRIMARY KEY(OrderNo, ProductName),
```

```
CONSTRAINT fKey_OrderDetails_ProductName
    FOREIGN KEY (ProductName) REFERENCES Products1(ProductName));
```

For example:

```
INSERT INTO OrderDetails (OrderNo, ProductName) VALUES (1, 'TV');
```

Output:

```
INSERT INTO OrderDetails (OrderNo, ProductName) VALUES (1, 'TV')
*
ERROR at line 1:
ORA-01400: cannot insert NULL into ("VAISHALI"."ORDERDETAILS"."COST")
Help: https://docs.oracle.com/error-help/db/ora-01400/
```

Viewing Defined Constraints

If a user desires to see the constraints defined on a particular table, the **DESC <TableName>** command can be useful to some extent, as it allows viewing the column names, data types, sizes, and **NOT NULL constraints**. However, information about other constraints, such as Primary Key, Foreign Key, etc., that are attached to the table columns, is not available using the DESC command.

Such detailed information is stored by Oracle in a table called **USER_CONSTRAINTS**. Querying USER_CONSTRAINTS provides comprehensive information about all constraints. Here are a few of the columns in the USER_CONSTRAINTS table:

Column Name	Description
OWNER	The owner of the constraint.
CONSTRAINT_NAME	The name of the constraint.
TABLE_NAME	The name of the table associated with the constraint.
CONSTRAINT_TYPE	The type of constraint: **P**: Primary Key Constraint **U**: Unique Constraint **R**: Foreign Key Constraint **C**: Check Constraint
SEARCH_CONDITION	The search condition used [for CHECK Constraints].
R_OWNER	The owner of the table used in the referential constraint.
R_CONSTRAINT_NAME	The name of the unique constraint definition for referenced table.

Let's take an example to display the constraints of the table OrderDetails:

```
SELECT OWNER, CONSTRAINT_NAME, CONSTRAINT_TYPE
  FROM USER_CONSTRAINTS WHERE TABLE_NAME = 'ORDERDETAILS';
```

Output:

```
OWNER                          CONSTRAINT_NAME                C
------------------------------ ------------------------------ -
VAISHALI                       ORDERDETAILS_PRODUCTS_FK1      R
VAISHALI                       SYS_C0010034                   C
```

```
VAISHALI                 ORDERDETAILS_EMPLOYEES_FK1    R
VAISHALI                 SYS_C0010035                  C
VAISHALI                 ORDERDETAILS_PK               P
```

The Default Constraint

When a table is created using the CREATE TABLE statement, a **default value** can be assigned to a column. Once a default value is applied as a constraint, whenever a record is inserted into the table and the column is left empty, Oracle automatically loads the column with the specified default value.

TIP: The data type of the default value should match the data type of the column.

Syntax:

```
<ColumnName> <Datatype>(<Size>) DEFAULT <Value>;
```

Let's create a table named Employees where the Salary column is set to a default value of zero if not entered:

```
CREATE TABLE Employees(
   EmployeeNo Number(10) PRIMARY KEY,
   FirstName Varchar2(25),
   LastName Varchar2(25),
   DateOfBirth Date,
   Gender Char(1),
   MaritalStatus Char(1),
   Address Varchar2(50),
   ContactNo Number(15),
   Salary Number(12, 2) DEFAULT 0,
   Designation Varchar2(25),
   ManagerNo Number(10) REFERENCES Employees(EmployeeNo),
   DeptNo Number(10) REFERENCES Departments,
   AboutMe Varchar2(4000),
   Username Varchar2(25),
   Password Varchar2(25));
```

Output:

```
Table created.
```

Character and date values in the DEFAULT constraint should be specified within single quotes.

When a column level constraint is defined on a column that has a default constraint, the default constraint must precede the constraint definition.

```
<ColumnName> <Datatype>(<Size>)
  DEFAULT <Value> <constraint definition>
```

Let's create a table named Employees where the column Salary is by default set to zero if not entered. Additionally, ensure that the value in the Salary column should not be less than zero:

```
CREATE TABLE Employees(
  EmployeeNo Number(10) PRIMARY KEY,
  FirstName Varchar2(25),
  LastName Varchar2(25),
  DateOfBirth Date,
  Gender Char(1),
  MaritalStatus Char(1),
  Address Varchar2(50),
  ContactNo Number(15),
  Salary Number(12, 2) DEFAULT 0 CHECK (Salary >=0),
  Designation Varchar2(25),
  ManagerNo Number(10) REFERENCES Employees(EmployeeNo),
  DeptNo Number(10) REFERENCES Departments,
  AboutMe Varchar2(4000),
  Username Varchar2(25),
  Password Varchar2(25));
```

Output:

```
Table created.
```

Identity Columns

Oracle 12c introduced the ability to define an **IDENTITY** clause against a table column defined using a numeric type. Identity columns automatically generate an auto-increment value upon row insertions. These columns are defined as NOT NULL.

Syntax:

```
GENERATED [ ALWAYS | BY DEFAULT [ ON NULL ] ]
  AS IDENTITY [ ( <Identity Options> ) ]
```

Let's take an example of creating a table with an ALWAYS identity column:

```
CREATE TABLE Students1(
  StudentNo NUMBER GENERATED ALWAYS AS IDENTITY,
  FirstName VARCHAR2(20),
  LastName VARCHAR2(20));
```

Output:

```
Table created.
```

Now let's input a record in the Students table:

```
INSERT INTO Students1(FirstName, LastName) VALUES('Sharanam', 'Shah');
```

Output:

```
1 row created.
```

Try the following INSERTs:

```
INSERT INTO Students1(StudentNo, FirstName, LastName)
  VALUES(2, 'Vaishali', 'Shah');
INSERT INTO Students1(StudentNo, FirstName, LastName)
  VALUES(NULL, 'Vaishali', 'Shah');
```

Output: (For both the INSERT statements)

```
INSERT INTO Students(StudentNo, FirstName, LastName)
                    *
ERROR at line 1:
ORA-32795: cannot insert into a generated always identity column
Help: https://docs.oracle.com/error-help/db/ora-32795/
```

ALWAYS clause forces the use of the identity. If an insert statement references the identity column, even to specify a NULL value, an error is produced.

Let's take an example of creating a table with a BY DEFAULT identity column:

```
CREATE TABLE Students(
  StudentNo NUMBER GENERATED BY DEFAULT AS IDENTITY,
  FirstName VARCHAR2(20),
  LastName VARCHAR2(20));
```

Output:

```
Table created.
```

Now let's input a record in the Students table:

```
INSERT INTO Students(FirstName, LastName) VALUES('Sharanam', 'Shah');
INSERT INTO Students(StudentNo, FirstName, LastName)
  VALUES(2, 'Vaishali', 'Shah');
```

Output: (For both the INSERT statements)

```
1 row created.
```

Try the following INSERT:

```
INSERT INTO Students(StudentNo, FirstName, LastName)
  VALUES(NULL, 'Vaishali', 'Shah');
```

Output:

```
        VALUES(NULL, 'Vaishali', 'Shah')
               *
ERROR at line 2:
ORA-01400: cannot insert NULL into ("VAISHALI"."STUDENTS"."STUDENTNO")
Help: https://docs.oracle.com/error-help/db/ora-01400/
```

BY DEFAULT allows using the identity if the column is not referenced in the INSERT statement, but if the column is referenced, the specified value will be used in place of the identity. Attempting to specify the value NULL in this case results in an error, since identity columns are always NOT NULL.

Let's take an example of creating a table with a BY DEFAULT ON NULL identity column:

```
CREATE TABLE Students(
  StudentNo NUMBER GENERATED BY DEFAULT ON NULL AS IDENTITY,
  FirstName VARCHAR2(20),
  LastName VARCHAR2(20));
```

Output:

```
Table created.
```

Now let's input a record in the Students table:

```
INSERT INTO Students(FirstName, LastName) VALUES('Sharanam', 'Shah');
INSERT INTO Students(StudentNo, FirstName, LastName)
  VALUES(2, 'Vaishali', 'Shah');
INSERT INTO Students(StudentNo, FirstName, LastName)
  VALUES(NULL, 'Vaishali', 'Shah');
```

Output: (For all the INSERT statements)

```
1 row created.
```

BY DEFAULT ON NULL allows the identity to be used if the identity column is referenced, but a value of NULL is specified.

Invisible Columns

In Oracle 11g, enhancements such as invisible indexes and virtual columns were introduced. Building on this, Oracle 12c introduced the concept of invisible columns.

In previous releases, to hide important data columns from being displayed in generic queries, a view was often created to hide the required information or to apply specific security conditions.

In Oracle 12c, there's now the option of defining an invisible column in a table. When a column is defined as invisible, it will not appear in generic queries unless explicitly referred to in the SQL statement or condition, or if the table definition is described.

Let's create a table named Employees with an invisible Salary column:

```
CREATE TABLE Employees(
   EmployeeNo Number(10) PRIMARY KEY,
   FirstName Varchar2(25),
   LastName Varchar2(25),
   DateOfBirth Date,
   Gender Char(1),
   MaritalStatus Char(1),
   Address Varchar2(50),
   ContactNo Number(15),
   Salary Number(12, 2) INVISIBLE,
   Designation Varchar2(25),
   ManagerNo Number(10) REFERENCES Employees(EmployeeNo),
   DeptNo Number(10) REFERENCES Departments,
   AboutMe Varchar2(4000),
   Username Varchar2(25),
   Password Varchar2(25));
```

Output:

```
Table created.
```

Let's insert a record in the Employees table:

```
INSERT INTO Employees VALUES (6, 'Chetan', 'Dedhia', '02-Sep-1965', 'M', 'U', 'Upendra
   Nagar, Mumbai', '40940094', 39000, 'HR', 4, 3, 'One year experience in Word. Contact No
   5544.988765.', null, null);
```

Output:

```
INSERT INTO Employees VALUES (6, 'Chetan', 'Dedhia', '02-Sep-1965', 'M', 'U', 'Upendra
            *
ERROR at line 1:
ORA-00913: too many values
Help: https://docs.oracle.com/error-help/db/ora-00913/
```

You need to refer the invisible column name explicitly in the INSERT statement to insert the data into invisible columns:

```
INSERT INTO Employees (EmployeeNo, FirstName, LastName, DateOfBirth, Gender,
   MaritalStatus, Address, ContactNo, Salary, Designation, ManagerNo, DeptNo, AboutMe,
   Username, Password) VALUES (6, 'Chetan', 'Dedhia', '02-Sep-1965', 'M', 'U', 'Upendra
   Nagar, Mumbai', '40940094', 39000.00, 'HR', 4, 3, 'One year experience in Word. Contact
   No 5544.988765.', null, null);
```

Output:

```
1 row created.
```

Let's alter the table Employees to make the Salary column visible:

```
ALTER TABLE Employees1 MODIFY (Salary VISIBLE);
```

Output:

```
Table altered.
```

Temporary tables, external tables and cluster tables do not support invisible columns.

Chapter

12

SECTION III: WORKING WITH DATA

Operators

Operators allow you to perform actions on one or more values, such as:

- Modifying the value held by one or more columns.
- Producing a new value by:
  - Combining values held by columns.
  - Performing calculations on existing column values. For example, calculating an employee's **annual salary** by multiplying their monthly salary by 12.

These actions are called **operations**. An operation requires at least one symbol and one value. The symbol used in an operation is known as an **Operator**, and a value involved in an operation is called an **Operand/Argument**. Operators are used in expressions or conditional statements.

Oracle provides several useful operators for data manipulation on data elements, enabling you to perform operations and return results.

Arithmetic Operators

Arithmetic operators are used to perform calculations on pairs of values and/or constants. These operators can be applied when viewing records from a table or during data manipulation operations, such as Insert, Update, and Delete.

The following table lists the available arithmetic operators:

Operator	Description	Usage
+ -	Positive/Negative expression	**SELECT** * **FROM** OrderDetails **WHERE** Qty = -1;
+	Addition	**SELECT** Salary + 2000 "Incremented Salary" **FROM** Employees
-	Subtraction	**SELECT** Salary - ProTax "Profession Tax Deduction" **FROM** Employees
*	Multiplication	**SELECT** Salary * 12 "Annual Salary" **FROM** Employees
**	Exponentiation	**SELECT** Salary ** 3 "Three Times Of Monthly Salary" **FROM** Employees
/	Division	**SELECT** Salary / 30 "Daily Wage" **FROM** Employees
( )	Enclosed operation	**SELECT** (Salary / 30) * 10 "Leave Deduction" **FROM** Employees

Let's take an example of displaying the product details of all the available products. Each product with its current price, 10% as the discount of the current product price and the product price after discount deduction:

```
SELECT ProductName, Price, Price*10/100, Price - (Price*10/100) FROM Products;
```

Output:

```
PRODUCTNAME                PRICE PRICE*10/100 PRICE-(PRICE*10/100)
------------------ ---------- ------------ --------------------
TV                         15000         1500                13500
LCD                        50000         5000                45000
Refrigerator               12000         1200                10800
DVD Player                  4000          400                 3600
AC                         13000         1300                11700
A4 Papers                    350           35                  315
Tables                       700           70                  630
Chairs                       700           70                  630

8 rows selected.
```

Here, ProductName and Price are table columns. However, Price*10/100 and Price - (Price*10/100) are not available in the table as column values. These values are produced using multiplication, division and subtraction operators on the Price column values. By default, Oracle uses the column names of the table Products as column headers when displaying column output.

Since Price*10/100 and Price - (Price*10/100) are not table columns Oracle performs the required arithmetic operations and uses the **arithmetic formula** as the **default** column header when displaying output:

```
PRODUCTNAME                    PRICE PRICE*10/100 PRICE-(PRICE*10/100)
------------------ ---------- ------------ --------------------
```

Alternatively, the same query can be written as:

```
SELECT ProductName, Price AS "Current Price", Price*0.10 AS "Discount",
  Price - Price*0.10 AS "Discounted Price" FROM Products;
```

Output:

```
PRODUCTNAME        Current Price   Discount Discounted Price
------------------ ------------- ---------- ----------------
TV                         15000       1500            13500
LCD                        50000       5000            45000
Refrigerator               12000       1200            10800
DVD Player                  4000        400             3600
AC                         13000       1300            11700
A4 Papers                    350         35              315
Tables                       700         70              630
Chairs                       700         70              630

8 rows selected.
```

This output looks meaningful instead of formulas as column headers, appropriate names are used.

The DUAL Work Table

There are times when calculations need to be performed on values that are not available in a database table. In such cases, tables are not referenced, and only **numeric values** are used. To perform these calculations, the SELECT query can output the calculated values. A SELECT statement always requires a table name in the FROM clause; otherwise, it **fails**.

To facilitate such calculations without referencing an existing table, Oracle provides a dummy table called **DUAL**. This table is owned by the user SYS. DUAL is a special one-row, one-column table. The column in this row holds the value *x*.

The structure of the DUAL table is as follows:

```
DESC DUAL;
```

Output:

```
Name        Null?          Type
----------- -------------- ------------------------------------
DUMMY                      VARCHAR2(1)
```

The data held by this table when queried is:

```
SELECT * FROM DUAL;
```

Output:

```
D
-
X
```

Let's take an example, where an employee's current salary is 5000. Display the following calculated values:

- Annual Salary
- 10% of the Current Salary as the increment
- Monthly Salary after increment
- Annual Salary after increment

```
SELECT 5000*12 AS "Annual Salary", 5000*10/100 AS "Increment",
  5000 + (5000*10/100) AS "Monthly Salary after increment",
  (5000*12) + (5000*10/100)*12 AS "Annual Salary after increment" FROM DUAL;
```

Output:

```
Annual Salary Increment Monthly Salary after increment Annual Salary after increment
------------- --------- ------------------------------ -----------------------------
        60000       500                           5500                         66000
```

Optional FROM Clause

For years, if you wanted to retrieve data from a database using SQL, the FROM clause in your SELECT statement was as essential as the SELECT keyword itself. It's how you told the database where to get the information. Think of it like telling a librarian which shelf to find a book on. You wouldn't just say "Give me a book!" - you'd specify the genre, author, or title location. The FROM clause was your database's "shelf location."

However, Oracle 23 has introduced a change that might surprise you: the FROM clause is now optional in certain SELECT statements. This brings Oracle in line with other popular database systems like MS SQL Server, MySQL, and PostgreSQL, improving compatibility and making it easier for developers working across different platforms.

Previously, Oracle required the FROM clause even if you weren't actually selecting data from a table. For instance, if you just wanted to get the current date and time, you'd have to use a "dummy" table, often DUAL. This table contains only one row and one column, and it served as a placeholder so that the FROM clause was syntactically correct.

Let's illustrate with an example. In versions of Oracle prior to 23, if you wanted to see the current date, you'd have to write something like this:

```
SELECT sysdate FROM DUAL;
```

sysdate is a function that returns the current date and time. **DUAL** is the dummy table. Even though you weren't really retrieving data from dual, you still had to include it to satisfy the SQL syntax rules.

If you tried to leave out the FROM clause, you'd get an error. Imagine the database saying, "I understand you want something, but you haven't told me where to look!"

Oracle 23 has changed this. Now, if you're selecting a value that doesn't come from a table (like the result of a function, a constant, or a system variable), you can omit the FROM clause entirely.

So, in Oracle 23, the following statement is perfectly valid:

```
SELECT sysdate;
```

This is much cleaner and more intuitive. You're simply asking the database to evaluate the sysdate function and return the result. No need for the dual table or any other placeholder.

Output:

```
sysdate
---------
11-FEB-25
```

Let's take the above example of an an employee's current salary and calculating its increment:

```
SELECT 5000*12 AS "Annual Salary", 5000*10/100 AS "Increment",
  5000 + (5000*10/100) AS "Monthly Salary after increment",
  (5000*12) + (5000*10/100)*12 AS "Annual Salary after increment";
```

Output:

```
Annual Salary Increment Monthly Salary after increment Annual Salary after increment
------------- --------- ------------------------------ -----------------------------
        60000       500                           5500                         66000
```

This change primarily improves compatibility with other database systems. Developers who are used to writing SQL on other platforms won't have to remember to add the FROM dual clause when working with version Oracle 23 onwards. It simplifies the syntax in certain cases, making SQL code more readable and easier to write.

It's important to remember that the FROM clause is not completely obsolete. You still need it whenever you're selecting data from one or more tables. The change only applies to situations where you're not retrieving data directly from a table. If you're querying a table, joining tables, or using any other table-related operation, the FROM clause is still absolutely essential.

Logical Operators

A logical operator is used to test whether the result of a condition is TRUE or FALSE. The result of a logical operation is always a Boolean value—TRUE or FALSE. There are three logical operators: AND, OR, and NOT.

These operators compare two conditions at a time to determine whether a row can be selected for the output. Logical operators are very useful when specified in the WHERE or HAVING clause of a SELECT statement, allowing the combination of more than one condition.

The AND Operator

The AND operator is used to fetch rows that satisfy all the given conditions. This operator requires that each condition must be met for the record to be included in the result set. It can be used in any valid SQL statement such as SELECT, INSERT, UPDATE, and DELETE.

When the AND operator is used, Oracle processes all the available records in the table and displays the result only after **all** the conditions specified using the **AND** operator are satisfied.

Display all those customers who have purchased products worth more than or equal to Rs. 20,000 but less than Rs. 30,000 on a monthly basis:

```
SELECT CustomerName, OrderDate, SUM(Cost) FROM OrderDetails
  GROUP BY CustomerName, OrderDate
     HAVING SUM(Cost) >= 20000 AND SUM(Cost) < 30000;
```

Output:

```
CUSTOMERNAME              ORDERDATE  SUM(COST)
------------------------- --------- ----------
Anil Mayekar              11-NOV-07      28400
```

Run the following query to understand how the AND operator functions:

```
SELECT CustomerName, OrderDate, SUM(Cost) FROM OrderDetails
  GROUP BY CustomerName, OrderDate;
```

Output:

```
CUSTOMERNAME              ORDERDATE  SUM(COST)
------------------------- --------- ----------
Hansel                    28-FEB-07      66350
Sharanam Chaitanya Shah   03-JAN-08      69350
Vaishali Sharanam Shah    09-FEB-08       5750
Chaitanya Kantilal Shah   09-DEC-08      15000
Sharanam Chaitanya Shah   14-OCT-07      14750
Anil Mayekar              11-NOV-07      28400

6 rows selected.
```

The following table describes how logical AND operator selects a row:

	Condition 1	Operator	Condition 2	Display Row
Row No	SUM(Cost) >= 20000	AND	SUM(Cost) < 30000	
1	√	AND	**X**	**X**
2	√	AND	**X**	**X**

	Condition 1	Operator	Condition 2	Display Row
Row No	SUM(Cost) >= 20000	AND	SUM(Cost) < 30000	
3	X	AND	√	X
4	X	AND	√	X
5	X	AND	√	X
6	√	AND	√	√

After the AND operator is applied on this data using the HAVING clause, only the record numbered 6 is displayed. [The GROUP BY and HAVING clauses are explained later in this book.]

The OR Operator

The OR operator is used to fetch rows that satisfy at least one of the given conditions. This operator requires that any one condition must be met for the record to be included in the result set. It can be used in any valid SQL statement such as SELECT, INSERT, UPDATE, and DELETE.

When the OR operator is used, Oracle processes all the available records in the table and displays the result only after any of the conditions specified with the **OR** operator are satisfied.

Display all those customers whose names begin with S or V:

```
SELECT CustomerNo, CustomerName FROM Customers
  WHERE CustomerName LIKE 'S%' OR CustomerName LIKE 'V%';
```

Output:

```
CUSTOMERNO CUSTOMERNAME
---------- -------------------------
        21 Sharanam Chaitanya Shah
        22 Vaishali Sharanam Shah
        26 Shravan Ashwin Benegal
        28 Stuti Kapil Khanna
```

Run the following query to understand how the OR operator functions:

```
SELECT CustomerNo, CustomerName FROM Customers;
```

Output:

```
CUSTOMERNO CUSTOMERNAME
---------- -------------------------
        21 Sharanam Chaitanya Shah
        22 Vaishali Sharanam Shah
        23 Anil Mayekar
        24 Hansel
        25 Chaitanya Kantilal Shah
        26 Shravan Ashwin Benegal
```

```
        27 Prakash K Chouduary
        28 Stuti Kapil Khanna
        29 Deepika Anil Bakshi
        30 Manali Narendra Naik
        31 Amit Paul

11 rows selected.
```

The following table describes how logical OR operator selects a row:

	Condition 1	Operator	Condition 2	Display Row
Row No	CustomerName **LIKE** "S%"	OR	CustomerName **LIKE** "V%"	
1	√	OR	X	√
2	X	OR	√	√
3	X	OR	X	X
4	X	OR	X	X
5	X	OR	X	X
6	√	OR	X	√
7	X	OR	X	X
8	√	OR	X	√
9	X	OR	X	X
10	X	OR	X	X
11	X	OR	X	X

After the OR operator is applied on this data using the WHERE clause, only the records numbered 1, 2, 6 and 8 are displayed.

The NOT Operator

Every condition that is evaluated by a set of logical operators can be negated to change the condition's perspective. The NOT operator is usually used to determine rows that do not satisfy a given condition. The NOT operator reverses the given condition. This means, if the condition **is met**, then the row is **not displayed**.

Display all those customers whose names do not begin with S or V:

```
SELECT CustomerNo, CustomerName FROM Customers
  WHERE NOT (CustomerName LIKE 'S%' OR CustomerName LIKE 'V%');
```

Output:

```
CUSTOMERNO CUSTOMERNAME
---------- -------------------------
        23 Anil Mayekar
        24 Hansel
        25 Chaitanya Kantilal Shah
        27 Prakash K Chouduary
        29 Deepika Anil Bakshi
```

```
        30 Manali Narendra Naik
        31 Amit Paul

7 rows selected.
```

Run the following query to understand how the OR operator functions:

```
SELECT CustomerNo, CustomerName FROM Customers;
```

Output:

```
CUSTOMERNO CUSTOMERNAME
---------- -------------------------
        21 Sharanam Chaitanya Shah
        22 Vaishali Sharanam Shah
        23 Anil Mayekar
        24 Hansel
        25 Chaitanya Kantilal Shah
        26 Shravan Ashwin Benegal
        27 Prakash K Chouduary
        28 Stuti Kapil Khanna
        29 Deepika Anil Bakshi
        30 Manali Narendra Naik
        31 Amit Paul

11 rows selected.
```

The following table describes how logical OR operator selects a row:

	Condition 1	**Operator**	**Condition 2**	**Display Row**
Row No	CustomerName **LIKE** "S%"	OR	CustomerName **LIKE** "V%"	
1	√	OR	X	X
2	X	OR	√	X
3	X	OR	X	√
4	X	OR	X	√
5	X	OR	X	√
6	√	OR	X	X
7	X	OR	X	√
8	√	OR	X	X
9	X	OR	X	√
10	X	OR	X	√
11	X	OR	X	√

After the NOT operator is applied on this data using the WHERE clause, only the records numbered 3, 4, 5, 7, 9, 10 and 11 is displayed.

Nested Logical Operators

The **NOT, AND** and **OR** operators can be combined in a single SQL statement.

When combining these conditions, it is important to use round brackets to indicate the evaluation order. When the logical operators are combined in a SELECT statement, the order in which the statement is processed is:

- NOT
- AND
- OR

> The order in which the conditions are phrased is very important, as changing order can lead to different results.

When these operators are used together, Oracle processes all rows in a table and displays the result only when:

- **All** of the conditions specified using the **NOT** operator **are not met**.
- **All** of the conditions specified using the **AND** operator **are met**.
- **Any of** the conditions specified using the **OR** operator **are met**.

Display all those customers whose name does not begin with 'S' and who have purchased:

1. Products worth more than or equal to Rs. 20,000 but less than Rs. 30,000 on a monthly basis

OR

2. Quantity of products more than 10 but less than or equal to 50 on a monthly basis

Only for the year 2007:

```
SELECT CustomerName, OrderDate, SUM(Cost) FROM OrderDetails
   WHERE CustomerName NOT LIKE 'S%'
        AND EXTRACT(YEAR FROM OrderDate) = '2007'
             GROUP BY CustomerName, OrderDate
                  HAVING (SUM(Cost) >= 20000 AND SUM(Cost) < 30000)
                       OR (SUM(Qty) > 10 AND SUM(Qty) <= 50);
```

Filters the records before grouping them using the following conditions:

```
CustomerName NOT LIKE 'S%'
AND
EXTRACT(YEAR FROM OrderDate) = '2007'
```

Only those records are grouped and further filtered using the following conditions:

```
(SUM(Cost) >= 20000 AND SUM(Cost) < 30000)
OR
(SUM(Qty) > 10 AND SUM(Qty) <= 50)
```

After grouping, all the records that satisfy the first two conditions are returned:

```
(SUM(Cost) >= 20000 AND SUM(Cost) < 30000)
```

The GROUP BY and HAVING clauses are explained later in this book.

- If the first two conditions **are met**, then the next two conditions **are not evaluated** for that row and the **row is displayed**.

- If the first two conditions **fail** then the next two conditions **are evaluated**.

```
(SUM(Qty) > 10 AND SUM(Qty) <= 50)
```

- If the next two conditions **are met**, then the **row is displayed**. If the next two conditions also **fail**, then the **row is not displayed**.

The brackets determine the order in which the **AND / OR** conditions are evaluated.

```
(SUM(Cost) >= 20000 AND SUM(Cost) < 30000)
OR
(SUM(Qty) > 10 AND SUM(Qty) <= 50)
```

In this case, the first two conditions are in a pair of round brackets, which indicate that these conditions will be evaluated first followed by the next two conditions.

Output:

```
CUSTOMERNAME                ORDERDATE  SUM(COST)
-------------------------- --------- ----------
Anil Mayekar                11-NOV-07       28400
```

Comparison Operators

The following are the comparison operators available in Oracle.

Equality (=)

Display customer details of the customer name Sharanam Chaitanya Shah:

```
SELECT CustomerNo, CustomerName, DateOfBirth, Address FROM Customers
  WHERE CustomerName = 'Sharanam Chaitanya Shah';
```

Output:

```
CUSTOMERNO CUSTOMERNAME            DATEOFBIR ADDRESS
---------- ----------------------- --------- --------------------------------------
        21 Sharanam Chaitanya Shah 03-JAN-81 20, Makanji Mansion, MG Road, 400076
```

Inequality (!= / ^= / <>)

Display customer details of the customers other than Sharanam Chaitanya Shah:

```
SELECT CustomerNo, CustomerName, DateOfBirth, Address FROM Customers
  WHERE CustomerName != 'Sharanam Chaitanya Shah';
```

```
SELECT CustomerNo, CustomerName, DateOfBirth, Address FROM Customers
  WHERE CustomerName ^= 'Sharanam Chaitanya Shah';
```

```
SELECT CustomerNo, CustomerName, DateOfBirth, Address FROM Customers
  WHERE CustomerName <> 'Sharanam Chaitanya Shah';
```

Output:

```
CUSTOMERNO CUSTOMERNAME                DATEOFBIR ADDRESS
---------- -------------------------- --------- ----------------------------------------
        22 Vaishali Sharanam Shah     22-NOV-81 Krishna Kunj, Thakur Lane, 400078
        23 Anil Mayekar               22-NOV-56 Advani Apts, Mumbai
        24 Hansel                     29-OCT-90 Jay Chambers, 7 Juhu
        25 Chaitanya Kantilal Shah    03-JAN-81 14, Raheja Tower, 347236
        26 Shravan Ashwin Benegal     22-SEP-79 3, Shankar Bldg, Mahim
        27 Prakash K Chouduary        07-JUL-90 1st Floor, Kapod Nivas, Mulund
        28 Stuti Kapil Khanna         05-JUN-67 3, Godrej Villa, Powai
        29 Deepika Anil Bakshi        30-JAN-81 Queensland Palace, India
        30 Manali Narendra Naik       22-JAN-81 Hiranadani Mansion, Lion Road
        31 Amit Paul                  22-NOV-56 Advani Apts, Mumbai

10 rows selected.
```

Greater Than & Less Than (> & <)

Display the order details of the orders placed after 2007:

```
SELECT * FROM OrderDetails WHERE EXTRACT(YEAR FROM OrderDate) > '2007';
```

Output:

```
ORDERNO ORDERDATE PRODUCTNAME COST     QTY    EMPLOYEENO CUSTOMERNAME
------- --------- ----------- -------- ------ ---------- -------------------------
1       03-JAN-08 A4 Papers   350      10     6          Sharanam Chaitanya Shah
2       09-FEB-08 Tables      700      100    5          Vaishali Sharanam Shah
1       03-JAN-08 LCD         50000    10     3          Sharanam Chaitanya Shah
2       09-FEB-08 Chairs      700      10     1          Vaishali Sharanam Shah
1       03-JAN-08 TV          15000    5      7          Sharanam Chaitanya Shah
2       09-FEB-08 DVD Player  4000     1      4          Vaishali Sharanam Shah
2       09-FEB-08 A4 Papers   350      3      6          Vaishali Sharanam Shah
1       03-JAN-08 DVD Player  4000     1      9          Sharanam Chaitanya Shah
6       09-DEC-08 TV          15000    1      1          Chaitanya Kantilal Shah

9 rows selected.
```

Display the order details of the orders placed before 2008:

```
SELECT * FROM OrderDetails WHERE EXTRACT(YEAR FROM OrderDate) < '2008';
```

Output:

```
ORDERNO ORDERDATE PRODUCTNAME    COST    QTY    EMPLOYEENO CUSTOMERNAME
------- --------- -------------- ------- ------ ---------- -------------------------
3       14-OCT-07 AC             13000   2      4          Sharanam Chaitanya Shah
4       11-NOV-07 Refrigerator   12000   4      3          Anil Mayekar
3       14-OCT-07 A4 Papers      350     2      5          Sharanam Chaitanya Shah
4       11-NOV-07 Tables         700     3      2          Anil Mayekar
5       28-FEB-07 DVD Player     4000    50     1          Hansel
3       14-OCT-07 Chairs         700     2      10         Sharanam Chaitanya Shah
4       11-NOV-07 Chairs         700     15     9          Anil Mayekar
5       28-FEB-07 A4 Papers      350     3      1          Hansel
5       28-FEB-07 LCD            50000   1      2          Hansel
4       11-NOV-07 TV             15000   4      2          Anil Mayekar
3       14-OCT-07 Tables         700     3      5          Sharanam Chaitanya Shah
5       28-FEB-07 Refrigerator   12000   1      5          Hansel

12 rows selected.
```

Greater Than Or Equal To & Less Than Or Equal To (>= & <=)

Display customer details of the customers born in and after the year 1980:

```
SELECT CustomerNo, CustomerName, DateOfBirth, Address FROM Customers
  WHERE EXTRACT(YEAR FROM DateOfBirth) >= '1980';
```

Output:

```
CUSTOMERNO CUSTOMERNAME              DATEOFBIR ADDRESS
---------- ------------------------- --------- ------------------------------------------
        21 Sharanam Chaitanya Shah   03-JAN-81 20, Makanji Mansion, MG Road, 400076
        22 Vaishali Sharanam Shah    22-NOV-81 Krishna Kunj, Thakur Lane, 400078
        24 Hansel                    29-OCT-90 Jay Chambers,  7 Juhu, 774463524
        25 Chaitanya Kantilal Shah   03-JAN-81 14, Raheja Tower, 347236
        27 Prakash K Chouduary       07-JUL-90 1st Floor, Kapod Nivas, Mulund
        29 Deepika Anil Bakshi       30-JAN-81 Queensland Palace,  India
        30 Manali Narendra Naik      22-JAN-81 Hiranadani Mansion,            Lion Road

7 rows selected.
```

Display customer details of the customers born in and before the year 1980:

```
SELECT CustomerNo, CustomerName, DateOfBirth, Address FROM Customers
  WHERE EXTRACT(YEAR FROM DateOfBirth) <= '1980';
```

Output:

```
CUSTOMERNO CUSTOMERNAME              DATEOFBIR ADDRESS
---------- ------------------------- --------- ------------------------------
        23 Anil Mayekar              22-NOV-56 Advani Apts, Mumbai, 665534256
        26 Shravan Ashwin Benegal    22-SEP-79 3, Shankar Bldg,  Mahim
        28 Stuti Kapil Khanna        05-JUN-67 3, Godrej Villa, Powai
        31 Amit Paul                 22-NOV-56 Advani Apts, Mumbai

4 rows selected.
```

Equal To Any Member Of (IN / = ANY)

In case a value needs to be compared to a list of values then the **IN** operator is used. The IN operator helps reduce using multiple OR conditions.

Display customer details of all those customers who had placed orders:

```
SELECT CustomerNo, CustomerName, DateOfBirth, Address FROM Customers
  WHERE CustomerName IN(SELECT CustomerName FROM OrderDetails);
```

```
SELECT CustomerNo, CustomerName, DateOfBirth, Address FROM Customers
  WHERE CustomerName = ANY(SELECT CustomerName FROM OrderDetails);
```

Output:

```
CUSTOMERNO CUSTOMERNAME            DATEOFBIRTH ADDRESS
---------- ----------------------- ----------- -----------------------------------
21         Sharanam Chaitanya Shah 03-JAN-81   20, Makanji Mansion, MG Road, 400076
22         Vaishali Sharanam Shah  22-NOV-81   Krishna Kunj, Thakur Lane, 400078
23         Anil Mayekar            22-NOV-56   Advani Apts, Mumbai,  665534256
24         Hansel                  29-OCT-90   Jay Chambers,  7 Juhu, 774463524
```

```
25          Chaitanya Kantilal Shah 03-JAN-81   14, Raheja Tower, 347236

5 rows selected.
```

Not Equal To Any Member Of (NOT IN / != ALL)

Display customer details of the customers other than the ones who had placed orders:

```
SELECT CustomerNo, CustomerName, DateOfBirth, Address FROM Customers
  WHERE CustomerName NOT IN (SELECT CustomerName FROM OrderDetails);
```

```
SELECT CustomerNo, CustomerName, DateOfBirth, Address FROM Customers
  WHERE CustomerName != ALL(SELECT CustomerName FROM OrderDetails);
```

Output:

```
CUSTOMERNO CUSTOMERNAME           DATEOFBIR ADDRESS
---------- ---------------------- --------- ---------------------------------------
        29 Deepika Anil Bakshi    30-JAN-81 Queensland Palace,  India
        28 Stuti Kapil Khanna     05-JUN-67 3, Godrej Villa, Powai
        27 Prakash K Chouduary    07-JUL-90 1st Floor, Kapod Nivas, Mulund
        31 Amit Paul              22-NOV-56 Advani Apts, Mumbai
        26 Shravan Ashwin Benegal 22-SEP-79 3, Shankar Bldg,  Mahim
        30 Manali Narendra Naik   22-JAN-81 Hiranadani Mansion,            Lion Road

6 rows selected.
```

Equal To Any Value In A List Or Returned By A Query (ANY / SOME)

Display customer details of all those customers who had placed orders:

```
SELECT CustomerNo, CustomerName, DateOfBirth, Address FROM Customers
  WHERE CustomerName =  ANY(SELECT CustomerName FROM OrderDetails);
```

```
SELECT CustomerNo, CustomerName, DateOfBirth, Address FROM Customers
  WHERE CustomerName = SOME(SELECT CustomerName FROM OrderDetails);
```

This operator **must be preceded by** =, !=, >, <, <=, >= operators.

Output:

```
CUSTOMERNO CUSTOMERNAME              DATEOFBIR ADDRESS
---------- ------------------------- --------- -------------------------------------
        21 Sharanam Chaitanya Shah   03-JAN-81 20, Makanji Mansion, MG Road, 400076
        22 Vaishali Sharanam Shah    22-NOV-81 Krishna Kunj, Thakur Lane, 400078
        23 Anil Mayekar              22-NOV-56 Advani Apts, Mumbai, 665534256
        24 Hansel                    29-OCT-90 Jay Chambers,  7 Juhu, 774463524
        25 Chaitanya Kantilal Shah   03-JAN-81 14, Raheja Tower, 347236
```

Equal To Every Value In A List Or Returned By A Query (ALL)

Display customer details of customers whose annual income is more than 350000 and less than 450000:

```
SELECT CustomerNo, CustomerName, DateOfBirth, AnnualIncome FROM Customers
  WHERE AnnualIncome > ALL(450000, 350000);
```

This operator **must be preceded by** =, !=, >, <, <=, >= operators.

Output:

```
CUSTOMERNO CUSTOMERNAME              DATEOFBIR ANNUALINCOME
---------- ------------------------- --------- ------------
        21 Sharanam Chaitanya Shah   03-JAN-81      5000000
        24 Hansel                    29-OCT-90       784000
        25 Chaitanya Kantilal Shah   03-JAN-81       890000
        26 Shravan Ashwin Benegal    22-SEP-79       783500
        29 Deepika Anil Bakshi       30-JAN-81      5000000
```

Exists

Display customer details of all those customers who had placed orders:

```
SELECT CustomerNo, CustomerName, DateOfBirth, Address FROM Customers
  WHERE EXISTS (SELECT * FROM OrderDetails
     WHERE OrderDetails.CustomerName = Customers.CustomerName);
```

This operator returns **TRUE**, if the subquery returns at least one row.

Output:

```
CUSTOMERNO CUSTOMERNAME              DATEOFBIRTH ADDRESS
---------- ------------------------- ----------- -------------------------------------
21         Sharanam Chaitanya Shah   03-JAN-81   20, Makanji Mansion, MG Road, 400076
22         Vaishali Sharanam Shah    22-NOV-81   Krishna Kunj, Thakur Lane, 400078
23         Anil Mayekar              22-NOV-56   Advani Apts, Mumbai, 665534256
24         Hansel                    29-OCT-90   Jay Chambers,  7 Juhu, 774463524
25         Chaitanya Kantilal Shah   03-JAN-81   14, Raheja Tower, 347236
```

NULL Values (IS [NOT] NULL)

Display employee details of employees who do not report to a manager:

```
SELECT DISTINCT(EmployeeNo), FirstName, LastName FROM Employees
  WHERE ManagerNo IS NULL;
```

Output:

```
EMPLOYEENO FIRSTNAME                 LASTNAME
---------- ------------------------- -------------------------
         1 Sharanam                  Shah
```

Display employee details of employees who report to a manager:

```
SELECT DISTINCT(EmployeeNo), FirstName, LastName FROM Employees
  WHERE ManagerNo IS NOT NULL;
```

Output:

```
EMPLOYEENO FIRSTNAME                 LASTNAME
---------- ------------------------- -------------------------
         2 Vaishali                  Shah
         3 Keyur                     Kapoor
         4 Amit                      Haria
         5 Abhishek                  Benegal
         6 Chetan                    Dedhia
         7 Narendra                  Dodhia
         8 Meenal                    Doshi
         9 Anil                      Mayekar
        10 Chaitanya                 Kapoor
        11 Amit                      Paul

10 rows selected.
```

The BETWEEN Operator

The BETWEEN operator allows selecting rows that contain values within a specified lower and upper limit. The range specified after the word BETWEEN is **inclusive**, meaning both boundary values are included. The values in the range are separated using the **AND** keyword. The BETWEEN operator can be used with string, numeric, and date data types. However, the data types cannot be mixed, i.e., you cannot have the lower value from a character column and the upper value from a numeric column. If any of the values is NULL, the BETWEEN AND operator also returns NULL.

Display all those customers who have purchased products worth more than or equal to Rs. 20,000 but less than Rs. 30,000 in the months from July to December:

```
SELECT CustomerName, OrderDate, SUM(Cost) FROM OrderDetails
  WHERE EXTRACT(MONTH FROM OrderDate) BETWEEN '07' AND '12'
     GROUP BY CustomerName, OrderDate
        HAVING SUM(Cost) >= 20000 AND SUM(Cost) < 30000;
```

Equivalent to:

```
SELECT CustomerName, OrderDate, SUM(Cost) FROM OrderDetails
  WHERE EXTRACT(MONTH FROM OrderDate) >= '07'
     AND EXTRACT(MONTH FROM OrderDate) <= '12'
        GROUP BY CustomerName, OrderDate
           HAVING SUM(Cost) >= 20000 AND SUM(Cost) < 30000;
```

Output:

```
CUSTOMERNAME              ORDERDATE  SUM(COST)
------------------------- --------- ----------
Anil Mayekar              11-NOV-07      28400
```

The NOT operator can also be used with BETWEEN. For example: Display all those customers who have purchased products worth more than or equal to Rs. 50,000 but less than Rs. 70,000 in the months other than July to December:

```
SELECT CustomerName, OrderDate, SUM(Cost) FROM OrderDetails
  WHERE EXTRACT(MONTH FROM OrderDate) NOT BETWEEN '07' AND '12'
     GROUP BY CustomerName, OrderDate
        HAVING SUM(Cost) >= 50000 AND SUM(Cost) < 70000;
```

Output:

```
CUSTOMERNAME              ORDERDATE  SUM(COST)
------------------------- --------- ----------
Hansel                    28-FEB-07      66350
Sharanam Chaitanya Shah   03-JAN-08      69350
```

Date Operators (+ / -)

Example:

```
SELECT SYSDATE, SYSDATE - 10 FROM Dual;
```

Output:

```
SYSDATE   SYSDATE-1
--------- ---------
09-DEC-24 29-NOV-24
```

Example:

```
SELECT DateOfBirth, DateOfBirth + 5 FROM Customers;
```

Output:

```
DATEOFBIRTH               DATEOFBIRTH+5
------------------------- -------------------------
03-JAN-81                 08-JAN-81
22-NOV-81                 27-NOV-81
22-NOV-56                 27-NOV-56
29-OCT-90                 03-NOV-90
03-JAN-81                 08-JAN-81
22-SEP-79                 27-SEP-79
07-JUL-90                 12-JUL-90
05-JUN-67                 10-JUN-67
30-JAN-81                 04-FEB-81
22-JAN-81                 27-JAN-81

10 rows selected.
```

> **TIP** **SYSDATE** is a pseudo column that contains the current date and time. It requires no arguments and returns the current date.

The LIKE Operator

The **LIKE** operator allows comparing one string value with another string value, which is not identical. This is achieved by using wildcard characters. The following wildcards are available:

- % allows to match any string of any length [including zero length].

Examples	Descriptions
SHA%	All those strings that begin with the letters 'SHA' are matched.
%HAH	All those strings that end with the letters HAH are matched.
%ARA%	All those strings that contain letters ARA are matched.

- _ allows to match a single character.

Examples	Descriptions
SHA_	All those strings that begin with the letters SHA and have one letter after it are matched.
_HAH	All those strings that begin with any single letter and end with the letters HAH are matched.
ARA	All those strings that contain letters ARA with any single letter as the first letter and as the last letter are matched.

Let's display customer details of customers whose name begin with "Sh":

```
SELECT CustomerNo, CustomerName, DateOfBirth, Address FROM Customers
  WHERE CustomerName LIKE 'Sh%';
```

Output:

```
CUSTOMERNO CUSTOMERNAME            DATEOFBIRTH ADDRESS
---------- ----------------------- ----------- ---------------------------------------
21         Sharanam Chaitanya Shah 03-JAN-81   20, Makanji Mansion, MG Road, 400076
26         Shravan Ashwin Benegal  22-SEP-79   3, Shankar Bldg,  Mahim
```

The % indicates that any number of characters can follow the letters **Sh**.

Let's display customer details of customers whose name have second character as "a" or "h":

```
SELECT CustomerNo, CustomerName, DateOfBirth, Address FROM Customers
  WHERE CustomerName LIKE '_a%' OR CustomerName LIKE '_h%';
```

Output:

```
CUSTOMERNO CUSTOMERNAME            DATEOFBIRTH ADDRESS
---------- ----------------------- ----------- ----------------------------------------
21         Sharanam Chaitanya Shah 03-JAN-81   20, Makanji Mansion, MG Road, 400076
22         Vaishali Sharanam Shah  22-NOV-81   Krishna Kunj, Thakur Lane, 400078
24         Hansel                  29-OCT-90   Jay Chambers, 7 Juhu, 774463524
25         Chaitanya Kantilal Shah 03-JAN-81   14, Raheja Tower, 347236
```

```
26         Shravan Ashwin Benegal  22-SEP-79   3, Shankar Bldg,  Mahim
30         Manali Narendra Naik    22-JAN-81   Hiranadani Mansion, Lion Road

6 rows selected.
```

All those customers with names having the second character as **a** or **h** are retrieved.

Let's display customer details of customers whose name have the sixth and seventh character as "al":

```
SELECT CustomerNo, CustomerName, DateOfBirth, Address FROM Customers
  WHERE CustomerName LIKE '_____al%';
```

Output:

```
CUSTOMERNO CUSTOMERNAME           DATEOFBIRTH ADDRESS
---------- ---------------------- ----------- ----------------------------------
22         Vaishali Sharanam Shah 22-NOV-81   Krishna Kunj, Thakur Lane, 400078
```

All those customers, with names of eight characters, having the sixth and seventh characters as **a** and **l** respectively, are retrieved.

Escaping Characters

It is also possible to escape special characters such as % and _ which are used as wild characters with the LIKE operator. Escaping these characters enables finding all those words that have % or _ within. Only a single character can be escaped.

Example:

```
SELECT CustomerNo, CustomerName, DateOfBirth, Address FROM Customers
  WHERE CustomerName LIKE '\%' ESCAPE '\';
```

The **ESCAPE** clause identifies the backslash '\' as the escape character. Since the % character is escaped, this query will retrieve all customers whose name is %.

Output:

```
CUSTOMERNO CUSTOMERNAME  DATEOFBIR ADDRESS
---------- ------------- --------- ---------------
        31 %             31-JUL-82 Krishna Kunj
```

Example:

```
SELECT CustomerNo, CustomerName, DateOfBirth, Address FROM Customers
  WHERE CustomerName LIKE 'S%\%' ESCAPE '\';
```

This query returns all those customers whose name begins with the letter S and ends with the character %.

Output:

```
CUSTOMERNO CUSTOMERNAME  DATEOFBIR ADDRESS
---------- ------------- --------- ---------------
        31 S%            31-JUL-82 Krishna Kunj
```

Example:

```
SELECT CustomerNo, CustomerName, DateOfBirth, Address FROM Customers
  WHERE CustomerName LIKE 'S%!_' ESCAPE '!';
```

This query returns all those customers whose name beings with a letter S and ends with a character _.

Output:

```
CUSTOMERNO CUSTOMERNAME  DATEOFBIR ADDRESS
---------- ------------- --------- ---------------
        31 S_            31-JUL-82 Krishna Kunj
```

IS NAN And IS INFINITE Operators

Starting from Oracle 10g, two new operators were introduced to support the BINARY_FLOAT and BINARY_DOUBLE data types. These data types can store values such as NaN (Not a Number) and Infinity. The following operators are provided to handle such values:

- *IS NAN/IS NOT NAN*: Matches **NaN** value.
- *IS INFINITE/IS NOT INFINITE*: Matches **INFINITE** value.

Let's display all those records where the order amount holds the value NaN or Infinity:

```
SELECT * FROM Orders WHERE OrderAmount IS NAN OR OrderAmount IS INFINITE;
```

Output:

```
ORDERNO ORDERDATE CUSTOMERNO ORDERAMOUNT ORDERSTATUS           ORDERCODE
------- --------- ---------- ----------- --------------------- ---------
8       08-FEB-08 25         Inf         Void                  MD/0203
7       09-DEC-08 25         NaN         Authorization Failed  MD/0503
```

Operator Precedence

Now that we are familiar with the operators Oracle provides, let's delve into their precedence. **Precedence** is an important property of an operator that determines the order in which Oracle evaluates different operators within the same expression. When an expression contains multiple operators, Oracle evaluates those with higher precedence first before moving on to operators with lower precedence. Operators with equal precedence are evaluated from left to right within an expression.

Solution:

```
SELECT Salary, Salary + 1000 * 3 FROM Employees;
```

Output:

```
SALARY                 SALARY+1000*3
---------------------- ----------------------
82500                  85500
55000                  58000
22000                  25000
22660                  25660
13334.2                16334.2
13553.1                16553.1
13578.4                16578.4
49500                  52500
31207                  34207
1320                   4320
31207                  34207

11 rows selected.
```

Since the multiplication operator has a higher precedence than the addition operator, Oracle multiplies the value 1000 by 3 and then adds the result to Salary.

Parentheses can be used in an expression to override operator precedence. Oracle evaluates expressions inside parentheses before evaluating those outside. If an expression has nested parentheses, the most deeply nested expression is evaluated first.

Solution:

```
SELECT Salary, (Salary + 1000) * 3 FROM Employees;
```

Output:

```
SALARY                 (SALARY+1000)*3
---------------------- ----------------------
82500                  250500
55000                  168000
22000                  69000
22660                  70980
13334.2                43002.6
13553.1                43659.3
13578.4                43735.2
49500                  151500
31207                  96621
1320                   6960
31207                  96621

11 rows selected.
```

Since the expression holds Salary + 1000 in parentheses, Oracle adds 1000 to Salary and then multiplies the result by 3.

Operator precedence plays a significant role of determining the sequence in which, the operations are performed in complex expressions, with multiple operators. The order of execution significantly affects the resulting value.

The following table indicates the precedence of the various operators:

<table>
<tr><th>Order</th><th>Operator</th><th>Description</th></tr>
<tr><td>1</td><td>+
-</td><td>Positive or Negative expression</td></tr>
<tr><td>2</td><td>*
/</td><td>Multiplication, Division</td></tr>
<tr><td>3</td><td>+
-
||</td><td>Addition, Subtraction, Concatenation</td></tr>
<tr><td>4</td><td>=
!=
<
>
<=
>=
IS NULL
LIKE
BETWEEN</td><td>Comparison</td></tr>
<tr><td>5</td><td>**
NOT</td><td>Exponentiation, Logical Negation</td></tr>
<tr><td>6</td><td>AND</td><td>Logical AND</td></tr>
<tr><td>7</td><td>OR</td><td>Logical OR</td></tr>
</table>

Subquery is explained later in this book.

Chapter

13

SECTION III: WORKING WITH DATA

Character/String Functions

A **function** is a one-word command that returns a single value, typically determined by input parameters. However, some functions, like CURRENT_TIME, do not require any input parameters to return a value.

Oracle offers a comprehensive set of character/string functions that:

- **Retrieve** information about strings.
- **Modify** the contents of strings.

These functions operate on character values, accepting one or more character values as parameters and return either a character or a numeric value.

For a string function:

- If the input argument is Char/Varchar2, the value returned is Varchar2.
- If the input argument is Nchar/NVarchar2, the value returned is NVarchar2.
- For functions that return Char/Varchar2, if the length of the return value exceeds the limit, Oracle truncates it and returns the result without an error message.

- For functions that return CLOB values, if the length of the return values exceeds the limit, Oracle raises an error and returns no data.

Concatenating Strings

The **CONCAT()** function allows combining two strings. It accepts two parameters and returns a concatenation of the values held by both the parameters. It can accept the following data types:

CHAR VARCHAR2 NCHAR NVARCHAR2 CLOB NCLOB

The string that is returned after concatenation is in the same character set as the first string. The data type depends on the data types of the arguments. If two strings of different data types are concatenated, this function returns the data type that results a lossless conversion.

For example:

- If one of the arguments is a LOB, then the returned value is a LOB.
- If one of the arguments is a national data type, then the returned value is a national data type.
- CONCAT(CLOB, NCLOB) returns NCLOB
- CONCAT(NCLOB, NCHAR) returns NCLOB
- CONCAT(NCLOB, CHAR) returns NCLOB
- CONCAT(NCHAR, CLOB) returns NCLOB

This function is equivalent to the concatenation operator [| |], which allows concatenating two or more strings together.

```
<String1> || <String2> || <StringN>
```

Where,

- *String1* is the first string to concatenate
- *String2* is the second string to concatenate
- *StringN* is the nth string to concatenate

Create an English sentence for every customer, by joining predetermined string values with appropriate column values retrieved from the **OrderDetails** table as:

Customer <CustomerName> has purchased products worth Rs. <SUM(Cost)> till MAX(OrderDate).

Solution (Using | |):

```
SELECT 'Customer ' || OrderDetails.CustomerName ||
   ' has purchased products worth Rs. ' || SUM(Cost) || ' till ' || MAX(OrderDate)
      AS "Cost of products purchased" FROM OrderDetails, Customers
         WHERE Customers.CustomerName = OrderDetails.CustomerName
            GROUP BY OrderDetails.CustomerName;
```

Solution (Using CONCAT):

```
SELECT CONCAT('Customer ', CONCAT(OrderDetails.CustomerName,
   CONCAT(' has purchased products worth Rs. ', CONCAT(SUM(Cost),
   CONCAT(' till ', MAX(OrderDate)))))) AS "Cost of products purchased"
      FROM OrderDetails, Customers
         WHERE Customers.CustomerName = OrderDetails.CustomerName
            GROUP BY OrderDetails.CustomerName;
```

Output:

```
Cost of products purchased
-----------------------------------------------------------------------------------------
Customer Anil Mayekar has purchased products worth Rs. 28400 till 11-NOV-07
Customer Chaitanya Kantilal Shah has purchased products worth Rs. 15000 till 09-DEC-08
Customer Vaishali Sharanam Shah has purchased products worth Rs. 5750 till 09-FEB-08
Customer Sharanam Chaitanya Shah has purchased products worth Rs. 84100 till 03-JAN-08
Customer Hansel has purchased products worth Rs. 66350 till 28-FEB-07
```

The Concatenation operator can be used intelligently to get some useful tasks done. One of such tasks would be to generate SQL queries.

Solution:

```
SELECT 'DROP TABLE ' || Table_Name || ';' AS "Drop Table Commands"
  FROM USER_TABLES;
```

The **||** operator is used to concatenate the SQL command with the available table names. **User_Tables** is an Oracle table that holds the details of the tables in the currently logged in user's schema. The **Table_Name** column holds the actual table names.

Output:

```
Drop Table Commands
------------------------------------------
DROP TABLE EMPLOYEEMUSTER;
DROP TABLE DISCONNECTEDSUBSCRIBERS;
. . .
DROP TABLE REGULARPRODUCTSSALES;
DROP TABLE ECONOMICPRODUCTS;

50 rows selected.
```

Operating On String Case

Lower Case

The **LOWER()** function accepts a string and returns it in lowercase. Non-letter characters within the string remain unaffected by this function.

Solution:

```
SELECT LOWER(CustomerName) "Lower" FROM Customers;
```

Output:

```
Lower
-------------------------
sharanam chaitanya shah
vaishali sharanam shah
anil mayekar
hansel
chaitanya kantilal shah
shravan ashwin benegal
prakash k chouduary
stuti kapil khanna
deepika anil bakshi
manali narendra naik
amit paul

11 rows selected.
```

Title Case

The **INITCAP()** function accepts a string and returns it with the first letter of each word in **uppercase** and the remaining letters of each word in lowercase.

Solution:

```
SELECT INITCAP(CustomerName) "InitCap" FROM Customers;
```

Output:

```
InitCap
-------------------------
Sharanam Chaitanya Shah
Vaishali Sharanam Shah
Anil Mayekar
Hansel
Chaitanya Kantilal Shah
Shravan Ashwin Benegal
Prakash K Chouduary
Stuti Kapil Khanna
Deepika Anil Bakshi
Manali Narendra Naik
Amit Paul

11 rows selected.
```

Upper Case

The **UPPER()** function accepts a string and returns it in uppercase. Non-letter characters within the string remain unaffected by this function.

Solution:

```
SELECT UPPER(CustomerName) "Upper" FROM Customers;
```

Output:

```
Upper
-------------------------
SHARANAM CHAITANYA SHAH
VAISHALI SHARANAM SHAH
ANIL MAYEKAR
HANSEL
CHAITANYA KANTILAL SHAH
SHRAVAN ASHWIN BENEGAL
PRAKASH K CHOUDUARY
STUTI KAPIL KHANNA
DEEPIKA ANIL BAKSHI
MANALI NARENDRA NAIK
AMIT PAUL

11 rows selected.
```

Comparing Strings

The Customers table contains a column named CustomerName with names stored in various cases, such as "Shah", "SHAH" or "shah." To find all customers with names containing the word "shah," regardless of how it is stored, you can use a case-insensitive search:

```
SELECT CustomerNo,CustomerName, DateOfBirth, Address FROM Customers
  WHERE UPPER(CustomerName) LIKE ('%SHAH%');
SELECT CustomerNo,CustomerName, DateOfBirth, Address FROM Customers
  WHERE UPPER(CustomerName) LIKE UPPER('%Shah%');
SELECT CustomerNo,CustomerName, DateOfBirth, Address FROM Customers
  WHERE UPPER(CustomerName) LIKE UPPER('%shah%');
```

Output:

```
CUSTOMERNO CUSTOMERNAME            DATEOFBIRTH ADDRESS
---------- ----------------------- ----------- -----------------------------------
21         Sharanam Chaitanya Shah 03-JAN-81   20, Makanji Mansion, MG Road, 400076
22         Vaishali Sharanam Shah  22-NOV-81   Krishna Kunj, Thakur Lane, 400078
25         Chaitanya Kantilal Shah 03-JAN-81   14, Raheja Tower, 347236
```

Extracting String Portions

The **SUBSTR()** function extracts a portion of the string based on specified parameters.

```
SUBSTR(<String>, <StartPosition>, [<Length>])
```

Where,

- *String:* The source string.
- *Length:* (Optional) The number of characters to extract.
- *StartPosition:* The position within the string where extraction begins.

Example:

```
SELECT SUBSTR('This is a test', 6, 2) "Example 1" FROM DUAL;
```

Output:

```
Example 1
---------
is
```

Example:

```
SELECT SUBSTR('This is a test', 6) "Example 2" FROM DUAL;
```

Output:

```
Example 2
---------
is a test
```

Example:

```
SELECT SUBSTR('TechOnTheWeb', -3, 3) "Example 3" FROM DUAL;
```

Output:

```
Example 3
---------
Web
```

Strings And ASCII Values

ASCII

The **ASCII()** function returns the numeric code in the database character set that represents the specified character. This function takes one parameter, which is the character for which you want to retrieve the numeric code. If more than one character is entered as the function parameter, the function returns the code for the first character and ignores the rest.

Solution:

```
SELECT ASCII('a') "ASCII 1", ASCII('A') "ASCII 2",  ASCII('A2') "ASCII 3" FROM DUAL;
```

Output:

```
   ASCII 1    ASCII 2    ASCII 3
---------- ---------- ----------
        97         65         65
```

The ASCII 3 column returns the same value as ASCII 2, as more than one character is specified as the function parameter value.

CHR

The **CHR()** function returns the character associated with a specified collating code. It is the inverse of the ASCII() function. The CHR() function takes one parameter, which is a number specifying the location in the collating sequence. The CHR() function is particularly useful when referencing non-printable character in the code.

For example, the location of the newline character in the standard ASCII collating sequence is ten. Using the CHR() function allows you to search for the linefeed control character in a string and perform operations based on its presence. Additionally, a linefeed can be inserted into a character string using the CHR() function.

Create a report that displays the names and addresses of customers that can be printed as visiting cards:

```
SELECT FirstName || ' ' || LastName ||
   DECODE (BuildingName, NULL, NULL, CHR (10) || BuildingName) ||
   DECODE (Road, NULL, NULL, CHR (10) || Road) ||
   DECODE (Area, NULL, NULL, CHR (10) || Area) ||
   DECODE (City, NULL, NULL, CHR (10) || City) ||
   DECODE (Pincode, NULL, NULL, CHR (10) || Pincode) ||
   CHR (10) AS "Customer Details" FROM SubscriberMaster;
```

Output:

```
Customer Details
--------------------------------------------------
Sharanam Shah
Flora Deccan
M. G. Road
Andheri
Mumbai
400058
Vaishali Shah
Blue Queens
S. V. Road
Bandra
Pune
400050
Kanchan Toprani
Shankar Apts
L. J. Road
Wadala
Delhi
400031
Anil Naik
Makanji Kunj
Savarkar Road
Matunga
Bangalore
```

```
400025
Nikhil Arora
Krishna Kunj
Edenwala Road
King Circle
Mumbai
400024
Stuti Shah
Aashirwad
Gadhakari Road
Colaba
Mumbai
400012
Anuraddha Iyer
Raj Bldg
Navy Road
Khar
Pune
400087
Mital Gandhi
Prakash Towers
Cadell Road
Borivali
Delhi
400045
Chaitanya Malhotra
Advani Bldg
Bal., Govinddas, Road
Dahisar
Mumbai
400090
Narendra Dodhia
Pheonix Towers
Phoenix Road
Sewree
Delhi
400021
10 rows selected.
```

The query returns a single formatted column per customer. The DECODE statement is used to specify IF-THEN-ELSE conditions within SQL and executes as follows: If the address string is NULL then concatenate NULL, otherwise insert a linefeed character followed by the address string.

The same report can also be presented as follows:

```
SELECT FirstName || ' ' || LastName || CHR (10) || BuildingName || ', ' || Road || ', '
  || Area || ', ' || City || ' ' || Pincode AS "Customer Details" FROM SubscriberMaster;
```

Output:

```
Customer Details
-----------------------------------------------------------
Sharanam Shah
```

```
Flora Deccan, M. G. Road, Andheri, Mumbai 400058
Vaishali Shah
Blue Queens, S. V. Road, Bandra, Pune 400050
Kanchan Toprani
Shankar Apts, L. J. Road, Wadala, Delhi 400031
Anil Naik
Makanji Kunj, Savarkar Road, Matunga, Bangalore 400025
Nikhil Arora
Krishna Kunj, Edenwala Road, King Circle, Mumbai 400024
Stuti Shah
Aashirwad, Gadhakari Road, Colaba, Mumbai 400012
Anuraddha Iyer
Raj Bldg, Navy Road, Khar, Pune 400087
Mital Gandhi
Prakash Towers, Cadell Road, Borivali, Delhi 400045
Chaitanya Malhotra
Advani Bldg, Bal., Govinddas, Road, Dahisar, Mumbai 400090
Narendra Dodhia
Pheonix Towers, Phoenix Road, Sewree, Delhi 400021
10 rows selected.
```

ASCIISTR

The **ASCIISTR()** function converts a given string from any character set to an ASCII string using the database character set.

Solution:

```
SELECT ASCIISTR('F D Y Ä Ê') "ASCIISTR 1", ASCIISTR('A B C Õ Ø') "ASCIISTR 2",
  ASCIISTR('A B C Ä Ê Í Õ Ø') "ASCIISTR 3" FROM DUAL;
```

Output:

```
ASCIISTR 1    ASCIISTR 2 ASCIISTR 3
------------- ---------- --------------------
F D Y \017D E A B C O O  A B C \017D E I O O
```

CONVERT

The **CONVERT()** function allows for the conversion of character data between different character sets. It converts the binary representation of a character string from one character set to another.

```
CONVERT(<Char>, <DestinationCharacterSet>, <SourceCharacterSet>)
```

Where,

- *SourceCharacterSet:* The original character set of the data.
- *DestinationCharacterSet:* The target character set to which the data will be converted.

Solution:

```
SELECT CONVERT('? ? ? ? ? A B C D E', 'US7ASCII', 'WE8ISO8859P1') FROM DUAL;
```

Output:

```
CONVERT('?????ABCDE
-------------------
? ? ? ? ? A B C D E
```

Searching For A Set Of Characters In A String

The **INSTR()** function returns the position of a substring within a string. It is typically used for simple or sophisticated searches within a string, indicating where the specified substring is found.

```
INSTR(<String1>, <String2>, [<StartPosition>], [<NthAppearance>])
```

Where,

- *String1:* The string to search.
- *String2:* The substring to search for within ***String1***.
- *StartPosition:* The position in ***String1*** where the search begins (Optional).
- *NthAppearance:* The *nth* appearance of ***String2*** to locate (Optional).

Solution:

```
SELECT
  INSTR('Oracle For Professionals By Sharanam And Vaishali', 'S') "S Found At",
  INSTR('Oracle For Professionals By Sharanam And Vaishali', 'V') "V Found At"
     FROM DUAL;
```

Output:

```
S Found At V Found At
---------- ----------
        29         42
```

Replacing String

TRANSLATE

The **TRANSLATE()** function replaces a sequence of characters in a string with another set of characters.

```
TRANSLATE(<String>, <StringToReplace>, <ReplacementString>)
```

Where,

- *String:* The string where the replacement will take place.
- *StringToReplace:* The string that will be searched for within ***<String>***.
- *ReplacementString:* The string that will replace characters in ***StringToReplace***.

Characters are replaced one at a time. This means, the first character in StringToReplace is replaced with the first character in the ReplacementString. The second character in StringToReplace is replaced with the second character in the ReplacementString and so on.

Solution:

```
SELECT TRANSLATE('1. Oracle For Professionals Edition I By Sharanam And
  Vaishali', '1.', '2)') "Change" FROM DUAL;
```

Output:

```
Change
------------------------------------------------------------
2) Oracle For Professionals Edition I By Sharanam And Vaishali
```

REPLACE

The **REPLACE()** function replaces a sequence of characters in a string with another set of characters.

```
REPLACE(<String>, <StringToReplace>, <ReplacementString>)
```

Where,

- ***String:*** The string where the replacement will take place.
- ***StringToReplace:*** The string that will be searched for within **<*String*>**.
- ***ReplacementString:*** The string that will replace all occurrences of ***StringToReplace*** in *String*. If the ***ReplacementString*** is omitted, the function simply removes all occurrences of ***StringToReplace*** and returns the resulting string.

While TRANSLATE() and REPLACE() are syntactically similar, they produce different results:

- TRANSLATE replaces characters by position. This means, the first character of StringToReplace is replaced by the first character of ReplacementString. The second character of StringToReplace is replaced by the second character of ReplacementString, and so on. If there are characters in StringToReplace that do not have positional equivalents in ReplacementString, they are dropped.
- REPLACE replaces the entire string to match with the replacement string. When replacing a single character, the operation is similar to TRANSLATE.

Solution:

```
SELECT REPLACE('1. Oracle For Professionals 1st Edition By Sharanam And Vaishali',
  '1', 'First') "Change" FROM DUAL;
```

Output:

```
Change
--------------------------------------------------------------------
First. Oracle For Professionals Firstst Edition By Sharanam And Vaishali
```

Determining String Length

The **LENGTH()** function returns the length of a given string, including letters, spaces and any other characters that are part of the string.

Example:

```
SELECT LENGTH('SHARANAM') "Length" FROM DUAL;
```

Output:

```
    Length
----------
         8
```

Example:

```
SELECT CustomerName FROM Customers ORDER BY LENGTH(CustomerName) DESC;
```

Output:

```
CUSTOMERNAME
-------------------------
Chaitanya Kantilal Shah
Sharanam Chaitanya Shah
Vaishali Sharanam Shah
Shravan Ashwin Benegal
Manali Narendra Naik
Prakash K Chouduary
Deepika Anil Bakshi
Stuti Kapil Khanna
Anil Mayekar
Amit Paul
Hansel

11 rows selected.
```

LENGTH() cannot be applied on a column that uses a LONG datatype.

Trimming Strings

LTRIM

The **LTRIM()** function removes all the specified set of characters from the beginning (left side) of a given string.

Example:

```
SELECT LTRIM('NISHA','N') "LTRIM 1", LTRIM('    NISHA') "LTRIM 2" FROM DUAL;
```

If the second parameter is omitted, the LTRIM() function removes all leading spaces from String.

Output:

```
LTRIM 1 LTRIM 2
------- -------
ISHA    NISHA
```

Example:

```
SELECT LTRIM('5437Books','0123456789') "Numbers Removed" FROM DUAL;
```

Output:

```
Numbers Removed
---------------
Books
```

RTRIM

The **RTRIM()** function removes all specified characters from the end (right side) of a given string.

Example:

```
SELECT RTRIM('NISHAAAAAA', 'A') "RTRIM 1", RTRIM('NISHA  ') "RTRIM 2" FROM DUAL;
```

If the second parameter is omitted, the RTRIM() function removes all trailing spaces from String.

Output:

```
RTRIM 1 RTRIM 2
------- -------
NISH    NISHA
```

Example:

```
SELECT RTRIM('Books347548','0123456789') "Numbers Removed" FROM DUAL;
```

Output:

```
Numbers Removed
---------------
Books
```

TRIM

The **TRIM()** function removes all specified characters from both sides (left and right) of a given string.

Syntax:

```
TRIM( [leading | trailing | both [<TrimCharacter> FROM ] ] <String1> )
```

Where,

- *leading:* Removes characters from the beginning of the string.
- *trailing:* Removes characters from the end of the string.
- *both:* Removes characters from both the beginning and end of the string. If none of the above parameters are specified, the TRIM() function removes characters from both the beginning and end of the string.
- *TrimCharacter:* A set of characters to be removed from *String1*.
- *String1:* The string to be trimmed.

Example:

```
SELECT TRIM('  Sharanam And Vaishali   ') "Trim Spaces" FROM DUAL;
```

Output:

```
Trim Spaces
---------------------
Sharanam And Vaishali
```

Example:

```
SELECT TRIM(LEADING 'x' FROM 'xxxOracleForProfessionalsxxx') "Remove prefixes"
  FROM DUAL;
```

Output:

```
Remove prefixes
-------------------------
OracleForProfessionalsxxx
```

Example 3:

```
SELECT TRIM(BOTH 'x' FROM 'xxxOracleForProfessionalsxxx') "Remove prefixes N
  suffixes" FROM DUAL;
```

Output:

```
Remove prefixes N suffixes
--------------------------
OracleForProfessionals
```

Example:

```
SELECT TRIM(BOTH '*' FROM '***Oracle***') "Remove prefixes N suffixes" FROM DUAL;
```

Output:

```
Remove prefixes N suffixes
--------------------------
Oracle
```

String Padding

LPAD

The **LPAD()** function pads the left side of a string with a specific set of characters. It returns the **String**, left-padded to length **n** with the sequence of characters specified in **StringToBePadded**. If ***n*** is smaller than the original string, LPAD() truncates the string to the size of n.

```
LPAD(<String>,<N> [,<StringToBePadded>])
```

Solution:

```
SELECT LPAD('Oracle', 10, '@') "LPAD" FROM DUAL;
```

Output:

```
LPAD
----------
@@@@Oracle
```

RPAD

The **RPAD()** function pads the right side of a string with a specific set of characters. It returns the **String**, right-padded to length **n** with the sequence of characters specified in **StringToBePadded**. If **StringToBePadded** is omitted, blanks are used by default. If **n** is smaller than the original string, RPAD() truncates the string to the size of n.

```
RPAD(<String>,<N> [,<StringToBePadded>])
```

Solution:

```
SELECT RPAD('Oracle', 10, '@') "RPAD" FROM DUAL;
```

Output:

```
RPAD
----------
Oracle@@@@
```

Number Of Bytes In A String

The **VSIZE()** function returns the number of bytes in the internal representation of a String.

Example:

```
SELECT VSIZE(' Oracle For Professionals By Sharanam And Vaishali ')
  "StringSizeInBytes" FROM DUAL;
```

Output:

```
StringSizeInBytes
-----------------
               51
```

Example 2:

```
SELECT VSIZE('') "StringSizeInBytes 1", VSIZE(' ') "StringSizeInBytes 2",
  VSIZE(NULL) "StringSizeInBytes 3" FROM DUAL;
```

Output:

```
StringSizeInBytes 1 StringSizeInBytes 2 StringSizeInBytes 3
------------------- ------------------- -------------------
                                      1
```

Number To String

The **TO_NUMBER()** function converts a given string and returns it as a NUMBER data type.

```
TO_NUMBER(<String>, [<FormatMask>])
```

Where,

- *String:* The string that will be converted to a number.
- *FormatMask:* (Optional) The format used to convert the String to a Number.

Solution:

```
SELECT TO_NUMBER('0210.70', '9999.99') "Number 1",
  TO_NUMBER('5554', '9999') " Number 2", TO_NUMBER('030', '999') " Number 3",
  TO_NUMBER('3455.2300') " Number 4" FROM DUAL;
```

Output:

```
  Number 1   Number 2   Number 3   Number 4
---------- ---------- ---------- ----------
     210.7       5554         30    3455.23
```

Replacing NULL Values

NVL

Not all columns in a table will hold values, and sometimes a column may not hold a value at all. In such a case, the column holds NULL. When records from such tables are displayed, NULL values are shown as blanks. To make this more readable, Oracle provides the **NVL()** function. The NVL() function allows replacing NULL values with another meaningful value when displaying such records.

This function accepts two parameters. The first parameter is the **column name** to be checked for NULL values. The second parameter is the value that will be used instead of displaying a blank. If the first parameter (i.e., the column name) holds a NULL value, the function returns the **value** specified in the second parameter. Otherwise, it returns the value held by the column.

In the Employees table, not all employees have a phone number, so some records have the ContactNo column set to NULL. Display all employees with their phone numbers. For those who do not have a phone number, indicate "Not Available".

```
SELECT FirstName || ' ' || LastName AS "Employees", NVL(ContactNo, 'Not Available')
  AS "Phone Number" FROM Employees;
```

Output:

```
Employees                          Phone Number
---------------------------------- --------------------
Sharanam Shah                      91-022-24440094
Vaishali Shah                      91-022-31040094
Keyur Kapoor                       91-022-27740094
Amit Haria                         91-022-34340094
Abhishek Benegal                   91-022-37640094
Chetan Dedhia                      91-022-40940094
Narendra Dodhia                    91-022-44240094
Meenal Doshi                       91-022-47540094
Anil Mayekar                       Not Available
Chaitanya Kapoor                   91-022-54140094
Amit Paul                          Not Available

11 rows selected.
```

NVL2

Oracle provides the **NVL2()** function, which allows converting both NULL and NOT NULL values into desired values. The NVL2() function accepts three parameters:

- ***Column Name:*** The name of the column to be checked for NULL values.
- ***Value1:*** The value used if the column holds a NOT NULL value.
- ***Value2:*** The value used if the column holds a NULL value.

If the column specified in the first parameter holds a value, the function returns ***Value1*** (the second parameter). Otherwise, it returns ***Value2*** (the third parameter).

Display all employees with their phone number availability status indicating **Available** if a phone number is present or **Not Available** if it is not:

```
SELECT FirstName || ' ' || LastName AS "Employees",
  NVL2(ContactNo, 'Available', 'Not Available') AS "Phone No Availability Status"
     FROM Employees;
```

Output:

```
Employees                           Phone No Availability Status
----------------------------------- ----------------------------
Sharanam Shah                       Available
Vaishali Shah                       Available
Keyur Kapoor                        Available
Amit Haria                          Available
Abhishek Benegal                    Available
Chetan Dedhia                       Available
Narendra Dodhia                     Available
Meenal Doshi                        Available
Anil Mayekar                        Not Available
Chaitanya Kapoor                    Available
Amit Paul                           Not Available

11 rows selected.
```

Phonetic String Representation

Many people have names that sound similar but are spelled differently. For example:

- Micheal or Michel
- Geeta or Gita
- Deepa or Dipa
- Seeta or Sita
- Pooja or Puja

Databases may hold records with such variations. For instance, the Accounts table could have customers with similar sounding names but different spellings. Occasionally, it is necessary to find all customers with similar sounding names. Oracle allows you to do this using the **SOUNDEX()** function.

The SOUNDEX() function returns a String that is a phonetic representation of a given string. This function is case-insensitive, meaning both uppercase and lowercase characters will generate the same SOUNDEX return value. The phonetic representation system uses a simple algorithm to reduce each name to a four-character alphanumeric code. The first letter of the code corresponds to the first letter of the word, and the remainder of the code consists of three digits derived from the syllables of the word.

The SOUNDEX Algorithm

The SOUNDEX algorithm works by retaining the first letter of the string and removing all occurrences of the letters 'a', 'e', 'h', 'i', 'o', 'u', 'w', 'y'. Only the first five consonants are used to determine the **numeric** portion of the return value, except if the first letter of the string is a vowel. If two or more letters with the same number are found adjacent to the original name or adjacent except for any intervening 'h' and 'w', then all such characters are omitted except for the first.

To search for a customer whose name sounds like "Gita" or "Seeta", use the SOUNDEX() function to find all similar-sounding names in the database:

```
SELECT AccountNo, AccountHolderName, AccountOpeningDate, CurrentBalance
  FROM Accounts WHERE SOUNDEX(AccountHolderName) = SOUNDEX('Gita')
     OR SOUNDEX(AccountHolderName) = SOUNDEX('Seeta');
```

Output:

```
ACCOUNTNO  ACCOUNTHOLDERNAME          ACCOUNTOP  CURRENTBALANCE
---------- -------------------------- ---------  --------------
         3 Gita                       08-JUN-06         2375.89
         4 Geeta                      01-JAN-05        46892.08
         8 Sita                       20-OCT-03            1234
         7 Seeta                      07-JUL-03            3000
```

To understand the working of this function issue the following command:

```
SELECT SOUNDEX(AccountHolderName), AccountHolderName, SOUNDEX('DEEP')
  FROM Accounts;
```

Output:

```
SOUNDEX(ACCOUNTHOLDERNAME) ACCOUNTHOLDERNAME SOUNDEX('DEEP')
-------------------------- ----------------- ---------------
S655                       Sharanam          D100
V240                       Vaishali          D100
G300                       Gita              D100
M240                       Michel            D100
M240                       Micheal           D100
G300                       Geeta             D100
P200                       Puja              D100
P200                       Pooja             D100
D100                       Dipa              D100
D100                       Deepa             D100
S300                       Sita              D100
S300                       Seeta             D100

12 rows selected.
```

The output shows how Oracle converts the words into numbers followed by a comparison between the two words and finally displays the output for the matching ones.

Examining The Column Content

Oracle allows examining the contents of a table column using the **DUMP()** function. DUMP() returns a Varchar2 value that includes the data type code, the length in bytes and the internal representation of the expression.

```
DUMP(<Expression>, [<ReturnFormat>], [<StartPosition>], [<Length>] )
```

Where,

- *Expression:* The expression to examine.
- *ReturnFormat:* (Optional) Determines the format of the return value. This parameter can be any of the following values:

Value	Explanation
8	Octal notation
10	Decimal notation
16	Hexadecimal notation
17	Single characters
1008	Octal notation with the character set name
1010	Decimal notation with the character set name
1016	Hexadecimal notation with the character set name
1017	Single characters with the character set name

- *StartPosition:* (Optional) Determines the starting position of the internal representation to display.
- *Length:* (Optional) Determines the length of the internal representation to display.

Extract the column details of the FirstName column from the Employees table:

```
SELECT DUMP(FirstName), FirstName FROM Employees;
```

Output:

```
DUMP(FIRSTNAME)                                FIRSTNAME
---------------------------------------------- -----------------
Typ=1 Len=8: 83,104,97,114,97,110,97,109      Sharanam
Typ=1 Len=8: 86,97,105,115,104,97,108,105     Vaishali
Typ=1 Len=5: 75,101,121,117,114               Keyur
Typ=1 Len=4: 65,109,105,116                   Amit
Typ=1 Len=8: 65,98,104,105,115,104,101,107    Abhishek
Typ=1 Len=6: 67,104,101,116,97,110            Chetan
Typ=1 Len=8: 78,97,114,101,110,100,114,97     Narendra
Typ=1 Len=6: 77,101,101,110,97,108            Meenal
Typ=1 Len=4: 65,110,105,108                   Anil
Typ=1 Len=9: 67,104,97,105,116,97,110,121,97 Chaitanya
Typ=1 Len=4: 65,109,105,116                   Amit
11 rows selected.
```

Explanation:

- *Typ = 1:* Indicates the column is Varchar2.
- *Len:* Indicates the length of the value held in the column.
- Values such as 83,104,97,114,97,110,97,109 indicate the ASCII code of the value held in that column.

Chapter

14

SECTION III: WORKING WITH DATA

Numeric Functions

Often, it is necessary to perform calculations on numeric values available as data in database tables. Oracle provides numerous numeric functions to facilitate these calculations. These functions:

- Accept an input number. The input number can be:
  - Fetched from a numeric column in a table.
  - An expression that evaluates to a number.
- Perform the required calculation.
- Return a number.

Aggregate Functions

Aggregate functions return a single result row based on groups of rows. They appear in:

- SELECT lists
- ORDER BY clause
- HAVING clause

However, they are commonly used with the GROUP BY clause in a SELECT statement, where Oracle splits the rows of a queried table or view into groups.

In a query containing a GROUP BY clause, the elements of the select list can be aggregate functions, GROUP BY expressions, constants, or expressions involving one of these. Oracle applies the aggregate functions to each group of rows and returns a single result row for each group. If the GROUP BY clause is omitted, Oracle applies aggregate functions in the select list to all the rows in the queried table or view.

Aggregate functions are used in the HAVING clause to eliminate groups from the output based on the results of the aggregate functions, rather than on the values of the individual rows of the queried table or view.

Most aggregate functions accept a single argument except for:

- *DISTINCT:* Causes an aggregate function to consider only distinct values of the argument expression.
- *ALL:* Causes an aggregate function to consider all values including duplicates.

If neither option is specified, the default is ALL.

For example:
The DISTINCT average of: 500 + 500 + 500 + **300** = **400**

The ALL average: 500 + 500 + 500 + 300 = 450

All aggregate functions except COUNT(*) and GROUPING ignore NULL values. It is good practice to use the NVL function as an argument to an aggregate function, to substitute a value for NULL. COUNT never returns NULL; it returns either a number or zero. For all other aggregate functions, if the dataset contains no rows or only rows with NULL as arguments to the aggregate function, the function returns NULL.

The following are the available aggregate functions:

Finding Average Value

The **AVG()** function returns an average value of expression, **ignoring** the NULL values in a column.

To calculate the average salary paid to employees of an organization, considering only distinct salaries:

```
SELECT AVG(DISTINCT Salary) "Average Salary" FROM Employees;
```

Output:

```
Average Salary
--------------
      30465.27
```

> In the above SELECT statement, AVG() is used to calculate the average balance of all distinct salary. The selected column is renamed as **Average Salary** in the output.

Explanation:
In this scenario, Oracle considers only the distinct salaries when the DISTINCT augment is used in the aggregate function.

Based on the data available in the Employees table:
(82500+55000+22000+22660+13334.2+13553.1+13578.4+49500+31207+1320)/10 = 30465.27 (excluding the repeated salary)

Out of the 11 records, a salary of 31207 is omitted as it repeats.

Finding The Minimum Value

The **MIN()** function returns the minimum value of an expression.

Display the minimum salary paid by the organization to its employees:

```
SELECT MIN(Salary) "Minimum Salary" FROM Employees;
```

Output:

```
Minimum Salary
--------------
          1320
```

Counting The Records

The **COUNT()** function returns the number of rows where the expression is not null.

Display the total number of subscribers who have subscribed:

```
SELECT COUNT(AccountNo) "Number Of Subscribers" FROM SubscriberMaster;
```

Output:

```
Number Of Subscribers
---------------------
                   10
```

The **COUNT(*)** function returns the total number of rows in a table, including duplicates and rows with NULL values.

Finding The Maximum Value

The **MAX()** function returns the maximum value of expression.

Display the maximum salary paid by the organization to its employees:

```
SELECT MAX(Salary) "Maximum Salary" FROM Employees;
```

Output:

```
Maximum Salary
--------------
         82500
```

Finding The Total Value

The **SUM()** function returns the sum of the values of an expression.

Display the total salary paid by the organization to its employees:

```
SELECT SUM(Salary) "Total Salary" FROM Employees;
```

Output:

```
Total Salary
------------
    335859.7
```

The Returning Clause

Consider a scenario where a row in the table is updated. The person performing the update wishes to view the results. The usual step to achieve this are:

- Update the table.
- Execute a SELECT query to view the updated values.

The **RETURNING** clause can simplify this process. It allows viewing the results of a DML operation without executing a separate SELECT query. The RETURNING clause can return values from aggregate functions such as AVG(), SUM(), COUNT(), and so on. This clause can only be used with DML statements that return single row results. To understand this clause, follow these steps:

- Declare a variable named **TotalSalary**.
- Increase the salary by 10%. After the increase, determine and return the total salary.
- Print the returned value.

Solution:

```
VARIABLE TotalSalary NUMBER;
UPDATE Employees SET Salary = Salary * 1.10
  RETURNING SUM(Salary) INTO :TotalSalary;
```

Output:

```
10 rows updated.
```

```
PRINT TotalSalary
```

Output:

```
TOTALSALARY
-----------
  369445.67
```

Numeric Functions

Absolute Function

The **ABS()** function returns the absolute value of an expression.

Solution:

```
SELECT ABS(-30) "Absolute" FROM DUAL;
```

Output:

```
  Absolute
----------
        30
```

Power Function

The **POWER()** function returns an expression raised to the **n**th power. The value of **n** must be an integer; otherwise, an error will be returned.

Solution:

```
SELECT POWER(64,2) "Raised" FROM DUAL;
```

Output:

```
    Raised
----------
      4096
```

Rounding The Numeric Value

The **ROUND()** function returns an expression, rounded to **n** places to the right of a decimal point. The value of **n** can be negative to round off digits to the left of the decimal point. **n** must be an integer.

Solution:

```
SELECT ROUND(20.14, 1) "Round" FROM DUAL;
```

Output:

```
     Round
----------
      20.1
```

Square Root

The **SQRT()** function returns the square root of an expression. If the value of the expression is less than zero, a NULL value is returned. The SQRT() function returns a **real** result.

Solution:

```
SELECT SQRT(64) "Square Root" FROM DUAL;
```

Output:

```
Square Root
-----------
          8
```

Exponentiation

The **EXP()** function returns **e** raised to the **nth** power, where **e = 2.71828183**.

Solution:

```
SELECT EXP(10) "Exponent" FROM DUAL;
```

Output:

```
  Exponent
----------
22026.4658
```

Finding The Greatest Value

The **GREATEST()** function returns the greatest value in a list of expressions.

```
GREATEST (<Expression1>,<Expression2>,. . ., <ExpressionN>)
```

Where, ***Expression1, Expression2, . . . ExpressionN*** are the expressions evaluated by the GREATEST() function.

Solution:

```
SELECT GREATEST(7, 13, 25) "Number", GREATEST('7', '13', '25') "Text"
  FROM DUAL;
```

Output:

```
    Number Text
---------- ----
        25 7
```

Finding The Least Value

The **LEAST()** function returns the least value in a list of expressions.

```
LEAST (<Expression1>,<Expression2>,. . ., <ExpressionN>)
```

Where, ***Expression1, Expression2, . . . ExpressionN*** are the expressions evaluated by the LEAST() function.

Solution:

```
SELECT LEAST(7, 13, 25) "Number", LEAST('7', '13', '25') "Text" FROM DUAL;
```

Output:

```
    Number Text
---------- ----
         7 13
```

In the **GREATEST()** and **LEAST()** functions, if the data types of the expressions are different, all expressions will be converted to the data type of the first expression in the list. If the comparison is based on character comparison, a character is considered greater than another if it has a higher character set value.

Finding The Remainder

The **MOD()** function returns the remainder of the first number divided by the second number passed as a parameter. If the second number is zero, the result is the same as the first number.

Solution:

```
SELECT MOD(256, 2) "Mod1", MOD(100.57, 7) "Mod2" FROM DUAL;
```

Output:

```
      Mod1       Mod2
---------- ----------
         0       2.57
```

Truncating A Number Value

The **TRUNC()** function returns a number truncated to a certain number of decimal places. The decimal place value must be an integer. If this parameter is omitted, TRUNC() truncates the number to 0 decimal places.

Solution:

```
SELECT TRUNC(125.815, 1) "Trunc1", TRUNC(125.815, -2) "Trunc2" FROM DUAL;
```

Output:

```
    Trunc1     Trunc2
---------- ----------
     125.8        100
```

Returning The Largest Integer Value

The **FLOOR()** function returns the largest integer value that is equal to or less than a given number.

Solution:

```
SELECT FLOOR(36.45) "Floor1", FLOOR(45.15) "Floor2" FROM DUAL;
```

Output:

```
    Floor1     Floor2
---------- ----------
        36         45
```

Returning The Smallest Integer Value

The **CEIL()** function returns the smallest integer value that is greater than or equal to a given number.

Solution:

```
SELECT CEIL(36.45) "Ceil1", CEIL(45.15) "Ceil2" FROM DUAL;
```

Output:

```
     Ceil1      Ceil2
---------- ----------
        37         46
```

Trigonometric Functions

The following are the available trigonometric functions:

Functions	Description
SIN	Returns the sine of the specified angle. The angle must be expressed in radians. A radian is equal to 180/pi or roughly 57.29578
ASIN	Returns the inverse sine. The value returned is between -pi/2 and pi/2

Functions	Description
SINH	Returns the hyperbolic sine
COS	Returns the cosine of the specified angle. The angle must be expressed in radians. A radian is equal to 180/pi or roughly 57.29578
ACOS	Returns the inverse cosine. The value returned is between 0 and pi
COSH	Returns the hyperbolic cosine
TAN	Returns the tangent of the specified angle. The angle must be expressed in radians. A radian is equal to 180/pi or roughly 57.29578
TANH	Returns the hyperbolic tangent. The value returned is between -pi/2 and pi/2

Syntax:

```
SIN (<n>) | SIN (<AngleInDegree>/57.29578)
ASIN (<n>)
SINH (<n>)
COS (<n>) | COS (<AngleInDegree>/57.29578)
ACOS (<n>)
COSH (<n>)
TAN (<n>) | TAN (<AngleInDegree>/57.29578)
TANH (<n>)
```

Create a table named Trigonometry with a column named TrigoNo. Add the following data to it, for running the examples to follow:

TrigoNo
0
1
1.570796
3.141592
-1
-1.570796
-3.141592

Example:

```
SELECT TrigoNo, SIN(TrigoNo), ASIN(MOD(TrigoNo, 1)), SINH(TrigoNo)
  FROM Trigonometry;
```

Output:

```
  TRIGONO SIN(TRIGONO) ASIN(MOD(TRIGONO,1)) SINH(TRIGONO)
--------- ------------ -------------------- -------------
        0            0                    0             0
        1    .84147098                    0     1.1752012
1.5707963            1            .60747537     2.3012989
3.1415927    4.626E-19            .14207009     11.548739
       -1     -.841471                    0     -1.175201
-1.570796           -1           -.6074754     -2.301299
```

```
-3.141593    -4.63E-19              -.1420701     -11.54874

7 rows selected.
```

Example:

```
SELECT TrigoNo, COS (TrigoNo), ACOS(MOD(TrigoNo, 1)), COSH(TrigoNo)
  FROM Trigonometry;
```

Output:

```
  TRIGONO COS(TRIGONO) ACOS(MOD(TRIGONO,1)) COSH(TRIGONO)
--------- ------------ -------------------- -------------
        0            1            1.5707963             1
        1    .54030231            1.5707963     1.5430806
1.5707963    2.313E-19            .96332096     2.5091785
3.1415927           -1            1.4287262     11.591953
       -1    .54030231            1.5707963     1.5430806
-1.570796    2.313E-19            2.1782717     2.5091785
-3.141593           -1            1.7128664     11.591953

7 rows selected.
```

Example:

```
SELECT TrigoNo, TAN (TrigoNo), TANH(TrigoNo) FROM Trigonometry;
```

Output:

```
  TRIGONO TAN(TRIGONO) TANH(TRIGONO)
--------- ------------ -------------
        0            0             0
        1    1.5574077     .76159416
1.5707963    4.323E+18     .91715234
3.1415927    -4.63E-19     .99627208
       -1    -1.557408     -.7615942
-1.570796    -4.32E+18     -.9171523
-3.141593    4.626E-19     -.9962721

7 rows selected.
```

Returning The Value Of Sign Of A Number

The **SIGN()** function returns the sign of the specified number. SIGN() returns one of the following three values:

- **-1:** If the specified number is less than zero.
- **1:** If the specified number is greater than zero.
- **0:** If the specified number is equal to zero.

Solution:

```
SELECT SIGN(-36.45) "Sign1", SIGN(45.15) "Sign2" FROM DUAL;
```

Output:

```
     Sign1      Sign2
---------- ----------
        -1          1
```

Conversion Of Number To Character

The **TO_CHAR()** function converts a value of a **Number** data type to a **character** data type, using an optional format string. TO_CHAR() accepts a **number (n)** and a **numeric format (fmt)** in which the number should appear. All number format models cause the number to be rounded to the specified number of significant digits.

The following table displays the available number formats:

Elements	Description
, [comma]	Returns a comma in the specified position. Example: 9,999
. [period]	Returns a decimal point, which is a period [.] in the specified position. Example: 99.99
$	Returns value with a leading dollar sign. Example: **$**9999
0	Returns leading or trailing zeros. Example: **0**999 or 999**0**
9	Returns value with the specified number of digits with a leading space if positive or with a leading minus if negative. Example: **9999**
B	Returns blanks for the integer part of a fixed-point number when the integer part is zero [regardless of "0"s in the number format]. Example: **B**9999
C	Returns the ISO currency symbol in the specified position [the current value of the NLS_ISO_CURRENCY parameter]. Example: **C**9999
D	Returns the decimal character in the specified position, which is the current value of the NLS_ISO_CURRENCY parameter. The default is a period [.]. Example: 99**D**99
EEEE	Returns a value using scientific notation. Example: 9.9**EEEE**
FM	Returns a value with no leading or trailing blanks. Example: **FM**90.9
G	Returns the group separator in the specified position [the current value of the NLS_NUMERIC_CHARACTER parameter]. Example: 9**G**999
L	Returns the local currency symbol in the specified position [the current value of the NLS_CURRENCY parameter]. Example: **L**999
MI	Returns a negative value with a trailing minus sign [-]. Returns positive value with a trailing blank. Example: 9999**MI**
PR	Returns negative value in <angle brackets>. Returns positive value with a leading and trailing blank. Example: 9999**PR**
RN / rn	Returns a value as Roman numerals in uppercase or lowercase. The value can be an integer between 1 and 3999. Example: **RN.** Example: **rn**

Elements	Description
S	Returns: ❑ Negative value with a leading minus sign [-]. ❑ Positive value with a leading plus sign [+]. ❑ Negative value with a trailing minus sign [-]. ❑ Positive value with a trailing plus sign [+]. Example: **S**9999. Example: 9999**S**
V	Returns a value multiplied by 10n [and if necessary, rounded up], where n is the number of 9's after the "V". Example: 999**V**99

Example:

```
SELECT TO_CHAR(Salary, '$999,999') "Salary" FROM Employees;
```

Output:

```
Salary
---------
  $82,500
  $55,000
  $22,000
  $22,660
  $13,334
  $13,553
  $13,578
  $49,500
  $31,207
   $1,320
  $31,207

11 rows selected.
```

Example:

```
SELECT TO_CHAR(Salary, '99,99,999.99') "Salary" FROM Employees;
```

Output:

```
Salary
-------------
    82,500.00
    55,000.00
    22,000.00
    22,660.00
    13,334.20
    13,553.10
    13,578.40
    49,500.00
    31,207.00
     1,320.00
    31,207.00

11 rows selected.
```

Example:

```
SELECT TO_CHAR(EmployeeNo, 'RN') "Employee No" FROM Employees;
```

Output:

```
Employee No
---------------
              I
             II
            III
             IV
              V
             VI
            VII
           VIII
             IX
              X
             XI

11 rows selected.
```

Chapter

15

SECTION III: WORKING WITH DATA

Date Functions

Most business data stored in a database usually includes date-time columns. Such dates often require modifications, such as changes in the date formats or data types, and calculations, such as adding or subtracting days from a date. Dates are stored in the database as a number that contains both calendar data and time information.

Oracle offers several date functions that allow modifying, calculating, and comparing date data types. For example, by default, Oracle uses the format DD-MON-YYYY to represent a date; however, using date functions, this format can be changed as desired.

Viewing The System Date And Time

SYSDATE

The **SYSDATE** function returns the current date.

Solution:

```
SELECT SYSDATE FROM DUAL;
```

Output:

```
SYSDATE
---------
18-DEC-24
```

CURRENT_DATE

The **CURRENT_DATE** function returns the current date in the session time zone, in a value in the Gregorian calendar of data type DATE.

Solution:

```
SELECT SESSIONTIMEZONE, CURRENT_DATE FROM DUAL;
```

The **SESSIONTIMEZONE** function returns the current session's time zone as a time zone offset or a time zone region name.

Output:

```
SESSIONTIMEZONE                                 CURRENT_D
---------------------------------------------   ---------
+05:30                                          18-DEC-24
```

SYSTIMESTAMP

The **SYSTIMESTAMP** function returns the system date, including fractional seconds and the time zone of the database. The return type is TIMESTAMP WITH TIME ZONE.

Solution:

```
SELECT SYSTIMESTAMP FROM DUAL;
```

Output:

```
SYSTIMESTAMP
-----------------------------------
18-DEC-24 09.58.51.638996 AM +05:30
```

Extracting A Date Or Interval Value

The **EXTRACT()** function extracts and returns the value of a specified datetime field from a datetime or interval value expression.

```
EXTRACT( {YEAR | MONTH | DAY | HOUR | MINUTE | SECOND | TIMEZONE_HOUR |
  TIMEZONE_MINUTE | TIMEZONE_REGION | TIMEZONE_ABBR}
```

```
FROM { <DateValue> | <IntervalValue> } )
```

A date can be used only to extract YEAR, MONTH, and DAY, while a timestamp with a time zone data type can be used only to extract TIMEZONE_HOUR and TIMEZONE_MINUTE. When TIMEZONE_REGION or TIMEZONE_ABBR (time zone abbreviation) is used, the value returned is a string containing the appropriate time zone name or abbreviation.

Solution:

```
SELECT EXTRACT(YEAR FROM DATE '2007-07-07') "Year",
  EXTRACT(MONTH FROM SYSDATE) "Month" FROM DUAL;
```

Output:

```
Year                   Month
---------------------- ----------------------
2007                   12
```

Date Conversion Functions

The Date data type is used to store date and time information. It has special properties that include storing information about the century, year, month, day, hour, minute, and second for each date value.

The value in a column of a Date data type **is always** stored in a specific **default** format, 'DD-MON-YY HH:MI:SS'. Therefore, when a date has to be inserted in a date field, its value must be specified in this format. Additionally, values of Date columns are always displayed in the **default** format when **retrieved** from the table.

TO_DATE

If data from a date column needs to be viewed in any format other than the default, Oracle provides the **TO_DATE** function to specify the required format. The TO_DATE function converts a character field to a date field.

This function can also be used to store a date in a Date field in a particular format other than the default. This is done by specifying the date value along with the format in which it is to be inserted. The TO_DATE() function also allows partial insertion of a Date value into a column, for example, only the day and month portions of the date value. To enter the time portion of a date, the TO_DATE function must be used with a **format mask** indicating the time portion.

Solution:

```
INSERT INTO BankBook (BookNo, AccountNo, BookDate, OpBal, ClBal)
  VALUES(5, 'SB110', TO_DATE('04-Jan-2008 10:55 A.M.', 'DD-MON-YY HH:MI
     A.M.'), 324.7f, 642.7d);
```

Output:

```
1 row created.
```

TO_CHAR

The **TO_CHAR()** function converts a value of a **Date** data type to a **Char** value. TO_CHAR() accepts a date as well as the format in which the date has to appear. The TO_CHAR function facilitates the retrieval of data in a format different from the default format. It can also extract a part of the date, i.e., the date, month, or year from the date value and use it for sorting or grouping data according to the date, month, or year.

```
TO_CHAR(<Date> [, <Format>])
```

The ***Format*** must be a date format. If the Format is omitted, the date is converted to a character value using the default date format i.e. "DD-MON-YY".

List the customer details in order of the months. The **Date of birth** should be displayed in the format '**DD/MM/YY**':

```
SELECT CustomerNo, CustomerName, TO_CHAR(DateOfBirth, 'DD/MM/YY')
  "Date Of Birth" FROM Customers ORDER BY TO_CHAR(DateOfBirth, 'MM');
```

The value held in the DateOfBirth field is formatted using the TO_CHAR() function to display the date in the **DD/MM/YY** format. The ordering of the output data set is based on the **month** segment of the data in the DateOfBirth column. This is achieved by using **TO_CHAR()** in the ORDER BY clause, extracting only the **month** segment of the DateOfBirth to sort the data.

Output:

```
CUSTOMERNO              CUSTOMERNAME               Date Of Birth
----------------------- -------------------------  -------------
21                      Sharanam Chaitanya Shah    03/01/81
30                      Manali Narendra Naik       22/01/81
29                      Deepika Anil Bakshi        30/01/81
25                      Chaitanya Kantilal Shah    03/01/81
28                      Stuti Kapil Khanna         05/06/67
27                      Prakash K Chouduary        07/07/90
26                      Shravan Ashwin Benegal     22/09/79
24                      Hansel                     29/10/90
23                      Anil Mayekar               22/11/56
22                      Vaishali Sharanam Shah     22/11/81
31                      Amit Paul                  22/11/56

11 rows selected.
```

Special Date Formats

Sometimes, date values need to be displayed in special formats. For example, instead of displaying the date as 03-JAN-81, it might be required to display it as 03rd of January, 1981. To achieve this, Oracle provides **special attributes** that can be used in the format specified with the **TO_CHAR** and **TO_DATE** functions.

Display the customer details:

```
SELECT CustomerNo, CustomerName, DateOfBirth FROM Customers
  ORDER BY TO_CHAR(DateOfBirth, 'MM');
```

Output:

```
CUSTOMERNO             CUSTOMERNAME              DATEOFBIRTH
---------------------- ------------------------- --------------
21                     Sharanam Chaitanya Shah   03-JAN-81
30                     Manali Narendra Naik      22-JAN-81
29                     Deepika Anil Bakshi       30-JAN-81
25                     Chaitanya Kantilal Shah   03-JAN-81
28                     Stuti Kapil Khanna        05-JUN-67
27                     Prakash K Chouduary       07-JUL-90
26                     Shravan Ashwin Benegal    22-SEP-79
24                     Hansel                    29-OCT-90
23                     Anil Mayekar              22-NOV-56
22                     Vaishali Sharanam Shah    22-NOV-81
31                     Amit Paul                 22-NOV-56

11 rows selected.
```

Variations in this output can be achieved as follows:

Use Of TH In The TO_CHAR() Function

DDTH places TH, RD, ND for the date [DD], for example, 2ND, 3RD, 08TH and so on:

```
SELECT CustomerNo, CustomerName, TO_CHAR(DateOfBirth, 'DDTH-MON-YY')
  "Date Of Birth"  FROM Customers ORDER BY TO_CHAR(DateOfBirth, 'MM');
```

Output:

```
CUSTOMERNO CUSTOMERNAME              Date Of Birth
---------- ------------------------- -------------
21         Sharanam Chaitanya Shah   03RD-JAN-81
30         Manali Narendra Naik      22ND-JAN-81
29         Deepika Anil Bakshi       30TH-JAN-81
25         Chaitanya Kantilal Shah   03RD-JAN-81
28         Stuti Kapil Khanna        05TH-JUN-67
27         Prakash K Chouduary       07TH-JUL-90
26         Shravan Ashwin Benegal    22ND-SEP-79
24         Hansel                    29TH-OCT-90
23         Anil Mayekar              22ND-NOV-56
22         Vaishali Sharanam Shah    22ND-NOV-81
31         Amit Paul                 22ND-NOV-56

11 rows selected.
```

Use Of DDSP In The TO_CHAR() Function

DDSP indicates that the date [DD] must be displayed by spelling the date such as ONE, TWELVE and so on:

```
SELECT CustomerNo, CustomerName, TO_CHAR(DateOfBirth, 'DDSP')
```

```
  "Date Of Birth" FROM Customers ORDER BY TO_CHAR(DateOfBirth, 'MM');
```

Output:

```
CUSTOMERNO CUSTOMERNAME              Date Of Birth
---------- ------------------------- -------------
21         Sharanam Chaitanya Shah   THREE
30         Manali Narendra Naik      TWENTY-TWO
29         Deepika Anil Bakshi       THIRTY
25         Chaitanya Kantilal Shah   THREE
28         Stuti Kapil Khanna        FIVE
27         Prakash K Chouduary       SEVEN
26         Shravan Ashwin Benegal    TWENTY-TWO
24         Hansel                    TWENTY-NINE
23         Anil Mayekar              TWENTY-TWO
22         Vaishali Sharanam Shah    TWENTY-TWO
31         Amit Paul                 TWENTY-TWO

11 rows selected.
```

Use Of SPTH In The TO_CHAR Function

SPTH displays the date [DD] with **th** added to the spelling fourteen**th**, twelf**th:**

```
SELECT CustomerNo, CustomerName, TO_CHAR(DateOfBirth, 'DDSPTH')
  "Date Of Birth" FROM Customers ORDER BY TO_CHAR(DateOfBirth, 'MM');
```

Output:

```
CUSTOMERNO CUSTOMERNAME              Date Of Birth
---------- ------------------------- --------------
21         Sharanam Chaitanya Shah   THIRD
30         Manali Narendra Naik      TWENTY-SECOND
29         Deepika Anil Bakshi       THIRTIETH
25         Chaitanya Kantilal Shah   THIRD
28         Stuti Kapil Khanna        FIFTH
27         Prakash K Chouduary       SEVENTH
26         Shravan Ashwin Benegal    TWENTY-SECOND
24         Hansel                    TWENTY-NINTH
23         Anil Mayekar              TWENTY-SECOND
22         Vaishali Sharanam Shah    TWENTY-SECOND
31         Amit Paul                 TWENTY-SECOND

11 rows selected.
```

Translating Numbers To Words Using Julian Date Conversion

In some commercial applications, **amounts** must be represented as words. For instance, while printing bank drafts, the system provides the draft amount in both **numbers** and **words**. In Oracle, this can be achieved using Julian Date conversion.

Display the amount in words for the monthly sales in the year 2007 from the OrderDetails table:

```
SELECT OrderNo, EXTRACT(MONTH FROM OrderDate) AS "Order Month",
```

```
TO_CHAR(TO_DATE(SUM(Cost), 'J'), 'JSP') AS "Amount In Words"
    FROM OrderDetails WHERE EXTRACT(YEAR FROM OrderDate) = '2007'
        GROUP BY OrderNo, EXTRACT(MONTH FROM OrderDate);
```

Output:

```
ORDERNO Order Month Amount In Words
------- ----------- -------------------------------------
      4          11 TWENTY-EIGHT THOUSAND FOUR HUNDRED
      5           2 SIXTY-SIX THOUSAND THREE HUNDRED FIFTY
      3          10 FOURTEEN THOUSAND SEVEN HUNDRED FIFTY
```

Similarly, the output can be displayed in Title Case using:

```
TO_CHAR(TO_DATE(SUM(Cost), 'J'), 'JsP')
```

Output:

```
   ORDERNO Order Month Amount In Words
---------- ----------- ----------------------------------------
         4          11 Twenty-Eight Thousand Four Hundred
         5           2 Sixty-Six Thousand Three Hundred Fifty
         3          10 Fourteen Thousand Five Hundred Fifty
```

And in lower case using:

```
TO_CHAR(TO_DATE(SUM(Cost), 'J'), 'jSP')
```

Output:

```
   ORDERNO Order Month Amount In Words
---------- ----------- ----------------------------------------
         4          11 twenty-eight thousand four hundred
         5           2 sixty-six thousand three hundred fifty
         3          10 fourteen thousand five hundred fifty
```

The minimum JULIAN number allowed is 1 and the maximum JULIAN number allowed is 5373484. Amount larger than the maximum JULIAN number cannot be converted to words. This conversion only works with integer amounts. If rupees and paise are also required in the output, the amount should be split into its integer and decimal parts and handle the case of a zero amount such as:

```
SELECT AccountNo, DECODE(TRUNC(CurrentBalance), 0, 'ZERO',
  TO_CHAR(TO_DATE(TRUNC(CurrentBalance), 'J'), 'JSP')) || ' AND ' ||
     DECODE(TRUNC(MOD(CurrentBalance, 1)*100), 0, 'ZERO',
        TO_CHAR(TO_DATE(TRUNC(MOD(CurrentBalance, 1)*100), 'J'), 'JSP'))
           || ' Paise' "Amount" FROM Accounts;
```

Output:

```
ACCOUNTNO Amount
--------- ------------------------------------------------------------------
        1 THIRTEEN THOUSAND FIVE HUNDRED FIFTY-EIGHT AND NINETY Paise
        2 FIVE THOUSAND AND ZERO Paise
```

```
         3 TWO THOUSAND THREE HUNDRED SEVENTY-FIVE AND EIGHTY-NINE Paise
         6 THREE THOUSAND AND ZERO Paise
         5 FOUR THOUSAND AND ZERO Paise
         4 FORTY-SIX THOUSAND EIGHT HUNDRED NINETY-TWO AND EIGHT Paise
        12 FOUR THOUSAND FIVE HUNDRED AND ZERO Paise
        11 ONE HUNDRED TWENTY-THREE THOUSAND EIGHT HUNDRED NINETY AND ZERO Paise
        10 ONE THOUSAND TWO HUNDRED FORTY-FIVE AND ZERO Paise
         9 ONE THOUSAND AND ZERO Paise
         8 ONE THOUSAND TWO HUNDRED THIRTY-FOUR AND ZERO Paise
         7 THREE THOUSAND AND ZERO Paise

12 rows selected.
```

Manipulating Dates

To manipulate and extract values from the date column of a table, Oracle provides several date functions.

Adding Dates

The **ADD_MONTHS()** function returns a date after adding the number of months specified in the function.

Solution:

```
SELECT ADD_MONTHS(SYSDATE, 4) "Add Months" FROM DUAL;
```

Output:

```
Add Months
-------------------------
18-APR-25
```

Retrieving The Last Date

The **LAST_DAY()** function returns the last date of the month specified by the function.

Solution:

```
SELECT SYSDATE, LAST_DAY(SYSDATE) "LastDay" FROM DUAL;
```

Output:

```
SYSDATE                   LastDay
------------------------- -------------------------
18-DEC-24                 31-DEC-24
```

Finding Months Between Dates

The **MONTHS_BETWEEN()** function returns number of months between ***Date1*** and ***Date2***. The following are the rules that apply to MONTHS_BETWEEN():

- If ***Date1*** comes after ***Date2***, then MONTHS_BETWEEN returns a positive number.
- If ***Date1*** comes before ***Date2***, then MONTHS_BETWEEN returns a negative number.
- If ***Date1*** and ***Date2*** are in the same month, then MONTHS_BETWEEN returns a fraction [a value between -1 and +1].
- If ***Date1*** and ***Date2*** both fall on the last day of their respective months, then MONTHS_BETWEEN returns a whole number [no fractional component].
- If ***Date1*** and ***Date2*** are in different months and at least one of the dates is not a last day in the month, then MONTHS_BETWEEN returns a fractional number. The fractional component is calculated on a 31-day month basis and also takes into account any differences in the time component of ***Date1*** and ***Date2***.

Solution:

```
SELECT MONTHS_BETWEEN('07-Jun-2008', '07-Jan-2008') "Months" FROM DUAL;
```

Output:

```
    Months
----------
         5
```

Retrieving The First Day Of The Week

The **NEXT_DAY()** function returns the date of the first weekday, named by character, that is after the date named by Date. The character must be a day of the week.

Solution:

```
SELECT NEXT_DAY('17-JAN-17', 'Saturday') "NEXT DAY" FROM DUAL;
```

Output:

```
NEXT DAY
----------
21-JAN-17
```

Converting A Date Time Across Time Zones

The **NEW_TIME()** function returns the date after converting it from ***time zone1*** to a date in ***time zone2***.

```
NEW_TIME(<Date>, <Zone1>, <Zone2>)
```

The following are the valid time zones:

Value	Description	Value	Description
AST	Atlantic Standard Time	ADT	Atlantic Daylight Time
BST	Bering Standard Time	BDT	Bering Daylight Time
CST	Central Standard Time	CDT	Central Daylight Time
EST	Eastern Standard Time	EDT	Eastern Daylight Time
GMT	Greenwich Mean Time	HST	Alaska-Hawaii Standard Time
HDT	Alaska-Hawaii Daylight Time	MST	Mountain Standard Time
MDT	Mountain Daylight Time	NST	Newfoundland Standard Time
PST	Pacific Standard Time	PDT	Pacific Daylight Time
YST	Yukon Standard Time	YDT	Yukon Daylight Time

Converts an **A**tlantic **S**tandard **T**ime into a **M**ountain **S**tandard **T**ime:

```
SELECT NEW_TIME(TO_DATE(SYSDATE, 'yyyy/mm/dd HH24:MI'), 'AST', 'MST')
  "MST" FROM DUAL;
```

Output:

```
MST
---------
18-DEC-18
```

Retrieving A Rounded Date

The **ROUND()** function returns a date rounded to a specific unit of measure. If the second parameter is omitted, the ROUND() function will round the date to the nearest day.

```
ROUND(<Date>, [<Format>])
```

The following are the valid format parameters:

Unit	Format parameters	Rounding Rule
Year	SYYYY, YYYY, YEAR, SYEAR, YYY, YY, Y	Rounds up on July 1st.
ISO Year	IYYY, IY, I	
Quarter	Q	Rounds up on the 16th day of the second month of the quarter.
Month	MONTH, MON, MM, RM	Rounds up on the 16th day of the month.
Week	WW	Same day of the week as the first day of the year.
IW	IW	Same day of the week as the first day of the ISO year.
W	W	Same day of the week as the first day of the month.
Day	DDD, DD, J	
Hour	HH, HH12, HH24	

Unit	Format parameters	Rounding Rule
Start day of the week	DAY, DY, D	
Minute	MI	

Solution:

```
SELECT ROUND(TO_DATE(SYSDATE), 'YYYY') "Year" FROM DUAL;
```

Output:

```
Year
-------------------------
01-JAN-25
```

When performing time-based calculations, Oracle allows for the addition or subtraction of values from a datetime column. For instance, each time a customer rents a movie, the checkout time is recorded in the RentDate column of the Rentals table. Upon returning the movie, the check-in time is noted.

The ReturnDate column in the Rentals table must be updated each time a movie is returned. Typically, customers return movies a few hours later. Therefore, the ReturnDate should be calculated by adding the rental duration to the RentDate for that movie. In date calculations, adding 1 to a date generally increments the date by one day.

In this case, fractions will be used to add hours, minutes, or seconds to the RentDate, thus advancing the date by those specific units. For example, in the solution provided below, the ReturnDate is calculated as the RentDate plus 4 hours, 30 minutes, and 40 seconds.

Currently, the details of rent number 13 are as follows:

```
SELECT RentNo, TO_CHAR(RentalDate, 'DD-MON-YYYY HH:MI:SS')
  AS "Rental Date", TO_CHAR(ReturnDate, 'DD-MON-YYYY HH:MI:SS')
     AS "Return Date" FROM Rentals WHERE RentNo=13;
```

Output:

```
    RENTNO Rental Date          Return Date
---------- -------------------- --------------------
        13 06-DEC-2007 12:00:00 10-DEC-2007 12:00:00
```

Solution:

```
UPDATE Rentals SET ReturnDate = RentalDate + 4/24 + 1/48 + 40/86400
  WHERE RentNo = 13;
```

Output:

```
1 row updated.
```

Retrieve the record for the RentNo 13 to see the change:

```
    RENTNO Rental Date          Return Date
---------- -------------------- --------------------
        13 06-DEC-2007 12:00:00 06-DEC-2007 04:30:40
```

The following are a few examples of working with dates.

Example: Tomorrow / next day

```
SELECT TO_CHAR(SYSDATE, 'DD-MON-YYYY HH:MI:SS') AS "Current Date",
  TO_CHAR(SYSDATE + 1, 'DD-MON-YYYY HH:MI:SS') AS "Tomorrow / next day"
     FROM DUAL;
```

Output:

```
Current Date                  Tomorrow / next day
----------------------------- -----------------------------
18-DEC-2024 10:42:33          19-DEC-2024 10:42:33
```

Example: Seven days from now

```
SELECT TO_CHAR(SYSDATE, 'DD-MON-YYYY HH:MI:SS') AS "Current Date",
  TO_CHAR(SYSDATE + 7, 'DD-MON-YYYY HH:MI:SS') AS "Seven days from now"
     FROM DUAL;
```

Output:

```
Current Date                  Seven days from now
----------------------------- -----------------------------
18-DEC-2024 10:43:23          25-DEC-2024 10:43:23
```

Example: One hour from now

```
SELECT TO_CHAR(SYSDATE, 'DD-MON-YYYY HH:MI:SS') AS "Current Date",
  TO_CHAR(SYSDATE + 1/24, 'DD-MON-YYYY HH:MI:SS') AS "One hour from now"
     FROM DUAL;
```

Output:

```
Current Date                  One hour from now
----------------------------- -----------------------------
18-DEC-2024 10:43:59          18-DEC-2024 11:43:59
```

Example: Three hours from now

```
SELECT TO_CHAR(SYSDATE, 'DD-MON-YYYY HH:MI:SS') AS "Current Date",
  TO_CHAR(SYSDATE + 3/24, 'DD-MON-YYYY HH:MI:SS') AS "Three hours from now"
     FROM DUAL;
```

Output:

```
Current Date                  Three hours from now
----------------------------- -----------------------------
18-DEC-2024 10:46:09          18-DEC-2024 01:46:09
```

Example: An half hour from now

```
SELECT TO_CHAR(SYSDATE, 'DD-MON-YYYY HH:MI:SS') AS "Current Date",
  TO_CHAR(SYSDATE + 1/48, 'DD-MON-YYYY HH:MI:SS') AS "An half hour from now"
     FROM DUAL;
```

Output:

```
Current Date                  An half hour from now
----------------------------- -----------------------------
18-DEC-2024 10:46:36          18-DEC-2024 11:16:36
```

Example: Ten minutes from now

```
SELECT TO_CHAR(SYSDATE, 'DD-MON-YYYY HH:MI:SS') AS "Current Date",
  TO_CHAR(SYSDATE + 10/1440, 'DD-MON-YYYY HH:MI:SS')
     AS "Ten minutes from now" FROM DUAL;
```

Output:

```
Current Date                  Ten minutes from now
----------------------------- -----------------------------
18-DEC-2024 10:47:08          18-DEC-2024 10:57:08
```

Example: Thrity seconds from now

```
SELECT TO_CHAR(SYSDATE, 'DD-MON-YYYY HH:MI:SS') AS "Current Date",
  TO_CHAR(SYSDATE + 30/86400, 'DD-MON-YYYY HH:MI:SS')
     AS "Thirty seconds from now" FROM DUAL;
```

Output:

```
Current Date                  Thirty seconds from now
----------------------------- -----------------------------
18-DEC-2024 10:47:29          18-DEC-2024 10:47:59
```

Example: Tomorrow at 12 midnight

```
SELECT TO_CHAR(SYSDATE, 'DD-MON-YYYY HH:MI:SS') AS "Current Date",
  TO_CHAR(TRUNC(SYSDATE + 1), 'DD-MON-YYYY HH:MI:SS')
     AS "Tomorrow at 12 midnight" FROM DUAL;
```

Output:

```
Current Date                  Tomorrow at 12 midnight
----------------------------- -----------------------------
18-DEC-2024 10:47:59          19-DEC-2024 12:00:00
```

Example: Tomorrow at 8 AM

```
SELECT TO_CHAR(SYSDATE, 'DD-MON-YYYY HH:MI:SS') AS "Current Date",
  TO_CHAR(TRUNC(SYSDATE + 1) + 8/24, 'DD-MON-YYYY HH:MI:SS')
     AS "Tomorrow at 8 AM" FROM DUAL;
```

Output:

```
Current Date                   Tomorrow at 8 AM
------------------------------ -----------------------------
18-DEC-2024 10:48:20           19-DEC-2024 08:00:00
```

Example: Next Monday at 12:00 noon

```
SELECT TO_CHAR(SYSDATE, 'DD-MON-YYYY HH:MI:SS') AS "Current Date",
  TO_CHAR(NEXT_DAY(TRUNC(SYSDATE), 'MONDAY') + 12/24,
      'DD-MON-YYYY HH:MI:SS') AS "Next Monday at 12:00 noon" FROM DUAL;
```

Output:

```
Current Date                   Next Monday at 12:00 noon
------------------------------ -----------------------------
18-DEC-2024 10:48:56           23-DEC-2024 12:00:00
```

Example: First day of the month at 12 midnight

```
SELECT TO_CHAR(SYSDATE, 'DD-MON-YYYY HH:MI:SS') AS "Current Date",
  TO_CHAR(TRUNC(LAST_DAY(SYSDATE) + 1), 'DD-MON-YYYY HH:MI:SS')
      AS "1st day - month at 12 midnight" FROM DUAL;
```

Output:

```
Current Date                   1st day - month at 12 midnigh
------------------------------ -----------------------------
18-DEC-2024 10:49:31           01-JAN-2025 12:00:00
```

Example: The next Monday, Wednesday or Friday at 9 AM

```
SELECT TO_CHAR(SYSDATE, 'DD-MON-YYYY HH:MI:SS') AS "Current Date",
  TO_CHAR(TRUNC(LEAST(NEXT_DAY(SYSDATE, 'MONDAY'),
      NEXT_DAY(SYSDATE, 'WEDNESDAY'),
          NEXT_DAY(SYSDATE, 'FRIDAY'))) + (9/24), 'DD-MON-YYYY HH:MI:SS')
              AS "Next Mon, Wed or Fri – 9 AM" FROM DUAL;
```

Output:

```
Current Date                   Next Mon, Wed or Fri - 9 AM
------------------------------ -----------------------------
18-DEC-2024 10:49:54           20-DEC-2024 09:00:00
```

Chapter 16

SECTION III: WORKING WITH DATA

Grouping Data

The Concept Of Grouping

A GROUP BY statement in SQL specifies that an SQL SELECT statement returns a list grouped by one or more columns, usually to apply some sort of aggregate function to certain columns. When aggregate functions such as SUM are invoked, the return value is the aggregate of all column values. To determine the sum for each individual group of column values, GROUP BY is used.

Here are a few common grouping [aggregation] functions:

- Count(expression): Quantity of matching records per group.
- Sum(expression): Summation of given value per group.
- Min(expression): Minimum of given value per group.
- Max(expression): Maximum of given value per group.
- Avg(expression): Average of given value per group.

The GROUP BY clause is one of the most complex concepts for those new to the SQL language, and the easiest way to understand it is through examples.

The **GROUP BY** clause can also be associated with the **HAVING** clause, similar to how the ORDER BY clause can be associated with the WHERE clause, except that GROUP BY and HAVING operate on record sets, **not** individual records, like ORDER BY and WHERE do.

Here are the rules for using the GROUP BY and HAVING clauses:

- Columns listed in the SELECT statement must be listed in the GROUP BY clause.
- Columns listed in the GROUP BY clause do not need to be listed in the SELECT statement.
- Only group functions can be used in the HAVING clause.
- The group functions listed in the HAVING clause do not need to be listed in the SELECT statement.

GROUP BY Clause

The GROUP BY clause is used with the SELECT statement. This optional clause instructs Oracle to group rows based on distinct values for **specified columns**. The GROUP BY clause creates a dataset containing several sets of records **grouped together** based on a condition.

```
SELECT <ColumnName1>, <ColumnName2>, <ColumnNameN>,
  AGGREGATE_FUNCTION (<Expression>) FROM <TableName>
     WHERE <Condition>
        GROUP BY <ColumnName1>, <ColumnName2>, <ColumnNameN>;
```

Currently the OrderDetails table holds the following data:

ORDERNO	ORDERDATE	PRODUCTNAME	COST	QTY	EMPLOYEENO	CUSTOMERNAME
1	03-JAN-08	A4 Papers	350	10	6	Sharanam Chaitanya Shah
2	09-FEB-08	Tables	700	100	5	Vaishali Sharanam Shah
3	14-OCT-07	AC	13000	2	4	Sharanam Chaitanya Shah
4	11-NOV-07	Refrigerator	12000	4	3	Anil Mayekar
1	03-JAN-08	LCD	50000	10	3	Sharanam Chaitanya Shah
2	09-FEB-08	Chairs	700	10	1	Vaishali Sharanam Shah
3	14-OCT-07	A4 Papers	350	2	5	Sharanam Chaitanya Shah
4	11-NOV-07	Tables	700	3	2	Anil Mayekar
5	28-FEB-07	DVD Player	4000	50	1	Hansel
1	03-JAN-08	TV	15000	5	7	Sharanam Chaitanya Shah
2	09-FEB-08	DVD Player	4000	1	4	Vaishali Sharanam Shah
3	14-OCT-07	Chairs	700	2	10	Sharanam Chaitanya Shah
4	11-NOV-07	Chairs	700	15	9	Anil Mayekar
5	28-FEB-07	A4 Papers	350	3	1	Hansel
5	28-FEB-07	LCD	50000	1	2	Hansel
4	11-NOV-07	TV	15000	4	2	Anil Mayekar
3	14-OCT-07	Tables	700	3	5	Sharanam Chaitanya Shah
2	09-FEB-08	A4 Papers	350	3	6	Vaishali Sharanam Shah
1	03-JAN-08	DVD Player	4000	1	9	Sharanam Chaitanya Shah
5	28-FEB-07	Refrigerator	12000	1	5	Hansel
6	09-DEC-08	TV	15000	1	1	Chaitanya Kantilal Shah

Display the total number of products ordered by each customer:

```
SELECT CustomerName, SUM(Qty) "Total No. Of Products" FROM OrderDetails
  GROUP BY CustomerName;
```

Output:

```
CUSTOMERNAME              Total No. Of Products
------------------------- ---------------------
Anil Mayekar                                 26
Chaitanya Kantilal Shah                       1
Vaishali Sharanam Shah                      114
Sharanam Chaitanya Shah                      35
Hansel                                       55
```

In this example, the SELECT query specifies two columns: CustomerName and SUM(Qty). The SUM(Qty) function returns a single value, even though the table contains multiple customers. Therefore, the existing columns need to be grouped in such a way that the total quantity of products for each group of customers can be calculated.

The GROUP BY clause accomplishes this. In the SELECT query, the GROUP BY clause ensures that the SUM function is executed for each unique customer in the table. Thus, the GROUP BY clause operates similarly to the DISTINCT clause, considering only unique customers.

Let's count the number of products per order from the OrderDetails table:

```
SELECT OrderNo, COUNT(*) "No. Of Products Per Order" FROM OrderDetails
  GROUP BY OrderNo;
```

Output:

```
   ORDERNO No. Of Products Per Order
---------- -------------------------
         1                         4
         2                         4
         3                         4
         4                         4
         5                         4
         6                         1

6 rows selected.
```

Simplifying GROUP BY with Aliases

A helpful new feature in Oracle 23: using aliases in the GROUP BY clause makes your SQL queries cleaner and easier to read, especially when dealing with complex calculations.

Before we dive into GROUP BY aliases, let's quickly recap what an alias is. In SQL, an **alias** is a temporary name you give to a column or a calculated expression. It's like giving a **nickname**. This nickname makes your queries more readable and manageable.

Syntax:

```
SELECT <ColumnName> "<AliasName>" FROM <TableName>;
```

Previously, when you wanted to group data based on a calculated value, you had to repeat that entire calculation in the GROUP BY clause.

For example, imagine you want to find the average balance per year of account opening:

```
SELECT EXTRACT(YEAR FROM AccountOpeningDate) AS OpeningYear,
  AVG(CurrentBalance) AS AverageBalance FROM Accounts
     GROUP BY EXTRACT(YEAR FROM AccountOpeningDate);
```

Notice how **EXTRACT(YEAR FROM AccountOpeningDate)** is written twice. This can become cumbersome and error-prone, especially if the calculation is more complex.

Oracle 23 simplifies this by allowing you to use the alias directly in the GROUP BY clause. So, the above query can now be written as:

```
SELECT EXTRACT(YEAR FROM AccountOpeningDate) AS OpeningYear,
  AVG(CurrentBalance) AS AverageBalance FROM Accounts
     GROUP BY OpeningYear;
```

We calculate the average account balance for each year in which accounts were opened once and then simply refer to it by its alias, "OpeningYear", in the GROUP BY clause.

Benefits of Using Aliases in GROUP BY:

- ***Improved Readability:*** Queries become easier to understand and maintain. You don't have to decipher complex expressions multiple times.
- ***Reduced Errors:*** Repeating calculations increases the risk of typos or inconsistencies. Using aliases minimizes this risk.
- ***Better Compatibility:*** This feature aligns Oracle with other popular database systems like Teradata, MySQL, and PostgreSQL, making it easier to port code between systems.

HAVING Clause

The **HAVING** clause is always used in conjunction with the GROUP BY clause. It serves as a condition applied to the result set generated by the GROUP BY clause.

> Each column referenced in the HAVING clause **must be used** within a statistical function or listed among the columns specified in the GROUP BY clause.

Display all customers who have purchased products worth more than 10000 rupees:

```
SELECT CustomerName, SUM(Cost) "Total Amount Spent" FROM OrderDetails
  GROUP BY CustomerName HAVING SUM(Cost) > 10000;
```

Output:

```
CUSTOMERNAME              Total Amount Spent
------------------------- ------------------
Anil Mayekar                           28400
Chaitanya Kantilal Shah                15000
Sharanam Chaitanya Shah                84100
Hansel                                 66350
```

In the given SELECT query, two columns are specified: CustomerName and SUM(Cost). The SUM(Cost) function returns a single value, whereas the table holds data for multiple customers. In such a situation, the columns must be grouped, allowing the total cost for each group to be calculated.

The GROUP BY clause in the SELECT query ensures that the SUM function is executed for each unique customer in the table. Additionally, to display only those customers who have purchased products worth more than ₹10,000, a condition is applied to the retrieved result set.

The HAVING clause imposes this condition, filtering out customers who do not meet the specified criteria.

Here's another example. Display all customers who have purchased products worth more than ₹10,000 in orders placed **after 1st January 2008:**

```
SELECT CustomerName, SUM(Cost) "Total Amount Spent" FROM OrderDetails
  WHERE OrderDate > '01-Jan-2008' GROUP BY CustomerName
     HAVING SUM(Cost) > 10000;
```

Output:

```
CUSTOMERNAME              Total Amount Spent
------------------------- ------------------
Chaitanya Kantilal Shah                15000
Sharanam Chaitanya Shah                69350
```

To consider only those orders placed after 1st January 2008, a row-level condition must be imposed using the WHERE clause. The WHERE clause **filters out** all records with an OrderDate earlier than 1st January 2008. As a result, only records that meet this condition are available for the grouping process.

Determining Whether Values Are Unique

One significant issue with the **DISTINCT** clause is that while it eliminates duplicates, **it does not show which values were duplicated** in the original data. The HAVING clause, on the other hand, can identify unique and non-unique values. This makes the HAVING clause useful for finding unique values in situations where DISTINCT does not apply.

Display all customers who have bought only one product till date:

```
SELECT CustomerName, SUM(Qty) "Total No. Of Products" FROM OrderDetails
  GROUP BY CustomerName HAVING COUNT(Qty) = 1;
```

Output:

```
CUSTOMERNAME              Total No. Of Products
------------------------- ---------------------
Chaitanya Kantilal Shah                       1
```

In this query, the **SUM()** function is applied to the **Qty** field, which holds the number of products bought by each customer. This information is **grouped** based on the Customer.

To retrieve only those customers who have purchased **exactly one product**, the HAVING clause is used to apply a condition on the aggregate value returned by SUM(). This clause ensures that only records where the sum of Qty equals exactly 1 are displayed.

Now, let's retrieve all customers who were executed in the earlier query. This means displaying all customers who have bought **more than** one product to date:

```
SELECT CustomerName, SUM(Qty) "Total No. Of Products" FROM OrderDetails
  GROUP BY CustomerName HAVING COUNT(Qty) > 1;
```

Output:

```
CUSTOMERNAME              Total No. Of Products
------------------------- ---------------------
Anil Mayekar                                 26
Vaishali Sharanam Shah                      114
Sharanam Chaitanya Shah                      35
Hansel                                       55
```

In this query, the **SUM()** function is applied to the **Qty** field, which holds the number of products bought by each customer. This information is **grouped** based on the Customer.

To retrieve only those customers who have purchased **more than one** product, the **HAVING** clause is used to apply a condition on the aggregate value returned by SUM(). This clause ensures that only records where the sum of Qty is **greater** than 1 are displayed.

Grouping Using The ROLLUP Operator

The **ROLLUP** operator is used to calculate aggregates and super aggregates for expressions within a GROUP BY statement. Report writers typically use this operator to extract statistics and summaries from a result set.

Create a report on customers, providing the **quantity of products** and the **price** Per Order as well as on a Per Customer basis:

```
SELECT CustomerName, OrderNo, SUM(Qty), SUM(Cost) FROM OrderDetails
  GROUP BY ROLLUP (CustomerName, OrderNo);
```

Output:

```
CUSTOMERNAME                ORDERNO   SUM(QTY)  SUM(COST)
------------------------- ---------- ---------- ----------
Hansel                             5         55      66350
Hansel                                       55      66350
Anil Mayekar                       4         26      28400
Anil Mayekar                                 26      28400
Vaishali Sharanam Shah             2        114       5750
Vaishali Sharanam Shah                      114       5750
Chaitanya Kantilal Shah            6          1      15000
Chaitanya Kantilal Shah                       1      15000
                                                  Per Order
Sharanam Chaitanya Shah            1         26      69350

Sharanam Chaitanya Shah            3          9      14750


Sharanam Chaitanya Shah                      35      84100
                                            231     199600

                                                  Per Customer
12 rows selected.
```

The OrderDetails table holds all the orders placed by the available customers, along with order details such as the quantity and price of products. The query is written to display the columns CustomerName, OrderNo, **SUM(**Qty**)**, and **SUM(**Cost**)**. The SUM(Qty) and SUM(Cost) functions enable displaying the **quantity of products** and the **total price** Per Order.

Once this information is retrieved, the aggregate values need to be further aggregated (super-aggregated) on a per-customer basis. To achieve this, the grouping is done using the ROLLUP operator. In the output, it is clear that the customer named Sharanam Chaitanya Shah has placed two orders, hence two order numbers are associated with that customer.

The ROLLUP operator first calculates the standard aggregate values for the groups specified in the GROUP BY clause (i.e., the **sum** of **quantity** and **price** for each order number). Then, it creates higher-level subtotals, moving from right to left through the list of grouping columns (i.e., the **sum** of **quantity** and **price** for each customer).

Grouping Using The CUBE Operator

The **CUBE** operator can be applied to aggregate functions such as AVG(), SUM(), MAX(), MIN(), and COUNT() within a GROUP BY statement. This operator is typically used by report writers to extract cross-tabular reports from a result set.

The CUBE operator produces subtotals for all possible combinations of groupings specified in the GROUP BY clause, along with a grand total. This is in contrast to the ROLLUP operator, which only produces a subset of possible subtotal combinations.

Create a report on the customers, providing the **quantity of products** and the **price** Per Order as well as on a Per Customer basis along with a GRAND TOTAL:

```
SELECT CustomerName, OrderNo, SUM(Qty), SUM(Cost) FROM OrderDetails
  GROUP BY CUBE (CustomerName, OrderNo);
```

Output:

```
CUSTOMERNAME                ORDERNO   SUM(QTY)  SUM(COST)
------------------------- ---------- ---------- ----------
                                            231     199600
                                                  Grand Total
                                                  Total Per Order
                                   1         26      69350
                                   2        114       5750
                                   3          9      14750
                                   4         26      28400
                                   5         55      66350
                                   6          1      15000
Hansel                                       55      66350
Hansel                             5         55      66350
Anil Mayekar                                 26      28400
Anil Mayekar                       4         26      28400
Vaishali Sharanam Shah                      114       5750
Vaishali Sharanam Shah             2        114       5750
Chaitanya Kantilal Shah                       1      15000
Chaitanya Kantilal Shah            6          1      15000
                                                  Per Customer
Sharanam Chaitanya Shah                      35      84100
                                                  Per Order
Sharanam Chaitanya Shah            1         26      69350
Sharanam Chaitanya Shah            3          9      14750

18 rows selected.
```

The OrderDetails table holds all the orders placed by available customers, along with order details such as the quantity and price of products. The query is written to display the columns CustomerName, OrderNo, SUM(Qty), and SUM(Cost). The SUM(Qty) and SUM(Cost) functions enable displaying the quantity of products and the price per order.

Once this information is retrieved, the aggregate values need to be further aggregated (super aggregated) on a per-customer basis. To achieve this, the grouping is done using the CUBE operator.

The **CUBE** operator is used to display:

- The quantity and price per OrderNo.
- The total quantity and price per Customer.
- The total per OrderNo irrespective of the customer.

- The grand total for all orders across all customers.

The CUBE operator first calculates the standard aggregate values for the groups specified in the GROUP BY clause (i.e., the sum of quantity and price for each OrderNo). It then creates higher-level subtotals, moving from right to left through the list of grouping columns (i.e., the sum of quantity and price for each customer).

Additionally, the CUBE operator displays the total balance per OrderNo irrespective of the customer and the grand total of all orders for all customers.

Chapter

17

SECTION III: WORKING WITH DATA

Subqueries

A **subquery** is an SQL statement contained within another SQL statement, also known as a **nested query**. The query within parenthesis is called the **inner query**, while the containing query is referred to as the **outer query**. A subquery can be specified within:

- WHERE clause
- FROM clause
- SELECT clause

Subqueries are used to:

- Insert records into a target table.
- Update records in a target table.
- Create tables and insert records into the newly created tables.
- Create views.
- Provide values for **conditions** in WHERE and HAVING clauses, and for operators such as IN used with SELECT, UPDATE, and DELETE statements.

Subquery In The WHERE Clause

Display all the books authored by "Sharanam Shah" and "Vaishali Shah":

```
SELECT ISBN, BookName, NoOfChapters, Category FROM Books
```

```
WHERE AuthorNo IN(SELECT AuthorNo FROM Authors
    WHERE AuthorName = 'Sharanam Shah' OR  AuthorName = 'Vaishali Shah');
```

Output:

```
ISBN             BOOKNAME                                   NOOFCHAPTERS CATEGORY
---------------- ------------------------------------------ ------------ --------
783-983242-23    Oracle For Professionals                   43           Database
90-987532-234    Professional Projects On PHP And Oracle    19           Project
234-82911-1      Oracle and Data Warehouse and Data Mining  12           Database
2364-90452       Database Concepts                          27           Database
978-34-13394-1   Professional MySQL                         16           Database
```

In this scenario, there are two tables: the **Authors** table holds all the authors, each identified by an AuthorNo (Primary Key), and the **Books** table holds a list of books, each identified by an ISBN (Primary Key). The Books table also includes a foreign key, AuthorNo, which identifies which book is written by which author.

To display all books authored by "Sharanam Shah" and "Vaishali Shah":

1. Identify the AuthorNo of both authors using the inner query:

```
SELECT AuthorNo FROM Authors WHERE AuthorName = 'Sharanam Shah'
  OR AuthorName = 'Vaishali Shah';
```

This query will retrieve the AuthorNo for both authors:

```
  AUTHORNO
----------
         1
         3
```

2. Pass this result set (i.e. the AuthorNo) to the outer query:

```
SELECT ISBN, BookName, NoOfChapters, Category FROM Books
  WHERE AuthorNo IN(1, 3);
```

TIP: Since the result holds more than one record, the **IN** operator is used, which accepts multiple values at once.

Choosing Between The = And IN Operators

Consider the following SQL query, which retrieves only a single value:

```
SELECT AuthorNo FROM Authors WHERE AuthorName = 'Sharanam Shah';
```

If an SQL query is written as a subquery:

```
SELECT ISBN, BookName, NoOfChapters, Category FROM Books
  WHERE AuthorNo = (SELECT AuthorNo FROM Authors
      WHERE AuthorName = 'Sharanam Shah');
```

Even this SQL subquery will retrieve **one and only one** value.

However, if you need to work with more than one value in a condition, the IN operator can be used:

```
SELECT ISBN, BookName, NoOfChapters, Category FROM Books
  WHERE AuthorNo IN(SELECT AuthorNo FROM Authors
     WHERE AuthorName = 'Sharanam Shah' OR AuthorName = 'Vaishali Shah');
```

This query retrieves all books authored by authors identified by the AuthorNo 1 and 3:

```
ISBN            BOOKNAME                                      NOOFCHAPTERS CATEGORY
--------------  --------------------------------------------  ------------ --------
783-983242-23   Oracle For Professionals                      43           Database
90-987532-234   Professional Projects On PHP And Oracle       19           Project
234-82911-1     Oracle and Data Warehouse and Data Mining     12           Database
2364-90452      Database Concepts                             27           Database
978-34-13394-1  Professional MySQL                            16           Database
```

Since more than one author name is specified in the subquery, more than one value will be retrieved. Hence, the IN operator is used because it accepts multiple values.

If the IN operator is replaced with the = operator, an error is returned:

```
SELECT ISBN, BookName, NoOfChapters, Category FROM Books
  WHERE AuthorNo = (SELECT AuthorNo FROM Authors
     WHERE AuthorName = 'Sharanam Shah' OR AuthorName = 'Vaishali Shah');
```

Output:

```
        WHERE AuthorNo = (SELECT AuthorNo FROM Authors
                          *
ERROR at line 2:
ORA-01427: single-row subquery returns more than one row
Help: https://docs.oracle.com/error-help/db/ora-01427/
```

Nested Subqueries

Display all books that have been authored with specialties in Oracle:

```
SELECT ISBN, BookName, NoOfChapters, Category FROM Books WHERE AuthorNo
  IN (SELECT AuthorNo FROM Authors WHERE SpecialtyNo =
     (SELECT SpecialtyNo FROM Specialties WHERE Specialty = 'Oracle'));
```

Output:

```
ISBN          BOOKNAME                                        NOOFCHAPTERS CATEGORY
------------- ----------------------------------------------- ------------ --------
783-983242-23 Oracle For Professionals                                  43 Database
90-987532-234 Professional Projects On PHP And Oracle                   19 Project
234-82911-1   Oracle and Data Warehouse and Data Mining                 12 Database
808-97365-80  Oracle SQL and SQL*Plus                                   17 Database
```

In the example above, the data to be retrieved is available in the **Books** table, making the outer query bound to this table.

To fulfill the condition of finding authors who have written books with specialties in Oracle, the **Specialties** table is queried. To understand the solution, the query needs to be simplified by handling the innermost subqueries first, followed by the outer queries.

1. Identify the SpecialtyNo of the specialty Oracle:

```
SELECT SpecialtyNo FROM Specialties WHERE Specialty = 'Oracle';
```

Output:

```
SPECIALTYNO
-----------
          1
```

2. Simplify the immediate outer query using the output from the inner query:

```
SELECT ISBN, BookName, NoOfChapters, Category FROM Books
  WHERE AuthorNo IN (SELECT AuthorNo FROM Authors WHERE SpecialtyNo = (1));
```

3. Identify the AuthorNo of all authors who have written books with specialties in Oracle using SpecialtyNo **1**:

```
SELECT AuthorNo FROM Authors WHERE SpecialtyNo = (1);
```

Output:

```
  AUTHORNO
----------
         1
         6
         7
```

4. Simplify the outermost query using the result set:

```
SELECT ISBN, BookName, NoOfChapters, Category FROM Books
  WHERE AuthorNo IN (1, 6, 7);
```

When the above SQL query is executed, the resulting output is equivalent to the desired output of the SQL query using two levels of Subqueries.

Let's display all books with highest number of chapters:

```
SELECT ISBN, BookName, NoOfChapters, Category FROM Books
  WHERE NoOfChapters = (SELECT MAX(NoOfChapters) FROM Books);
```

Output:

```
ISBN          BOOKNAME                 NOOFCHATPERS CATEGORY
------------- ------------------------ ------------ -----------
783-983242-23 Oracle For Professionals           43 Database
```

This result is achieved through the following two steps:

- Determine the highest number of chapters from the Books table.

- Based on the retrieved value, identify the books with the number of chapters matching the highest value.

1. Retrieve the highest number of chapters:

```
SELECT MAX(NoOfChapters) FROM Books;
```

2. Retrieve books based on the highest number of chapters, for example 43:

```
SELECT ISBN, BookName, NoOfChapters, Category FROM Books
  WHERE NoOfChapters = 43;
```

3. The simplest solution to form a subquery is to replace the value 43 with the inner query that retrieves the highest number of chapters. Hence, the complete SQL query will be:

```
SELECT ISBN, BookName, NoOfChapters, Category FROM Books
  WHERE NoOfChapters = (SELECT MAX(NoOfChapters) FROM Books);
```

4. Since the innermost query executes first, the outer query can be simplified as:

```
SELECT ISBN, BookName, NoOfChapters, Category FROM Books
  WHERE NoOfChapters = (43);
```

Often times, developers have the following question:

Why cannot the same query can be written as:

```
SELECT ISBN, BookName, NoOfChapters, Category FROM Books
  WHERE NoOfChapters = MAX(NoOfChapters);
```

OR

```
SELECT ISBN, BookName, NoOfChapters, Category FROM Books
  WHERE MAX(NoOfChapters) = NoOfChapters;
```

If these queries are executed, they will not run successfully. The reason is that a condition in the WHERE clause cannot hold aggregate or group functions unless a subquery is used.

Subquery In The FROM Clause

A subquery written in the **FROM** clause of a **SELECT** statement is known as an **inline view**. Since anything written in the FROM clause serves as the data source for that specific SELECT statement, subqueries in the FROM clause will also represent a **data source**.

Display all authors and the total number of books written by them:

```
SELECT AuthorName, B.NoOfBooks FROM Authors A,
  (SELECT AuthorNo, COUNT(ISBN) AS NoOfBooks FROM Books
     GROUP BY AuthorNo) B WHERE A.AuthorNo = B.AuthorNo;
```

Output:

```
AUTHORNAME                 NOOFBOOKS
------------------------- ----------
Sharanam Shah                      3
```

```
Hansel Colaco                    1
Vaishali Shah                    2
Chaitanya Naik                   1
Ashwini Kolapure                 1
Daniel Joshua                    1

6 rows selected.
```

The required data is available in two tables: Authors and Books. The Author names are stored as a column value in the Authors table.

1. However, the total number of books is not available as a column in either of the tables. This value can be calculated by counting the number of books available in the Books table for each author:

```
SELECT COUNT (ISBN) AS NoOfBooks FROM Books GROUP BY AuthorNo
```

Since such a value is not readily available, a subquery needs to be written and attached to another query that will retrieve author names.

2. Query to retrieve author names:

```
SELECT AuthorName, B.NoOfBooks FROM Authors
```

3. The subquery returns a value that becomes part of the output. Since the subquery acts as a data source, it is placed in the **FROM** clause of the outer query and given an alias **B:**

```
SELECT AuthorName, B.NoOfBooks FROM Authors A,
   (SELECT AuthorNo, COUNT (ISBN) AS NoOfBooks FROM Books
       GROUP BY AuthorNo) B
```

Once the data is available from both tables, it needs to be associated with each other. This means every author name should be associated with the total number of books written by that author. To do this association, a join is used, mapping the data retrieved from the inner query with the data retrieved from the outer query using AuthorNo as the mapping element, i.e., [A.AuthorNo = B.AuthorNo].

Subqueries In A HAVING Clause

Placing a subquery in the HAVING clause of an outer query allows filtering records based on the result returned by the subquery.

Display all authors whose total number of chapters written are fewer than the author with highest number of chapters written:

```
SELECT AuthorName FROM Authors WHERE AuthorNo IN (SELECT AuthorNo
   FROM Books GROUP BY AuthorNo HAVING SUM(NoOfChapters) <
       (SELECT MAX(NoOfChapters) FROM Books));
```

Output:

```
AUTHORNAME
-------------------------
Daniel Joshua
Hansel Colaco
Chaitanya Naik
Ashwini Kolapure
```

1. The innermost query calculates the highest number of chapters written by an author:

```
SELECT MAX(NoOfChapters) FROM Books;
```

Output:

```
MAX(NOOFCHAPTERS)
-----------------
               43
```

2. The result returned by the innermost query is passed on to the immediate outer query, which returns the AuthorNo of all those authors who have written fewer chapters than the author with the highest number of chapters written:

```
SELECT AuthorNo FROM Books GROUP BY AuthorNo
  HAVING SUM(NoOfChapters) < (43);
```

Output:

```
  AUTHORNO
----------
         6
         2
         4
         5
```

Once the AuthorNo of all such authors are retrieved, they are passed on to the outermost query that retrieves the Author names.

Correlated Subqueries

A subquery becomes **correlated** when it references a column from a table in the parent query. A correlated subquery is evaluated once for each row processed by the parent statement, which can be a SELECT, DELETE, or UPDATE statement. It is a way of reading every row in a table and comparing values in each row against related data. Correlated subqueries are used when a subquery must return a different result for each candidate row considered by the parent query.

The **EXISTS** operator is usually used with correlated subqueries. This operator determines whether a value retrieved by the outer query exists in the result set of the inner query. If the subquery returns at least one row, the operator returns **TRUE**. If no value exists, it returns **FALSE**. The EXISTS operator ensures that the search in the inner query terminates when at least one match is found.

Similarly, the **NOT EXISTS** operator determines whether a value retrieved by the outer query is not a part of the result set of the inner query.

Display all authors who have written at least one book:

```
SELECT AuthorName, ContactNo FROM Authors WHERE EXISTS
  (SELECT AuthorNo FROM Books WHERE Authors.AuthorNo = Books.AuthorNo);
```

Output:

```
AUTHORNAME                CONTACTNO
------------------------- ----------
Sharanam Shah               27385653
Hansel Colaco               74321547
Vaishali Shah               22356753
Chaitanya Naik              21324764
Ashwini Kolapure            27341939
Daniel Joshua               35793857

6 rows selected.
```

1. The parent query, which retrieves the author names and contact numbers, is executed first:

```
SELECT AuthorName, ContactNo FROM Authors
```

2. The WHERE EXISTS clause is used for correlation. The subquery checks if there is at least one corresponding entry in the Books table for each author in the Authors table:

```
SELECT AuthorNo FROM Books WHERE Authors.AuthorNo = Books.AuthorNo
```

Execution process:

- For every row of Parent query, the subquery is executed once.
- The subquery returns Boolean value [True or False].
- If the subquery returns TRUE, the parent query includes the row in its result.
- If the subquery returns FALSE, the parent query does not include the row in its result.

Display all books with a number of chapters greater than the average number of chapters by the same author:

```
SELECT ISBN, BookName, NoOfChapters FROM Books A
  WHERE NoOfChapters > (SELECT AVG(NoOfChapters) FROM Books
     WHERE AuthorNo = A.AuthorNo);
```

Output:

```
ISBN                 BOOKNAME                     NOOFCHAPTERS
-------------------- ---------------------------- ------------
783-983242-23        Oracle For Professionals               43
2364-90452           Database Concepts                      27
```

The retrieved data is available in the Books table. Hence, the primary query references this table:

```
SELECT ISBN, BookName, NoOfChapters FROM Books A
```

The output needs to be filtered to show only those books that have more chapters than the average number of chapters written by the same author. A subquery is used to determine this average.

Both queries are correlated using the condition:

```
AuthorNo = A.AuthorNo
```

The parent query retrieves book details. For each book:

- The subquery calculates the average number of chapters for books by the same author.
- The number of chapters for the current book is compared to this average.
- If the book's chapter count is greater, the book is included in the output.

Subquery With Multi Columns

Display all authors who have the same names as the employees:

```
SELECT AuthorNo, AuthorName, ContactNo FROM Authors
  WHERE (AuthorName) IN(SELECT FirstName || ' ' || LastName FROM Employees);
```

Output:

```
  AUTHORNO AUTHORNAME                CONTACTNO
---------- ------------------------- ----------
         3 Vaishali Shah               22356753
         1 Sharanam Shah               27385653
```

Here, AuthorName column of every row retrieved by the outer query is compared with both the columns of every row retrieved by the inner query.

Subquery As Part Of The Between Operator

Display all books with number of chapters more than the minimum number of chapters and less than the average number of chapters:

```
SELECT ISBN, BookName, NoOfChapters FROM Books
  WHERE (NoOfChapters BETWEEN (SELECT MIN(NoOfChapters) FROM Books)
      AND (SELECT AVG(NoOfChapters) FROM Books));
```

Output:

```
ISBN              BOOKNAME                                  NOOFCHAPTERS
----------------- ----------------------------------------- ------------
808-97365-80      Oracle SQL and SQL*Plus                             17
978-34-13394-1    Professional MySQL                                  16
21-783592-1       PHP Tips And Tricks                                 10
1-34523-880       Ajax With JSF                                        8
234-82911-1       Oracle and Data Warehouse and Data Mining           12
978-0-470-13394-1 Mastering phpMyAdmin                                13

6 rows selected.
```

Subquery In CASE Expressions

Display the author details along with a Status [Published or Unpublished] that indicates if the author has published at least one book:

```
SELECT AuthorName, ContactNo, (CASE WHEN AuthorNo IN(SELECT AuthorNo
  FROM Books) THEN 'Published' ELSE 'Unpublished' END) "Status" FROM Authors;
```

Output:

```
AUTHORNAME                       CONTACTNO Status
------------------------- ---------- -----------
Sharanam Shah                     27385653 Published
Hansel Colaco                     74321547 Published
Vaishali Shah                     22356753 Published
Chaitanya Naik                    21324764 Published
Ashwini Kolapure                  27341939 Published
Daniel Joshua                     35793857 Published
Anil Vaidya                       98758362 Unpublished

7 rows selected.
```

In the above example, the inner query returns AuthorNo. If the AuthorNo available in the Authors table is available in the values returned by the inner query, then the Status column is set to display Published otherwise Unpublished.

Subquery In An ORDER BY clause

Display all books in the order of the author names of authors who have published them:

```
SELECT ISBN, BookName, NoOfChapters FROM Books B
  ORDER BY (SELECT AuthorName FROM Authors A
     WHERE A.AuthorNo = B.AuthorNo);
```

Output:

```
ISBN              BOOKNAME                                 NOOFCHAPTERS
----------------- ---------------------------------------- ------------
978-0-470-13394-1 Mastering phpMyAdmin                     13
21-783592-1       PHP Tips And Tricks                      10
808-97365-80      Oracle SQL and SQL*Plus                  17
1-34523-880       Ajax With JSF                            8
783-983242-23     Oracle For Professionals                 43
90-987532-234     Professional Projects On PHP And Oracle  19
234-82911-1       Oracle and Data Warehouse and Data Mining 12
2364-90452        Database Concepts                        27
978-34-13394-1    Professional MySQL                       16

9 rows selected.
```

In the above example, the output needs to be ordered on the basis of author names of authors who have published those books. The book details are available in the Books table. The output needs to be ordered on the basis of author names, which are available in the AuthorName column of the **Authors** table.

Since two different tables are involved, a subquery is used. The inner query returns author names in an alphabetic order. The records returned by the inner query are correlated with the outer query using AuthorNo column, which is a common column in both the tables.

Subquery In An UPDATE Statement

In an UPDATE statement, column values can be set to a value returned by a single-row subquery.

Update the NoOfChapters column value of all books to the average number of chapters:

```
UPDATE Books SET NoOfChapters = (SELECT AVG(NoOfChapters) FROM Books);
```

Output:

```
9 rows updated.
```

The subquery calculates and returns the average number of books. Using this value, the NoOfChapters column value is updated.

Subquery In A Delete Statement

Subqueries can also be used in a DELETE statement's WHERE clause.

Delete all books that have been published by a Publisher named "BpB":

```
DELETE FROM Books WHERE PublisherNo IN (SELECT PublisherNo
  FROM Publishers WHERE PublisherName = 'BpB');
```

Output:

```
1 row deleted.
```

Chapter 18

SECTION III: WORKING WITH DATA

Joins

A **join** is an SQL query that combines records from two or more tables. Oracle executes a join whenever multiple tables appear in the FROM clause. The **JOIN** operator specifies how to relate these tables in the SQL query. In many cases, data needs to be retrieved from more than one table to make the end result complete. Joins allow multiple tables to be treated as a single entity.

To retrieve joined data from two or more tables, there must be a meaningful relationship between them. The tables to be joined must possess a column or columns that share a common set of values, enabling them to be linked meaningfully. This column or columns are called the **join key** or **common key**.

Most often, the join key is the primary key of one table and a foreign key in another table. As long as the data in these columns match, the join can be performed successfully.

Types Of JOIN

Inner Join

An **Inner Join**, also known as an **Equi Join**, represents the default join type in SQL. In an Inner Join, the WHERE condition compares two columns from two tables using the equality operator (=). This join combines rows that have equivalent values in the specified columns, making it the most commonly used type of join.

An Inner Join requires each record in both joined tables to have a matching record. When applied, it combines every record from Table A with every record in Table B, but only those records that satisfy the join condition are considered. This type of join is ideal for situations where you need to select only those rows that have values in common in the specified columns.

Outer Join

An **Outer Join** does not require each record in the two joined tables to have a matching record. The joined table retains each record, even if no matching record exists in the other table. An Outer Join returns all the rows that are returned by an Inner Join and also includes all rows from one table that **do not have matching** rows in the other table. The plus (+) operator is used to indicate an Outer Join.

Outer joins can be categorized into three types:

Left Outer Join

The result of a **Left Outer Join** for tables A and B always contains all records from the left table (A), even if the join condition does not find any matching records in the right table (B). If there is no matching join predicate, the result will include NULL in place of the non-matching record from table B.

> TIP: To qualify a table as left or right, its name has to appear after the FROM or JOIN keyword, respectively.

Right Outer Join

A **Right Outer Join** closely resembles a Left Outer Join, except with the tables reversed. Every record from the right table (B) appears in the joined table at least once. If no matching row from the left table (A) exists, NULL appears in the columns from A for those records that have no match in A.

Full Outer Join

A **Full Outer Join** combines the results of both Left and Right Outer Joins. The joined table contains all records from both tables, with NULLs for missing matches on either side.

Cross Join

A **Cross Join** always returns a Cartesian product. It combines every row from the left table with every row from the right table. This type of join is useful when it is desired to select all possible combinations of rows and columns from both tables.

> However, this kind of join is usually not preferred, as it may run for a very long time and produce a huge result set that may not be useful.

Cartesian Product

The condition in a join plays an important role. However, if the condition is not specified, the query returns all rows from one table with all the rows from the other table. This result set is known as a **Cartesian product**. Such queries usually return a large number of rows.

For example, if a table named Employees holds 100 records and another table named Departments holds 20 records, joining these tables **without a join condition** will result in 2,000 records. This is because each row from the Employees table is combined with each row from the Departments table, yielding a total of 100 rows multiplied by 20 rows, which equals 2,000 rows.

Self Join

A join does not always have to involve two different tables. A table can be joined to itself, creating a **Self Join**. This is useful when values from one column need to be compared with other values in the same column of the same table.

To join a table to itself, **two** copies of the same table have to be opened in memory. A Self Join is created by listing the table twice in the FROM clause and distinguishing them by assigning different aliases to each table name:

```
FROM <TableName> [<Alias1>], <TableName> [<Alias2>] ...
```

Self Join queries are executed by logically making two copies of the same table.

Non-Equi Joins

A Non-Equi join uses an operator other than the equality operator [=] in joins and is relatively rare. The operators used in Non-Equi joins include:

- Not-equal [<>]
- Less than [<]
- Greater than [>]
- Less than or equal to [<=]
- Greater than or equal to [>=]
- LIKE
- IN
- BETWEEN

A JOIN can be written using **ANSI** as well as **Theta** style.

ANSI Style

In the ANSI SQL-92 standards, joins are performed in the JOIN clause of the query, known as the **ANSI style:**

```
SELECT <ColumnName1>, <ColumnName2>, <ColumnNameN>
  FROM <TableName1> <JOIN TYPE> <TableName2>
     ON <TableName1>.<ColumnName1>=<TableName2>.<ColumnName2>
        WHERE <Condition>
           ORDER BY <ColumnName1>, <ColumnName2>, <ColumnNameN>
```

Joins in the ANSI style are more readable than those in Theta style, as the query clearly indicates which table is on the left in a LEFT JOIN and which table is on the right in a RIGHT JOIN.

Theta Style

In non-ANSI standard implementations, the join operation is performed in the WHERE clause, known as the **Theta style:**

```
SELECT <ColumnName1>, <ColumnName2>, <ColumnNameN>
  FROM <TableName1>, <TableName2>
     WHERE <TableName1>.<ColumnName1>=<TableName2>.<ColumnName2>
        AND <Condition>
           ORDER BY <ColumnName1>, <ColumnName2>, <ColumnNameN>
```

Where:

- ***ColumnName1*** in ***TableName1*** is usually that table's **Primary Key**.
- ***ColumnName2*** in ***TableName2*** is a **Foreign Key** in that table.
- ***ColumnName1*** and ***ColumnName2*** must have the **same Data Type** and for certain data types, the same size.

Inner Join Examples

Display all employees along with the department names to which they belong.

Solution (Ansi-style):

```
SELECT FirstName, LastName, Designation, DepartmentName FROM Employees
  INNER JOIN Departments ON Employees.DeptNo = Departments.DeptNo;
```

The join condition:

```
ON Employees.DeptNo = Departments.DeptNo;
```

can be simplified with the USING clause. The **USING clause** can only be applied to an Equi Join and the columns in the Equi Join must have the same name. This means the Primary Key column of one table will have the same name as the Foreign Key column of another table.

Solution (Ansi-style with USING clause):

```
SELECT FirstName, LastName, Designation, DepartmentName
  FROM Employees INNER JOIN Departments USING (DeptNo);
```

Do not use a table name or alias when referencing columns used in a USING clause:

```
SELECT FirstName, LastName, Designation, DepartmentName
  FROM Employees INNER JOIN Departments USING (Employees.DeptNo);
```

This displays an error:

```
        FROM Employees INNER JOIN Departments USING (Employees.DeptNo)
                                                                 *

ERROR at line 2:
ORA-01748: only simple column names allowed here
Help: https://docs.oracle.com/error-help/db/ora-01748/
```

Solution (Theta-style):

```
SELECT FirstName, LastName, Designation, DepartmentName
  FROM Employees, Departments WHERE Employees.DeptNo = Departments.DeptNo;
```

If the column names on which the **join** is specified are the same in each table, reference the columns using **TableName.ColumnName**.

Output:

```
FIRSTNAME LASTNAME DESIGNATION          DEPARTMENTNAME
--------- -------- -------------------- -------------------------
Sharanam  Shah     Technical Writing    Helpline Department
Vaishali  Shah     Database Management  HR Department
Keyur     Kapoor   Testing              Purchase Department
Amit      Haria    Programming          HR Department
Abhishek  Benegal  Sales                Sales Department
Chetan    Dedhia   HR                   Technical Department
Narendra  Dodhia   Accounts             Technical Department
```

```
Meenal    Doshi    Auditing                 IT Department
Anil      Mayekar  Peon                     Technical Department
Chaitanya Kapoor   Peon                     Customer Care Department

10 rows selected.
```

Here, DeptNo is the primary key in the Departments table and is a foreign key in the Employees table. The **DeptNo** column in the Employees table is used to refer to the departments available in the Departments table without using their names.

Using this common key, the records are related to each other using the following Equi Join condition:

```
WHERE Employees.DeptNo = Departments.DeptNo
```

If some employees are not assigned to any department, meaning the DeptNo in the Employees table holds NULL, such employees will not be considered in the output. This happens because an Inner Join is used, which requires matching records in both tables.

Let's take an example of displaying all employees along with their departments and order details.

Solution (Ansi-style):

```
SELECT FirstName, LastName, DepartmentName, OrderDate, ProductName, Cost, Qty
  FROM Employees E
    INNER JOIN OrderDetails O ON E.EmployeeNo = O.EmployeeNo
    INNER JOIN Departments D ON E.DeptNo = D.DeptNo;
```

Solution (Theta-style):

```
SELECT FirstName, LastName, DepartmentName, OrderDate, ProductName, Cost, Qty
  FROM Employees E, OrderDetails O, Departments D
    WHERE E.EmployeeNo = O.EmployeeNo AND E.DeptNo = D.DeptNo;
```

TIP: When writing a SELECT statement that joins tables, precede the column name with the table name for clarity.

Output:

```
FIRSTNAME LASTNAME DEPARTMENTNAME             ORDERDATE PRODUCTNAME   COST    QTY
--------- -------- -------------------------- --------- ------------- ------- -----
Chetan    Dedhia   Technical Department       03-JAN-08 A4 Papers     350     10
Abhishek  Benegal  Sales Department           09-FEB-08 Tables        700     100
Amit      Haria    HR Department              14-OCT-07 AC            13000   2
Keyur     Kapoor   Purchase Department        11-NOV-07 Refrigerator  12000   4
Keyur     Kapoor   Purchase Department        03-JAN-08 LCD           50000   10
Sharanam  Shah     Purchase Department        09-FEB-08 Chairs        700     10
Abhishek  Benegal  Sales Department           14-OCT-07 A4 Papers     350     2
Vaishali  Shah     HR Department              11-NOV-07 Tables        700     3
Sharanam  Shah     Purchase Department        28-FEB-07 DVD Player    4000    50
Narendra  Dodhia   Technical Department       03-JAN-08 TV            15000   5
Amit      Haria    HR Department              09-FEB-08 DVD Player    4000    1
```

```
Chaitanya Kapoor   Customer Care Department  14-OCT-07 Chairs        700     2
Anil      Mayekar  Technical Department      11-NOV-07 Chairs        700     15
Sharanam  Shah     Purchase Department       28-FEB-07 A4 Papers     350     3
Vaishali  Shah     HR Department             28-FEB-07 LCD           50000   1
Vaishali  Shah     HR Department             11-NOV-07 TV            15000   4
Abhishek  Benegal  Sales Department          14-OCT-07 Tables        700     3
Chetan    Dedhia   Technical Department      09-FEB-08 A4 Papers     350     3
Anil      Mayekar  Technical Department      03-JAN-08 DVD Player    4000    1
Abhishek  Benegal  Sales Department          28-FEB-07 Refrigerator  12000   1
Sharanam  Shah     Purchase Department       09-DEC-08 TV            15000   1

21 rows selected.
```

The data required is available in three tables i.e. Employees, Departments and OrderDetails. All three tables are linked using common field.

- In **Employees** table:
  - **EmployeeNo** is the primary key.
  - **DeptNo** is the foreign key that allows referencing departments in the **Departments** table without using the department names.
- In **Departments** table:
  - **DeptNo** is the primary key.
- In **OrderDetails** table:
  - **EmployeeNo** is the foreign key that allows mapping each record to an employee in the **Employees** table.

Since all the three tables are related to each other, data can be retrieved using Inner Join. To retrieve the required data, all three tables have to be linked on the basis of a common column:

- E.EmployeeNo = O.EmployeeNo
- E.DeptNo = D.DeptNo

By joining these tables, the data can be retrieved as if they are all in one table.

Let's take another example. Display employees with a salary higher than 30000 along with their departments and order details.

Solution (Ansi-style):

```
SELECT FirstName, LastName, DepartmentName, OrderDate, ProductName, Cost, Qty
  FROM Employees E
     INNER JOIN OrderDetails O ON E.EmployeeNo = O.EmployeeNo
     INNER JOIN Departments D ON E.DeptNo = D.DeptNo WHERE Salary > 30000;
```

Solution (Theta-style):

```
SELECT FirstName, LastName, DepartmentName, OrderDate, ProductName, Cost, Qty
  FROM Employees E, OrderDetails O, Departments D
     WHERE E.EmployeeNo = O.EmployeeNo AND E.DeptNo = D.DeptNo
        AND Salary > 30000;
```

TIP If the same column name appears in more than one table, the column name must be prefixed with the table name for clarity.

Output:

```
FIRSTNAME  LASTNAME  DEPARTMENTNAME            ORDERDATE PRODUCTNAME   COST     QTY
---------- --------- ------------------------- --------- ------------- -------- ----
Sharanam   Shah      Purchase Department       09-FEB-08 Chairs        700      10
Vaishali   Shah      HR Department             11-NOV-07 Tables        700      3
Sharanam   Shah      Purchase Department       28-FEB-07 DVD Player    4000     50
Anil       Mayekar   Technical Department      11-NOV-07 Chairs        700      15
Sharanam   Shah      Purchase Department       28-FEB-07 A4 Papers     350      3
Vaishali   Shah      HR Department             28-FEB-07 LCD           50000    1
Vaishali   Shah      HR Department             11-NOV-07 TV            15000    4
Anil       Mayekar   Technical Department      03-JAN-08 DVD Player    4000     1
Sharanam   Shah      Purchase Department       09-DEC-08 TV            15000    1

9 rows selected.
```

Since only those employees with a salary more than 30000 are required, a WHERE condition (Salary > 30000) is used in the SQL query along with the join conditions.

Let's take another example. Display employees along with their departments and a consolidated order summary (Total amount spent and Total number of products purchased).

Solution (Ansi-style):

```
SELECT FirstName, LastName, DepartmentName, SUM(Cost), SUM(Qty)
  FROM Employees E
     INNER JOIN OrderDetails O ON E.EmployeeNo = O.EmployeeNo
     INNER JOIN Departments D ON E.DeptNo = D.DeptNo
        GROUP BY FirstName, LastName, DepartmentName;
```

Solution (Theta-style):

```
SELECT FirstName, LastName, DepartmentName, SUM(Cost), SUM(Qty)
  FROM Employees E, OrderDetails O, Departments D
     WHERE E.EmployeeNo = O.EmployeeNo AND E.DeptNo = D.DeptNo
        GROUP BY FirstName, LastName, DepartmentName;
```

Output:

```
FIRSTNAME     LASTNAME   DEPARTMENTNAME            SUM(COST) SUM(QTY)
------------- ---------- ------------------------- --------- --------
Sharanam      Shah       Purchase Department       20050     64
Vaishali      Shah       HR Department             65700     8
Chaitanya     Kapoor     Customer Care Department  700       2
Chetan        Dedhia     Technical Department      700       13
Anil          Mayekar    Technical Department      4700      16
Abhishek      Benegal    Sales Department          13750     106
Amit          Haria      HR Department             17000     3
Keyur         Kapoor     Purchase Department       62000     14
Narendra      Dodhia     Technical Department      15000     5

9 rows selected.
```

The SQL query selects all distinct employees with details such as employee names and departments, and computes the sum of cost and quantity. Since the OrderDetails table holds individual records of all order details by an employee, these records are grouped on an employee basis.

Outer Join Examples

Display all employees along with department details (if any).

Solution (Left Join: Ansi-style):

```
SELECT FirstName, LastName, DepartmentName FROM Employees E
  LEFT JOIN Departments D ON E.DeptNo = D.DeptNo;
```

Solution (Left Join: Theta-style):

```
SELECT FirstName, LastName, DepartmentName FROM Employees E, Departments D
  WHERE E.DeptNo = D.DeptNo (+);
```

Solution (Right Join: Ansi-style):

```
SELECT FirstName, LastName, DepartmentName FROM Departments D
  RIGHT JOIN Employees E ON D.DeptNo = E.DeptNo;
```

Solution (Right Join: Theta-style):

```
SELECT FirstName, LastName, DepartmentName FROM Departments D, Employees E
  WHERE D.DeptNo (+) = E.DeptNo;
```

Output:

```
FIRSTNAME        LASTNAME        DEPARTMENTNAME
---------------- --------------- -------------------------
Meenal           Doshi           IT Department
Abhishek         Benegal         Sales Department
Amit             Haria           HR Department
Vaishali         Shah            HR Department
Anil             Mayekar         Technical Department
Narendra         Dodhia          Technical Department
Chetan           Dedhia          Technical Department
Keyur            Kapoor          Purchase Department
Sharanam         Shah            Purchase Department
Chaitanya        Kapoor          Customer Care Department
Amit             Paul

11 rows selected.
```

The requirement is to display the details of all employees, even if they are not assigned to a department. This means listing all employee details even if their corresponding DeptNo column holds NULL.

Since the DeptNo may hold NULL for some employees, an Inner Join will not meet the requirement, as it will not show those employees who do not have a corresponding DeptNo. In such a situation, the OUTER JOIN can be used:

- Left Join returns all the rows from the first table (Employees), even if there are no matches in the second table (Departments). This means, if there are employees in **Employees** who do not have any departments in the **Departments** table, those rows will also be listed.
- Right Join returns all the rows from the second table (Employees), even if there are no matches in the first table (Departments). This means, if there are employees in **Employees** who do not have any departments in the **Departments** table, those rows will also be listed.

Notice the **(+)** in the second solution (Theta-style). For Left Join, **(+)** is always on the right table's column in the condition, which is equivalent to writing Left Join. For Right Join, **(+)** is always on the left table's column in the condition, which is equivalent to writing Right Join.

Let's take another example. Display all departments along with employees they hold, if any.

Solution (Left Join: Ansi-style):

```
SELECT DepartmentName, FirstName, LastName FROM Departments D
  LEFT JOIN Employees E ON D.DeptNo = E.DeptNo;
```

Solution (Left Join: Theta-style):

```
SELECT DepartmentName, FirstName, LastName FROM Departments D, Employees E
  WHERE D.DeptNo = E.DeptNo (+);
```

Solution (Right Join: Ansi-style):

```
SELECT DepartmentName, FirstName, LastName FROM Employees E
  RIGHT JOIN Departments D ON E.DeptNo = D.DeptNo;
```

Solution (Right Join: Theta-style):

```
SELECT DepartmentName, FirstName, LastName FROM Employees E, Departments D
  WHERE E.DeptNo (+) = D.DeptNo;
```

Output:

```
DEPARTMENTNAME              FIRSTNAME        LASTNAME
-------------------------   ---------------- -----------------
Purchase Department         Sharanam         Shah
HR Department               Vaishali         Shah
Purchase Department         Keyur            Kapoor
HR Department               Amit             Haria
Sales Department            Abhishek         Benegal
Technical Department        Chetan           Dedhia
Technical Department        Narendra         Dodhia
IT Department               Meenal           Doshi
Technical Department        Anil             Mayekar
Customer Care Department    Chaitanya        Kapoor
Helpline Department
Accounts

12 rows selected.
```

Here, the requirement is to display all the departments irrespective of the employees they hold. This means all the departments have to be listed even though their corresponding DeptNo column in the Employees table holds NULL. To achieve this:

- Left Join returns all the rows from the first table (Departments), even if there are no matches in the second table (Employees). This means if there are departments that do not have employees assigned to them, those rows will also be listed.
- Right Join returns all the rows from the second table (Departments), even if there are no matches in the first table (Employees). This means if there are departments that do not have employees assigned to them, those rows will also be listed.

Using the appropriate join ensures that departments are included in the result set regardless of whether they have associated employees. This approach allows us to get a complete list of departments and any employees they might have, even if some departments are currently empty.

Cross Join Examples

To categorize customer spending according to a Discount Chart, which includes three types of discounts, an organization requires a report projecting the customer's order-wise discounts. This task can be efficiently accomplished using a cross join. The report should display the following columns:

- OrderNo
- CustomerNo
- OrderAmount
- Discounted Cost

Solution:

```
SELECT OrderNo, CustomerNo, OrderAmount, Discount,
  (OrderAmount - OrderAmount * Discount / 100) AS "Discounted Cost" FROM Orders
      CROSS JOIN Discounts;
```

Output:

```
ORDERNO  CUSTOMERNO ORDERAMOUNT DISCOUNT Discounted Cost
-------- ---------- ----------- -------- ---------------
1        21         69350.0     5        65882.5
2        22         5750.0      5        5462.5
3        21         14750.0     5        14012.5
4        23         28400.0     5        26980.0
5        24         66350.0     5        63032.5
8        25         Infinity    5        NaN
6        25         15000.0     5        14250.0
7        25         NaN         5        NaN
1        21         69350.0     10       62415.0
2        22         5750.0      10       5175.0
3        21         14750.0     10       13275.0
4        23         28400.0     10       25560.0
5        24         66350.0     10       59715.0
8        25         Infinity    10       NaN
6        25         15000.0     10       13500.0
7        25         NaN         10       NaN
1        21         69350.0     15       58947.5
2        22         5750.0      15       4887.5
3        21         14750.0     15       12537.5
4        23         28400.0     15       24140.0
5        24         66350.0     15       56397.5
8        25         Infinity    15       NaN
6        25         15000.0     15       12750.0
7        25         NaN         15       NaN

24 rows selected.
```

In this scenario, the Orders table contains details of individual orders placed by customers, the Discounts table includes three discount percentages: 5%, 10% and 15%. Each discount is applied to every customer's order amount.

The report will compute the discounted amount as follows:

For each order amount in the Orders table

For each discount available in the Discounts table

A Cross Join is used to achieve this as it combines each record from the left table (Orders) with every record from the right table (Discounts). In this example, the cross join merges each order amount from the Orders table with each discount record in the Discounts table.

For Oracle versions **prior to 9i** that do not support an explicit cross join, the same result can be obtained using the following statement:

```
SELECT OrderNo, CustomerNo, OrderAmount, Discount,
  (OrderAmount - OrderAmount * Discount / 100) AS "Discounted Cost"
     FROM Orders, Discounts;
```

Self Join Examples

Display all employees along with the Managers to whom they report to:

```
SELECT E.EmployeeNo AS "Employee Code", E.FirstName || ' ' || E.LastName
  AS "Employee", M.EmployeeNo AS "Manager Code", M.FirstName || ' ' ||
  M.LastName AS "Reports To" FROM Employees E, Employees M
     WHERE E.ManagerNo = M.EmployeeNo;
```

Output:

```
Employee Code Employee             Manager Code Reports To
------------- -------------------- ------------ ----------------
11            Amit Paul            1            Sharanam Shah
10            Chaitanya Kapoor     1            Sharanam Shah
9             Anil Mayekar         1            Sharanam Shah
7             Narendra Dodhia      2            Vaishali Shah
5             Abhishek Benegal     3            Keyur Kapoor
6             Chetan Dedhia        4            Amit Haria
4             Amit Haria           7            Narendra Dodhia
3             Keyur Kapoor         8            Meenal Doshi
8             Meenal Doshi         9            Anil Mayekar
2             Vaishali Shah        10           Chaitanya Kapoor

10 rows selected.
```

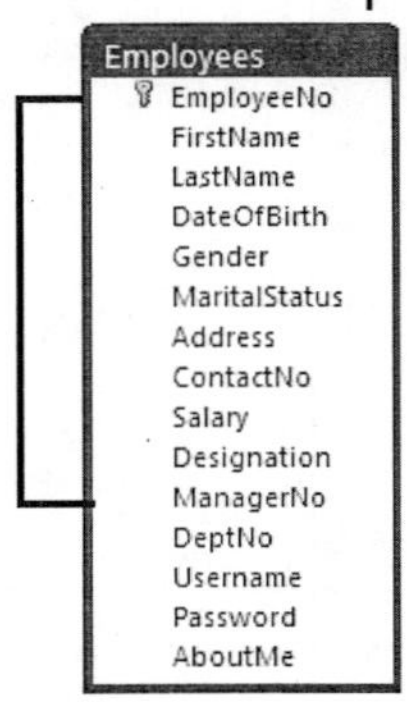

In this scenario, the **Employees** table is treated as two separate tables, **E** and **M**. The Employees table contains employee numbers, their names, and the manager numbers to whom they report. A manager number is a foreign key in the Employees table that refers to the EmployeeNo column, which is the primary key in the same table. Every manager is also an employee in this table.

Currently the Employees table contains the following data:

```
EMPLOYEENO FIRSTNAME    LASTNAME         MANAGERNO
---------- ------------ -------------- ----------
         1 Sharanam     Shah
         2 Vaishali     Shah                   10
         3 Keyur        Kapoor                  8
         4 Amit         Haria                   7
         5 Abhishek     Benegal                 3
         6 Chetan       Dedhia                  4
         7 Narendra     Dodhia                  2
         8 Meenal       Doshi                   9
         9 Anil         Mayekar                 1
        10 Chaitanya    Kapoor                  1
        11 Amit         Paul                    1
```

In the above data, for example, the employee named **Chaitanya**, identified by employee number **10**, reports to a manager (who is also an employee) named **Sharanam**, with employee number **1**. Similarly, employees numbered **6**, **7**, **8**, **9**, and **3** report to managers numbered **4**, **2**, **9**, **1**, and **8**, respectively.

From the data available in the Employees table, it is possible to extract the manager number to whom the employee reports. However, the requirement is to display the Employee Name and the Manager Name, **not just the Manager Number**. To extract the manager's name (who is also an employee), a reference to the same table must be made using a Self Join.

To retrieve the required data, both copies of the same tables must be linked based on the following common column:

- **E.**ManagerNo = **M.**EmployeeNo

Let's take another example. Display all the customers who reside in same city:

```
SELECT DISTINCT A.CustomerName AS "Customer 1", B.CustomerName
  AS "Customer 2", A.City FROM Customers A, Customers B
     WHERE A.City = B.City AND A.CustomerNo <> B.CustomerNo
        ORDER BY A.City;
```

Output:

```
Customer 1                Customer 2                CITY
------------------------- ------------------------- -----------
Vaishali Sharanam Shah    Sharanam Chaitanya Shah   Mumbai
Sharanam Chaitanya Shah   Vaishali Sharanam Shah    Mumbai
```

There can be more than one customer who stays in the same city. Since "city" is also a column in the same table, to compare a customer's record with another customer's record, a copy of the same table is created. The **Customers** table is treated as two separate tables: **A** and **B**. The Customers table holds customer names and the city.

To retrieve the required data, both copies of the same tables must be linked on the basis of common columns as:

- **A.**City = **B.**City

The most standard way of writing this query would be:

```
SELECT DISTINCT A.CustomerName AS "Customer 1",
  B.CustomerName AS "Customer 2", A.City FROM Customers A, Customers B
    WHERE A.City = B.City ORDER BY A.City;
```

However, this query when executed will return incorrect results:

```
Customer 1                Customer 2                CITY
------------------------- ------------------------- -----------
Hansel                    Hansel                    Bangalore
Manali Narendra Naik      Manali Narendra Naik      Hyderabad
Deepika Anil Bakshi       Deepika Anil Bakshi       Indore
Chaitanya Kantilal Shah   Chaitanya Kantilal Shah   Kottayam
Prakash K Chouduary       Prakash K Chouduary       Ludhania
Shravan Ashwin Benegal    Shravan Ashwin Benegal    Mount Abu
Sharanam Chaitanya Shah   Sharanam Chaitanya Shah   Mumbai
Vaishali Sharanam Shah    Sharanam Chaitanya Shah   Mumbai
Sharanam Chaitanya Shah   Vaishali Sharanam Shah    Mumbai
Vaishali Sharanam Shah    Vaishali Sharanam Shah    Mumbai
Stuti Kapil Khanna        Stuti Kapil Khanna        Patna
Anil Mayekar              Anil Mayekar              Pune

12 rows selected.
```

Here, a customer is compared to the same customer, and hence the output includes unnecessary rows, which could have been eliminated.

To eliminate comparison of a customer from the first table with the same customer of the second table (copy) a <> operator is used:

```
  AND A.CustomerNo <> B.CustomerNo
```

This ensures that a customer identified by a Customer number will not be considered when being compared with other customers having the same Customer number.

Non-Equi Join Examples

The SpendingCategory table holds categories along with the minimum and maximum amounts for each category. The goal is to display the spending category against every product ordered by a customer:

```
SELECT CustomerName, Category, Cost FROM OrderDetails, SpendingCategory
  WHERE Cost BETWEEN MinAmount AND MaxAmount
    ORDER BY CustomerName, Cost DESC;
```

Output:

```
CUSTOMERNAME              CATEGORY                        COST
------------------------- ------------------------- ----------
Anil Mayekar              Spent A Lot                    15000
Anil Mayekar              Spent A Lot                    12000
Anil Mayekar              Optimistically spent             700
Anil Mayekar              Optimistically spent             700
Chaitanya Kantilal Shah   Spent A Lot                    15000
Hansel                    Spent A Lot                    12000
Hansel                    Spent A Lot                     4000
Hansel                    Hardly Spent                     350
Sharanam Chaitanya Shah   Spent A Lot                    15000
Sharanam Chaitanya Shah   Spent A Lot                    13000
Sharanam Chaitanya Shah   Spent A Lot                     4000
Sharanam Chaitanya Shah   Optimistically spent             700
Sharanam Chaitanya Shah   Optimistically spent             700
Sharanam Chaitanya Shah   Hardly Spent                     350
Sharanam Chaitanya Shah   Hardly Spent                     350
Vaishali Sharanam Shah    Spent A Lot                     4000
Vaishali Sharanam Shah    Optimistically spent             700
Vaishali Sharanam Shah    Optimistically spent             700
Vaishali Sharanam Shah    Hardly Spent                     350

19 rows selected.
```

Here, a Non-Equi Join is used. The BETWEEN operator returns true if the customer's spending is between the minimum and maximum amounts for that category. For all the records where the operator returns True, the current category is the customer's spending category.

Chapter

19

SECTION III: WORKING WITH DATA

Union, Intersect And Minus

Union Clause

Sometimes, applications might require data to be picked up from more than one table. For example, sales for the year 2007 are stored in a table named OrderDetails2007, and sales for the year 2008 are stored in a table named OrderDetails2008. Both tables are identical in structure, but the data they hold differs.

There are also situations where data held in both tables might be the same to some extent. For example, a table named Customers holds customer details, and a table named Employees holds employee details.

An employee can also buy products and thus be a customer to the same organization. Since an employee has bought a product, both tables will hold that employee's details - Employees table will hold them as an employee and Customers table will hold them as a customer.

To generate a report that lists all employees as well as customers, two queries will be fired, and their results will be combined using the **UNION clause**. UNION allows putting together multiple queries and combines the output generated by those queries. The UNION clause merges the output of two or more queries into a single set of rows and columns.

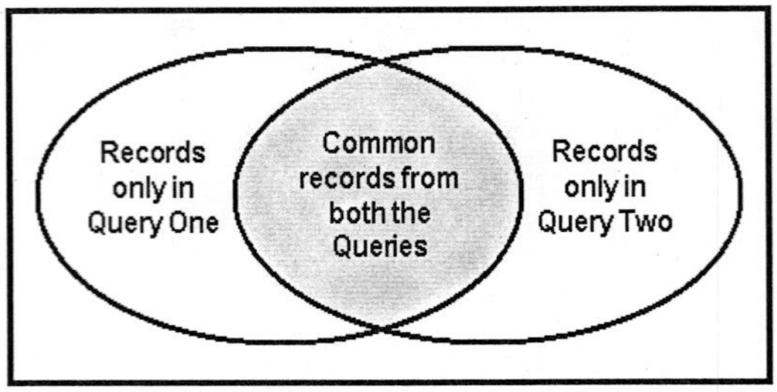

UNION Clause Output: Records from query one **+** Records from query two **+** A single set of records common to both queries.

Syntax:

```
SELECT <Column1>, ... <ColumnN> FROM <DerivedTable>
UNION [ALL]
SELECT <Column1>, ... <ColumnN> FROM <DerivedTable>
```

TIP The **ALL** keyword along with the UNION operator includes duplicate rows in the combined result set.

Each SQL statement within the Union query must have the same number of columns in the result set with similar data types. However,

- The names of the columns need not be identical.
- The width of columns can be different.

The UNION Clause applies to every column specified in the SELECT query. It displays only distinct values (similar to SELECT DISTINCT) and **NULL** values are **not ignored** during duplicate checking.

In a UNION query:

- Only aliases of the columns of the first query are considered.
- The ORDER BY clause is the last clause after the last query.
- Subqueries cannot be used.
- Aggregate functions cannot be used.

Display the following details for all the employees and customers of the organization:

- Name (FirstName LastName)
- DateOfBirth
- Address
- ContactNo

Solution:

```
SELECT CustomerName AS "Customers and Employees", DateOfBirth, Address,
  ContactNo  FROM Customers
```

```
UNION
SELECT FirstName || ' ' || LastName, DateOfBirth, Address, ContactNo
  FROM Employees;
```

In this example, both tables have different number of columns. However, the required columns in the output are same, hence UNION can be applied. Notice the following issue:

- The Customers table holds Customer names as a single column (CustomerName).
- The Employees table holds Employee names as two different columns (FirstName and LastName).

The UNION clause will not accept this as the number of columns in the SELECT query differs. To resolve this issue, the FirstName and LastName columns of the Employees table are concatenated with a space between the first and the last name:

```
FirstName || ' ' || LastName
```

Execution of the first query:

```
SELECT CustomerName AS "Customers and Employees", DateOfBirth, Address,
  ContactNo FROM Customers;
```

Output of the first query:

```
Customers and Employees DATEOFBIRTH ADDRESS                                        CONTACTNO
----------------------- ----------- ---------------------------------------------- ---------------
Sharanam Chaitanya Shah 03-JAN-81   20, Makanji Mansion, MG Road, 400076           91-022-24440094
Vaishali Sharanam Shah  22-NOV-81   Krishna Kunj, Thakur Lane, 400078              91-022-27740094
Anil Mayekar            22-NOV-56   Advani Apts, Mumbai, 665534256
Hansel                  29-OCT-90   Jay Chambers,  7 Juhu, 774463524               91-022-34340094
Chaitanya Kantilal Shah 03-JAN-81   14, Raheja Tower, 347236                       91-022-37640094
Shravan Ashwin Benegal  22-SEP-79   3, Shankar Bldg,  Mahim                        91-022-40940094
Prakash K Chouduary     07-JUL-90   1st Floor, Kapod Nivas, Mulund                 91-022-47540094
Stuti Kapil Khanna      05-JUN-67   3, Godrej Villa, Powai                         91-022-54140094
Deepika Anil Bakshi     30-JAN-81   Queensland Palace,  India                      91-022-57440094
Manali Narendra Naik    22-JAN-81   Hiranadani Mansion,              Lion Road     91-022-60740094
Amit Paul               22-NOV-56   Advani Apts, Mumbai

11 rows selected.
```

Execution of the second query:

```
SELECT FirstName || ' ' || LastName, DateOfBirth, Address, ContactNo
  FROM Employees;
```

Output of the second query:

```
FIRSTNAME||''||LASTNAME DATEOFBIRTH ADDRESS                  CONTACTNO
----------------------- ----------- ------------------------ ---------------
Sharanam Shah           03-JAN-81   Makanji Mansion          91-022-24440094
Vaishali Shah           09-FEB-81   Makanji Mansion, Mumbai  91-022-31040094
Keyur Kapoor            14-OCT-84   Sita Sadan, Delhi        91-022-27740094
Amit Haria              11-NOV-72   Krishna Kunj, Mumbai     91-022-34340094
Abhishek Benegal        28-FEB-59   Thakur Complex, Mumbai   91-022-37640094
Chetan Dedhia           20-SEP-65   Upendra Nagar, Mumbai    91-022-40940094
Narendra Dodhia         23-JUN-80   Gokul Vihar, Mumbai      91-022-44240094
Meenal Doshi            12-DEC-87   Prakash Towers, Mumbai   91-022-47540094
```

```
Anil Mayekar              22-NOV-56   Advani Apts, Mumbai
Chaitanya Kapoor          04-APR-62   Tilak Nagar, Mumbai     91-022-54140094
Amit Paul                 22-NOV-56   Advani Apts, Mumbai

11 rows selected.
```

The **UNION** clause combines the **common records** as well as the individual records from both queries:

```
Customers and Employees  DATEOFBIRTH ADDRESS                                  CONTACTNO
------------------------ ----------- ---------------------------------------- ---------------
Abhishek Benegal         28-FEB-59   Thakur Complex, Mumbai                   91-022-37640094
Amit Haria               11-NOV-72   Krishna Kunj, Mumbai                     91-022-34340094
Amit Paul                22-NOV-56   Advani Apts, Mumbai
Anil Mayekar             22-NOV-56   Advani Apts, Mumbai
Anil Mayekar             22-NOV-56   Advani Apts, Mumbai, 665534256
Chaitanya Kantilal Shah  03-JAN-81   14, Raheja Tower, 347236                 91-022-37640094
Chaitanya Kapoor         04-APR-62   Tilak Nagar, Mumbai                      91-022-54140094
Chetan Dedhia            20-SEP-65   Upendra Nagar, Mumbai                    91-022-40940094
Deepika Anil Bakshi      30-JAN-81   Queensland Palace,  India                91-022-57440094
Hansel                   29-OCT-90   Jay Chambers,  7 Juhu, 774463524         91-022-34340094
Keyur Kapoor             14-OCT-84   Sita Sadan, Delhi                        91-022-27740094
Manali Narendra Naik     22-JAN-81   Hiranadani Mansion,            Lion Road 91-022-60740094
Meenal Doshi             12-DEC-87   Prakash Towers, Mumbai                   91-022-47540094
Narendra Dodhia          23-JUN-80   Gokul Vihar, Mumbai                      91-022-44240094
Prakash K Chouduary      07-JUL-90   1st Floor, Kapod Nivas, Mulund           91-022-47540094
Sharanam Chaitanya Shah  03-JAN-81   20, Makanji Mansion, MG Road, 400076     91-022-24440094
Sharanam Shah            03-JAN-81   Makanji Mansion                          91-022-24440094
Shravan Ashwin Benegal   22-SEP-79   3, Shankar Bldg,  Mahim                  91-022-40940094
Stuti Kapil Khanna       05-JUN-67   3, Godrej Villa, Powai                   91-022-54140094
Vaishali Shah            09-FEB-81   Makanji Mansion, Mumbai                  91-022-31040094
Vaishali Sharanam Shah   22-NOV-81   Krishna Kunj, Thakur Lane, 400078        91-022-27740094

21 rows selected.
```

By default, the output is sorted in ascending order of the first column of the **SELECT** clause.

Only the alias that is assigned to the first query will be applied in the final output irrespective of the alias assigned to the second query.

When using UNION ALL instead of UNION, all records from both queries are included, even duplicates:

```
SELECT CustomerName AS "Customers and Employees", DateOfBirth, Address,
  ContactNo  FROM Customers
UNION ALL
SELECT FirstName || ' ' || LastName, DateOfBirth, Address, ContactNo
  FROM Employees;
```

Output:

```
Customers and Employees  DATEOFBIRTH ADDRESS                                  CONTACTNO
------------------------ ----------- ---------------------------------------- ---------------
Sharanam Chaitanya Shah  03-JAN-81   20, Makanji Mansion, MG Road, 400076     91-022-24440094
Vaishali Sharanam Shah   22-NOV-81   Krishna Kunj, Thakur Lane, 400078        91-022-27740094
Anil Mayekar             22-NOV-56   Advani Apts, Mumbai, 665534256
Hansel                   29-OCT-90   Jay Chambers,  7 Juhu, 774463524         91-022-34340094
```

```
Chaitanya Kantilal Shah  03-JAN-81  14, Raheja Tower, 347236                         91-022-37640094
Shravan Ashwin Benegal   22-SEP-79  3, Shankar Bldg,  Mahim                          91-022-40940094
Prakash K Chouduary      07-JUL-90  1st Floor, Kapod Nivas, Mulund                   91-022-47540094
Stuti Kapil Khanna       05-JUN-67  3, Godrej Villa, Powai                           91-022-54140094
Deepika Anil Bakshi      30-JAN-81  Queensland Palace,  India                        91-022-57440094
Manali Narendra Naik     22-JAN-81  Hiranadani Mansion,               Lion Road      91-022-60740094
Amit Paul                22-NOV-56  Advani Apts, Mumbai
Sharanam Shah            03-JAN-81  Makanji Mansion                                  91-022-24440094
Vaishali Shah            09-FEB-81  Makanji Mansion, Mumbai                          91-022-31040094
Keyur Kapoor             14-OCT-84  Sita Sadan, Delhi                                91-022-27740094
Amit Haria               11-NOV-72  Krishna Kunj, Mumbai                             91-022-34340094
Abhishek Benegal         28-FEB-59  Thakur Complex, Mumbai                           91-022-37640094
Chetan Dedhia            20-SEP-65  Upendra Nagar, Mumbai                            91-022-40940094
Narendra Dodhia          23-JUN-80  Gokul Vihar, Mumbai                              91-022-44240094
Meenal Doshi             12-DEC-87  Prakash Towers, Mumbai                           91-022-47540094
Anil Mayekar             22-NOV-56  Advani Apts, Mumbai
Chaitanya Kapoor         04-APR-62  Tilak Nagar, Mumbai                              91-022-54140094
Amit Paul                22-NOV-56  Advani Apts, Mumbai

22 rows selected.
```

The UNION ALL operator picks up **all records**, including duplicates, from both queries. This means that if an individual appears in both the Customers and Employees tables, they will appear multiple times in the output.

In contrast, the UNION operator combines the results and eliminates duplicates, displaying only distinct rows.

Intersect Clause

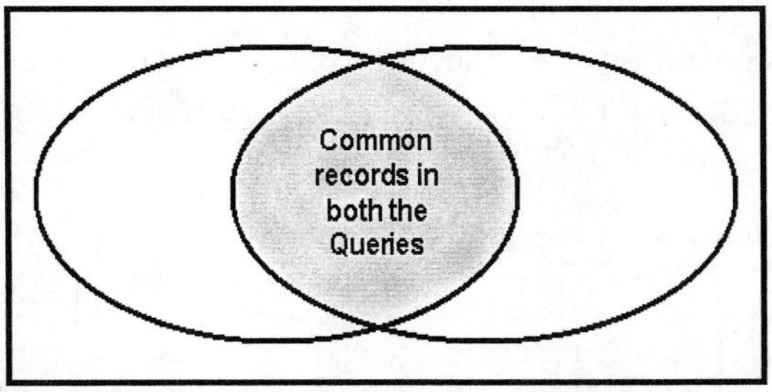

Multiple queries can be combined using the INTERSECT Clause. The **INTERSECT clause** outputs only rows that are common to **both** queries meaning it includes only those rows retrieved by both queries:

```
SELECT <Column1>, ... <ColumnN> FROM <DerivedTable>
INTERSECT
SELECT <Column1>, ... <ColumnN> FROM <DerivedTable>
```

The output of both the queries will be as displayed above. The final output of the Intersect clause will be: **Output =** A single set of records which are common in both queries.

Display the following details of all those employees who are also customers of the organization:

- Name (FirstName LastName)
- DateOfBirth
- Address
- ContactNo

Solution:

```
SELECT CustomerName AS "Customers and Employees", DateOfBirth, Address,
```

```
  ContactNo FROM Customers
INTERSECT
SELECT FirstName || ' ' || LastName, DateOfBirth, Address, ContactNo
  FROM Employees;
```

Execution of the first query: Retrieves data from the Customers table:

```
SELECT CustomerName AS "Customers and Employees", DateOfBirth, Address,
  ContactNo FROM Customers;
```

Output of the first query:

```
Customers and Employees DATEOFBIRTH ADDRESS                                   CONTACTNO
----------------------- ----------- ----------------------------------------- --------------
Sharanam Chaitanya Shah 03-JAN-81   20, Makanji Mansion, MG Road, 400076      91-022-24440094
Vaishali Sharanam Shah  22-NOV-81   Krishna Kunj, Thakur Lane, 400078         91-022-27740094
Anil Mayekar            22-NOV-56   Advani Apts, Mumbai, 665534256
Hansel                  29-OCT-90   Jay Chambers,  7 Juhu, 774463524          91-022-34340094
Chaitanya Kantilal Shah 03-JAN-81   14, Raheja Tower, 347236                  91-022-37640094
Shravan Ashwin Benegal  22-SEP-79   3, Shankar Bldg,  Mahim                   91-022-40940094
Prakash K Chouduary     07-JUL-90   1st Floor, Kapod Nivas, Mulund            91-022-47540094
Stuti Kapil Khanna      05-JUN-67   3, Godrej Villa, Powai                    91-022-54140094
Deepika Anil Bakshi     30-JAN-81   Queensland Palace,  India                 91-022-57440094
Manali Narendra Naik    22-JAN-81   Hiranadani Mansion,             Lion Road 91-022-60740094
Amit Paul               22-NOV-56   Advani Apts, Mumbai

11 rows selected.
```

Execution of the second query: Retrieves data from the Employees table:

```
SELECT FirstName || ' ' || LastName, DateOfBirth, Address, ContactNo
  FROM Employees;
```

Output of the second query:

```
FIRSTNAME||''||LASTNAME DATEOFBIRTH ADDRESS                 CONTACTNO
----------------------- ----------- ----------------------- ---------------
Sharanam Shah           03-JAN-81   Makanji Mansion         91-022-24440094
Vaishali Shah           09-FEB-81   Makanji Mansion, Mumbai 91-022-31040094
Keyur Kapoor            14-OCT-84   Sita Sadan, Delhi       91-022-27740094
Amit Haria              11-NOV-72   Krishna Kunj, Mumbai    91-022-34340094
Abhishek Benegal        28-FEB-59   Thakur Complex, Mumbai  91-022-37640094
Chetan Dedhia           20-SEP-65   Upendra Nagar, Mumbai   91-022-40940094
Narendra Dodhia         23-JUN-80   Gokul Vihar, Mumbai     91-022-44240094
Meenal Doshi            12-DEC-87   Prakash Towers, Mumbai  91-022-47540094
Anil Mayekar            22-NOV-56   Advani Apts, Mumbai
Chaitanya Kapoor        04-APR-62   Tilak Nagar, Mumbai     91-022-54140094
Amit Paul               22-NOV-56   Advani Apts, Mumbai

11 rows selected.
```

The **INTERSECT** clause picks up records that are common in both queries:

```
Customers and Employees DATEOFBIRTH ADDRESS             CONTACTNO
----------------------- ----------- ------------------- --------------------
Amit Paul               22-NOV-56   Advani Apts, Mumbai
```

Minus Clause

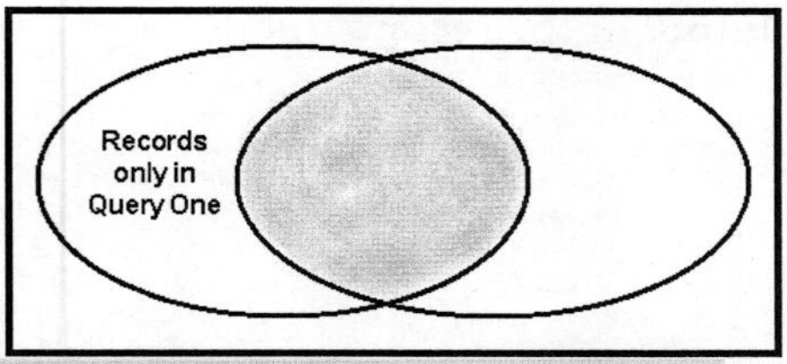

Multiple queries can be combined using the MINUS Clause. The **MINUS clause** outputs the rows produced by the first query after **removing** the rows retrieved by the second query:

```
SELECT <Column1>, ... <ColumnN> FROM <DerivedTable>
MINUS
SELECT <Column1>, ... <ColumnN> FROM <DerivedTable>
```

The final output of the MINUS clause will be:
Output = Records only in query one.

Display the following details of all those employees who are not customers to the organization:

- Name (FirstName LastName)
- DateOfBirth
- Address
- ContactNo

Solution:

```
SELECT FirstName || ' ' || LastName AS "Customers and Employees", DateOfBirth,
   Address, ContactNo FROM Employees
MINUS
SELECT CustomerName, DateOfBirth, Address, ContactNo FROM Customers;
```

Execution of the first query: Retrieves data from the Employees table:

```
SELECT FirstName || ' ' || LastName AS "Customers and Employees", DateOfBirth,
   Address, ContactNo FROM Employees;
```

Output of the first query:

```
Customers and Employees DATEOFBIRTH ADDRESS                  CONTACTNO
----------------------- ----------- ------------------------ ---------------
Sharanam Shah           03-JAN-81   Makanji Mansion          91-022-24440094
Vaishali Shah           09-FEB-81   Makanji Mansion, Mumbai  91-022-31040094
Keyur Kapoor            14-OCT-84   Sita Sadan, Delhi        91-022-27740094
Amit Haria              11-NOV-72   Krishna Kunj, Mumbai     91-022-34340094
Abhishek Benegal        28-FEB-59   Thakur Complex, Mumbai   91-022-37640094
Chetan Dedhia           20-SEP-65   Upendra Nagar, Mumbai    91-022-40940094
Narendra Dodhia         23-JUN-80   Gokul Vihar, Mumbai      91-022-44240094
Meenal Doshi            12-DEC-87   Prakash Towers, Mumbai   91-022-47540094
Anil Mayekar            22-NOV-56   Advani Apts, Mumbai
Chaitanya Kapoor        04-APR-62   Tilak Nagar, Mumbai      91-022-54140094
Amit Paul               22-NOV-56   Advani Apts, Mumbai

11 rows selected.
```

Execution of the second query: Retrieves data from the Customers table:

```
SELECT CustomerName, DateOfBirth, Address, ContactNo FROM Customers;
```

Output of the second query:

```
CUSTOMERNAME           DATEOFBIRTH ADDRESS                                    CONTACTNO
---------------------- ----------- ------------------------------------------ ---------------

Sharanam Chaitanya Shah 03-JAN-81  20, Makanji Mansion, MG Road, 400076       91-022-24440094
Vaishali Sharanam Shah  22-NOV-81  Krishna Kunj, Thakur Lane, 400078          91-022-27740094
Anil Mayekar            22-NOV-56  Advani Apts, Mumbai, 665534256
Hansel                  29-OCT-90  Jay Chambers,  7 Juhu, 774463524           91-022-34340094
Chaitanya Kantilal Shah 03-JAN-81  14, Raheja Tower, 347236                   91-022-37640094
Shravan Ashwin Benegal  22-SEP-79  3, Shankar Bldg,  Mahim                    91-022-40940094
Prakash K Chouduary     07-JUL-90  1st Floor, Kapod Nivas, Mulund              91-022-47540094
Stuti Kapil Khanna      05-JUN-67  3, Godrej Villa, Powai                     91-022-54140094
Deepika Anil Bakshi     30-JAN-81  Queensland Palace,  India                  91-022-57440094
Manali Narendra Naik    22-JAN-81  Hiranadani Mansion,              Lion Road 91-022-60740094
Amit Paul               22-NOV-56  Advani Apts, Mumbai

11 rows selected.
```

The **MINUS** clause picks up records in the first query after filtering out the records retrieved by the second query:

```
Customers and Employees DATEOFBIRTH ADDRESS                   CONTACTNO
----------------------- ----------- ------------------------- ---------------

Abhishek Benegal        28-FEB-59   Thakur Complex, Mumbai    91-022-37640094
Amit Haria              11-NOV-72   Krishna Kunj, Mumbai      91-022-34340094
Anil Mayekar            22-NOV-56   Advani Apts, Mumbai
Chaitanya Kapoor        04-APR-62   Tilak Nagar, Mumbai       91-022-54140094
Chetan Dedhia           20-SEP-65   Upendra Nagar, Mumbai     91-022-40940094
Keyur Kapoor            14-OCT-84   Sita Sadan, Delhi         91-022-27740094
Meenal Doshi            12-DEC-87   Prakash Towers, Mumbai    91-022-47540094
Narendra Dodhia         23-JUN-80   Gokul Vihar, Mumbai       91-022-44240094
Sharanam Shah           03-JAN-81   Makanji Mansion           91-022-24440094
Vaishali Shah           09-FEB-81   Makanji Mansion, Mumbai   91-022-31040094

10 rows selected.
```

Combining Union, Intersect, Minus

More than two queries can be combined using multiple set operators, with the results returned from one operator feeding into the next operator. Set operators are evaluated from top to bottom. The order can be enforced using parentheses.

Display the following details of all the employees and customers to the organization **excluding the old ones:**

- Name (FirstName LastName)
- DateOfBirth
- Address
- ContactNo

Solution:

```
(SELECT FirstName || ' ' || LastName AS "Customers and Employees", DateOfBirth,
   Address, ContactNo FROM Employees
UNION SELECT CustomerName, DateOfBirth, Address, ContactNo FROM Customers)
MINUS
(SELECT FirstName || ' ' || LastName, DateOfBirth, Address, ContactNo
```

```
  FROM OldEmployees UNION
SELECT CustomerName, DateOfBirth, Address, ContactNo FROM OldCustomers);
```

First Record Set:

- Employees table holds existing as well as a few old employees.
- Customers table holds existing as well as a few old customers.
- OldEmployees table holds only old employees.
- OldCustomers table holds only old customers.

The UNION operator is used to combine the results from the Employees and Customers tables. Hence only the non-duplicate records are retrieved by these queries.

Output of first record set:

```
Customers and Employees DATEOFBIRTH ADDRESS                                   CONTACTNO
----------------------- ----------- ----------------------------------------- ---------------
Abhishek Benegal        28-FEB-59   Thakur Complex, Mumbai                    91-022-37640094
Amit Haria              11-NOV-72   Krishna Kunj, Mumbai                      91-022-34340094
Amit Paul               22-NOV-56   Advani Apts, Mumbai
Anil Mayekar            22-NOV-56   Advani Apts, Mumbai
Anil Mayekar            22-NOV-56   Advani Apts, Mumbai, 665534256
Chaitanya Kantilal Shah 03-JAN-81   14, Raheja Tower, 347236                  91-022-37640094
Chaitanya Kapoor        04-APR-62   Tilak Nagar, Mumbai                       91-022-54140094
Chetan Dedhia           20-SEP-65   Upendra Nagar, Mumbai                     91-022-40940094
Deepika Anil Bakshi     30-JAN-81   Queensland Palace,  India                 91-022-57440094
Hansel                  29-OCT-90   Jay Chambers,  7 Juhu, 774463524          91-022-34340094
Keyur Kapoor            14-OCT-84   Sita Sadan, Delhi                         91-022-27740094
Manali Narendra Naik    22-JAN-81   Hiranadani Mansion,             Lion Road 91-022-60740094
Meenal Doshi            12-DEC-87   Prakash Towers, Mumbai                    91-022-47540094
Narendra Dodhia         23-JUN-80   Gokul Vihar, Mumbai                       91-022-44240094
Prakash K Chouduary     07-JUL-90   1st Floor, Kapod Nivas, Mulund            91-022-47540094
Sharanam Chaitanya Shah 03-JAN-81   20, Makanji Mansion, MG Road, 400076      91-022-24440094
Sharanam Shah           03-JAN-81   Makanji Mansion                           91-022-24440094
Shravan Ashwin Benegal  22-SEP-79   3, Shankar Bldg,  Mahim                   91-022-40940094
Stuti Kapil Khanna      05-JUN-67   3, Godrej Villa, Powai                    91-022-54140094
Vaishali Shah           09-FEB-81   Makanji Mansion, Mumbai                   91-022-31040094
Vaishali Sharanam Shah  22-NOV-81   Krishna Kunj, Thakur Lane, 400078         91-022-27740094

21 rows selected.
```

This result is combined [using MINUS operator] with:

Second Record Set:

The records returned by combining the results from the OldEmployees and OldCustomers tables using the UNION operator. Hence only the non-duplicate records are retrieved by these queries.

Output of the second record set:

```
FIRSTNAME||''||LASTNAME  DATEOFBIRTH ADDRESS                                   CONTACTNO
------------------------ ----------- ----------------------------------------- ---------------
Amit Haria               11-NOV-72   Krishna Kunj, Mumbai                      91-022-34340094
Anil Mayekar             22-NOV-56   Advani Apts, Mumbai
Ashwin Dedhia            20-SEP-65   Upendra Nagar, Mumbai                     91-022-40940094
Gopi Kapoor              04-APR-62   Tilak Nagar, Mumbai                       91-022-54140094
Hansel                   29-OCT-90   Jay Chambers,  7 Juhu                     91-022-34340094
Hitesh                   30-JAN-81   Queensland Palace,  India                 91-022-57440094
Kantilal Shah            03-JAN-81   14, Raheja Tower, 347236                  91-022-37640094
Katrina Mayekar          22-NOV-56   Advani Apts, Mumbai
```

```
Keyur Kapoor              14-OCT-84   Sita Sadan, Delhi                                91-022-27740094
Kirti Benegal             28-FEB-59   Thakur Complex, Mumbai                           91-022-37640094
Madhuri Doshi             12-DEC-87   Prakash Towers, Mumbai                           91-022-47540094
Manali Dodhia             23-JUN-80   Gokul Vihar, Mumbai                              91-022-44240094
Parul                     05-JUN-67   3, Godrej Villa, Powai                           91-022-54140094
Raghu Bhatt               07-JUL-90   1st Floor, Kapod Nivas, Mulund                   91-022-47540094
Ramdass                   22-SEP-79   3, Shankar Bldg,  Mahim                          91-022-40940094
Ravi Sejpal               22-JAN-81   Hiranadani Mansion,              Lion Road       91-022-60740094
Sharanam Chaitanya Shah   03-JAN-81   20, Makanji Mansion, MG Road, 400076             91-022-24440094
Sharanam Shah             03-JAN-81   Makanji Mansion                                  91-022-24440094
Vaishali Shah             09-FEB-81   Makanji Mansion, Mumbai                          91-022-31040094
Vaishali Sharanam Shah    22-NOV-81   Krishna Kunj, Thakur Lane, 400078                91-022-27740094

20 rows selected.
```

Using the MINUS clause, the **first record set** is picked up after filtering out the records retrieved by the **Second Record Set**. Parentheses are used to distinguish between the first and the second record sets.

Final Output:

```
Customers and Employees   DATEOFBIRTH  ADDRESS                                          CONTACTNO
------------------------  -----------  -----------------------------------------------  ---------------
Abhishek Benegal          28-FEB-59    Thakur Complex, Mumbai                           91-022-37640094
Amit Paul                 22-NOV-56    Advani Apts, Mumbai
Anil Mayekar              22-NOV-56    Advani Apts, Mumbai, 665534256
Chaitanya Kantilal Shah   03-JAN-81    14, Raheja Tower, 347236                         91-022-37640094
Chaitanya Kapoor          04-APR-62    Tilak Nagar, Mumbai                              91-022-54140094
Chetan Dedhia             20-SEP-65    Upendra Nagar, Mumbai                            91-022-40940094
Deepika Anil Bakshi       30-JAN-81    Queensland Palace,  India                        91-022-57440094
Hansel                    29-OCT-90    Jay Chambers,  7 Juhu, 774463524                 91-022-34340094
Manali Narendra Naik      22-JAN-81    Hiranadani Mansion,              Lion Road       91-022-60740094
Meenal Doshi              12-DEC-87    Prakash Towers, Mumbai                           91-022-47540094
Narendra Dodhia           23-JUN-80    Gokul Vihar, Mumbai                              91-022-44240094
Prakash K Chouduary       07-JUL-90    1st Floor, Kapod Nivas, Mulund                   91-022-47540094
Shravan Ashwin Benegal    22-SEP-79    3, Shankar Bldg,  Mahim                          91-022-40940094
Stuti Kapil Khanna        05-JUN-67    3, Godrej Villa, Powai                           91-022-54140094

14 rows selected.
```

Chapter 20

SECTION III: WORKING WITH DATA

Regular Expressions

Regular expressions have been around since the time of Perl or UNIX shell scripting. A regular expression is a template against which strings are compared to determine if they fit the template. Oracle Database (10g onwards) supports regular expressions, which can be used in both SQL and PL/SQL. Regular expressions enable powerful search and manipulation operations on the available data.

TIP: Regular expressions in Oracle comply with the **P**ortable **O**perating **S**ystem for UNI**X** (POSIX) standard, which is controlled by the **I**nstitute of **E**lectrical and **E**lectronics **E**ngineers (IEEE) for ASCII data matching semantics and syntax. Oracle's multi-lingual capabilities extend the matching capabilities of the operators **beyond** the POSIX standard.

Why Use Regular Expressions?

The LIKE operator in Oracle is the nearest match to regular expressions for pattern matching. However, for complex pattern matching, regular expressions provide a more efficient and concise solution compared to the LIKE operator.

To search for all customers whose name holds the string "Shah":

```
SELECT CustomerNo, CustomerName, Address, City, State FROM Customers
  WHERE CustomerName LIKE '%Shah%';
```

Using the **REGEXP_LIKE function**, the same result can be achieved:

```
SELECT CustomerNo, CustomerName, Address, City, State FROM Customers
  WHERE REGEXP_LIKE (CustomerName, '\Shah\');
```

Output:

```
CUSTOMERNO CUSTOMERNAME            ADDRESS                              CITY     STATE
---------- ----------------------- ------------------------------------ -------- -----------
21         Sharanam Chaitanya Shah 20, Makanji Mansion, MG Road, 400076 Mumbai   Maharashtra
22         Vaishali Sharanam Shah  Krishna Kunj, Thakur Lane, 400078    Mumbai   Maharashtra
25         Chaitanya Kantilal Shah 14, Raheja Tower, 347236             Kottayam Kerala
```

If the same result can be achieved using LIKE, why use REGEXP_LIKE? The LIKE operator allows simple pattern matching, but for complex patterns, it requires multiple OR and LIKE combinations. Regular expressions can combine such multiple OR cases into a single pattern for comparison.

Suppose you want to search for all customers whose name contains either "Shah" or "Sharanam". Using LIKE, it would look like this:

```
SELECT CustomerNo, CustomerName, Address, City, State FROM Customers
  WHERE CustomerName LIKE '%Sha%';
```

This would also list customers such as:

Shantanu **Sh**anti Ni**sha** Ai**sha**

This is not what is desired. The LIKE operator will therefore have to be more precise with multiple conditions as:

```
SELECT CustomerNo, CustomerName, Address, City, State FROM Customers
  WHERE CustomerName LIKE '%Sharanam%' OR CustomerName LIKE '%Shah%';
```

The same can be achieved with much ease using REGEXP_LIKE as:

```
SELECT CustomerNo, CustomerName, Address, City, State FROM Customers
  WHERE REGEXP_LIKE (CustomerName, '\Sha(ranam|h)\');
```

Output:

```
CUSTOMERNO CUSTOMERNAME            ADDRESS                              CITY     STATE
---------- ----------------------- ------------------------------------ -------- ------------
21         Sharanam Chaitanya Shah 20, Makanji Mansion, MG Road, 400076 Mumbai   Maharashtra
22         Vaishali Sharanam Shah  Krishna Kunj, Thakur Lane, 400078    Mumbai   Maharashtra
25         Chaitanya Kantilal Shah 14, Raheja Tower, 347236             Kottayam Kerala
```

Regular expressions are far more powerful than standard pattern matching operators in Oracle. They can be used in complex searches, such as extracting URLs from a block of text, locating words where every second character is a vowel, validating an email address using CHECK constraints, and much more.

Regular Expression Functions In Oracle

Here are the four regular expression functions introduced in Oracle Database 10g, which can be used in SQL as well as PL/SQL:

REGEXP_LIKE

The **REGEXP_LIKE** function is similar to the LIKE operator but performs regular expression matching instead of simple pattern matching. It returns TRUE if the first argument matches a regular expression. This function is typically used in the WHERE clause of a SQL query to return rows that match the specified pattern.

Syntax:

```
REGEXP_LIKE(SRCSTR, PATTERN [,MATCH_OPTION])
```

Where:

- *SRCSTR:* A character expression that serves as the search value. It can be of any of the following data types: CHAR, VARCHAR2, NCHAR, NVARCHAR2, CLOB or NCLOB.
- *PATTERN:* The regular expression to match. It is usually a text literal and can be of any of the following data types: CHAR, VARCHAR2, NCHAR or NVARCHAR2. It can contain up to 512 bytes.
- *MATCH_OPTION (optional):* Options to change default matching behaviour. This parameter can hold one or more of the following values:

Value	Description
'c'	Use case sensitive matching (DEFAULT).
'i'	Use case insensitive matching.
'n'	Allows the match-any-character operator.
'm'	Treats source string as multiple line.

REGEXP_INSTR

The **REGEXP_INSTR** function searches a string for a specified occurrence of a regular expression pattern. The function allows specifying the occurrence to be found and the start position for the search. It returns an integer indicating the position in the string where the match is found. This function is similar to the INSTR function, but it allows for greater versatility by using a pattern instead of a specific search string.

Syntax:

```
REGEXP_INSTR(SRCSTR, PATTERN [, POSITION [, OCCURRENCE [,
  RETURN_OPTION [, MATCH_OPTION]]]])
```

Where:

- *POSITION (optional):* A positive integer indicating the character of SRCSTR where Oracle should begin the search. The default is **1**, meaning the search begins at the first character of SRCSTR.
- *OCCURRENCE (optional):* A positive integer indicating which occurrence of the pattern in SRCSTR Oracle should search for. The default is **1**, meaning Oracle searches for the first occurrence of the pattern.
- *RETURN_OPTION (optional):* Specifies what Oracle should return in relation to the occurrence:
  - If 0 is specified, Oracle returns the position of the first character of the occurrence (**default**).
  - If 1 is specified, Oracle returns the position of the character following the occurrence.

REGEXP_REPLACE

The **REGEXP_REPLACE** function searches for a pattern in a character column and replaces each occurrence of that pattern with the specified replacement string.

Syntax:

```
REGEXP_REPLACE(SRCSTR, PATTERN [, REPLACESTR [, POSITION [,
  OCCURRENCE [, MATCH_OPTION]]]])
```

Where, ***REPLACESTR*** is the replacement string. It can be of any of the following data types: CHAR, VARCHAR2, NCHAR, NVARCHAR2, CLOB, or NCLOB. If REPLACESTR is a CLOB or NCLOB, Oracle truncates it to **32K**. REPLACESTR can contain up to 500 backreferences to subexpressions in the form **\n**, where n is a number from 1 to 9. If \ is the backslash character in REPLACESTR, then it must be preceded with the escape character ****.

REGEXP_SUBSTR

The **REGEXP_SUBSTR** function returns the substring that matches a specified regular expression pattern within a given string.

Syntax:

```
REGEXP_SUBSTR(SRCSTR, PATTERN [, POSITION [, OCCURRENCE [,
  MATCH_OPTION]]])
```

> All these functions support only CHAR, VARCHAR2, CLOB, NCHAR, NVARCHAR and NCLOB data types.

REGEXP_COUNT

The **REGEXP_COUNT** function complements the functionality of the REGEXP_INSTR function by returning the number of times a pattern occurs in a source string. This function evaluates strings using characters as defined by the input character set. It returns an integer indicating the number of occurrences of the pattern. If no match is found, the function returns 0.

Syntax:

```
REGEXP_COUNT(SRCSTR, PATTERN [, POSITION [,          MATCH_OPTION]]])
```

META Characters

A regular expression is composed of two types of characters:

- *Meta Characters:* These are operators that specify algorithms for performing the search.
- *Literals:* These are the actual characters to search for.

Oracle Database supports a set of common Meta characters for use in regular expressions.

Anchoring Meta Characters

Beginning of Line Anchor

Meta Character	Description
^	Matches the start of a line.

End of Line Anchor

Meta Character	Description
$	Matches the end of a line.

Quantifiers or Repetition Operators

Zero or More - Star Quantifier

Meta Character	Description
*	Matches zero or more occurrences of the preceding character.

Zero or One - Question Mark Quantifier

Meta Character	Description
?	Matches zero or one occurrence of the preceding character.

One or More - Plus Quantifier

Meta Character	Description
+	Matches one or more occurrences of the preceding character.

Any Character - Dot

Meta Character	Description
.	Matches any single character except newline.

Interval - Exact Count

Meta Character	Description
{m}	Matches exactly m occurrences of the preceding character.

Interval - At Least Count

Meta Character	Description
{m, }	Matches m or more occurrences of the preceding character.

Interval - Between Count

Meta Character	Description
{m, n}	Matches between m and n occurrences of the preceding character.

Alternate Matching and Grouping of Expressions

Matching Character List

Meta Character	Description
[ ]	Matches any one of the enclosed characters. Example: [abc] matches a, b, or c.

Or

<table>
<tr><th>Meta Character</th><th>Description</th></tr>
<tr><td>|</td><td>Separates alternates, often used with grouping operator ().</td></tr>
</table>

Sub Expression or Grouping

Meta Character	Description
( )	Groups patterns together. Example: (abc)+ matches one or more occurrences of abc.

Predefined POSIX Character Classes

Meta Character	Description
[:alnum:]	All alphanumeric characters.
[:alpha:]	All alphabetic characters.
[:cntrl:]	All control characters [nonprinting].
[:digit:]	All numeric digits.
[:lower:]	All lowercase alphabetic characters.
[:print:]	All printable characters.
[:punct:]	All punctuation characters.
[:space:]	All space characters [nonprinting].
[:upper:]	All uppercase alphabetic characters.

Others

Non-Matching Character List

Meta Character	Description
[^exp]	Negates the expression [If the caret is inside the brackets].

Escape Character

Meta Character	Description
\	Signifies: 1. Stand for itself. 2. Quote the next character. 3. Introduce an operator. 4. Do nothing.

Backreference

Meta Character	Description
\n	Backreference expression.

Example: Display all PAN numbers that have characters:

```
SELECT PANNo FROM Customers WHERE REGEXP_LIKE(PANNo, '[^[:digit:]]');
```

Output:

```
PANNO
---------------
JDH7823J
HSB9845
HSGD897
KSI841J
```

```
GDY8734J
SKDI894
AJDH19024
HGTF190287

8 rows selected.
```

The regular expression **[^[:digit:]]** is used to identify strings that contain at least one character that is not a digit. The **^** inside the brackets negates the class, meaning it matches any character that is not a digit (0-9). This query effectively filters out PAN numbers that contain non-digit characters, as required.

Example: Display all customers having the 2nd last and the 4th last character of their names as vowels i.e. A, E, I, O, U:

```
SELECT CustomerName FROM Customers
  WHERE REGEXP_LIKE(CustomerName, '[AEIOU].[AEIOU].$','i');
```

Output:

```
CUSTOMERNAME
-------------------------
Anil Mayekar
Shravan Ashwin Benegal
```

The regular expression **[AEIOU].[AEIOU].$** is used to match customer names that end with a specific pattern. Let's break it down:

- *[AEIOU]:* Matches any vowel (A, E, I, O, U).
- *.:* Matches any single character.
- *[AEIOU]:* Matches another vowel.
- *.:* Matches any single character.
- *$:* Asserts that the position is at the end of the string.

So, this regular expression essentially matches names where:

- The 2nd last character is a vowel.
- The 4th last character is a vowel.
- The name ends with any character.

The **i** in the third parameter makes the search case-insensitive, meaning it treats both uppercase and lowercase vowels the same.

This function helps identify all customers whose names meet the specified vowel pattern criteria.

Example: Display all orders having the order number beginning with the following:

- MU/0203 – Indicates Mumbai Orders placed on 2nd March.
- DL/0203 – Indicates Delhi Orders placed on 2nd March.
- KL/0203 – Indicates Kolkatta Orders placed on 2nd March.
- MD/0203 – Indicates Madras Orders placed on 2nd March.

Solution:

```
SELECT OrderNo, OrderCode, OrderAmount, OrderStatus FROM Orders
  WHERE REGEXP_LIKE(OrderCode, '[MDKLU]/0203');
```

Output:

```
ORDERNO ORDERCODE  ORDERAMOUNT ORDERSTATUS
------- ---------  ----------- --------------------
1       MU/0203    69350.0     Confirmed
2       DL/0203    5750.0      Void
3       KL/0203    14750.0     Confirmed
4       MD/0203    28400.0     Void
8       MD/0203    Infinity    Void
```

The regular expression **[MDKLU]/0203** is used to match order codes that begin with specific prefixes. Let's break down the expression:

- *[MDKLU]:* Matches any single character from the set (M, D, K, L, U).
- **/0203:** Matches the literal string /0203.

Therefore, the regular expression matches order codes that:

- Start with "MU/", "DL/", "KL/", or "MD/"
- Followed by "0203"

In summary, this query retrieves all orders with order numbers indicating specific locations (Mumbai, Delhi, Kolkata, and Madras) and dates (2nd March).

Example: Display all employees whose name begin with S and ending with M:

```
SELECT EmployeeNo, FirstName, LastName, ContactNo FROM Employees
  WHERE REGEXP_LIKE(FirstName, '^S[A-Z]*M$', 'i');
```

Output:

```
EMPLOYEENO FIRSTNAME   LASTNAME       CONTACTNO
---------- ----------- -------------- ----------------
         1 Sharanam     Shah          91-022-24440094
```

- *^S:* Indicates that the string must begin with 'S'.
- *[A-Z]*:* Indicates that the string can have any number of alphabets after the first character 'S'.
- ^S[A-Z]**M$:* Indicates the last character in the string must be 'M'.
- The ***i*** in the third parameter makes the search case-insensitive.

This function helps to identify all employees whose names meet the specified pattern criteria.

Example: Display all Building names with road names containing two punctuation marks:

```
SELECT BuildingName, Road FROM SubscriberMaster
  WHERE REGEXP_LIKE(Road, '[[:punct:]]{2}');
```

Output:

```
BUILDINGNAME                 ROAD
-------------------------    -------------------------
Advani Bldg                  Bal., Govinddas, Road
```

The regular expression **[[:punct:]]{2}** is used to match strings that contain exactly two consecutive punctuation marks. Let's break it down:

- *[[:punct:]]:* This matches any punctuation character.
- *{2}:* This quantifier specifies that the preceding element (in this case, a punctuation mark) must occur exactly twice.

So, this regular expression matches roads that have two punctuation marks together within the string.

This query effectively retrieves all building names where the road names contain two consecutive punctuation marks, as demonstrated in the output.

Example: Display all customers who have mentioned their surname along with their names:

```
SELECT CustomerNo, CustomerName FROM Customers
  WHERE REGEXP_LIKE(CustomerName, '[[:space:]].');
```

Output:

```
CUSTOMERNO CUSTOMERNAME
---------- -------------------------
        21 Sharanam Chaitanya Shah
        22 Vaishali Sharanam Shah
        23 Anil Mayekar
        25 Chaitanya Kantilal Shah
        26 Shravan Ashwin Benegal
        27 Prakash K Chouduary
        28 Stuti Kapil Khanna
        29 Deepika Anil Bakshi
        30 Manali Narendra Naik
        31 Amit Paul

10 rows selected.
```

The regular expression **[[:space:]].** is used to identify customer names that include both the first name and the surname. Here's what the pattern indicates:

- *[[:space:]]:* Matches a whitespace character.
- *.:* Matches any single character following the whitespace.

Therefore, this regular expression matches strings where a space is immediately followed by a character, effectively identifying names that include a first name and a surname.

This query helps list all customers who have mentioned their surname along with their names.

Example: Display the start position of the digit in the Customer's Address (if one exists):

```
SELECT CustomerNo, Address, REGEXP_INSTR(Address, '[[:digit:]]') DigitPosition
  FROM Customers;
```

Output:

```
CUSTOMERNO ADDRESS                                         DIGITPOSITION
---------- ----------------------------------------- -------------
        21 20, Makanji Mansion, MG Road, 400076                  1
        22 Krishna Kunj, Thakur Lane, 400078                    28
        23 Advani Apts, Mumbai, 665534256                       22
        24 Jay Chambers,  7 Juhu, 774463524                     16
        25 14, Raheja Tower, 347236                              1
        26 3, Shankar Bldg,  Mahim                               1
        27 1st Floor, Kapod Nivas, Mulund                        1
        28 3, Godrej Villa, Powai                                1
        29 Queensland Palace,  India                             0
        30 Hiranadani Mansion,               Lion Road           0
        31 Advani Apts, Mumbai                                   0

11 rows selected.
```

The regular expression [[:digit:]] is used to identify digits in the address. This pattern is passed to the REGEXP_INSTR function, which returns the position of the first digit found in the string.

- ***[[:digit:]]:*** Matches any digit (0-9).
- ***REGEXP_INSTR(Address, '[[:digit:]]'):*** Returns the position of the first digit in the Address column. If no digit is found, it returns 0.

This query effectively lists the start position of the first digit in each customer's address, helping to locate numeric values within the addresses.

Example: Determine the start position of the Pincode in the Customer's Address:

```
SELECT Address, REGEXP_INSTR(Address, '[[:digit:]]{6}$') "PinCodePosition"
  FROM Customers;
```

Output:

```
ADDRESS                                   PinCodePosition
----------------------------------------- ---------------
20, Makanji Mansion, MG Road, 400076                   31
Krishna Kunj, Thakur Lane, 400078                      28
Advani Apts, Mumbai, 665534256                         25
Jay Chambers,  7 Juhu, 774463524                       27
14, Raheja Tower, 347236                               19
3, Shankar Bldg,  Mahim                                 0
1st Floor, Kapod Nivas, Mulund                          0
3, Godrej Villa, Powai                                  0
Queensland Palace,  India                               0
Hiranadani Mansion,               Lion Road             0
Advani Apts, Mumbai                                     0

11 rows selected.
```

- *[[:digit:]]:* Matches any digits (0-9).
- *{6}:* Matches exactly six consecutive digits.
- *$:* Matches a string that ends with exactly six consecutive digits.

This query returns the position in the address where a six-digit Pincode starts, assuming it appears at the end of the address string. If no six-digit Pincode is found at the end, it returns 0.

This helps identify customer addresses containing a six-digit Pincode and pinpoints its starting position within the address.

Example: The Customer's Address can either hold a four-digit or a four + five-digit Pincode along with the address. Determine the start position of the Pincode in the Customer's Address:

```
SELECT Address,
  REGEXP_INSTR(Address, '[[:digit:]]{4}(-[[:digit:]]{5})?$') "PinCodePosition"
     FROM Customers;
```

Output:

```
ADDRESS                                   PinCodePosition
----------------------------------------- ---------------
20, Makanji Mansion, MG Road, 400076                   33
Krishna Kunj, Thakur Lane, 400078                      30
Advani Apts, Mumbai, 665534256                         27
Jay Chambers,  7 Juhu, 774463524                       29
14, Raheja Tower, 347236                               21
3, Shankar Bldg,  Mahim                                 0
1st Floor, Kapod Nivas, Mulund                          0
3, Godrej Villa, Powai                                  0
Queensland Palace,  India                               0
Hiranadani Mansion,          Lion Road                  0
Advani Apts, Mumbai                                     0

11 rows selected.
```

- ***[[:digit:]]*** - Indicates only digits.
- *[[:digit:]]**{4}*** - Indicates 4 consecutive digits.
- *[[:digit:]]{4}**(-[[:digit:]]{5})**?$* - Indicates a string that ends with 4 consecutive digits **OR** a string that ends with nine consecutive digits.

The sub-expression (-[[:digit:]]{4}) is repeated zero or one times, as indicated by the ? repetition operator. This means the string may end with a four-digit Pincode or a nine [4+5] digit Pincode, as the sub-expression may or may not repeat.

Example: Locate the 2nd occurrence of book names that contain the word "and" followed by a space:

```
SELECT BookName,
  REGEXP_INSTR(BookName, 'and[[:space:]]', 1, 2) "Position Of 2nd and"
     FROM Books;
```

Output:

```
BOOKNAME                                  Position Of 2nd and
----------------------------------------- -------------------
Oracle SQL and SQL*Plus                                     0
```

```
Professional MySQL                                  0
PHP Tips And Tricks                                 0
Ajax With JSF                                       0
Oracle For Professionals                            0
Oracle and Data Warehouse and Data Mining          27
Professional Projects On PHP And Oracle             0
Database Concepts                                   0
Mastering phpMyAdmin                                0

9 rows selected.
```

REGEXP_INSTR(BookName, **'and[[:space:]]'**, 1, 2**)** indicates a string that contains a word "and" followed by a space. The second parameter indicates to begin the search from the first character. The third parameter indicates to consider the second occurrence.

Example: The Address column is composed of Flat No, Building Name, Road Name, Locality, City and Pincode. Display only the Building Names from the Customer Addresses:

```
SELECT REGEXP_SUBSTR(Address, ', [^,]*,') "Building Name" FROM Customers;
```

Output:

```
Building Name
--------------------------------------------------
, Makanji Mansion,
, Thakur Lane,
, Mumbai,
,  7 Juhu,
, Raheja Tower,
, Shankar Bldg,
, Kapod Nivas,
, Godrej Villa,

11 rows selected.
```

, [^,]*, indicates a string that begins with a comma (,) followed by a space and zero or more characters that are not commas, (**[^,]***), and further followed by another comma (,).

Example: The InvoiceNo is composed of Inv12/02032007/29.
Display the Invoice No in the following format: INV12-02032007-29
Invoice Number = Inv12
InvoiceDate = /02032007
CustomerNo = /29

Solution:

```
SELECT REGEXP_SUBSTR(InvoiceNo, '[^/]+') InvoiceNumber,
   REGEXP_SUBSTR(InvoiceNo, '/[^/]+') InvoiceDate,
   REGEXP_SUBSTR(InvoiceNo, '/[^/]+',1,2) CustomerNo FROM Invoices;
```

Output:

```
INVOICENUMBER INVOICEDATE  CUSTOMERNO
------------- ------------ --------------
INV1          /03012008    /21
INV2          /06012008    /22
INV3          /04022008    /21
INV4          /07022008    /23
INV5          /05012008    /24
INV6          /08012008    /25
INV7          /06012008    /25

7 rows selected.
```

- *REGEXP_SUBSTR(InvoiceNo, '/[^/]+')* - Extracts one or more characters before a /.
- *REGEXP_SUBSTR(InvoiceNo, '/[^/]+', 1)* - Extracts a / followed by one or more characters before encountering a /, starting from the first character.
- *REGEXP_SUBSTR(InvoiceNo, '/[^/]+', 1, 2)* - Extracts a / followed by one or more characters before encountering a /, considering the second occurrence of such a pattern.

Example: The Employees table holds an About Me column, which might include employees' telephone number. For example, the AboutMe column could hold:

- I can work with PHP, MySQL, Apache, Oracle, JSP. My Contact No is 8121-451969.
- I am comfortable working with Word, Powerpoint, Excel. My Phone No is 7131.461962.

Retrieve such telephone numbers that are embedded within the About Me column:

```
SELECT FirstName, REGEXP_SUBSTR(AboutMe, '[0-9]{4}[-.][0-9]{6,6}') "PhoneNo"
  FROM Employees WHERE REGEXP_LIKE(AboutMe, '[0-9]{4}[-.][0-9]{6,6}');
```

Output:

```
FIRSTNAME                 PhoneNo
------------------------- ------------------
Sharanam                  8121-451969
Vaishali                  7131.461962
Keyur                     3131.987344
Amit                      2671.978344
Abhishek                  3322.554433
Chetan                    5544.988765
Narendra                  9844.983335
Anil                      6644.983335
Amit                      6644.983335

9 rows selected
```

- *[0-9]* - Indicates any digit.
- *{4}* - Repeats the previous element four times, meaning it should be a four-digit number.
- *[-.]* - The four-digit number can be followed by either hyphen (-) **OR** a period (.).
- *[0-9]{6,6}* - Indicates a six-digit number. {6,6} specifies that the digit should repeat exactly six times.

Example: The Employees table holds the Contact No column. This column should only contain phone numbers in the format: 91-022-24440094. Add a constraint to enforce this format:

```
ALTER TABLE Employees ADD (CONSTRAINT ContactNoFormat
  CHECK (REGEXP_LIKE(ContactNo, '^[[:digit:]]{2}-[[:digit:]]{3}-[[:digit:]]{8}$')));
```

Output:

```
Table altered.
```

Test the constraint by issuing the following commands:

Solution (Invalid Number):

```
INSERT INTO Employees (EmployeeNo, FirstName, LastName, ContactNo)
  VALUES (12, 'Meenal', 'Shah','91.021.2224013');
```

Output:

```
INSERT INTO Employees (EmployeeNo, FirstName, LastName, ContactNo)
*
ERROR at line 1:
ORA-02290: check constraint (VAISHALI.CONTACTNOFORMAT) violated
```

Solution (Valid Number):

```
INSERT INTO Employees (EmployeeNo, FirstName, LastName, ContactNo)
  VALUES (12, 'Meenal', 'Shah','91-021-22240123');
```

Output:

```
1 row created.
```

Example: The Knowledge Base table contains all the knowledge gathered within an organization. The URL column holds the web address of the knowledge source. The URL column may contain data such as:

- http://www.sharanamshah.com/articles/Oracle/Chap1.html
- http://www.sharanamshah.com/articles/PHP/Chap7.html
- http://www.vaishalishahonline.com/Downloads/Apache/Setup.html

Retrieve only the unique web addresses without the complete path:

```
SELECT DISTINCT REGEXP_SUBSTR(URL, 'http://([[:alnum:]]+\.?){3,4}/?')
  "Web Address" FROM KnowledgeBase;
```

Output:

```
Web Address
---------------------------------------------------
http://www.vaishalishahonline.com/
http://specials.rediff.com/
http://www.sharanamshah.com/
http://www.rediff.com/
```

- ***http://*** - Indicates a string that begins with **http://**.
- *http://([[:**alnum**:]]+\.?)* - Indicates a string that begins with **http://**, followed by a substring composed of one or more alphanumeric characters and optionally a period (.).
- *http://([[:alnum:]]+\.?)***{3,4}/?** - Indicates a string that begins with **http://**, followed by substring composed of one or more alphanumeric characters and optionally a period (.). This substring may repeat at least three times and at most four times. The string may or may not end with a /.

Example: Some addresses in the Address column of the Customers table contain **double spaces**. Replace double spaces with a single space wherever applicable in the given string:

```
SELECT REGEXP_REPLACE(Address, '  ', ' ') "Address" FROM Customers;
```

Output:

```
Address
-----------------------------------------------------------
20, Makanji Mansion, MG Road, 400076
Krishna Kunj, Thakur Lane, 400078
Advani Apts, Mumbai, 665534256
Jay Chambers, 7 Juhu, 774463524
14, Raheja Tower, 347236
3, Shankar Bldg, Mahim
1st Floor, Kapod Nivas, Mulund
3, Godrej Villa, Powai
Queensland Palace, India
Hiranadani Mansion,       Lion Road
Advani Apts, Mumbai

11 rows selected.
```

The first parameter contains two spaces, which indicates the search target of two consecutive spaces. The second parameter contains a single space, which will be used to replace two consecutive spaces.

Example: Some addresses in the Address column of the Customers table contain **more than one space**. Replace all instances of multiple spaces with a single space wherever applicable in the given string:

```
SELECT REGEXP_REPLACE(Address, '( ){2,}', ' ') "Address" FROM Customers;
```

Output:

```
Address
-----------------------------------------------------
20, Makanji Mansion, MG Road, 400076
Krishna Kunj, Thakur Lane, 400078
Advani Apts, Mumbai, 665534256
Jay Chambers, 7 Juhu, 774463524
14, Raheja Tower, 347236
3, Shankar Bldg, Mahim
1st Floor, Kapod Nivas, Mulund
```

```
3, Godrej Villa, Powai
Queensland Palace, India
Hiranadani Mansion, Lion Road
Advani Apts, Mumbai

11 rows selected.
```

The first parameter *( ){2,}* indicates two or more consecutive spaces. The second parameter contains a single space, which will be used to replace such instances of multiple spaces.

Example: Count the number of times the word "and" appears in the BookName column of the Books table:

```
SELECT REGEXP_COUNT(BookName, 'and', 1,'i') "CountAnds" FROM Books;
```

This function returns the number of times the word "and" appears in the BookName column.

Output:

```
CountAnds
----------
         1
         0
         1
         0
         0
         2
         1
         0
         0

9 rows selected.
```

Backreferences

A useful feature of regular expressions is the ability to store sub-expressions for reuse later. This is known as **backreferencing**. It allows sophisticated replace capabilities, such as swapping patterns into new positions or indicating repeated word or letter occurrences. The matched part of the sub-expression is stored in a temporary buffer. The buffer is numbered from left to right and accessed with the \digit notation, where digit is a number between 1 and 9 and matches the digitth sub-expression, as indicated by a set of parentheses.

Example: The CustomerName column of the Customers table holds names in the format:
FirstName MiddleName LastName
For viewing purpose, it is required to change this format as:
LastName, FirstName MiddleName

Solution:

```
SELECT REGEXP_REPLACE(CustomerName, '(.*) (.*) (.*)', '\3, \1 \2')
  "CustomerName" FROM Customers;
```

Output:

```
CustomerName
---------------------------------------------
Shah, Sharanam Chaitanya
Shah, Vaishali Sharanam
Anil Mayekar
Hansel
Shah, Chaitanya Kantilal
Benegal, Shravan Ashwin
Chouduary, Prakash K
Khanna, Stuti Kapil
Bakshi, Deepika Anil
Naik, Manali Narendra
Amit Paul

11 rows selected.
```

(.*) (.*) (.*) indicates three different sub-expressions. Each one retrieves a set of characters until a space is encountered. Once the values are retrieved (in this case, FirstName MiddleName LastName), they are reformatted as desired using back references. Since three sub-expressions are used, three back references are created. The first sub-expression is assigned **\1**, the second **\2** and so on.

These backreferences are used in the last parameter of this function as ***\3, \1 \2***, which effectively returns the replacement substrings and places them in the desired format (including commas and spaces).

Example 2: The phone numbers of the customers in the Customers table need to be stored in a more readable format. Currently, they are stored as**:** 9102224356476
These need to be stored as**:** 91-022-24356476

Query the Customers table to view the existing contact numbers:

```
CONTACTNO
--------------------
9102224440094
9102231040094
9102227740094
9102234340094
9102237640094
9102240940094
9102244240094
9102247540094

9102254140094


11 rows selected.
```

Solution:

```
UPDATE Customers
  SET ContactNo = REGEXP_REPLACE(ContactNo, '(.{2})(.{3})(.*)', '\1-\2-\3');
```

Output:

```
10 rows updated.
```

Query the Customers table to view the changes:

```
CONTACTNO
--------------------
91-022-24440094
91-022-31040094
91-022-27740094
91-022-34340094
91-022-37640094
91-022-40940094
91-022-44240094
91-022-47540094

91-022-54140094

11 rows selected.
```

- *(.){2}* - Indicates the first two characters.
- *(.){3}* - Indicates the next three characters.
- *(.*)* - Indicates the remaining characters.

Three sub-expressions are created, and each one can be referred using backreferences. The first sub-expression is assigned **\1**, the second **\2**, and the third **\3**. Using backreferences, the values are retrieved and placed in the desired format (**\1-\2-\3**).

Chapter 21

SECTION III: WORKING WITH DATA

Working With RowID And RowNum

RowID

A **RowID** is a pseudo column provided by Oracle that uniquely identifies a row within a table.

> TIP: A Pseudo column is data associated with table data, similar to columns, but not actually stored in the database.

A RowID does not represent the data in the database table itself but rather maps the physical location of a row within a specific datafile. Since a RowID points directly to the physical location of a row, it allows faster updates or deletes compared to performing a full table scan or looking up the RowID in an index and then performing the same action.

Deleting Duplicate Rows

A table called Customers holds duplicate rows. The following is what the Customers table currently holds:

CustomerNo	CustomerName	Address
1	*Ivan*	*Makanji Mansion, Mumbai*
1	*Ivan*	*Makanji Mansion, Mumbai*
1	*Ivan*	*Makanji Mansion, Mumbai*
2	Amit	Krishna Kunj, Mumbai
3	Maya	Advani Apts, Pune
4	Peter	Jay Chambers, Bangalore
5	Mandhar	Raheja Tower, Kottayam
6	Sonal	Shankar Bldg, Mount Abu
7	Anil	Kapod Nivas, Ludhania
8	Seema	Swarg Bldg, Bangalore
9	Vikram	Godrej Villa, Patna
10	Anjali	Sita Sadan, Mumbai

Since this table holds a lot of duplicate records, it is desired to delete all the duplicates, retaining the original entry. The most common solution is to use the DELETE command with a WHERE clause to indicate the duplicate **CustomerNo** to be deleted:

```
DELETE FROM Customers WHERE CustomerNo IN(1, 2, 3);
```

However, this command deletes all customers with CustomerNo 1, 2 or 3, **including the original entry**, which is not desired. The original entry **should be retained** while deleting the duplicates.

To achieve this, a record should be uniquely identifiable, which seems impossible if all column values hold duplicate data. In this scenario, Oracle's pseudo column RowID can be used. A RowID is unique for every record in the table, even if those records hold duplicate data. Each record in a block of the data file is given a unique record number, ensuring the RowID column value is always unique.

The DELETE command can be written with a WHERE clause using the **RowID** pseudo column:

```
DELETE FROM Customers WHERE RowID NOT IN(SELECT MIN(RowID)
  FROM Customers GROUP BY CustomerNo, CustomerName, Address);
```

Output:

```
2 rows deleted.
```

The values for the WHERE clause in the DELETE command are provided by a subquery that retrieves the RowID of the first row in each set of duplicate records in the table:

```
SELECT MIN(RowID) FROM Customers
```

```
GROUP BY CustomerNo, CustomerName, Address;
```

Query when executed returns:

```
MIN(ROWID)
------------------
AAASSCAAEAAADOvAAP
AAASSCAAEAAADOvAAU
AAASSCAAEAAADOvAAM
AAASSCAAEAAADOvAAR
AAASSCAAEAAADOvAAV
AAASSCAAEAAADOvAAX
AAASSCAAEAAADOvAAT
AAASSCAAEAAADOvAAW
AAASSCAAEAAADOvAAS
AAASSCAAEAAADOvAAQ

10 rows selected.
```

This query groups duplicate records and extracts the RowID of the first row in each set of duplicates using the **MIN()** function, which returns the minimum value from a set of values. The parent query's WHERE clause using the **NOT IN** operator skips deleting all those RowIDs that the subquery returns. Since the subquery returns the lowest RowID of every set of duplicate records, one record from each set is retained.

During execution, the subquery' results are held in memory and passed to the parent query:

```
MIN(ROWID)         CUSTOMERNO CUSTOMERNAME ADDRESS
------------------ ---------- ------------ -----------------------
AAASSCAAEAAADOvAAP          2 Sharanam     Krishna Kunj, Mumbai
AAASSCAAEAAADOvAAU          7 Anil         Kapod Nivas, Ludhania
AAASSCAAEAAADOvAAM          1 Ivan         Makanji Mansion, Mumbai
AAASSCAAEAAADOvAAR          4 Peter        Jay Chambers, Bangalore
AAASSCAAEAAADOvAAV          8 Seema        Swarg Bldg, Bangalore
AAASSCAAEAAADOvAAX         10 Amit         Sita Sadan, Mumbai
AAASSCAAEAAADOvAAT          6 Sonal        Shankar Bldg, Mount Abu
AAASSCAAEAAADOvAAW          9 Vikram       Godrej Villa, Patna
AAASSCAAEAAADOvAAS          5 Mandhar      Raheja Tower, Kottayam
AAASSCAAEAAADOvAAQ          3 Vaishali     Advani Apts, Pune

10 rows selected.
```

After the subquery completes execution, Oracle replaces the values in the parent query's WHERE clause with the lowest RowIDs. Thus the delete command becomes:

```
DELETE FROM Customers WHERE RowID NOT IN(
  'AAASSCAAEAAADOvAAP', 'AAASSCAAEAAADOvAAU',
  'AAASSCAAEAAADOvAAM', 'AAASSCAAEAAADOvAAR',
  'AAASSCAAEAAADOvAAV', 'AAASSCAAEAAADOvAAX',
  'AAASSCAAEAAADOvAAT', 'AAASSCAAEAAADOvAAW',
  'AAASSCAAEAAADOvAAS', 'AAASSCAAEAAADOvAAQ');
```

RowNum

RowNum is a pseudo column provided by Oracle to number the records in a result set. When an SQL query is executed and records are retrieved after meeting the criteria in the WHERE clause (if any), the first record that is retrieved is assigned a RowNum of 1. Every subsequent record is assigned the next RowNum in sequence (i.e., 2, 3, 4, and so on). This means Oracle assigns an incrementing number starting from 1 to each row returned by the SQL query. These RowNum values can be retrieved using a SELECT statement.

Solution:

```
SELECT RowNum, CustomerNo, CustomerName FROM Customers;
```

Output:

```
    ROWNUM CUSTOMERNO CUSTOMERNAME
---------- ---------- -------------------------
         1         21 Sharanam Chaitanya Shah
         2         22 Vaishali Sharanam Shah
         3         23 Anil Mayekar
         4         24 Hansel
         5         25 Chaitanya Kantilal Shah
         6         26 Shravan Ashwin Benegal
         7         27 Prakash K Chouduary
         8         28 Stuti Kapil Khanna
         9         29 Deepika Anil Bakshi
        10         30 Manali Narendra Naik
        11         31 Amit Paul

11 rows selected.
```

Limiting Number Of Rows Returned By A Query

RowNum can be used to limit the number of rows retrieved.

Retrieve the first three rows from the Customers table using RowNum:

```
SELECT RowNum, CustomerNo, CustomerName FROM Customers WHERE RowNum < 4;
```

Output:

```
    ROWNUM CUSTOMERNO CUSTOMERNAME
---------- ---------- -------------------------
         1         21 Sharanam Chaitanya Shah
         2         22 Vaishali Sharanam Shah
         3         23 Anil Mayekar
```

The ORDER BY clause works differently when used with RowNum to restrict query results. It works accurately only if the column on which the ORDER BY clause is applied is the primary key of the table.

Example: (CustomerNo is the primary key of the Customers table)

```
SELECT CustomerName, Address FROM Customers WHERE RowNum < 5
  ORDER BY CustomerNo;
```

Output:

```
CUSTOMERNAME                 ADDRESS
-------------------------    ------------------------------------
Sharanam Chaitanya Shah      20, Makanji Mansion, MG Road, 400076
Vaishali Sharanam Shah       Krishna Kunj, Thakur Lane, 400078
Anil Mayekar                 Advani Apts, Mumbai, 665534256
Hansel                       Jay Chambers,  7 Juhu, 774463524
```

If the same query is executed on the Customers table with the ORDER BY clause applied to a column that is not the Primary key of the table, the results vary.

Example: (CustomerName is not the primary key of the Customers table)

```
SELECT CustomerName, Address FROM Customers WHERE RowNum < 5
  ORDER BY CustomerName;
```

Output:

```
CUSTOMERNAME                 ADDRESS
-------------------------    ------------------------------------
Anil Mayekar                 Advani Apts, Mumbai, 665534256
Hansel                       Jay Chambers,  7 Juhu, 774463524
Sharanam Chaitanya Shah      20, Makanji Mansion, MG Road, 400076
Vaishali Sharanam Shah       Krishna Kunj, Thakur Lane, 400078
```

A **RowNum** value is assigned to each row as it is retrieved, **before the rows are sorted** on the column(s) in the ORDER BY clause. The order in which data is retrieved depends on the indexes created on the table. If an index is created on the column(s) used in the ORDER BY clause, Oracle uses the index to retrieve data in a sorted order. Thus, the RowNum will be in the order of the rows retrieved from the index.

If an index is not created on the column(s) used in the ORDER BY clause, Oracle retrieves data from the table in the order of data insertion, and thus an ORDER BY clause does not affect the RowNum of each row. A RowNum cannot be compared with a value greater than a positive integer.

Example:

```
SELECT * FROM Customers WHERE RowNum > 1;
```

Output:

```
no rows selected.
```

The first row that is fetched is assigned a RowNum of 1. Because of this, the condition in the WHERE clause returns false.

The second row to be fetched now becomes the first row and is also assigned a RowNum of 1, which again returns false. All rows subsequently fail to satisfy the condition, so no rows are returned.

Display Every Nth Row From A Table

Example:

```
SELECT RowNum, CustomerNo, CustomerName FROM Customers
  WHERE (RowID, 0) IN (SELECT RowID, MOD(RowNum, 2) FROM Customers);
```

Output:

```
    ROWNUM CUSTOMERNO CUSTOMERNAME
---------- ---------- -------------------------
         1         22 Vaishali Sharanam Shah
         2         24 Hansel
         3         26 Shravan Ashwin Benegal
         4         28 Stuti Kapil Khanna
         5         30 Manali Narendra Naik
```

Here, using a Subquery on the same table, only even rows are displayed. The WHERE clause compares a list of values **(**ROWID, 0**)** with two values returned by the subquery:

```
(SELECT RowID, MOD(RowNum, 2) FROM Customers)
```

This query returns the RowID and the modulus of RowNum and 2. For every modulus result that is 0, the parent query returns a record.

Example:

```
SELECT * FROM (SELECT RowNum RN, CustomerNo, CustomerName
  FROM Customers) C WHERE MOD(C.RN, 2) = 0;
```

Output:

```
        RN CUSTOMERNO CUSTOMERNAME
---------- ---------- -------------------------
         2         22 Vaishali Sharanam Shah
         4         24 Hansel
         6         26 Shravan Ashwin Benegal
         8         28 Stuti Kapil Khanna
        10         30 Manali Narendra Naik
```

Here, using a dynamic view (i.e. a SQL query as the data source for the parent query), only even rows are displayed. The WHERE clause of the parent query displays only even rows of the data source by using the modulus of the inner query's RowNum and 2.

Example:

```
SELECT RowNum, CustomerNo, CustomerName FROM Customers
  GROUP BY RowNum, CustomerNo, CustomerName
     HAVING MOD(RowNum, 2) = 0 OR RowNum = 2-0;
```

Output:

```
    ROWNUM CUSTOMERNO CUSTOMERNAME
---------- ---------- -------------------------
         6         26 Shravan Ashwin Benegal
         8         28 Stuti Kapil Khanna
         2         22 Vaishali Sharanam Shah
        10         30 Manali Narendra Naik
         4         24 Hansel
```

Here, the records are grouped and filtered using the HAVING clause to consider only those rows which are even, using the following condition:

```
HAVING MOD(RowNum, 2) = 0 OR RowNum = 2-0;
```

Retrieve Only Rows X To Y From A Table

Retrieve the records available in the Customers table from row 4 onwards till 7:

```
SELECT * FROM (SELECT RowNum RN, CustomerName FROM Customers
  WHERE RowNum < 8) WHERE RN BETWEEN 4 AND 7;
```

Output:

```
        RN CUSTOMERNAME
---------- -------------------------
         4 Hansel
         5 Chaitanya Kantilal Shah
         6 Shravan Ashwin Benegal
         7 Prakash K Chouduary
```

Here, a dynamic view is used that retrieves all the records up to row 7. This result is then passed one level above to the parent query, which further filters the result set to display records from row 4 onwards till row 7.

Example:

```
SELECT RowNum RN, CustomerName FROM Customers
  GROUP BY RowNum, CustomerName HAVING RowNum BETWEEN 4 AND 7;
```

Output:

```
        RN CUSTOMERNAME
---------- -------------------------
         4 Hansel
         5 Chaitanya Kantilal Shah
         7 Prakash K Chouduary
         6 Shravan Ashwin Benegal
```

Here, the records are grouped, creating a subset of records. The HAVING clause is then applied to filter these records, displaying the 4th record onwards till the 7th.

Example:

```
SELECT RowNum RN, CustomerName FROM Customers WHERE RowID IN(
```

```
SELECT RowID FROM Customers WHERE RowNum <= 7
MINUS
SELECT RowID FROM Customers WHERE RowNum < 4);
```

Output:

```
        RN CUSTOMERNAME
---------- -----------------------
         1 Hansel
         2 Chaitanya Kantilal Shah
         3 Shravan Ashwin Benegal
         4 Prakash K Chouduary
```

Here, a subquery is used along with the MINUS set operator.

```
SELECT RowID FROM Customers WHERE RowNum <= 7
```

The first query in the SET operator retrieves RowIDs of the first seven records.

```
SELECT RowID FROM Customers WHERE RowNum < 4
```

The second query in the SET operator retrieves RowIDs of the first four records.

Using the MINUS Set operator, the difference is retrieved, which results in records from the 4th row onwards till the 7th row. Finally, all such RowIDs are passed to the parent query to display only those records identified by those RowIDs.

Generating Primary Key Values Using RowNum

RowNum is useful in situations where a table holds records without a unique identifier.

A table called Students exists with three columns:

- StudentNo
- StudentName
- Age

This table holds a few records without a unique identifier.

The data held in the table Students:

```
SELECT * FROM Students;
```

Output:

```
STUDENTNO  STUDENTNAME                      AGE
---------- ------------------------- ----------
           Sharanam                          28
           Vaishali                          28
           Stuti                             23
           Mandhar                           20
           Sonal                             30
           Anil                              31
           Seema                             32
           Vikram                            24
           Amit                              19
```

```
9 rows selected.
```

Issue the following command to generate a primary key for the column StudentNo:

```sql
UPDATE Students SET StudentNo = RowNum;
```

Output:

```
10 rows updated.
```

The data held in the table Students after update:

```sql
SELECT * FROM Students;
```

Output:

```
STUDENTNO  STUDENTNAME
---------- -------------------------
1          Sharanam
2          Vaishali
3          Stuti
4          Mandhar
5          Sonal
6          Anil
7          Seema
8          Vikram
9          Amit

9 rows selected.
```

Alternatively, use a sequence:

```sql
CREATE SEQUENCE SEQ_StudentNo START WITH 1 INCREMENT BY 1;
```

Output:

```
Sequence created.
```

```sql
UPDATE Students SET StudentNo = SEQ_StudentNo.NEXTVAL;
```

Output:

```
10 rows updated.
```

Finally, create a unique index on the column StudentNo as:

```sql
CREATE UNIQUE INDEX idx_StudentNo ON Students(StudentNo);
```

Output:

```
Index created.
```

This will now restrict the insertion of duplicate values:

```sql
INSERT INTO Students VALUES(1, 'Milind');
```

Output:

```
INSERT INTO Students VALUES(1, 'Milind')
            *
ERROR at line 1:
ORA-00947: not enough values
Help: https://docs.oracle.com/error-help/db/ora-00947/
```

Chapter

22

SECTION IV: SQL PERFORMANCE TUNING

Indexes

Indexes significantly enhance the speed of data retrieval. Consider a scenario where you have a book titled "Oracle For Beginners" and you want to find a section on Views. Instead of reading the book from cover to cover, you can refer to the index section at the end of the book, find the page number for Views, and go directly to that page. This approach saves a lot of time and is far more efficient.

The same concept applies to database tables. Without an index, Oracle would have to scan the entire table to find the required data. However, with an index, Oracle can quickly locate the index, determine the location of the required data, and retrieve it directly. This makes the process much faster.

Therefore, creating indexes on tables is highly recommended. An **index** is a physical storage structure that provides rapid access to rows of a table based on the values of one or more columns.

However, indexes do consume additional disk space and need to be updated whenever a row is added or an indexed column is updated in existing row.

How Does Indexing Work?

When an index is created on a table column, Oracle internally forms a two-dimensional matrix, independent of the table on which the index is based. One column in this matrix stores sorted data extracted from the table column(s) where the index is created. The other column stores the actual location/physical address of the records in the Oracle database table that holds the data.

Every time data is inserted into the table, Oracle automatically updates the index with the same value. Additionally, Oracle includes the **RowID** value for each indexed column in the matrix. This **RowID** specifies the exact location of the record in the table. When an SQL query containing a **WHERE** clause referencing an indexed column is executed, Oracle searches the Index matrix for the desired value. Once the value is located, Oracle uses the **RowID** to quickly find the associated record in the table.

TIP Each key in an index is associated with a RowID that points to the address of the corresponding row for fast access.

When To Use Indexes?

For relatively small tables, indexes may not significantly improve performance. Generally, indexes are most beneficial when created on fields used in table joins or when queries retrieve smaller datasets. If queries often fetch most of the data from the table, having indexes can actually slow down the retrieval process.

An index should be created in the following scenarios:

1. When the SQL SELECT query retrieves less than 25% of table data.
2. On Primary key columns.
3. On common columns used in JOIN operations.

It's important to note that all indexes are automatically updated by the system for all DML (**D**ata **M**anipulation **L**anguage) operations. However, the larger the number of indexes, the slower the DML operations become.

What Happens After An Index Is Created?

Each time a record is inserted into the table:

- Oracle locates free space in the blocks in the data files.

- Inserts a record in all the indexes associated with the table.
- The index entries are sorted in ascending order.

> It's important to note that if too many indexes are created on a table, Oracle takes longer to insert a record into the table. This is because index processing is done for each record that is inserted, updated, or deleted. While indexes speed up data retrieval, they can significantly slow down data insertion. Therefore, it's crucial to maintain a balance by indexing only those columns that are frequently used for data retrieval (i.e., querying the table).

How Does Oracle Choose An Index?

Oracle prepares a **query plan** to decide which index to use for specific data retrieval, based on the **WHERE** clause or the **ORDER BY** clause specified in the SELECT statement. Whenever a SELECT statement is executed, Oracle generates a query plan that outlines the data retrieval method. This query plan includes the name of the table from which data will be retrieved and the name of the index to be used.

If a SELECT statement is executed without a WHERE clause or an ORDER BY clause, Oracle **does not** use the indexes created on the table for data extraction. However, if a WHERE clause or an ORDER BY clause is specified, Oracle uses the index created on the column referenced by these clauses. If no index exists for the column specified in the WHERE clause or the ORDER BY clause, data is retrieved without using indexes.

When Oracle Invokes An Index?

Oracle will use an index, if it exists, under the following conditions:

- A SELECT query with a WHERE clause specified on the column on which an index exists.
- A SELECT query with an ORDER BY clause specified on the column on which an index exists.

When Oracle Does Not Invoke An Index?

An index, even if it exists, will not always be used by Oracle. Here are a few conditions when an index is not invoked:

- If a SELECT query is executed without a WHERE clause.
- If a SELECT query is executed with a WHERE clause on a column that does not have an index.
- If a SELECT query is executed with an ORDER BY clause on a column that does not have an index.

- If a SELECT query is executed with a WHERE clause that uses the != condition.
- If a SELECT query is executed with IS NULL or IS NOT NULL operators.

> NULL values are never stored in an index.

- Anytime a secondary index key is used.
- If a SELECT query includes a condition that uses the OR logical operator to compare column values, and only one of the columns is indexed.
- If a SELECT query includes a function or an expression on left-hand side of a relational operator.
- If an index is created on multiple table columns (e.g., Col1, Col2, and Col3). SQL queries that access only Col1 or only Col1 and Col2 will use the index. However, an SQL query that accesses only Col2, only Col3, or only Col2 and Col3 will not use the index.

Let's dive into the example! Given the Books table and the index created on the BookName column, the index named **idx_BookName** would hold sorted data for the book names along with the RowID for each book. Display the book details of the book named "Oracle For Professionals":

BookName	ROWID
PHP For Beginners	AAAHeeAABAAAMWCAAA
Java Server Programming For Professionals	AAAHeeAABAAAMWCAAC
Oracle For Professionals	AAAHeeAABAAAMWCAAE
MySQL For Professionals	AAAHeeAABAAAMWCAAG
Java Server Pages For Beginners	AAAHeeAABAAAMWCAAI
Ajax For Professionals	AAAHeeAABAAAMWCAAK
Oracle And PHP On Linux For Professionals	AAAHeeAABAAAMWCAAM
Java EE 5 For Beginners	AAAHeeAABAAAMWCAAO

Solution:

```
SELECT ISBN, BookName, Cost, NoOfPages, NoOfChapters FROM Books
  WHERE BookName = 'Oracle For Professionals';
```

When the SELECT query above is executed, Oracle locates the appropriate RowID from the index data by scanning the index for the specific data value (BookName = 'Oracle For Professionals'). Once the RowID is determined, Oracle uses this RowID to find the actual address of the record in the table and retrieves the record stored at that specified address.

Output:

```
ISBN          BOOKNAME                 COST  NOOFPAGES NOOFCHAPTERS
------------- ------------------------ ----- --------- ------------
783-983242-23 Oracle For Professionals 450   890       43

1 rows selected
```

Create Index

An index:

- Can be created on one or more columns.
- Can allow duplicate values.
- Can deny duplicate values.

Syntax (On A Single Column):

```
CREATE INDEX <IndexName> ON <TableName> (<ColumnName>);
```

Syntax (On Multiple Columns):

```
CREATE INDEX <IndexName>
  ON <TableName> (<ColumnName1>, <ColumnName2>);
```

Let's create an index on the **BookName** column of the **Books** table:

```
CREATE INDEX idx_BookName ON Books (BookName);
```

Output:

```
Index created.
```

Let's create an index on the **CustomerName** and **City** columns of the Customers table:

```
CREATE INDEX idx_CustNameCity ON Customers (CustomerName, City);
```

Output:

```
Index created.
```

Explicit Unique Indexes

The indexes created in the examples above do not enforce uniqueness, meaning the columns included in the index can hold duplicate values. Indexes can be either unique or non-unique. Unique indexes guarantee that no two rows in a table have duplicate values in the key column (or columns), while non-unique indexes do not impose this restriction on column values. To create a unique index, the keyword **UNIQUE** should be included in the CREATE INDEX command.

Syntax (On Single Column):

```
CREATE UNIQUE INDEX <IndexName> ON <TableName> (<ColumnName>);
```

Syntax (On Multiple Columns):

```
CREATE UNIQUE INDEX <IndexName>
  ON <TableName> (<ColumnName>, <ColumnName>);
```

Let's create a unique index on **BookName** column of the **Books** table:

```
CREATE UNIQUE INDEX idx_BookName ON Books (BookName);
```

Output:

```
Index created.
```

A unique index can be created on one or more columns.

Let's create a unique index on **OrderNo** and **ProductName** columns of the OrderDetails table:

```
CREATE UNIQUE INDEX idx_OrderProductName ON OrderDetails (OrderNo, ProductName);
```

Output:

```
Index created.
```

Where a unique index exists on a column, and a single value is being searched in that indexed column, Oracle is assured that there will be, at most, one matching row.

Implicit Unique Indexes

When a user defines a primary key or unique key constraint at the table or column level, Oracle automatically creates a **unique index** on the primary key or unique key column(s). Although Oracle creates these indexes implicitly, their creation can be explicitly controlled in the CREATE TABLE command using the USING INDEX clause.

The Using Index clause allows you to:

- Specify an existing index that Oracle should use to enforce the constraint.
- Specify a Create Index statement that Oracle should use to create the index and enforce the constraint.

Let's create a table named Books and override the explicit unique index creation on the UNIQUE constraint on the BookName column:

```
CREATE TABLE Books(
   ISBN Varchar2(25) PRIMARY KEY,
   BookName Varchar2(100) UNIQUE
   USING INDEX (CREATE INDEX idx_BookNamei ON Books (BookName)),
   NoOfChapters Number(25),
   AuthorID Number(10),
   PublisherID Number(10),
   Category Varchar2(100));
```

Output:

```
Table created.
```

Let's create a table named OrderDetails and override the explicit unique index creation on the UNIQUE constraint on the OrderNo and ProductName columns:

```
CREATE TABLE OrderDetails(
  OrderNo Number(10),
  OrderDate Date,
  ProductName Varchar2(25),
  Cost Number(12, 2),
  Qty Number(5),
  EmployeeNo Number(10),
  CustomerName Varchar2(25),
  CONSTRAINT unq_OrderProduct UNIQUE (OrderNo, ProductName)
  USING INDEX (CREATE UNIQUE INDEX idx_OrderProduct
  ON OrderDetails(OrderNo, ProductName)));
```

Output:

```
Table created.
```

There exists a table named Customers. An index named idx_Customer is created on the CustomerNo and CustomerName columns of the Customers table:

```
CREATE INDEX idx_Customer ON Customers (CustomerNo, CustomerName);
```

Output:

```
Index created.
```

To add a primary key constraint on the CustomerNo column with explicit instructions to use the already existing index named idx_Customer, you can alter the table structure as follows:

```
ALTER TABLE Customers
  ADD CONSTRAINT pk_CustomerNo PRIMARY KEY (CustomerNo)
      USING INDEX idx_customer;
```

Output:

```
Table altered.
```

Reverse Key Indexes

Creating a reverse key index, as opposed to a standard index, reverses the bytes of each indexed column (except the RowID) while keeping the column order. This reversal distributes data insertions more evenly across all leaf keys in the index.

Syntax:

```
CREATE INDEX <IndexName> ON <TableName> (<ColumnName>) REVERSE;
```

Why Reverse Indexes?

In the index leaf block, Oracle stores the indexed value along with the 6-byte RowID. For example, consider a table named Customers with a sequential primary key column CustomerNo. The uniqueness of the primary key value is guaranteed by a unique index, and the primary key value is always ascending. Suppose three individuals concurrently insert rows with CustomerNo values 101, 102, and 103. To see the actual values stored in the index leaf blocks for a non-reversed unique index, execute the following command:

```
SELECT DUMP(101), DUMP(102), DUMP(103) FROM DUAL;
```

Output:

```
DUMP(101)            DUMP(102)            DUMP(103)
-------------------- -------------------- --------------------
Typ=2 Len=3: 194,2,2 Typ=2 Len=3: 194,2,3 Typ=2 Len=3: 194,2,4
```

Notice the last byte differs for each CustomerNo. In this scenario, when these values are inserted, the index entries for CustomerNo 101, 102, and 103 will be in the same leaf block, causing buffer busy waits. If the index were a reverse unique index, the following values would be inserted in the index leaf blocks:

```
SELECT DUMP(101), DUMP(201), DUMP(301) FROM DUAL;
```

Output:

```
DUMP(101)            DUMP(201)            DUMP(301)
-------------------- -------------------- --------------------
Typ=2 Len=3: 194,2,2 Typ=2 Len=3: 194,3,2 Typ=2 Len=3: 194,4,2
```

Now, if data is inserted concurrently, it will not hit the same leaf block, thereby reducing contention and improving performance.

To create a reverse index on the CustomerNo column of the Customers table:

```
CREATE INDEX idxR_CustomerNo ON Customers (CustomerNo) REVERSE;
```

Output:

```
Index created.
```

When the values in the CustomerNo column, such as 421, 422, 423, are indexed, they are reversed to 124, 224, and 324, respectively. A reverse index provides a more even distribution of hits on the various leaf blocks. In a scenario where data is being inserted into the Customers table concurrently, instead of all transactions hitting the same block, the blocks being hit are spread out. This reduces the potentially expensive buffer busy waits.

However, the main disadvantage of reverse indexes is the inability to perform index range scans. Since values are now distributed all over the place, only fetch-by-key or full-index (table) scans can be performed.

A reverse index can be rebuilt into a normal non-reverse index using the **NOREVERSE** keyword:

```
ALTER INDEX <IndexName> REBUILD NOREVERSE;
```

To modify the reverse index created on the CustomerNo column of the Customer table to a normal index:

```
ALTER INDEX idxR_CustomerNo REBUILD NOREVERSE;
```

Output:

```
Index altered.
```

A normal index cannot be **rebuilt** as a reverse key index. The same can be achieved using the CREATE INDEX command.

In a non-reverse index, the rows are stored together in one block since the values are almost the same for all rows. In a reverse index, the column values are stored in different blocks as the starting values differ.

Bitmap Indexes

A bitmap index is advisable when:

- Dealing with low cardinality columns i.e. columns in which the number of distinct values is small compared to the number of rows in the table.
- SQL queries reference multiple, low cardinality values in the WHERE clause.
- Data is not frequently updated by many concurrent systems.

How Does Bitmap Indexing Work?

In bitmap indexes, Oracle creates a two-dimensional array with one column for every row in the table being indexed. Each column represents a distinct value within the bitmapped index. This two-dimensional array represents each value within the index multiplied by the number of rows in the table. When records are retrieved, Oracle decompresses the bitmap into the RAM data buffers to rapidly scan for matching values. These matching values are delivered to Oracle in the form of a list of RowIDs, which directly access the required information.

A bitmap index is useful when one table includes multiple bitmapped indexes. If each individual column has low cardinality, multiple bitmap indexes provide a powerful method for rapidly answering complex SQL queries.

Consider the table named Products with several low cardinality columns such as:

- ProductColor
- ProductMake
- ProductModel
- ManufacturingYear

Combining such indexes in a query can provide excellent response times.

To search a black monitor manufactured by LG in 2008:

```
SELECT ProductName, Price FROM Products WHERE ProductColor = 'Black'
  AND ProductMake = 'LG' AND ManufacturingYear = 2008;
```

Output:

```
PRODUCTNAME                          PRICE
-------------------------- ----------
TV                                   15000
```

Oracle uses a special optimizer method called bitmapped index merge to service this query. In a bitmapped index merge, each RowID is built independently using the bitmaps, and a special merge routine is used to compare the RowIDs and find the intersecting values.

AND and OR conditions in the WHERE clause of a query can be quickly resolved by performing the corresponding Boolean operations directly on the bitmaps before converting the resulting bitmap to RowIDs.

Syntax:

```
CREATE BITMAP INDEX <IndexName> ON <TableName> (<ColumnName>);
```

Create a bitmap index on MaritalStatus and Gender columns of the Employees table:

```
CREATE BITMAP INDEX btidx_Employees ON Employees (MaritalStatus, Gender);
```

Output:

```
Index created.
```

Function Based Index

Sometimes, even though an index exists, Oracle does not use it and instead performs a full table scan. This usually occurs when an index is created on a column, but the SQL query references that column with a function, an arithmetic expression, or an expression that uses a PL/SQL function, package function, or SQL function.

For example, an index is created on the City column of the Customers table, and the following query is executed to retrieve all customers from MUMBAI:

```
SELECT * FROM Customers WHERE UPPER(City)='MUMBAI';
```

This query references the City column with string function UPPER(), causing Oracle to bypass the index and perform a full table scan instead.

To address this issue, Oracle provides function-based indexes. A **function-based index** allows the creation of indexes based on a function or expression applied to one or more columns in a table.

TIP: Function-based indexes are particularly useful when the WHERE clause contains functions or expressions to evaluate a query.

The expression used to build the index can be an arithmetic expression. However, it **cannot contain** any aggregate functions.

Syntax:

```
CREATE INDEX <IndexName> ON <TableName> (<Function>(<ColumnName>));
```

Create a function-based index on the following columns of the Customers table:

- **UPPER(**City**)**
- **EXTRACT(MONTH FROM** DateOfBirth**)**

Solution:

```
CREATE INDEX fnidx_Customers
  ON Customers(UPPER(City), EXTRACT(MONTH FROM DateOfBirth));
```

Output:

```
Index created.
```

This will allow Oracle to invoke the index for SQL queries like:

```
SELECT CustomerNo, CustomerName, DateOfBirth, Address, City, ContactNo
  FROM Customers WHERE UPPER(City)='MUMBAI';
```

Output:

CUSTOMERNO	CUSTOMERNAME	DATEOFBIRTH	ADDRESS	CITY	CONTACTNO
21	Sharanam Chaitanya Shah	03-JAN-81	20, Makanji Mansion, MG Road, 400076	**Mumbai**	91-022-24440094
22	Vaishali Sharanam Shah	22-NOV-81	Krishna Kunj, Thakur Lane, 400078	**Mumbai**	91-022-27740094

```
SELECT CustomerNo, CustomerName, DateOfBirth, Address, City, ContactNo
  FROM Customers WHERE EXTRACT(MONTH FROM DateOfBirth)='01';
```

Output:

CUSTOMERNO	CUSTOMERNAME	DATEOFBIRTH	ADDRESS	CITY	CONTACTNO
21	Sharanam Chaitanya Shah	03-**JAN**-81	20, Makanji Mansion, MG Road, 400076	Mumbai	91-022-24440094
25	Chaitanya Kantilal Shah	03-**JAN**-81	14, Raheja Tower, 347236	Kottayam	91-022-37640094
29	Deepika Anil Bakshi	30-**JAN**-81	Queensland Palace, India	Indore	91-022-57440094
30	Manali Narendra Naik	22-**JAN**-81	Hiranadani Mansion, Lion Road	Hyderabad	91-022-60740094

Key Compressed Index

A **key compressed index** is a compressed index that allows for space savings, enabling more keys to be stored in each index block. This can lead to reduced I/O and better performance.

> However, while key compression reduces the storage requirements of an index, it increases the CPU time needed to reconstruct the key column values during an index scan.

Key compression is particularly useful when dealing with non-unique indexes.

How Does Key Compressed Index Work?

In a key compressed index, Oracle breaks an index key into a prefix and a suffix entry. Compression is achieved by sharing the prefix entries among all the suffix entries in an index block. Key compression can be useful:

- For a non-unique index with RowID appended to make the key unique. In this situation, the duplicate key is stored as a prefix entry on the index block without the RowID. The remaining rows become suffix entries consisting of only the RowID.
- For a unique multi-column index.

Compression can be enabled using the **COMPRESS** clause:

```
CREATE INDEX <IndexName> ON <TableName>
  (<ColumnName1>, <ColumnName2>, . . . ) COMPRESS
```

The prefix length, which is the number of key columns, can be specified along with the Compress clause to identify how the key columns are divided into a prefix and suffix entry.

Create a key compressed index on the FirstName column of the Employees table, which holds non-unique values:

```
CREATE INDEX kcidx_FirstName ON Employees(FirstName) COMPRESS;
```

Output:

```
Index created.
```

This command compresses duplicate occurrences of a key in the index leaf block.

The COMPRESS clause can also be specified during rebuild.

Disable compression on the index named kcidx_FirstName while rebuilding it:

```
ALTER INDEX kcidx_FirstName REBUILD NOCOMPRESS;
```

Output:

```
Index altered.
```

Multiple Indexes On Same Column

One of the standout features introduced with Oracle Database 12c is the ability to create multiple indexes on the same column list. Having multiple indexes on the same set of columns allows you to switch between them quickly, making it easier to test the impact of various indexes.

Prior to Oracle 12c, multiple indexes could not be created on the same column or set of columns in any form. For example, if there was an index on the column {CustomerNo} or columns {CustomerNo, OrderNo}, another index could not be created on the same column or set of columns in the same order. However, in Oracle 12c, you can have multiple indexes on the same column or set of columns as long as the index type is different. However, only one type of index is usable/visible at any given time.

First, let's create a Books table whose ISBN is the primary key:

```
CREATE TABLE Books(
   ISBN Varchar2(25) PRIMARY KEY,
   BookName Varchar2(100),
   NoOfChapters Number(25),
   AuthorID Number(10),
   PublisherID Number(10),
   Category Varchar2(100));
```

Output:

```
Table created.
```

Next, insert some records into the Books table:

```
INSERT INTO Books VALUES('B81-91', 'Oracle For Beginners', 250, 2, 4,
   'Computers');
INSERT INTO Books VALUES('B82-92', 'Oracle For Professionals', 500, 3, 4,
   'Computers');
INSERT INTO Books VALUES('B83-93', 'Core Java 8', 250, 2, 3, 'Computers');
```

Output for each INSERT statement:

```
1 row created.
```

Commit the transaction:

```
COMMIT;
```

Output:

```
Commit completed.
```

Create the first index on the BookName column of the Books table:

```
CREATE INDEX idx_bookName1 ON Books(BookName);
```

Output:

```
Index created.
```

Make the BookName a Unique key:

```
ALTER TABLE Books1 ADD CONSTRAINT unq_bookName UNIQUE(BookName);
```

Output:

```
Table altered.
```

Create a unique index on the BookName column of the Books table as:

```
CREATE UNIQUE INDEX idx_bookName2 ON Books(BookName);
```

Output:

```
CREATE UNIQUE INDEX idx_bookName2 ON Books(BookName)
                                          *

ERROR at line 1:
ORA-01408: such column list already indexed
Help: https://docs.oracle.com/error-help/db/ora-01408/
```

Creating a unique index on the same set of columns fails because it has the same attributes as the existing index.

Now, create a unique index, which is invisible, on the BookName column:

```
CREATE UNIQUE INDEX idx_bookName2 ON Books(BookName) INVISIBLE;
```

Output:

```
Index created.
```

Now, create a bitmap index, which is invisible, on the BookName column:

```
CREATE BITMAP INDEX idx_bookName3 ON Books1(BookName) INVISIBLE;
```

Output:

```
Index created.
```

Dropping Indexes

Indexes associated with tables can be removed using the **DROP INDEX** command:

```
DROP INDEX <indexname>;
```

Remove the index named kcidx_FirstName:

```
DROP INDEX kcidx_FirstName;
```

Output:

```
Index dropped.
```

When a table with indexes is dropped, all the associated indexes are automatically dropped.

Chapter

23

SECTION IV: SQL PERFORMANCE TUNING

Views

Relational databases provide a high degree of **data abstraction**. It's not feasible to determine the exact location on the Hard Disk Drive where the RDBMS stores each row of a table.

Information held by a single table row might be split up and spread across multiple disk drives. When a new column is added to a table with a large number of records, it becomes difficult to pinpoint where the RDBMS will place the new column values:

- Will it be placed next to the pre-existing columns?
- Will a new block of hard disk space be allocated to hold the new column values for all existing rows?

A developer will not know such information and doesn't need to be concerned about it. Similarly, from an SQL perspective, Oracle allows the creation of views. A view is a way of building an even higher level of data abstraction.

Data Abstraction

Data abstraction is typically required after a table is created and populated with data. Some tables may contain sensitive information that requires restricted access to ensure data security. To address these security concerns, several tables with appropriate columns can be created, and specific users can be assigned to each table as needed.

While this approach effectively addresses data security requirements, it can lead to significant redundant data within the database. To minimize **redundant data**, Oracle provides the use of virtual tables, known as **Views**.

What Is A View?

A **View** is a virtual table based on the result returned by a SELECT query. The content is derived from one or more tables using a query. The primary purpose of a view is to restrict access to specific columns or rows of a table, allowing different users to see only certain parts of the data.

Views help simplify database access by presenting the structure of the data in a manner that is most intuitive for each user. In terms of usage, a View behaves just like an actual table. Therefore, a View can be queried exactly as though it were a real table.

Views Are Slower

A query executed on a view will generally run slower than a query executed directly on a base table. This is because, every time a query is run, Oracle retrieves the View definition from its system catalog. Once the definition is retrieved, the base table(s) are identified and loaded into memory. The View is then constructed on top of the base table(s). Only after this process is complete does the query in the view definition actually execute and return the required data.

Composition Of View

A View is composed of rows and columns, similar to a table. The fields in a View are fields from one or more database tables. SQL functions, WHERE clauses, and JOIN statements can be applied to a View in the same manner as they are applied to a table.

View Storage

A View is not a part of the physical schema like ordinary tables; it is a dynamic, virtual table computed or collated from the data available in the database.

Changing the data in a base table alters the data shown by the View. Oracle does not store the View data. It recreates the data using the View's SELECT statement each time a user queries the View.

A View is stored only as a definition in Oracle's system catalog. When a reference is made to a View, its definition is scanned, the base table is opened, and the View is constructed on top of the base table. This means that a View never holds data until a specific call to the View is made, significantly reducing redundant data on the hard disk drive.

Kinds Of Views

Views can be either **read-only** or **updatable**. If the RDBMS is able to determine the reverse mapping from the view schema to the schema of the underlying base tables, then the view is updatable, allowing INSERT, UPDATE, and DELETE operations.

Views that do not allow INSERT, UPDATE, and DELETE operations are known as **Read-Only Views**. A view becomes read-only if the RDBMS cannot map the changes to the underlying base tables.

When an **Updatable View** is used to manipulate table data, the underlying base table remains invisible to the user, who is granted rights only to the view and not to the actual base table. This ensures the required level of data security.

Advantages Of View

- *Security:* Each user can be given permission to access only a set of views that contain specific data.
- *Query Simplicity:* A view can draw data from several different tables and present it as a single table, simplifying multiple table queries into single table queries against the view.
- *Structural Simplicity:* Views can give users a personalized view of the database structure, presenting the database as a set of virtual tables that makes sense for that user.
- *Data Integrity:* When data is accessed and entered through a view, the DBMS can automatically check the data to ensure that it meets specified integrity constraints.

Creating View

Once a view is created, it can be used within an SQL query, a stored procedure, or even another view.

Syntax:

```
CREATE VIEW <ViewName> AS SELECT <ColumnName1>, <ColumnName2>
```

```
FROM <TableName> WHERE <ColumnName> = <Expression List>
    GROUP BY <Grouping Criteria> HAVING <Predicate>;
```

The ORDER BY clause **cannot** be used while creating a view.

Privacy Protection Using Views

The most common purpose of using a view is to protect confidential data.

Let's take an example. An organization has numerous employees who work to serve its customers. This organization uses relational database tables to hold customers' confidential data and has several departments that need access to this information. However, not all departments can have access to all information.

For instance:

- The Marketing department should not be aware of a customer's PAN number, passport number, and annual income.
- The Finance & Investments department should have access to details relevant to its operations, such as PAN number, passport number, and annual income.

To achieve this:

- Marketing Department:

```
CREATE VIEW vw_CustomersForMarketing AS
  SELECT CustomerNo, CustomerName, Address, ContactNo, MaritalStatus
      FROM Customers;
```

Output:

```
View created.
```

- Finance & Investments Department:

```
CREATE VIEW vw_CustomersForFinanceInv AS
  SELECT CustomerNo, CustomerName, PANNo, PassportNo, AnnualIncome
      FROM Customers;
```

Output:

```
View created.
```

For user-based access, each department is assigned a unique database User ID. Appropriate permissions on specific views are granted to each department's user ID. After setting these permissions, each user can only view the information they are permitted to access.

Source Code Protection Using Views

An organization that handles shopping using credit cards regularly needs to extract data from the Orders table to indicate the order status. An order can hold one of the following statuses:

- Confirmed
- Authorization Failed
- Void

To fetch such information from the Orders table, the query would be:

```
SELECT * FROM Orders
  WHERE OrderStatus IN ('Confirmed', 'Authorization Failed', 'Void');
```

Output:

```
ORDERNO ORDERDATE CUSTOMERNO ORDERAMOUNT ORDERSTATUS          ORDERCODE
------- --------- ---------- ----------- -------------------- ---------
1       03-JAN-08 21         69350.0     Confirmed            MU/0203
2       09-FEB-08 22         5750.0      Void                 DL/0203
3       14-OCT-07 21         14750.0     Confirmed            KL/0203
4       11-NOV-07 23         28400.0     Void                 MD/0203
5       28-FEB-07 24         66350.0     Confirmed            DL/0303
8       08-FEB-08 25         Infinity    Void                 MD/0203
6       09-DEC-08 25         15000.0     Authorization Failed KL/0403
7       09-DEC-08 25         NaN         Authorization Failed MD/0503

8 rows selected.
```

This query reveals internal system flags such as:

- Confirmed
- Authorization Failed
- Void

This might not be a secure solution as any employee accessing such data using this query would be aware of the system flags.

Source code can be protected using views as follows:

```
CREATE VIEW vw_OrdersProcessed AS SELECT * FROM Orders
  WHERE OrderStatus IN ('Confirmed', 'Authorization Failed', 'Void');
```

Output:

```
View created.
```

Read-Only Views

An employee from the marketing department needs to know a customer's monthly buying capacity. This information is available in more than one table and can be easily retrieved using the following SQL query with aggregate functions:

```
SELECT Customers.CustomerName "Customer", EXTRACT(MONTH FROM OrderDate)
  "Month", SUM(Cost) "TotalPrice" FROM Customers, OrderDetails
     WHERE Customers.CustomerName = OrderDetails.CustomerName
        GROUP BY Customers.CustomerName,
           EXTRACT(MONTH FROM OrderDate);
```

Output:

```
Customer                  Month TotalPrice
------------------------- ---------- ----------
Vaishali Sharanam Shah        2       5750
Anil Mayekar                 11      28400
Hansel                        2      66350
Chaitanya Kantilal Shah      12      15000
Sharanam Chaitanya Shah       1      69350
Sharanam Chaitanya Shah      10      14750

6 rows selected.
```

Since this information is required daily, it is not feasible to use a complex SQL query that reveals the base table's structure and column names. To provide a simple solution, a view called vw_CustomerOrders can be created. This view will extract order details for each customer:

```
CREATE VIEW vw_CustomerOrders AS SELECT Customers.CustomerName
  "Customer", EXTRACT(MONTH FROM OrderDate) "Month", SUM(Cost) "TotalPrice"
    FROM Customers, OrderDetails
      WHERE Customers.CustomerName = OrderDetails.CustomerName
        GROUP BY Customers.CustomerName,
          EXTRACT(MONTH FROM OrderDate);
```

Output:

```
View created.
```

Now, the marketing department can use a simpler SQL query:

```
SELECT * FROM vw_CustomerOrders;
```

Output:

```
Customer                  Month TotalPrice
------------------------- ---------- ----------
Vaishali Sharanam Shah        2       5750
Anil Mayekar                 11      28400
Hansel                        2      66350
Chaitanya Kantilal Shah      12      15000
Sharanam Chaitanya Shah       1      69350
Sharanam Chaitanya Shah      10      14750

6 rows selected.
```

Since the view has been created, it can be queried exactly like a base table.

Syntax:

```
SELECT <ColumnName1>, <ColumnName2> FROM <ViewName>;
```

Instead of a **table** name in the FROM clause, a **view** name is used. The SELECT statement can include all standard clauses such as **WHERE** and **ORDER BY**.

This query does not reveal the base table's structure and column names. It provides a level of security that prevents the marketing department from accessing any information other than:

- Customer's Name
- Monthly Purchases

When a view is queried to retrieve results, Oracle expands the simple query as follows:

```
SELECT "Customer", "Month", "TotalPrice" FROM (SELECT Customers.CustomerName
  "Customer", EXTRACT(Month FROM OrderDate) "Month", SUM(Cost) "TotalPrice"
     FROM Customers, OrderDetails
        WHERE Customers.CustomerName = OrderDetails.CustomerName
           GROUP BY Customers.CustomerName,
              EXTRACT(Month FROM OrderDate));
```

Output:

```
Customer                       Month TotalPrice
------------------------- ---------- ----------
Vaishali Sharanam Shah             2       5750
Anil Mayekar                      11      28400
Hansel                             2      66350
Chaitanya Kantilal Shah           12      15000
Sharanam Chaitanya Shah            1      69350
Sharanam Chaitanya Shah           10      14750

6 rows selected.
```

Every column in the query is given an alias. These column aliases become the actual column names for the view. If an alias is not given, the column name defaults to the base table's column name.

Updateable Views

Views can also be used for manipulating the data available in the base tables (i.e., the user can perform INSERT, UPDATE, and DELETE operations). Views on which data manipulation can be done are called Updateable Views. If an INSERT, UPDATE, or DELETE SQL statement is executed on a view, modifications to the data in the view are passed to the underlying base table.

For a view to be updateable, it should meet the following criteria:

- Views must be defined from a Single table.
- If the user wants to **INSERT** records with the help of a view, the PRIMARY KEY column(s) and **all** the NOT NULL columns must be included in the view.
- The user can **UPDATE, DELETE** records with the help of a view even if the PRIMARY KEY and NOT NULL column(s) **are excluded** from the view definition.

Create a view on the Customers table so that all the mandatory column data can be manipulated using this view.

This table is structured as:

Column Name	Data Type	Width	Attributes
CustomerNo	Number	10	Primary key
CustomerName	Varchar2	50	Not Null
DateOfBirth	Date		Not Null
Address	Varchar2	75	
ContactNo	Number	12, 2	Not Null

Solution:

```
CREATE VIEW vw_Customers AS
   SELECT CustomerNo, CustomerName, DateOfBirth, ContactNo FROM Customers;
```

Output:

```
View created.
```

This view fulfils all the required rules:

- The view is defined on one table only.
- The PRIMARY KEY column(s) and **all** the NOT NULL columns are included in the view.

Data can be manipulated as follows:

- **INSERT operation performed on the view:**

```
INSERT INTO vw_Customers VALUES(100, 'Meenal Joshi', '12-Dec-1987', 34523575);
```

Output:

```
1 row created.
```

- **MODIFY operation performed on the view:**

```
UPDATE vw_Customers SET CustomerName = 'Manali Doshi'
   WHERE CustomerName='Meenal Joshi';
```

Output:

```
1 row updated.
```

- **DELETE operation performed on the view:**

```
DELETE FROM vw_Customers WHERE CustomerName = 'Manali Doshi';
```

Output:

```
1 row deleted.
```

A view can be created from more than one table. For the purpose of creating the view, these tables will be linked by a JOIN specified in the WHERE clause of the view definition. If a view is created on multiple base tables that do not share a relationship between them, the view's behavior will be as follows.

The INSERT, UPDATE or DELETE operation is **not allowed**. If attempted, Oracle displays the following error message:

For insert/modify:

```
ORA -01779: cannot modify a column, which maps to a non key-preserved table.
```

For delete:

```
ORA -01752: cannot delete from view without exactly one key-preserved table.
```

If the view's base tables share a relationship between them using Primary and Foreign keys, the behavior of the View varies for different operations:

- An **INSERT** operation is not allowed.
- **DELETE** or **MODIFY** operations **that do not** affect the Master table are allowed.

If a **DELETE** operation is executed on the view, the corresponding records from the **detail table** are deleted.

Table Name: Authors

Column Name	Data Type	Size	Attributes
AuthorNo	Number	10	Primary Key
AuthorName	VarChar2	25	
ContactNo	Number	10	
SpecialtyNo	Number	10	

Table Name: Books

Column Name	Data Type	Size	Attributes
ISBN	Varchar2	20	Primary Key
AuthorNo	Number	10	Foreign Key references AuthorNo of the Authors table.
BookName	varchar2	50	
Cost	Number	12, 2	
NoOfPages	Number	4	
NoOfChapters	Number	2	
PublisherNo	Number	10	
Category	Vachar2	25	

To create a view on both these tables:

```
CREATE VIEW vw_AuthorDetails AS SELECT Authors.AuthorNo, AuthorName, ISBN,
  BookName, Cost, NoOfPages, PublisherNo FROM Authors, Books
     WHERE Authors.AuthorNo = Books.AuthorNo;
```

Output:

```
View created.
```

An INSERT operation performed on the view:

```
INSERT INTO vw_AuthorDetails
  VALUES(1, 'Anil Vaidya', '739-923-2736', 'Computer Fundamentals', 400, 1600, 1);
```

Oracle returns the following error message:

```
INSERT INTO vw_AuthorDetails
*
ERROR at line 1:
ORA-01779: cannot modify a column which maps to a non key-preserved table
Help: https://docs.oracle.com/error-help/db/ora-01779/
```

A MODIFY operation performed on the view:

```
UPDATE vw_AuthorDetails SET BookName = 'Ajax For Professionals'
  WHERE ISBN = '2-9485769-90';
```

Oracle returns the following message:

```
1 row updated.
```

A DELETE operation performed on the view:

```
DELETE FROM vw_AuthorDetails WHERE ISBN = '2-9485769-90';
```

Oracle returns the following message:

```
1 row deleted.
```

For a view to be updateable, the view definition must not include:

- Aggregate functions
- DISTINCT, GROUP BY or HAVING clause
- Sub-queries
- UNION, INTERSECT or MINUS clause
- Constants, Strings or Value Expressions like SellPrice * 1.05
- If a view is defined from another view, the second view should be updateable

If the user tries to perform any of INSERT, UPDATE, or DELETE operation on a view created from a non-updateable view, Oracle returns the following error message:

```
ORA-01732: data manipulation operation not legal on this view
```

Solution:

```
CREATE VIEW vw_MumbaiCustomers
  AS SELECT * FROM Customers WHERE City = 'Mumbai';
```

Output:

```
View created.
```

This view is created using * which selects all the available columns in the table at the moment. However, if the table structure is updated to add more columns later, the view is not updated automatically until the view is recreated by issuing **CREATE OR REPLACE VIEW** command.

Re-Creating A View

To recreate a view without destroying it, the following syntax can be used:

```
CREATE OR REPLACE VIEW <ViewName> AS
  SELECT <ColumnName1>, <ColumnName2> FROM <TableName>
     WHERE <ColumnName> = <Expression List>
        GROUP BY <Grouping Criteria> HAVING <Predicate>;
```

Destroying A View

The **DROP VIEW** command is used to destroy a view from the database.

Destroy the view **vw_AuthorDetails** from the database:

```
DROP VIEW vw_AuthorDetails;
```

Output:

```
View dropped.
```

Materialized Views

In an ordinary view, when an SQL query is fired, Oracle locates the actual definition and extracts the appropriate data from the underlying base tables. A **materialized view** takes a different approach, caching the query result as a concrete table that may be updated from the original base tables periodically.

Like ordinary views, materialized views can also be used to build data abstraction. However, since materialized views hold data, they consume disk space.

A materialized view does not contain up-to-the-minute information. When an ordinary view is queried, the data retrieved includes changes made up to the last committed transaction. However, when a materialized view is queried, the data retrieved reflects the state when the view was created or last refreshed. The refresh intervals at which the materialized view will be automatically updated can be controlled.

A materialized view is a database object that contains the results of a query, unlike normal views that only contain the query definition and not the results. Materialized views are usually chosen when creating summary tables based on aggregations of a table's data. A materialized view can query tables, views, and other materialized views.

The commonly created materialized views are:

- Primary Key
- RowID
- Subquery

Syntax:

```
CREATE MATERIALIZED VIEW <Schema.Name>
  REFRESH [FAST | COMPLETE | FORCE] [ON DEMAND | COMMIT]
  START WITH DATE NEXT DATE WITH [PRIMARY KEY | RowID]
```

Where,

- ***REFRESH:*** Since the materialized view is built on underlying data that is periodically changed, specify how and when to refresh the data in the view. The following keywords can be used to create a schedule for recurring refresh operations:
  - ***FAST:*** Updates only the values in the materialized view, assuming that some preconditions are met.
  - ***COMPLETE:*** Recreates the entire materialized view.
  - ***FORCE:*** Performs a fast refresh if one is possible or a complete refresh otherwise. If no refresh clause is specified, the FORCE clause is the default.
  - ***ON COMMIT:*** Causes a refresh to occur whenever the underlying data is changed and the change is committed.
  - ***ON DEMAND:*** Performs a refresh when it is scheduled or explicitly called.
- ***START WITH DATE:*** Indicates when to perform the first replication from the master table to the local base table. It should evaluate to a future point in time.
- ***NEXT DATE:*** Indicates the time and interval at which the materialized view is to be refreshed next. The NEXT DATE clause specifies the interval between refreshes.
- ***WITH PRIMARY KEY:*** Indicates whether the materialized view is based on a Primary key.
- ***WITH RowID:*** Indicates whether the materialized view is based on RowID.

Primary Key Materialized Views

Primary key materialized views allow materialized view master tables to be reorganized without affecting the eligibility of the materialized view for fast refresh. Such a materialized view is based on the primary key of the master table instead of RowID.

PRIMARY KEY is the default option. To use the PRIMARY KEY clause, a PRIMARY KEY must be defined on the master table.

The following statement creates a primary-key materialized view on the Employees table:

```
CREATE MATERIALIZED VIEW mv_pk_Employees
   REFRESH FAST START WITH SYSDATE NEXT SYSDATE + 2
        WITH PRIMARY KEY AS SELECT * FROM Employees;
```

The **REFRESH** option specifies:

- The refresh method used by Oracle to refresh data in materialized view.
- Whether the view is primary key based or row-id based.
- The time and interval at which the view is to be refreshed.

```
START WITH SYSDATE NEXT SYSDATE + 2
```

Indicates that the first copy of the materialized view is made at SYSDATE and the refresh interval is set to every two days.

Output:

```
Materialized view created.
```

When a materialized view is created using the **FAST** option, a view log needs to be created on the master tables.

Solution:

```
CREATE MATERIALIZED VIEW LOG ON Employees;
```

Output:

```
Materialized view log created.
```

Materialized view output when queried:

```
EMPLOYEENO FIRSTNAME LASTNAME DATEOFBIR G M ADDRESS                 CONTACTNO
---------- --------- -------- --------- - - ----------------------- ---------------
SALARY DESIGNATION          MANAGERNO DEPTNO
------ -------------------- --------- ------
ABOUTME
-------------------------------------------------------------------------------------
USERNAME                  PASSWORD
------------------------- -------------------------
         1 Sharanam  Shah     03-JAN-81 M M Makanji Mansion         91-022-24440094
 75000 Technical Writing            6      5
I can work with PHP, MySQL, Apache, Oracle, JSP. My Contact No is 8121-451969.
         2 Vaishali  Shah     09-FEB-81 F M Makanji Mansion, Mumbai 91-022-31040094
 50000 Database Management  10      2      6
I am comfortable working with Word, Powerpoint, Excel. My Phone No is 7131.461962.
         3 Keyur     Kapoor   14-OCT-84 M U Sita Sadan, Delhi       91-022-27740094
 20000 Testing             8        4      0
I am comfortable working with only Word. My Phone No is 3131.987344.
         4 Amit      Haria    11-NOV-72 M M Krishna Kunj, Mumbai    91-022-34340094
 20000 Programming         7        2      1
Contact me at 2671.978344.
         5 Abhishek  Benegal  28-FEB-59 M M Thakur Complex, Mumbai  91-022-37640094
 12122 Sales               3        1      17
Call me at 3322.554433.
```

```
         6 Chetan    Dedhia   20-SEP-65 M U Upendra Nagar, Mumbai   91-022-40940094
 12321 HR                  4         3      3
One year experience in Word. Contact No 5544.988765.
         7 Narendra  Dodhia   23-JUN-80 M M Gokul Vihar, Mumbai     91-022-44240094
 12344 Accounts            2         3      2
One year experience in Excel. Contact No 9844.983335.
         8 Meenal    Doshi    12-DEC-87 F U Prakash Towers, Mumbai  91-022-47540094
 45000 Auditing            9         7      5
One year experience in Word.
         9 Anil      Mayekar  22-NOV-56 M U Advani Apts, Mumbai
  2500 Peon                1         3      30
One year experience in Word. Contact No 6644.983335.
        10 Chaitanya Kapoor   04-APR-62 M U Tilak Nagar, Mumbai     91-022-54140094
  1200 Peon                1         5      10
One year experience in Word.

10 rows selected.
```

Insert a record in the Employees table:

```
INSERT INTO Employees (EmployeeNo, FirstName, LastName, DateOfBirth, Salary,
  Designation, ManagerNo, DeptNo) VALUES(13,'Stuti', 'Khanna', '08-JUN-1984',
  28370, 'Consultant', 2, 1);
```

Query the materialized view and notice the output. It will still hold 10 records. This is because:

```
NEXT SYSDATE + 2
```

This indicates that the data will be refreshed every two days. Hence, if the same materialized view is queried after two days the output will include the 11th record.

RowID Materialized Views

RowID materialized views should have a single master table and cannot contain any of the following:

- Distinct or aggregate functions
- GROUP BY Clauses, Subqueries, Joins, and Set operations

The following statement creates the RowID materialized view on the Employees table:

```
CREATE MATERIALIZED VIEW mv_rowid_Employees
  REFRESH WITH RowID AS SELECT * FROM Employees;
```

Output:

```
Materialized view created.
```

Subquery Materialized Views

The following statement creates a subquery materialized view based on the Employees and Departments tables:

```
CREATE MATERIALIZED VIEW mv_sq_EmployeesDept
```

```
AS SELECT * FROM Employees E
WHERE EXISTS(SELECT * FROM Departments D WHERE E.DeptNo = D.DeptNo);
```

Output:

```
Materialized view created.
```

Chapter

24

SECTION IV: SQL PERFORMANCE TUNING

Clusters

Before deploying an application to a production environment, performance tuning is crucial to enhance throughput and overall performance. Clusters play a vital role in this tuning process. A **cluster** is a group of one or more tables that share common columns and are physically stored together.

A **table cluster** is a collection of tables sharing the same data blocks because they have common columns and are frequently used together. When cluster tables are created, Oracle physically stores all rows for each table within the same data blocks. The cluster key value represents the value of the cluster key columns for a particular row.

For instance, consider the Orders and OrderDetails tables, which have OrderNo as their common column. Typically, the OrderDetails table is accessed to retrieve the order details of orders available in the Orders table, meaning these tables are often used together.

To optimize performance, a cluster can be created to group these tables by sharing OrderNo as the common column. When a cluster is created, it stores the rows physically together, improving disk access time.

Clusters store data from different tables in the **same physical data blocks**. As a result, the rows from the detail table are stored in the same physical data block as those from the master table. This consolidation reduces the number of database block reads required to fulfill queries, thereby enhancing performance. Clusters are especially beneficial when records are frequently queried from multiple tables.

Similar to indexes, clusters do not affect application design. This means that creating a cluster after an application is deployed will not impact the application's functionality. Tables within a cluster remain transparent to users and applications, and data stored in a clustered table is accessed using SQL in the same manner as data stored in a non-clustered table. Each created cluster includes a cluster index, which is used to sort table data when needed.

When To Cluster

The following guidelines explain when to use clustering:

- ***Tables that are accessed frequently by an application using join statements. Do not cluster tables if:***
  - Tables are joined occasionally.
  - The common column values are frequently modified.

  Oracle takes longer to modify a row's cluster key than the value in a non-clustered table because it transfers the modified row to another block to maintain the cluster data.
- ***Tables that share a master-detail relationship***, such as Orders and OrderDetails, Departments and Employees, Customer and ContactDetails, etc. Typically, in master-detail tables, master records are retrieved along with the corresponding detail records. If such tables are clustered, the detail records are stored in the same data block(s) as the master record, so the detail records remain in memory when retrieved, requiring Oracle to perform less I/O.
- ***Do not cluster tables that are scanned fully (all rows, all columns)***. A full table scan of a clustered table takes longer than a full table scan of a non-clustered table because Oracle is likely to read more blocks since the tables are stored together.
- ***A detail table that is often queried for a single master record***. For example: Order Details of the Order No 71.

  This improves the performance of queries that select detail records of the same master but does not decrease the performance of a full table scan on the master table.

Types Of Clusters

Indexed Clusters

In an **indexed cluster**, Oracle stores together rows that share the same cluster key value. Each distinct cluster key value is stored only once in each data block, regardless of the number of tables and rows in which it occurs. This conserves disk space and enhances performance for many operations.

After an indexed cluster is created, an index must be created on the cluster key before any **D**ata **M**anipulation **L**anguage (DML) statements are issued against a table in the cluster. This index is called the **Cluster Index**.

A cluster index provides quick access to rows within a cluster based on the cluster key. When an SQL query searches for a row in the cluster based on its cluster key value, Oracle searches the cluster index for the cluster key value and then locates the row in the cluster based on its RowID.

Hash Clusters

In a **hash cluster**, Oracle stores together rows that have the same hash key value. The hash value for a row is the value returned by the cluster's hash function. Unlike indexed clusters, where Oracle locates rows using key values stored in a separate index, in a hash cluster, the database physically stores and retrieves rows according to the results of a hash function.

TIP: While hash values are not stored in the cluster, cluster key values are stored for every row in the cluster.

A hash cluster can be created either by using a custom hash function or Oracle's internal hash function. Oracle uses a hash function to generate a distribution of numeric values called hash values, based on specific cluster key values.

The key of a hash cluster, like that of an indexed cluster, can be a single column or a composite key. To find or store a row in a hash cluster, the database applies the hash function to the cluster key value of the row. The resulting hash value corresponds to a data block in the cluster, which the database then reads or writes. This process often results in less I/O compared to the indexed cluster because the index search is not required.

A cluster index cannot be created on a hash cluster, and there is no need to create an index on a hash cluster key.

Hashing is particularly useful when dealing with SQL queries that use equality operators on the cluster key. The cluster key in the equality condition is hashed, and the corresponding hash key is usually found with a single read. In contrast, for an indexed table, the key value must first be found in the index (usually several reads) and then the row is read from the table (another read).

Create Cluster

The **CREATE CLUSTER** command is used to create a cluster. A cluster is a schema object containing data from one or more tables, all of which share one or more columns. Oracle Database stores together all the rows from all tables that share the same cluster key.

```
CREATE CLUSTER <ClusterName> (<ColumnName> <DataType>
  [, <ColumnName> <DataType>] . . .) [<Other Options>];
```

Where,

- ***ClusterName:*** The name of the cluster to be created. It follows the table naming conventions. After a cluster is created and tables are added to it, the cluster becomes transparent. The clustered tables can be accessed using SQL statements in the same manner as non-clustered tables. A cluster can contain a maximum of 32 tables.
- ***ColumnName:*** Indicates one or more column names in the cluster key. Up to 16 cluster key columns can be specified. These columns must correspond in both data type and size to columns in each of the clustered tables. However, the columns need not correspond in name.
- ***DataType:*** Indicates the data type for the column specified.

Integrity constraints cannot be a part of the definition of a cluster key column. However, integrity constraints can be associated with the tables that belong to the cluster.

Cluster Key

The columns defined by the CREATE CLUSTER command make up the **cluster key**. These cluster columns must correspond in both data type and size to columns in each of the clustered tables, though they need not correspond in name. Since the cluster key columns determine the physical placement of rows within the cluster, the cluster key is usually the foreign key of one table that references the primary key of another table in the cluster.

In a cluster, a cluster key value is the value of the cluster key column for a particular row. Each cluster key value is stored only once in both the cluster and the cluster index, regardless of how many rows of different tables contain the value. After the cluster is created, the cluster index is created on the cluster key columns.

Once the cluster key index is created, data can be entered into the tables stored in the cluster. As rows are inserted, the database stores a cluster key and its associated rows in each of the cluster's blocks.

Consider two tables named Customers and Orders. Typically, you need to retrieve all orders for a particular customer. In a normal scenario, Oracle performs an I/O to fetch the desired customer row from the Customers table and then performs multiple I/Os to fetch each order for that customer from the Orders table.

The following SQL query fetches all the orders for a particular customer:

```
SELECT Customers.CustomerName, OrderNo, OrderAmount, OrderDate
  FROM Customers, Orders WHERE Customers.CustomerNo = Orders.CustomerNo
     AND Customers.CustomerName = 'Sharanam Chaitanya Shah';
```

Output:

```
CUSTOMERNAME                ORDERNO  ORDERAMOUNT ORDERDATE
-------------------------- -------- ----------- ----------
Sharanam Chaitanya Shah     1        69350.0     03-JAN-08
Sharanam Chaitanya Shah     3        14750.0     14-OCT-07

2 rows selected.
```

If this customer has ten orders, each on a different data block, eleven I/Os will be performed to return the query result - one I/O on the Customers table and ten I/Os on the Orders table.

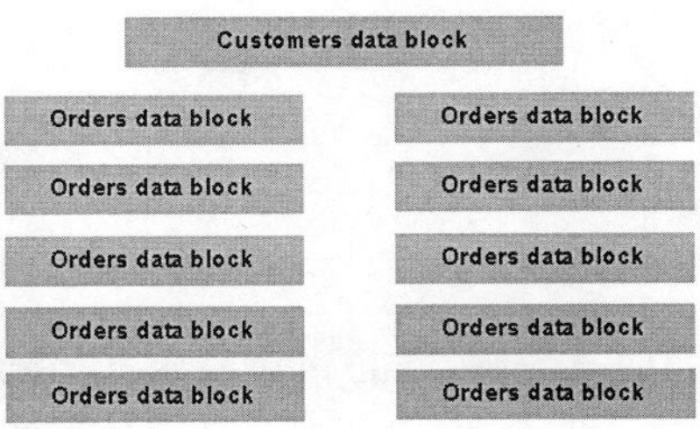

Oracle stores customers and orders as different physical data blocks as shown in adjoining diagram. To improve the performance, create an **indexed cluster** named cli_CustOrders and add both these tables to that Cluster.

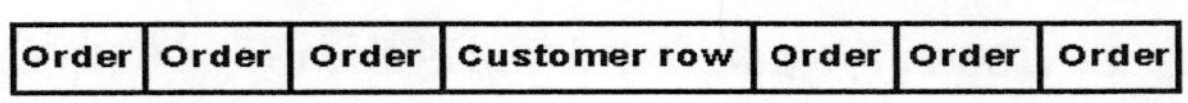

Creating Cluster

Solution:

```
CREATE CLUSTER cli_CustOrders (CustomerNo Number(10));
```

Output:

```
Cluster created.
```

Adding Tables To The Cluster

Example:

```
CREATE TABLE Customers(
   CustomerNo Number(10) PRIMARY KEY,
   CustomerName Varchar2(25),
   DateOfBirth Date,
   Address Varchar2(50),
   City Varchar2(25),
   State Varchar2(25),
   ContactNo Number(15),
   PANNo Varchar2(15),
   PassportNo Varchar2(15),
   AnnualIncome Number(12, 2),
   MaritalStatus Char(1))
   CLUSTER cli_CustOrders(CustomerNo);
```

Output:

```
Table created.
```

Example:

```
CREATE TABLE Orders(
   OrderNo Number(10) PRIMARY KEY,
   OrderDate Date,
   CustomerNo Number(10),
   OrderAmount Number(12, 2),
   OrderStatus Varchar2(20),
   OrderCode Varchar2(20))
   CLUSTER cli_CustOrders(CustomerNo);
```

Output:

```
Table created.
```

After a cluster is created and tables are added to the cluster, Oracle physically stores the Orders table rows on the same data block as the Customers table rows, thereby reducing I/O by a factor of ten.

The following statement creates the cluster index on the cluster key of CustomerNo:

```
CREATE INDEX idx_CustomerNo ON CLUSTER cli_CustOrders;
```

Output:

```
Index created.
```

After creating the cluster index, records can be inserted into either of the two tables.

Create a hash cluster named clh_CustOrders1 with the cluster key column as CustomerNo, a maximum of 503 hash key values, each of size 512 bytes, and following storage parameter values:

- INITIAL 100K
- NEXT 50K
- PCTINCREASE 10

Solution:

```
CREATE CLUSTER clh_CustOrders1(CustomerNo Number(10)) SIZE 512
  HASHKEYS 503 STORAGE (INITIAL 100K NEXT 50K PCTINCREASE 10);
```

Output:

```
Cluster created.
```

Here, the **HASH IS** clause is not specified; hence Oracle uses the internal hash function for the cluster.

Create a hash cluster named clh_CustOrders2 with the cluster key consisting of the columns OrderNo and EmployeeNo, using an SQL expression containing these columns for the hash function:

```
CREATE CLUSTER clh_CustOrders2(OrderNo Number(10), EmployeeNo Number(10))
  HASHKEYS 20 HASH IS MOD (OrderNo + EmployeeNo, 101);
```

Output:

```
Cluster created.
```

Listing Information About Clusters

To display the clusters in the current schema, issue the following command:

```
SELECT CLUSTER_NAME, TABLESPACE_NAME, PCT_FREE, KEY_SIZE,
  HASHKEYS, CACHE FROM USER_CLUSTERS;
```

Output:

```
CLUSTER_NAME     TABLESPACE_NAME          PCT_FREE KEY_SIZE HASHKEYS CACHE
---------------  ----------------------- -------- -------- -------- -----
CLI_CUSTORDERS   ORACLEFORPROFESSIONALS        10                  0     N
CLH_CUSTORDERS2  ORACLEFORPROFESSIONALS        10                 23     N
CLH_CUSTORDERS1  ORACLEFORPROFESSIONALS        10      512       503     N
```

To determine the tables clustered, issue the following command:

```
SELECT * FROM TAB;
```

Output:

```
TNAME                          TABTYPE  CLUSTERID
------------------------------ ------- ----------
ACCOUNTS                       TABLE
```

```
. . .
. . .
CITIZENEMPLOYMENTDETAILS        TABLE
CLH_CUSTORDERS1                 CLUSTER
CLH_CUSTORDERS2                 CLUSTER
CLI_CUSTORDERS                  CLUSTER          1
CUSTOMERS                       TABLE
. . .
. . .
TRIGONOMETRY                    TABLE
VW_CUSTOMERORDERS               VIEW
VW_CUSTOMERS                    VIEW
VW_CUSTOMERSFORFINANCEINV       VIEW
VW_CUSTOMERSFORMARKETING        VIEW
VW_MUMBAICUSTOMERS              VIEW
VW_ORDERSPROCESSED              VIEW

62 rows selected.
```

Here, notice the CLUSTER_ID column value, for the tables Orders and Customers. It holds a value of 1, indicating that these tables are in cluster whose CLUSTER_ID is 1.

Dropping Clusters

To drop a cluster, use the **DROP CLUSTER** command.

Drop the cluster named cli_CustOrders:

```
DROP CLUSTER cli_CustOrders;
```

Output:

```
Cluster dropped.
```

This command drops the cluster if the cluster is empty, i.e., no tables are held within it. If the cluster contains tables, they need to be dropped prior dropping the cluster.

Alternatively, the cluster can be dropped even with tables existing within it by issuing the following command:

```
DROP CLUSTER cli_CustOrders INCLUDING TABLES;
```

Output:

```
Cluster dropped.
```

Chapter 25

SECTION IV: SQL PERFORMANCE TUNING

Sequences

Data entered into a table needs to be uniquely identified. Only when data is uniquely identifiable can it be accurately queried and manipulated. For an individual row of data (record) in a table to be uniquely identifiable, a table column is dedicated to storing unique values only. For example, to identify an employee in the Employees table, an EmployeeNo serves as the unique identifier, allowing for the identification of an individual employee by their employee number.

Using EmployeeNo, specific records can be deleted, updated, and retrieved from the database table by using it in the WHERE clause:

```
SELECT * FROM Employees WHERE EmployeeNo = 6;
```

To ensure the values in the dedicated table column (in this case, EmployeeNo) remain unique, a data constraint (Primary Key or Unique and NOT NULL) is attached to that column. This ensures that the column is never left empty and that the values within it are unique.

However, even with such a data constraint, there is a risk that a person entering data might accidentally enter a duplicate value, thus violating the constraint and causing the entire row to be rejected. To prevent record rejections due to violations of the data constraint, this dedicated column can be automatically assigned unique values every time a record is inserted into the table.

Oracle provides a solution for this using an object called a **Sequence**. A sequence is an independent database object that can be used with any table that requires the automatic generation of unique numbers. A sequence is usually the choice when a unique auto-number, either in ascending or descending order, needs to be assigned to a primary key column.

TIP: Oracle allows setting intervals between the numbers generated by the Sequence.

Oracle also enables caching of sequence numbers in memory to speed up their availability.

Creating Sequences

A Sequence is created using the **CREATE SEQUENCE** command:

```
CREATE SEQUENCE <SequenceName>
   [INCREMENT BY <IntegerValue>
   START WITH <IntegerValue>
   MAXVALUE <IntegerValue> / NOMAXVALUE
   MINVALUE <integervalue> / NOMINVALUE
   CYCLE / NOCYCLE
   CACHE <IntegerValue> / NOCACHE
   ORDER   / NOORDER]
```

Where,

- *INCREMENT BY:* Indicates the interval between sequence numbers. This integer value can be any positive or negative integer, but cannot be zero. The absolute value must be less than the difference between MAXVALUE and MINVALUE. If negative, the sequence descends; if positive, the sequence ascends. If omitted, the interval defaults to 1.
- *START WITH:* Indicates the first sequence number to be generated. This clause is used to either start an ascending sequence at a value greater than its minimum or start a descending sequence at a value less than its maximum. Defaults to the minimum value for ascending sequences and the maximum value for descending sequences.
- *MAXVALUE:* Indicates the maximum value the sequence can generate. The value must be equal to or greater than START WITH and greater than MINVALUE.
- *NOMAXVALUE:* Indicates a maximum value of 1 followed by 27 zeros for an ascending sequence or -1 for a descending sequence. This is the default.

- *MINVALUE:* Indicates the minimum value the sequence can generate. The value must be less than or equal to START WITH and less than MAXVALUE.
- *NOMINVALUE:* Indicates a minimum value of 1 for an ascending sequence or -1026 for a descending sequence. This is the default.
- *CYCLE:* Indicates that the sequence continues to generate values after reaching its maximum or minimum value, cycling back to the minimum for ascending sequences and maximum for descending sequences.
- *NOCYCLE:* Indicates that the sequence cannot generate more values after reaching its maximum or minimum value. This is the default.
- *CACHE:* Indicates the number of sequence values that will be pre-allocated and kept in the memory for faster access. This integer value must be greater than or equal to 2 and less than the cycle' capacity for sequences that cycle. Cached values are lost if a system failure occurs.
- *NOCACHE:* Indicates that sequence values are not pre-allocated. If both CACHE and NOCACHE are omitted, the default is to cache 20 sequence numbers.
- *ORDER:* Indicates that sequence numbers are generated in order of request. Useful for timestamps, it guarantees ordered generation in Oracle Real Application Clusters.
- *NOORDER:* Indicates no guarantee for the order of generated sequence numbers. This is the default.

To create a sequence object, specify the starting number, the maximum number that can be generated, and the increment value for the next number.

> The ORDER, NOORDER clause have no significance if Oracle is configured with a Single Server option.

Let's create a sequence that automatically generates the DeptNo in the Departments table. The number generation will begin from 1 upto 100 in **ascending** order with an interval of 1:

```
CREATE SEQUENCE sq_DeptNo INCREMENT BY 1 START WITH 1
  MINVALUE 1 MAXVALUE 100;
```

Output:

```
Sequence created.
```

Retrieving The Current And Next Sequence Value

Sequence values can be referenced or retrieved using SQL statements with the help of the following Pseudo Columns:

- *CURRVAL:* Returns the current value of a sequence.

- *NEXTVAL:* Increments the sequence and returns the next value.
- CURRVAL and NEXTVAL pseudo columns must be qualified with the name of the sequence:

```
<SequenceName>.CURRVAL
<SequenceName>.NEXTVAL
```

- To refer to the current or next value of a sequence in the schema of another user, qualify the sequence with the schema containing it:

```
<SchemaName>.<SequenceName>.CURRVAL
<SchemaName>.<SequenceName>.NEXTVAL
```

  This will work only if appropriate permissions on that schema exist.

- To refer to the value of a sequence on a remote database, qualify the sequence with a complete or partial name of a database link:

```
<SchemaName>.<SequenceName>.CURRVAL@dblink
<SchemaName>.<SequenceName>.NEXTVAL@dblink
```

NEXTVAL

After a sequence is created using the CREATE SEQUENCE command the next value can be retrieved as:

```
SELECT <SequenceName>.NextVal FROM DUAL;
```

This query displays the next value held in the cache.

> The very first reference to NEXTVAL returns the sequence's initial value. Subsequent references to NEXTVAL **increment the sequence value** by the defined increment and return the new value.

CURRVAL

The following query extracts the current value in the sequence:

```
SELECT <SequenceName>.CURRVAL FROM DUAL;
```

NEXTVAL And CURRVAL Usage

Both pseudo columns can be used in:

- The SELECT list of a SELECT statement that is not contained in a subquery, materialized view or view:

```
SELECT sq_DeptNo.NextVal, DepartmentName FROM OldDepartments;
```

- The SELECT list of a subquery in an INSERT statement:

```
INSERT INTO Departments (DeptNo, DepartmentName)
  VALUES(SELECT sq_DeptNo.NextVal, DepartmentName FROM OldDepartments);
```

- The VALUES clause of an INSERT statement:

```
INSERT INTO Departments (DeptNo, DepartmentName)
  VALUES(sq_DeptNo.NextVal, 'Accounts');
```

- The SET clause of an UPDATE statement:

```
UPDATE Departments SET DeptNo = sq_DeptNo.NextVal
  WHERE DepartmentName = 'Accounts';
```

The CURRVAL and NEXTVAL pseudo columns cannot be used in:

- A subquery in a DELETE, SELECT, or UPDATE statement.
- A query of a view or a materialized view.
- A SELECT statement with the DISTINCT operator.
- A SELECT statement with a GROUP BY clause or ORDER BY clause.
- A SELECT statement that is combined with another SELECT statement with the UNION, INTERSECT, or MINUS set operator.
- The WHERE clause of a SELECT statement.
- The DEFAULT value of a column in a CREATE TABLE or ALTER TABLE statement.
- The condition of a CHECK constraint.

Using The Sequence Value

To add a new record in the Departments table using the sq_DeptNo sequence to generate the next department number for the DeptNo column:

```
INSERT INTO Departments1 (DeptNo, DepartmentName)
  VALUES(sq_DeptNo.NextVal, 'Accounts');
```

Output:

```
1 row created.
```

In the commercial application world, an automatically generated number is often an alphanumeric value.

For example, in the Orders table, the OrderNo may be composed of:

Company Initials	System Date	Running Number	OrderNo
ABC	03012007	1	ABC030120071
ABC	04022007	2	ABC040220072

This can be achieved using a sequence by concatenating it with the required values.

Create a sequence to allow automatic generation of the StudentNo in the Students table in the following format:

Student Division	System Date	Running Number	StudentNo
A	10052008	1	A100520081

The number generation will begin from 1 upto 999 in **ascending** order with an interval of 1. After the maximum value, the sequence number will restart from 1:

```
CREATE SEQUENCE sq_StudentNo INCREMENT BY 1 START WITH 1
  MINVALUE 1 MAXVALUE 999 CYCLE;
```

Output:

```
Sequence created.
```

The sequence will handle the numeric value in the StudentNo, while the other values will be generated on the fly and concatenated with the next sequence number during data insertion using the INSERT INTO statement.

Add a new record in the Students table using the sq_StudentNo sequence to generate the next student number (as per the specified format) for the StudentNo column:

```
INSERT INTO Students (StudentNo, StudentName, Age)
  VALUES('A' || TO_CHAR(SYSDATE, 'DDMMYYYY') ||
      TO_CHAR(sq_StudentNo.NextVal), 'Nita', 29);
```

Output:

```
1 row created.
```

Run the following query to ensure that the StudentNo was generated as per the required format:

```
SELECT StudentNo FROM Students;
```

Output:

```
STUDENTNO
--------------------
A200520081

1 row selected.
```

Let's take an example of adding a new record in the Students table using the sq_StudentNo sequence to generate the next student number (as per the specified format) for the StudentNo column. Additionally, use the same sequence number to add detail records to the StudentMarks table.

Master Table (Students) Insert:

```
INSERT INTO Students (StudentNo, StudentName, Age)
  VALUES('S' || TO_CHAR(SYSDATE, 'DDMMYYYY') ||
      TO_CHAR(sq_StudentNo.NextVal), 'Sanjana Kapur', 36);
```

Output:

```
1 row created.
```

Details Table (StudentMarks) Insert:

```
INSERT INTO StudentMarks (StudentNo, Semester, Subject, Marks)
  VALUES('S' || TO_CHAR(SYSDATE, 'DDMMYYYY') ||
      TO_CHAR(sq_StudentNo.CurrVal), 'SemesterII', 'English', 80);
INSERT INTO StudentMarks (StudentNo, Semester, Subject, Marks)
  VALUES('S' || TO_CHAR(SYSDATE, 'DDMMYYYY') ||
      TO_CHAR(sq_StudentNo.CurrVal), 'SemesterI', 'Maths', 97);
INSERT INTO StudentMarks (StudentNo, Semester, Subject, Marks)
  VALUES('S' || TO_CHAR(SYSDATE, 'DDMMYYYY') ||
      TO_CHAR(sq_StudentNo.CurrVal), 'SemesterII', 'Marathi', 57);
```

Output (For each INSERT statement):

```
1 row created.
```

Run the following query on the master table to ensure that the StudentNo was generated as per the required format:

```
SELECT StudentNo FROM Students;
```

Output:

```
STUDENTNO
--------------------
A200520081
S200520082

2 rows selected.
```

Run the following query on the details table to ensure that the same StudentNo was used for the child records in the StudentMarks table:

```
SELECT * FROM StudentMarks;
```

Output:

```
STUDENTNO   SEMESTER     SUBJECT     MARKS
----------- ------------ ----------- --------
S200520082  SemesterII   English     80
S200520082  SemesterI    Maths       97
S200520082  SemesterII   Marathi     57

3 rows selected.
```

Modifying An Existing Sequence

A sequence, once created, can be modified using the **ALTER SEQUENCE** command:

```
ALTER SEQUENCE <SequenceName>
  [INCREMENT BY <IntegerValue>
  MAXVALUE <IntegerValue> / NOMAXVALUE
```

```
MINVALUE <IntegerValue> / NOMINVALUE CYCLE / NOCYCLE
CACHE <IntegerValue> / NOCACHE ORDER / NOORDER]
```

The **START** value of the sequence cannot be altered.

Modify the sequence named sq_StudentNo to generate odd numbers and change the cache to 30:

```
ALTER SEQUENCE sq_StudentNo INCREMENT BY 2 CACHE 30;
```

Output:

```
Sequence altered.
```

The disadvantage of creating a sequence with a cache is that if a system failure occurs, all cached sequence values that have not been used are **lost**. This results in a **gap** in the assigned sequence values. When the system comes back up, Oracle caches new numbers from where it left off in the sequence, ignoring the so-called **lost** sequence values.

Modify the sequence named sq_StudentNo to ensure that no values are lost in case of system failure:

```
ALTER SEQUENCE sq_StudentNo NOCACHE;
```

Output:

```
Sequence altered.
```

NOCACHE means that none of the sequence values are stored in memory. This option reduces performance to some extent. However, it ensures that no gap occurs in the assigned sequence values in case of system failure.

Sometimes it is required to modify an already existing sequence's last value to a particular value without using it (using NextVal). Currently the value of sequence named sq_StudentNo is 2. To modify the last value of sequence to 126, so that the next value that is extracted using NextVal is 127, first determine the current value of the sequence:

```
SELECT sq_StudentNo.CurrVal FROM DUAL;
```

Output:

```
   CURRVAL
----------
         2
```

Since the current value is 2, modify the sequence by setting the ***INCREMENT BY*** to 124 (2 + 124 = 126):

```
ALTER SEQUENCE sq_StudentNo INCREMENT BY 124;
```

Output:

```
Sequence altered.
```

Execute the sequence using the NEXTVAL pseudo column to increment the value to 126:

```
SELECT sq_StudentNo.NextVal FROM DUAL;
```

Output:

```
   NEXTVAL
----------
       126
```

This changes the next value to 126, as the last value was 2, and the increment by was set to 124, increasing the sequence value to 126. Now reset the INCREMENT BY value to 1:

```
ALTER SEQUENCE sq_StudentNo INCREMENT BY 1;
```

Output:

```
Sequence altered.
```

Now the next value when retrieved will be 127. Test this by executing an INSERT INTO statement:

```
INSERT INTO Students (StudentNo, StudentName, Age)
  VALUES('C' || TO_CHAR(SYSDATE, 'DDMMYYYY') ||
      TO_CHAR(sq_StudentNo.NextVal), 'Gopi Shah', 48);
```

Output:

```
1 row created.
```

Query the Students table:

```
SELECT StudentNo FROM Students;
```

Output:

```
STUDENTNO
--------------------
A200520081
C20052008127
S200520082

3 rows selected.
```

Dropping A Sequence

The **DROP SEQUENCE** command is used to remove the sequence from the database.

To destroy the sequence named sq_DeptNo, use the following command:

```
DROP SEQUENCE sq_DeptNo;
```

Output:

```
Sequence dropped.
```

Sequence In PL/SQL

A sequence can also be used in traditional PL/SQL code specifications.

Prior To Oracle 11g Code Spec

Solution:

```
SET SERVEROUTPUT ON
DECLARE
   nxt NATURAL;
   cur NATURAL;
BEGIN
   SELECT sq_StudentNo.NEXTVAL, sq_StudentNo.CURRVAL INTO nxt, cur
        FROM DUAL;
   DBMS_OUTPUT.PUT_LINE(nxt);
   DBMS_OUTPUT.PUT_LINE(cur);
END;
/
```

Output:

```
PL/SQL procedure successfully completed.
```

In the above code, the next and the current sequence values are copied to memory variables using the SELECT INTO command before being used.

Starting from Oracle 11g, sequences can be directly assigned to memory variables. Before 11g, the SELECT INTO command was necessary to copy the sequence values into memory variables.

Oracle 11g Code Spec

Solution:

```
SET SERVEROUTPUT ON
DECLARE
   nxt NATURAL;
   cur NATURAL;
BEGIN
   nxt := sq_StudentNo.NEXTVAL;
```

```
    cur := sq_StudentNo.CURRVAL;
    DBMS_OUTPUT.PUT_LINE(nxt);
    DBMS_OUTPUT.PUT_LINE(cur);
END;
/
```

Alternatively:

```
SET SERVEROUTPUT ON
BEGIN
    DBMS_OUTPUT.PUT_LINE(sq_StudentNo.NEXTVAL);
    DBMS_OUTPUT.PUT_LINE(sq_StudentNo.CURRVAL);
END;
/
```

Output:

```
PL/SQL procedure successfully completed.
```

Querying Existing Sequences

Oracle stores all information related to sequences created in the USER_SEQUENCES table. This table describes all sequences owned by the current user and holds the following columns:

Column Name	Description
SEQUENCE_NAME	Name of the sequence.
MIN_VALUE	Minimum value of the sequence.
MAX_VALUE	Maximum value of the sequence.
INCREMENT_BY	Value by which sequence is incremented.
CYCLE_FLAG	Indicates if the sequence will wrap on reaching the limit.
ORDER_FLAG	Indicates if the sequence numbers are generated in order.
CACHE_SIZE	Number of sequence numbers to cache.
LAST_NUMBER	Last sequence number written to disk.

This table can be queried as follows:

```
SELECT Sequence_Name, Last_Number FROM USER_SEQUENCES;
```

Output:

```
SEQUENCE_NAME                  LAST_NUMBER
------------------------------ -----------
SQ_STUDENTNO                           131

1 row selected.
```

```
SELECT Sequence_Name, (Last_Number + Increment_By) "NextValue"
   FROM USER_SEQUENCES;
```

Output:

```
SEQUENCE_NAME                  LAST_NUMBER
------------------------------ -----------
SQ_STUDENTNO                           132
1 row selected.
```

Chapter

26

SECTION V: PL/SQL

Introduction To PL/SQL

PL/SQL stands for **P**rocedural **L**anguage/**S**tructured **Q**uery **L**anguage. It is a database-oriented programming language that extends Oracle SQL with procedural capabilities. By integrating programming constructs found in procedural languages, PL/SQL offers a more powerful and versatile language than SQL.

Developed by Oracle in the early 1990s, PL/SQL was created to enhance the capabilities of SQL. As a procedural language, it allows developers to write programs that specify a sequence of operations to achieve the desired results.

Key Features of PL/SQL:

- ***Selective Constructs:*** Conditional statements such as if...then...else.
- ***Iterative Constructs:*** Loop structures for repeated execution.
- ***Functions:*** Encapsulated reusable code blocks.
- ***Triggers:*** Automated actions in response to specific database events.
- ***Stored Procedures:*** Precompiled collections of SQL and PL/SQL statements.
- ***Packages:*** Groupings of related procedures, functions, and other program units.

PL/SQL is based on the ADA programming language, and as a result, it shares many syntax elements with Pascal.

Applications of PL/SQL:

- ***Oracle Relational Database:*** Used for creating and managing database applications.
- ***Oracle Server:*** Employed in server-side programming.
- ***Client-side Application Development:*** Utilized in tools such as Oracle Forms for building user interfaces.

PL/SQL v/s SQL

- **SQL Limitations: Lacks Procedural Capabilities:**
  - No Condition checking
  - No Looping
  - No Branching

  These capabilities are essential for testing data before permanent storage.
- **Advantages of PL/SQL:**
  - ***Enhanced Procedural Capabilities:*** Supports SQL data manipulation and provides procedural constructs such as conditional checking, branching, and looping.
  - ***Efficient Data Processing:*** SQL statements are passed one at a time to Oracle for execution, which increases network traffic and decreases processing speed, especially in multi-user environments. PL/SQL sends an entire block of SQL statements to Oracle in one go, minimizing communication between the program block and Oracle. This reduces network traffic and speeds up data processing as Oracle processes the entire block faster than individual commands.
  - ***Error Handling:*** SQL does not allow defining custom error messages; Oracle displays its own error messages during data manipulation errors. PL/SQL enables custom error handling, allowing for user-friendly error messages.
- **Superset and Portability:**
  - ***Superset of SQL:*** PL/SQL operates over the SQL command and is a superset of SQL.
  - ***Portability:*** Applications written in PL/SQL are portable to any computer hardware and operating system where Oracle is operational. PL/SQL code blocks written for a DOS version of Oracle will run on its Linux/UNIX version without modifications.
- **Client Application Integration:**
  - ***Modular Programming:*** Client application code that needs to communicate with the Oracle database typically uses PL/SQL programs. This approach provides generic modular programming with functional APIs disclosed while implementation remains hidden. It also helps reduce network round trips between the client and Oracle database.

- **Availability:**
  - ***Included in All Oracle Editions:*** PL/SQL is available in all editions of Oracle Database and does not require explicit installation or licensing.

Basic Structure Of PL/SQL

The fundamental unit in PL/SQL is a block. All PL/SQL programs consist of blocks, which can be nested within each other. Typically, each block performs a logical action in the program. A block has the following structure:

- The Declaration section [optional]
- The Execution section [mandatory]
- The Exception [or Error] Handling section [optional]

Structure of a basic PL/SQL block:

```
DECLARE
/* Declarative section: Variables, types and local subprograms. */
BEGIN
/* Executable section: Procedural and SQL statements are placed here. */
/* This is the only section of the block that is required. */
EXCEPTION
/* Exception handling section: Error handling statements are placed here.
*/
END;
```

The Declarative Section

Every PL/SQL block begins with a declarative section, which starts with the reserved keyword **DECLARE**. This section is **optional** and holds placeholder **declarations** used to manipulate data in the execution section, including:

- Variables
- Constants
- Records
- Cursors

These elements must be declared before they can be used in SQL statements for data manipulation.

The Execution Section

The Execution section of a PL/SQL block starts with the reserved keyword **BEGIN** and ends with **END**. This is a **mandatory** section that holds the **program logic**.

Begin Section

This section contains a set of SQL and PL/SQL statements. Each statement describes the process that will be carried out upon execution. Note that data definition statements such as CREATE, DROP, or ALTER are not allowed here.

All data manipulation commands and programming constructs used for assignments, branches, loops, procedure calls, triggers, and conditional statements are specified here.

End Section

This marks the end of a PL/SQL block.

The Exception Handling Section

The Exception Handling section of a PL/SQL block starts with the reserved keyword **EXCEPTION**. This section is **optional**. Any errors that occur in the program are handled here, allowing the PL/SQL code block to terminate gracefully. Errors typically arise due to syntax, logic, or validation rule violations, all of which can be handled in this section.

When an exception is raised within the execution section of a PL/SQL block, control passes to the exception section. PL/SQL scans through the exception handlers to determine if the exception is handled.

> If the PL/SQL Block contains exceptions that cannot be handled, the block terminates abruptly with errors.

Additional Notes

- Every statement in the three sections must end with a semicolon (;).
- PL/SQL code is not case-sensitive.
- C-style comments (/* ... */) can be used.

Comments

Comments can be used in PL/SQL code blocks in either of the following form:

- ***Single-Line Comments: Double Hyphen (--):*** A comment line begins with a double hyphen (--), and the entire line is treated as a comment.

```
-- This is a single-line comment
```

- ***Multi-Line Comments: Slash-Asterisk (/* ... */):*** A comment block begins with a slash followed by an asterisk (/*) and ends with an asterisk followed by a slash (*/). All lines within this block are treated as comments. This form of specifying comments can span across multiple lines and can also be used to temporarily isolate and ignore a section of a PL/SQL block.

```
/*
  This is a multi-line comment.
  It spans across multiple lines.
*/
```

Using comments effectively can help you document your code and make it more understandable to others (and to yourself when you return to it later).

PL/SQL Placeholders

Information can be transmitted between a PL/SQL code block and the database using placeholders, which can be variables, constants, or records. Placeholders are defined to store data temporarily, which can be used to manipulate data during the execution of a PL/SQL code block. A placeholder can be defined with a name and a data type.

A variable can be declared as follows:

```
<VariableName> [CONSTANT] DATATYPE [NOT NULL] [:= | DEFAULT InitialValue]
```

Where,

- ***VariableName:*** The name of the variable.
- ***CONSTANT:*** Flags that placeholder as a constant.
- ***DATATYPE:*** A valid PL/SQL data type.
- ***NOT NULL:*** An optional constraint that causes the creation of a variable or a constant that cannot be assigned a null value. If an attempt is made to assign the value NULL to such a variable or constant, Oracle raises an exception automatically and returns an internal error.
- ***DEFAULT InitialValue:*** An optional clause that allows initializing a variable.

> Each variable declaration is a separate statement and must be terminated by a semicolon (;).

PL/SQL Data Types

Below are some of the data types used to define placeholders in PL/SQL:

- Number(n, m)
- Char(n)
- Varchar2(n)
- Date
- Long
- Long raw
- Raw
- Blob

- Clob
- Nclob
- Bfile

These data types help define how data is stored and manipulated within PL/SQL code blocks.

Declaring Variables

Declaring a variable:

```
DECLARE ProductDescription Varchar2(100);
```

Declaring a constant:

```
DECLARE ProductPrice CONSTANT Numeric(8, 1) := 324765.49;
```

No further assignments are allowed to the constant after it is assigned a value during its declaration.

The following example will return an error:

```
DECLARE
  ProductPrice CONSTANT Numeric(8, 1);
BEGIN
  ProductPrice := 324765.49;
END;
```

A constant must be assigned a value during declaration. If a value is not assigned to a constant while declaring it and is instead assigned in the execution section, an error will occur.

Declaring a variable with an initial value:

```
DECLARE AuthorName Varchar2(20) := 'Sharanam Shah';
```

Declaring a variable as NOT NULL:

```
DECLARE BookName Varchar2(20) NOT NULL := "Oracle For Professionals";
```

When a variable or constant is declared as NOT NULL, it must be assigned a value. Therefore, every variable or constant declared as NOT NULL must be followed by a PL/SQL expression that assigns a value to it.

Assigning Values To Variables

A variable can be assigned a value using:

- Assignment operator (:=):

```
<VariableName> := <Value>;
```

- Direct assignment from the database table columns using a SELECT . . . INTO statement:

```
SELECT <ColumnName> INTO <VariableName> FROM <TableName>
  [WHERE <Condition>];
```

Solution:

```
SET SERVEROUTPUT ON
DECLARE
  varCustomerName Varchar2(40);
  varAddress Varchar2(100);
BEGIN
/* Using assignment operator. */
  varCustomerName := 'Sharanam Chaitanya Shah';
/* Using direct assignment from table column. */
  SELECT Address INTO varAddress FROM Customers
     WHERE CustomerName = varCustomerName;
/* Printing a message. */
  DBMS_OUTPUT.PUT_LINE('Address: ' || varAddress);
END;
/
```

Output:

```
Address: 20, Makanji Mansion, MG Road, 400076
PL/SQL procedure successfully completed.
```

- **SERVEROUTPUT** is a SQL*PLUS environment parameter that, when set to **ON**, displays the information passed as a parameter to the PUT_LINE function.
- **DBMS_OUTPUT** package includes several procedures and functions that accumulate information in a buffer, allowing it to be retrieved later. These functions can be used to display messages.
- **PUT_LINE** procedure puts a piece of information in the package buffer followed by an end-of-line marker. It can also be used to display a message and expects a single parameter of character data type (e.g., a message string).

Using these tools, you can effectively assign values to variables and display messages in PL/SQL.

Scope Of Variables

PL/SQL allows the nesting of code blocks within other code blocks. This means that the execution section of a code block can contain inner code block.

Variable Accessibility: A variable accessible to an outer code block is also accessible to all nested inner code blocks. However, variables declared in the inner code blocks are not accessible to outer code blocks.

Classification of variables:

- ***Local variable:*** Declared in an inner code block and cannot be referenced by outer code block.
- ***Global variable:*** Declared in an outer code block and can be referenced by the inner code blocks.

Solution:

```
SET SERVEROUTPUT ON
DECLARE
/* Global variables declared. */
  varGlobalVariable1 Number;
  varGlobalVariable2 Number;
/* *************** Outer code block starts. *************** */
BEGIN
/* Global variables assigned. */
  varGlobalVariable1 := 1000;
  varGlobalVariable2 := 2000;
/* *************** Inner code block starts. *************** */
  DECLARE
  /* Local variable declared. */
     varLocalVariable Number;
  BEGIN
  /* Local variable assigned using values from Global variables. */
     varLocalVariable := varGlobalVariable1 * varGlobalVariable2;
  /* Printing a message. */
     DBMS_OUTPUT.PUT_LINE('Value in the local variable: ' ||
        TO_CHAR(varLocalVariable));
  END;
/* *************** Inner code block ends. *************** */
END;
/* *************** Outer code block ends. *************** */
/
```

In the example, two global variables named **varGlobalVariable1** and **varGlobalVariable2** are declared and assigned values in the outer code block. A local variable named **varLocalVariable** is declared in the inner code block. The global variables are accessed in the inner block to assign a computed value to the local variable.

Output:

```
Value in the local variable: 2000000
PL/SQL procedure successfully completed.
```

Record Data Type

PL/SQL provides a special data type called ***Records***. A record data type is a composite data type formed by combining different scalar data types, such as Char, Varchar2, Number, and so on. A record data type is very similar to a row of data in the table.

Declaring A Record

Syntax:

```
TYPE <RecordName> IS RECORD
  (<ColumnName1> <DataType>, <ColumnNameN> <DataType>);
```

Where,

- ***RecordName:*** Indicates the name of the composite type begin defined.
- ***ColumnName:*** Are the columns within the record being defined.
- ***DataType:*** Indicates the data type for the column being defined.

Example:

```
DECLARE
   TYPE typCustomers IS RECORD
        (CustomerID Number(10),
        CustomerName Varchar2(25),
        CustomerAddress Varchar2(50));
```

Besides the above method, Oracle allows declaring a record using ***%TYPE***. %TYPE is useful if a variable of a record is based on a column from an existing database table:

```
<ColumnName> <TableName>.<ColumnName> %TYPE;
```

The %TYPE attribute allows declaring variables based on the definitions of columns in a table. If a column's attributes change, the variable's attributes will also change. This provides data independence, reduces maintenance costs, and allows programs to adapt to changes made to the table.

Example:

```
DECLARE
   TYPE typCustomers IS RECORD
        (CustomerID Customers.CustomerID%TYPE,
        CustomerName Customers.CustomerName%TYPE,
        CustomerAddress Customers.CustomerAddress%TYPE);
```

If all the fields of a record are based on all the columns of a table, a record can be declared using the following syntax:

```
<RecordName> <TableName>%ROWTYPE;
```

Example:

```
DECLARE typCustomers Customers%ROWTYPE
```

In this method, the column names of the table need not be explicitly declared as variables.

Assigning Values To Record

Values assigned to a record are assigned to individual field in that record:

```
<RecordName>.<ColumnName> := <Value>;
```

```
SELECT <ColumnName1>, <ColumnName2> INTO
  <RecordName>.<ColumnName>, <RecordName>.<ColumnName2>
     FROM <TableName> [WHERE <Condition>];
```

If %ROWTYPE is used to declare a record, values can be directly assigned to the entire record instead of one column at a time.

Syntax:

```
SELECT * INTO <RecordName> FROM <TableName> [WHERE <Condition>];
```

Example:

```
DECLARE
/* Defining a Record Type. */
  TYPE typCustomers IS RECORD
     (CustomerNo Customers.CustomerNo%TYPE,
     CustomerName Customers.CustomerName%TYPE,
     CustomerDOB Customers.DateOfBirth%TYPE);
/* Declaring a variable of type typCustomers. */
  varCustomers typCustomers;
BEGIN
  varCustomers.CustomerNo := 1;
  varCustomers.CustomerName := 'Sharanam Chaitanya Shah';
  varCustomers.CustomerDOB := '03-Jan-1981';
END;
/
```

Output:

```
PL/SQL procedure successfully completed.
```

Example:

```
DECLARE
  typCustomers Customers%ROWTYPE;
BEGIN
  SELECT * INTO typCustomers FROM Customers
     WHERE CustomerName = 'Sharanam Chaitanya Shah';
END;
/
```

Output:

```
PL/SQL procedure successfully completed.
```

Control Statements

PL/SQL provides the following control structures:

- Conditional Statements
- Iterative Statements
- Sequential Statements

Conditional Statements

In a program written using PL/SQL, the execution of a code block can be controlled using an **IF** statement. The **IF - THEN - ELSIF - ELSE - END IF** construct IN PL/SQL is very similar to the IF construct provided by other programming languages such as Java, PHP, C++, and others. This construct is primarily used in code blocks to specify conditions under which a specific block of code should be executed.

Syntax:

```
IF <Condition> THEN <Action>
ELSIF <Condition> THEN <Action>
ELSE <Action>
END IF;
```

Write a program using PL/SQL that:

- Accepts the EmployeeNo.
- Validates if the EmployeeNo is valid.
- If valid, accepts the attendance as **P** for **P**resent, **A** for **A**bsent and **S** for **S**ick Leave.
- Marks the attendance by inserting a record in the EmployeeMuster table.
- If Present, also inserts a timestamp in the InTime column.

Solution:

```
DECLARE
/* Declaration of memory variables and constants to be used in the
Execution section. */
  varEmpValid  Char(1) := 'N';
  varEmpAtd Char(1);
  varEmployeeNo Employees.EmployeeNo%TYPE;
BEGIN
/* Accepting the EmployeeNo */
  varEmployeeNo := &EmployeeNo;
/* Validating the existence of such an employee. */
  SELECT 'Y' INTO varEmpValid FROM Employees
       WHERE EmployeeNo = varEmployeeNo;
  IF varEmpValid = 'Y' THEN
  /* Accepting the Employee Attendance */
```

```
      varEmpAtd := '&Attendance';
   END IF;
/* Inserting a record in the EmployeeMuster table if the employee number
is valid. */
   IF varEmpAtd IS NOT NULL THEN
      IF varEmpAtd = 'P' THEN
         INSERT INTO EmployeeMuster (EmployeeNo, MusterDate, Attendance,
            Intime) VALUES(varEmployeeNo, SYSDATE, 'Present',
               CURRENT_TIMESTAMP);
      ELSIF varEmpAtd = 'S' THEN
         INSERT INTO EmployeeMuster (EmployeeNo, MusterDate, Attendance)
            VALUES(varEmployeeNo, SYSDATE, 'Sick Leave');
      ELSE
         INSERT INTO EmployeeMuster (EmployeeNo, MusterDate, Attendance)
            VALUES(varEmployeeNo, SYSDATE, 'Absent');
      END IF;
   END IF;
END;
/
```

Output:

```
Enter value for employeeno: 1
old   9:         varEmployeeNo := &EmployeeNo;
new   9:         varEmployeeNo := 1;
Enter value for attendance: A
old  17:                 varEmpAtd := '&Attendance';
new  17:                 varEmpAtd := 'A';

PL/SQL procedure successfully completed.
```

To verify that the PL/SQL program has achieved what it was supposed to, execute the following query and look at the output:

```
SELECT * FROM EmployeeMuster;
```

Output:

```
EMPLOYEENO MUSTERDATE ATTENDANCE INTIME                         OUTTIME
---------- ---------- ---------- ------------------------------ -------------------------

         1 06-JAN-25  Absent
         1 21-MAY-08  Absent
        21 07-APR-08  Absent
         3 02-MAY-08  Present    02-MAY-08 11.53.40.451359 PM
         1 01-MAY-08  Absent
         2 02-MAY-08  Present    02-MAY-08 09.53.40.451359 PM
         4 05-MAY-08  Present    05-MAY-08 10.03.21.075645 PM
         4 04-MAY-08  Present
         4 05-MAY-08  Absent

9 rows selected.
```

Iterative Statements

An iterative statement is used when the execution of one or more statements in the PL/SQL code block needs to be repeated for a specific number of times. These are similar to those in Java, PHP, C++, and so on.

PL/SQL provides the following three types of iterative statements:

- Simple Loop
- While Loop
- For Loop

Simple Loop

A **Simple Loop** repeats a set of statements in the PL/SQL code block at least once before the loop terminates.

> An EXIT condition **must be specified** in the loop, otherwise the loop enters into infinite iterations.

When the EXIT condition is satisfied the process exits from the loop.

Syntax:

```
LOOP
  <Sequence of statements>
END LOOP;
```

A single column table called **RandomNumbers** exists. This table holds a set of random numbers which are used by the application. Create a program using PL/SQL that:

- Accepts a number indicating how many random numbers to be generated.
- Generates that many random numbers.
- Stores them in the RandomNumbers table.

Solution:

```
SET SERVEROUTPUT ON
DECLARE
/* Declaration of memory variables and constants to be used in the
Execution section. */
  varHowManyTimes Number;
  varCtr Number := 0;
BEGIN
/* Accepting how many numbers to be generated. */
  varHowManyTimes := &HowManyNos;
/* Simple loop. */
  LOOP
  /* Incrementing the counter. */
```

```
        varCtr := varCtr + 1;
    /* Generating and inserting random numbers into the table. */
        INSERT INTO RandomNumbers (RandNo)
            VALUES (DBMS_RANDOM.RANDOM());
        EXIT WHEN varCtr >= varHowManyTimes;
    END LOOP;
/* Printing a message. */
    DBMS_OUTPUT.PUT_LINE(TO_CHAR(varCtr) || ' random numbers generated
        successfully.');
END;
/
```

Output:

```
Enter value for howmanynos: 10
old   7:         varHowManyTimes  := &HowManyNos;
new   7:         varHowManyTimes  := 10;
10 random numbers generated successfully.

PL/SQL procedure successfully completed.
```

TIP **DBMS_RANDOM.RANDOM()** returns a binary random integer as a value.

To verify the program's output, execute the following query:

```
SELECT * FROM RandomNumbers;
```

Output:

```
    RANDNO
----------
1181729147
1208756580
2087124120
-2.126E+09
-882648640
-801224308
1686205916
1429361842
-596130830
-458022947

10 rows selected.
```

WHILE Loop

A **While Loop** repeats a set of statements in the PL/SQL code block as long as a condition is true. The condition is evaluated when iteration begins and continues until the condition becomes false:

```
WHILE <Condition>
```

```
LOOP
  <Action>
END LOOP;
```

Using the same example as the **Simple Loop** section:

```
SET SERVEROUTPUT ON
DECLARE
/* Declaration of memory variables and constants to be used in the
Execution section. */
  varHowManyTimes Number;
  varCtr Number := 0;
BEGIN
/* Accepting how many numbers to be generated. */
  varHowManyTimes := &HowManyNos;
/* While loop. */
  WHILE varCtr < varHowManyTimes
  LOOP
  /* Generating and inserting random numbers into the table. */
     INSERT INTO RandomNumbers (RandNo)
        VALUES (DBMS_RANDOM.RANDOM());
  /* Incrementing the counter. */
     varCtr := varCtr + 1;
  END LOOP;
/* Printing a message. */
  DBMS_OUTPUT.PUT_LINE(TO_CHAR(varCtr) || ' random numbers generated
     successfully.');
END;
/
```

Output:

```
Enter value for howmanynos: 2
old   7:         varHowManyTimes  := &HowManyNos;
new   7:         varHowManyTimes  := 2;
2 random numbers generated successfully.

PL/SQL procedure successfully completed.
```

FOR Loop

A **For Loop** is used to execute a set of statements for a predetermined number of times. Iteration occurs between the given start and end integer values. The counter is always incremented by 1. The loop exits when the counter reaches the value of the end integer.

Syntax:

```
FOR <Variable> IN [REVERSE] <StartValue>..<EndValue>
LOOP
  <Action>
END LOOP;
```

Using the same example as the **Simple Loop** section:

```
SET SERVEROUTPUT ON
DECLARE
/* Declaration of memory variables and constants to be used in the
Execution section. */
  varHowManyTimes Number;
  varCtr Number := 0;
BEGIN
/* Accepting how many numbers to be generated. */
  varHowManyTimes := &HowManyNos;
/* For loop. */
  FOR varCtrTemp IN 1..varHowManyTimes
  LOOP
  /* Generating and inserting random numbers into the table. */
      INSERT INTO RandomNumbers (RandNo)
          VALUES (DBMS_RANDOM.RANDOM());
      varCtr := varCtrTemp;
  END LOOP;
/* Printing a message. */
  DBMS_OUTPUT.PUT_LINE(TO_CHAR(varCtr) || ' random numbers generated
      successfully.');
END;
/
```

Output:

```
Enter value for howmanynos: 4
old   7:         varHowManyTimes   := &HowManyNos;
new   7:         varHowManyTimes   := 4;
4 random numbers generated successfully.

PL/SQL procedure successfully completed.
```

In a For Loop:

1. The counter variable is implicitly declared in the declaration section, so it is not necessary to declare it explicitly.
2. The counter variable is incremented by 1 and does not need to be incremented explicitly.

GOTO Statement

Often, it is necessary to shift the control of the program from one set of statements to another. This means the statements in the code block will not execute in sequence as they usually do. The **GOTO** statement helps achieving this by allowing the control to shift from one block of code to another within a PL/SQL block. It is an unconditional branch that jumps execution to the label identified in the statement.

The entry point into such a block of code is marked using labels:

```
<<Any name to the code block that follows>>
```

The GOTO statement can then use this user-defined name to jump into that block of code for execution. The label must be in scope when the GOTO statement is encountered.

> When a GOTO statement is encountered, program execution jumps to the code directly after the label, so there must be at least one line of code after the label.

Syntax:

```
GOTO <CodeBlock Name>;
```

Write a program using PL/SQL that:

- Accepts the EmployeeNo.
- Validates if the EmployeeNo is valid.
- If valid, accepts the attendance as **P** for **P**resent, **A** for **A**bsent and **S** for **S**ick Leave.
- Marks the attendance by inserting a record in the EmployeeMuster table.
- If Present, also inserts a timestamp in the InTime column.

Solution:

```
DECLARE
/* Declaration of memory variables and constants to be used in the
Execution section. */
   varEmpValid Char(1) := 'N';
   varEmpAtd Char(1);
   varEmployeeNo Employees.EmployeeNo%TYPE;
BEGIN
/* Accepting the EmployeeNo */
   varEmployeeNo := &EmployeeNo;
/* Validating the existence of such an employee. */
   SELECT 'Y' INTO varEmpValid FROM Employees
       WHERE EmployeeNo = varEmployeeNo;
   IF varEmpValid = 'Y' THEN
   /* Accepting the Employee Attendance */
       varEmpAtd := '&Attendance';
   END IF;
/* Inserting a record in the EmployeeMuster table if the employee number
is valid. */
   IF varEmpAtd IS NOT NULL THEN
       IF varEmpAtd = 'P' THEN
           GOTO InsertPresent;
       ELSIF varEmpAtd = 'S' THEN
           GOTO InsertSickLeave;
       ELSE
           GOTO InsertAbsent;
       END IF;
```

```
  END IF;
/* GOTO code blocks. */
<<InsertPresent>>
  INSERT INTO EmplcyeeMuster (EmployeeNo, MusterDate, Attendance, Intime)
      VALUES(varEmployeeNo, SYSDATE,   'Present', CURRENT_TIMESTAMP);
<<InsertSickLeave>>
  INSERT INTO EmplcyeeMuster (EmployeeNo, MusterDate, Attendance)
      VALUES(varEmployeeNo, SYSDATE, 'Sick Leave');
<<InsertAbsent>>
  INSERT INTO EmplcyeeMuster (EmployeeNo, MusterDate, Attendance)
      VALUES(varEmployeeNo, SYSDATE, 'Absent');
END;
/
```

Output:

```
Enter value for employeeno: 4
old   9:        varEmployeeNo := &EmployeeNo;
new   9:        varEmployeeNo := 4;
Enter value for attendance: P
old  17:                varEmpAtd := '&Attendance';
new  17:                varEmpAtd := 'P';

PL/SQL procedure successfully completed.
```

Chapter

27

SECTION V: PL/SQL

Transactions

Oracle ensures integrity of data using transactions. A series of SQL statements that help manipulate data, when put together as a logical unit, form a transaction. This logical unit is treated as a single entity. Any change to the data in the database is a two-step process:

1. The changes that were requested are made.
2. These changes can either be made permanent by issuing a COMMIT statement or undone by issuing a ROLLBACK statement to undo all changes or partial changes.

A transaction begins with the first executable SQL statement after a **COMMIT, ROLLBACK,** or **CONNECTION** made to Oracle. A transaction ends by using either a **COMMIT** or a **ROLLBACK** statement.

Oracle provides the following commands to control transactions:

Commit

COMMIT makes permanent any database changes made during the current transaction. It ends the current transaction and makes permanent any changes made during the transaction.

All transactional locks acquired on tables are released:

```
COMMIT;
```

Rollback

ROLLBACK ends the current transaction and undoes any changes made since the transaction began. It performs the opposite action of COMMIT:

```
ROLLBACK [WORK] [TO [SAVEPOINT] <SavepointName>];
```

Where,

- ***WORK*** (optional) is provided for ANSI compatibility.
- ***SAVEPOINT*** (optional) is used to rollback a transaction partially, as far as the specified savepoint.
- ***SavepointName*** is a savepoint created during the current transaction.

A ROLLBACK operation performed without the SAVEPOINT clause leads to:

- Ends the transaction.
- Undoes all the changes in the current transaction.
- Releases the transactional locks.
- Erases all savepoints in that transaction.

A ROLLBACK operation performed with the TO SAVEPOINT clause leads to:

- Roll back a predetermined portion of the transaction.
- Retains the save point rolled back to, but loses those created after the named savepoint.
- Releases all transactional locks acquired since the savepoint was taken.

Savepoint

SAVEPOINT marks the current point in the processing of a transaction. When used with a ROLLBACK statement, parts of a transaction can be undone. An active SAVEPOINT is one that is specified since the last COMMIT or ROLLBACK:

```
SAVEPOINT <SavepointName>;
```

For example, every transaction carried out in a bank is recorded in the Transactions table. Every account maintained with the bank is held in a table called Accounts. When a customer deposits or withdraws money, a transaction is recorded in the Transactions table. After the transaction is recorded, the account holder's current balance in the Accounts table is updated. If the current balance falls below Rs. 500/- after a withdrawal, transaction should be rolled back. Each transaction is logged in the TransactionsLog table, and the Status column is updated with the transaction status (Success/Failure).

Write a program using PL/SQL that:

- Accept the account number and the amount to be withdrawn.
- Log the transaction.
- Record the transaction.
- Update the current balance.
- Roll back the transaction if the current balance falls below Rs. 500 after the withdrawal; otherwise, commit the transaction.
- Update the Status column of the TransactionsLog table to **Success** if the transaction was committed or **Failure** if it was rolled back.

Solution:

```
DECLARE
   varTransactionNo Number(20);
   varTransactionLogNo Number(20);
   varAccountNo Number(20);
   varTransactionAmount Number(8,2);
   varCurrentBalance Number(8,2);
BEGIN
   varAccountNo := &AccountNo;
   varTransactionAmount := &Amount;
/* Generating a transaction number. */
   SELECT MAX(TransactionNo) + 1 INTO varTransactionNo FROM Transactions;
   IF varTransactionNo IS NULL THEN
        varTransactionNo := 1;
   END IF;
/* Generating a transaction log number. */
   SELECT MAX(TransactionNo) + 1 INTO varTransactionLogNo
        FROM TransactionsLog;
   IF varTransactionLogNo IS NULL THEN
        varTransactionLogNo := 1;
   END IF;
/* Logging the transaction. */
   INSERT INTO TransactionsLog(TransactionNo, AccountNo, TransactionDate,
        Particulars, TransactionType, Amount) VALUES(varTransactionLogNo,
        varAccountNo, SYSDATE, 'Self Withdraw', 'Dr', varTransactionAmount);
/* Defining a savepoint for rollbacks. */
   SAVEPOINT WithdrawalTrans;
/* Recording the transaction. */
   INSERT INTO Transactions(TransactionNo, AccountNo, TransactionDate,
        Particulars, TransactionType, Amount) VALUES(varTransactionNo,
        varAccountNo, SYSDATE, 'Self Withdraw', 'Dr', varTransactionAmount);
/* Updating the current balance. */
   UPDATE Accounts SET CurrentBalance = CurrentBalance - varTransactionAmount
        WHERE AccountNo = varAccountNo;
/* Retrieving the current balance after update. */
   SELECT CurrentBalance INTO varCurrentBalance FROM Accounts
            WHERE AccountNo = varAccountNo;
/* Checking if current balance falls under 500. */
```

```
  IF varCurrentBalance < 500 THEN
  /* Undo the withdrawal transaction completely. */
     ROLLBACK To SAVEPOINT WithdrawalTrans;
  /* Updating the TransactionsLog table. */
     UPDATE TransactionsLog SET Status = 'Failure'
        WHERE TransactionNo = varTransactionLogNo;
  ELSE
  /* Making the changes permanent. */
     COMMIT;
  /* Updating the TransactionsLog table. */
     UPDATE TransactionsLog SET Status = 'Success'
        WHERE TransactionNo = varTransactionLogNo;
  END IF;
END;
/
```

After a record is inserted into the Transactions table and the Accounts table is updated, a savepoint called WithdrawalTrans is created. This savepoint ensures that if the current balance check fails, the entire withdrawal transaction (i.e., the INSERT INTO Transactions and UPDATE Accounts) can be rolled back. However, the data inserted into the TransactionsLog table is not rolled back because the savepoint is created after the data is inserted into the log table.

To verify that the PL/SQL program has performed as expected, execute the following queries/programs and review the output.

Querying Accounts Table:

```
SELECT * FROM Accounts;
```

Output (Data before running the program):

```
ACCOUNTNO ACCOUNTHOLDERNAME ACCOUNTOPENINGDATE ACCOUNTTYPE CURRENTBALANCE
--------- ----------------- ------------------ ----------- --------------
1         Sharanam          23-MAY-07          SB          13558.9
2         Vaishali          05-FEB-05          SB          5000
3         Gita              08-JUN-06          SB          2375.89
6         Michel            29-MAR-08          CA          3000
5         Micheal           20-OCT-03          SB          4000
4         Geeta             01-JAN-05          CA          46892.08
12        Puja              20-FEB-05          SB          4500
11        Pooja             07-JUL-03          CA          123890
10        Dipa              23-MAY-07          SB          1245
9         Deepa             08-JUN-06          SB          1000
8         Sita              20-OCT-03          SB          1234
7         Seeta             07-JUL-03          SB          3000

12 rows selected.
```

Running the PL/SQL program:

```
Enter value for accountno: 1
old  10:        varAccountNo := &AccountNo;
new  10:        varAccountNo := 1;
```

```
Enter value for amount: 200
old  11:         varTransactionAmount := &Amount;
new  11:         varTransactionAmount := 200;

PL/SQL procedure successfully completed.
```

Running the PL/SQL program:

```
Enter value for accountno: 2
old  10:         varAccountNo := &AccountNo;
new  10:         varAccountNo := 2;
Enter value for amount: 4600
old  11:         varTransactionAmount := &Amount;
new  11:         varTransactionAmount := 4600;

PL/SQL procedure successfully completed.
```

Querying Transactions Table:

```
SELECT * FROM Transactions;
```

Output:

```
TRANSACTIONNO  ACCOUNTNO TRANSACTI PARTICULARS               TR     AMOUNT
------------- ---------- --------- ------------------------- -- ----------
            1          1 06-JAN-25 Self Withdraw             Dr        200
```

Here, for the account number 2, since the amount to be withdrawn was 4600 which violates the minimum balance criteria, the withdrawal transaction is rolled back and hence, this table does not hold the record for the withdrawal.

Querying TransactionsLog Table:

```
SELECT * FROM TransactionsLog;
```

Output:

```
TRANSACTIONNO  ACCOUNTNO TRANSACTI PARTICULARS   TR     AMOUNT STATUS
------------- ---------- --------- ------------- -- ---------- ---------------
            1          1 06-JAN-25 Self Withdraw Dr        200 Success
            2          2 06-JAN-25 Self Withdraw Dr       4600 Failure
```

Here, for the account number 2, since the amount to be withdrawn was 4600 which violates the minimum balance criteria, the Status column holds Failure.

Querying Accounts Table:

```
SELECT * FROM Accounts;
```

Output:

```
ACCOUNTNO ACCOUNTHOLDERNAME ACCOUNTOPENINGDATE ACCOUNTTYPE CURRENTBALANCE
--------- ----------------- ------------------ ----------- --------------
1         Sharanam          23-MAY-07          SB          13358.9
2         Vaishali          05-FEB-05          SB          5000
3         Gita              08-JUN-06          SB          2375.89
```

6	Michel	29-MAR-08	CA	3000
5	Micheal	20-OCT-03	SB	4000
4	Geeta	01-JAN-05	CA	46892.08
12	Puja	20-FEB-05	SB	4500
11	Pooja	07-JUL-03	CA	123890
10	Dipa	23-MAY-07	SB	1245
9	Deepa	08-JUN-06	SB	1000
8	Sita	20-OCT-03	SB	1234
7	Seeta	07-JUL-03	SB	3000

12 rows selected.

Data Concurrency And Consistency

Oracle manages **data concurrency** and **consistency** using **locks**, which are critical components of any database management system. Oracle implicitly uses locking mechanisms, but manual locking can also be employed if necessary.

In multi-user environments, multiple users often operate on the same data simultaneously. To prevent data integrity issues, Oracle allows locking specific data blocks, thereby preventing other users from modifying the same data.

When a user modifies data through a transaction, the data is locked by that transaction until it is **committed** or **rolled back**. The lock persists until the transaction is complete, and only then is the data made available to other users. Oracle releases the locks when a COMMIT or ROLLBACK command is issued.

Oracle provides two types of locks:

- *Row Level Lock:*
  - Locks a particular row or set of rows for a transaction.
  - Allows other users to update rows in different tables but not the locked rows.
  - Displays the original copy of the locked row to other users.
  - Once the transaction is committed, users can see the updated data and modify the previously locked rows.
  - More efficient than Table Level Locking.

  A row level lock can be applied using the **SELECT ... FOR UPDATE** statement, which ensures that other users cannot update the locked rows. Once the transaction is committed, the rows are available for modification by other users. Oracle allows locking an unlimited number of rows.

- *Table Level Lock:*
  - Locks the entire table, preventing others from modifying any rows until the lock is released.
  - Automatically applied when a row-level lock is obtained to prevent DDL operations on the table.

For example, to increment the salaries of employees in the HR department and ensure other users cannot update these rows during the process, use the following PL/SQL block:

```
DECLARE
   varSalary Number(12,2);
   CURSOR curEmpSal IS
        SELECT Salary FROM Employees WHERE DeptNo =
             (SELECT DeptNo FROM Departments
                  WHERE DepartmentName = 'HR')
                       FOR UPDATE OF Salary;
BEGIN
   OPEN curEmpSal;
   LOOP
        FETCH curEmpSal INTO varSalary;
        EXIT WHEN curEmpSal%NOTFOUND;
        UPDATE Employees SET Salary = varSalary * 1.10
             WHERE CURRENT OF curEmpSal;
   END LOOP;
   CLOSE curEmpSal;
END;
/
```

Output:

```
PL/SQL procedure successfully completed.
```

This block locks the specified records, preventing other users from updating the same records.

Open two SQL sessions and in each session issue the following commands:

Session I

```
SELECT EmployeeNo, Salary FROM Employees WHERE DeptNo = (SELECT DeptNo
   FROM Departments WHERE DepartmentName = 'HR Department')
        FOR UPDATE OF Salary;
```

Session II

```
UPDATE Employees SET Salary = Salary * 1.10 WHERE DeptNo = (SELECT DeptNo
   FROM Departments WHERE DepartmentName = 'HR Department');
```

The transaction in Session II will not proceed because the row is locked in Session I. The transaction in Session II will only proceed after a COMMIT or ROLLBACK command is issued in Session I.

Session I

```
SELECT EmployeeNo, Salary FROM Employees WHERE DeptNo = (SELECT DeptNo
  FROM Departments WHERE DepartmentName = 'HR Department')
     FOR UPDATE OF Salary;
```

Output:

```
EMPLOYEENO     SALARY
---------- ----------
         2      55000
         4      22000
```

Do rollback in Session I:

```
ROLLBACK;
```

Output:

```
Rollback complete.
```

Session II

```
UPDATE Employees SET Salary = Salary * 1.10 WHERE DeptNo = (SELECT DeptNo
  FROM Departments WHERE DepartmentName = 'HR Department');
```

Output:

```
2 rows updated.
```

Explicit locking can also be achieved on tables using the **LOCK TABLE** command, which locks the entire table. Users who want to update the data in this table must wait until the lock is released.

Dead Lock

A **deadlock** occurs when two or more users are waiting for access to data that has been locked by each other, causing the transactions to become stuck and unable to proceed. In such cases, Oracle resolves the deadlock by forcing one or more transactions to roll back.

If Oracle's default locking mechanism is overridden, it is essential for the database administrator or application developer to ensure that the custom locking procedures operate correctly. These procedures must satisfy the following criteria:
Data integrity is guaranteed.
Data concurrency is acceptable.
Deadlocks are prevented and appropriately handled.

Chapter

28

SECTION V: PL/SQL

Cursors

In Oracle, a certain portion of memory is allocated for every SQL query that is executed. Using PL/SQL, this memory portion can be assigned a custom name, known as the **context area** or **Cursor**.

A cursor is essentially a pointer to the context area, representing a structure in memory. Through a PL/SQL program, this context area can be managed using the cursor. The data retrieved by the query from table(s) is stored in a cursor, which Oracle opens in memory. This data is then transferred to the client machine that requested it.

When a cursor is declared, it returns a pointer that initially points to nothing. Once the cursor is opened, the appropriate memory is allocated, and the cursor structure is created. The cursor variable then points to the memory area. When the cursor is closed, the allocated memory is released.

Cursors are commonly used to hold data retrieved from table(s) and to perform actions on that data, one row at a time.

Types Of Cursors

Oracle provides two kinds of cursors:

- ***Implicit Cursor:*** This type of cursor is automatically created by Oracle for its internal processing when an SQL statement is executed. The programmer does not explicitly declare or manage these cursors.
- ***Explicit Cursor:*** This type of cursor is created explicitly by the programmer within a PL/SQL block to process data on demand. It provides greater control over the context area and is used to fetch and manipulate data from tables.

Cursor Attributes

When an Implicit or Explicit cursor is spawned, Oracle makes the cursor control variables available to manage the execution of the cursor. These control variables help keep track of the current status of a cursor and can be accessed and used within a PL/SQL code block.

Cursor attributes are accessed by preceding the attribute with the cursor name. For implicit cursors, the cursor name is always "SQL". The values of cursor attributes always refer to the most recently executed SQL statement, regardless of where the statement appears.

Here are the attributes of a Cursor:

%ISOPEN

- ***For Explicit cursor:*** This is a Boolean variable that evaluates to **TRUE** if the cursor is opened; otherwise, it evaluates to **FALSE**.
- ***For Implicit cursor:*** %ISOPEN always evaluates to FALSE because Implicit cursors are automatically opened and closed after executing the SELECT, INSERT, UPDATE, or DELETE SQL queries. Consequently, the %ISOPEN attribute cannot be referenced outside its SQL query.

%FOUND

- This attribute evaluates to **TRUE** if a record was fetched successfully; otherwise, it evaluates to **FALSE**. If the cursor has not been opened, referencing the %FOUND attribute raises the ***INVALID_CURSOR*** exception.
- ***For Implicit Cursor:*** If Oracle has not opened an implicit cursor, references to the %FOUND attribute return **NULL** instead of raising the INVALID_CURSOR error.

%NOTFOUND

- This attribute evaluates to **TRUE** if a record was not fetched successfully; otherwise, it evaluates to **FALSE**. If the cursor has not been opened, referencing the %NOTFOUND attribute raises the ***INVALID_CURSOR*** exception.
- ***For Implicit Cursor:*** If Oracle has not opened an implicit cursor, references to the %NOTFOUND attribute return **NULL** instead of raising the INVALID_CURSOR error.

%ROWCOUNT

This attribute returns the number of rows fetched from a cursor at the time it is queried. If the cursor has not been opened, referencing the %ROWCOUNT attribute raises the ***INVALID_CURSOR*** exception.

Implicit Cursors

In PL/SQL, SQL queries that return a single row of data are declared as ***implicit cursors***. Implicit cursors are created and opened automatically when SQL SELECT statements are written in the execution section of a PL/SQL program. These cursors retrieve exactly one row.

Solution:

```
DECLARE
   varCustomerName Customers.CustomerName%TYPE;
   varDOB Customers.DateOfBirth%TYPE;
BEGIN
   SELECT CustomerName, DateOfBirth INTO varCustomerName, varDOB
      FROM Customers WHERE CustomerNo = 1;
```

Oracle implicitly declares cursors for all DML statements written in PL/SQL. Since the implicit cursor are managed internally by Oracle, the following functions are handled automatically:

- Reserving a portion of memory.
- Processing the data in the memory area.
- Populating this portion with appropriate data.
- Releasing the memory area when the processing is complete.

After the data in the cursor is processed, it is passed to the client who requested it.

For Implicit cursor, Oracle provides attributes that can be used to access status information such as:

- Last Insert
- Update
- Delete
- Single-row select statements

When an implicit cursor for a SELECT query does not return any rows, PL/SQL raises the **NO_DATA_FOUND** exception. When an implicit cursor for a SELECT query returns more than one row, PL/SQL raises the **TOO_MANY_ROWS** exception.

Example: The company desires to transfer a few employees across the available departments. Write a program using PL/SQL that:

- Accepts the EmployeeNo of the employee to be transferred.
- Validates the existence of that Employee.
- Accepts the new DeptNo of that employee.
- Updates the Department number of that employee to the new DeptNo.

After the employee has been successfully transferred, indicates the same using a message.

Solution:

```
SET SERVEROUTPUT ON
DECLARE
  varEmployeeNo Employees.EmployeeNo%TYPE;
  varDeptNo Employees.DeptNo%TYPE;
BEGIN
/* Accepting employee number */
  varEmployeeNo := &EmployeeNo;
/* Accepting department number */
  varDeptNo := &DeptNo;
/* Updating the department number */
  UPDATE Employees SET DeptNo = varDeptNo
      WHERE EmployeeNo = varEmployeeNo;
/* Displaying a message if the update is successful */
  IF SQL%FOUND THEN
      DBMS_OUTPUT.PUT_LINE('Employee ' || varEmployeeNo || ' Successfully Transferred to
          DeptNo: ' || varDeptNo);
  END IF;
/* Validating the existence of the employee and department */
  IF SQL%NOTFOUND THEN
      DBMS_OUTPUT.PUT_LINE('Employee ' || varEmployeeNo || ' does not exist.');
  END IF;
END;
/
```

Output:

```
Enter value for employeeno: 1
old   6:        varEmployeeNo := &EmployeeNo;
new   6:        varEmployeeNo := 1;
Enter value for deptno: 4
old   7:        varDeptNo := &DeptNo;
new   7:        varDeptNo := 4;
Employee 1 Successfully Transferred to DeptNo: 4

PL/SQL procedure successfully completed.
```

Example: The company maintains the attendance records of all its employees in the EmployeesMuster table. Write a program using PL/SQL that:

- Accepts a date.
- Determines the number of employees who were marked as sick.
- Updates the attendance column value to hold 'Present' instead of 'Sick'.
- Return this number with an appropriate message.

Solution:

```
SET SERVEROUTPUT ON
DECLARE
   varEmpSick Number(10);
   varDate EmployeeMuster.MusterDate%TYPE;
   varEmployeeNo EmployeeMuster.EmployeeNo%TYPE;
BEGIN
/* Accepting a date */
   varDate := '&EnterDate';
/* Updating the attendance column */
   UPDATE EmployeeMuster SET Attendance = 'Present'
      WHERE TO_CHAR(MusterDate,'DD-Mon-YY') = varDate
         AND Attendance = 'Sick Leave';
/* Determining the number of employee who is sick */
   varEmpSick := SQL%ROWCOUNT;
/* Returning the employee number with a message */
   IF varEmpSick > 0 THEN
      DBMS_OUTPUT.PUT_LINE(TO_CHAR(varEmpSick) || ' employees are found sick on '
         || varDate);
   ELSE
      DBMS_OUTPUT.PUT_LINE('All employees found present on ' || varDate);
   END IF;
END;
/
```

Query the EmployeeMuster table before executing the program:

```
EMPLOYEENO MUSTERDATE ATTENDANCE      INTIME                          OUTTIME
---------- ---------- --------------- ------------------------------- --------------------
4          21-MAY-08  Present         21-JAN-17 05.08.29.473718000 PM
4          21-MAY-08  Sick Leave
1          21-MAY-08  Absent
4          21-MAY-08  Absent
21         07-APR-08  Absent
3          02-MAY-08  Present         02-JAN-17 11.53.40.451359000 PM
1          01-MAY-08  Absent
2          02-MAY-08  Present         02-JAN-17 09.53.40.451359000 PM
4          05-MAY-08  Present         05-JAN-17 10.03.21.075645000 PM
4          04-MAY-08  Present
4          05-MAY-08  Absent

11 rows selected.
```

Execute the program:

```
Enter value for enterdate: 21-JAN-17
old   7:         varDate := '&EnterDate';
```

```
new   7:        varDate := '21-JAN-17';
1 employees are found sick on 21-JAN-17

PL/SQL procedure successfully completed.
```

Query the EmployeeMuster table after executing the program:

```
EMPLOYEENO MUSTERDATE ATTENDANCE      INTIME                          OUTTIME
---------- ---------- --------------- ------------------------------- --------------------
4          21-MAY-08  Present         21-JAN-17 05.08.29.473718000 PM
4          21-JAN-17  Present
1          21-MAY-08  Absent
4          21-MAY-08  Absent
21         07-APR-08  Absent
3          02-MAY-08  Present         02-JAN-17 11.53.40.451359000 PM
1          01-MAY-08  Absent
2          02-MAY-08  Present         02-JAN-17 09.53.40.451359000 PM
4          05-MAY-08  Present         05-JAN-17 10.03.21.075645000 PM
4          04-MAY-08  Present
4          05-MAY-08  Absent

11 rows selected.
```

Explicit Cursor

An **Explicit Cursor** is explicitly opened for processing data using a PL/SQL block. It is useful when individual records from a database table need to be processed. An explicit cursor is declared in the DECLARE section of a PL/SQL program.

Syntax:

```
CURSOR <CursorName> IS <SELECT Query>
```

Solution:

```
DECLARE
  CURSOR curCustomers IS SELECT CustomerName, CustomerNo, DateOfBirth
      FROM Customers;
BEGIN
END;
```

The declaration of an explicit cursor is merely an intimation to Oracle, and no memory allocation done at this point.

Explicit cursors are used in queries that return multiple rows. Processing multiple rows with explicit cursor is similar to processing a flat file.

A flat file can be processed as:

- Open the file.
- Process records.
- Close the file.

Similarly, an explicit cursor can be processed as:

- Declare a cursor mapped to an SQL SELECT query.
- Open the cursor.

- Fetch rows from the cursor one row at a time into memory variables.
- Process the data held in the memory variables as required using a loop.
- Exit from the loop after processing is complete.
- Close the cursor.

Once the cursor is declared, it can be used by opening it, fetching the data, and finally closing it when no longer needed.

Opening Cursor

Once a cursor is declared, it needs to be opened:

```
OPEN <CursorName>;
```

Solution:

```
DECLARE
   CURSOR curCustomers IS SELECT CustomerName, CustomerNo, DateOfBirth
       FROM Customers;
BEGIN
   OPEN curCustomers;
END;
```

The OPEN command:

- Defines a named portion in the memory.
- Executes the associated SQL query.
- Creates the **Active Data Set** by retrieving data and populating the named portion of the memory.
- Establishes a row pointer and sets it to point to the first row in the **Active Data Set**.

Fetching Data From Cursor

Once the data is available in the cursor (Active Data Set), it needs to be fetched into a set of memory variables for manipulation. The **FETCH** command allows moving such data into memory variables, retrieving one row at a time:

```
FETCH <CursorName> INTO <Variable1>, <Variable2>, . . .;
```

Solution:

```
DECLARE
   varCustomerName Customers.CustomerName%TYPE;
   varCustomerNo Customers.CustomerNo%TYPE;
   varContactNo Customers.ContactNo%TYPE;
   CURSOR curCustomers IS SELECT CustomerName, CustomerNo, ContactNo
       FROM Customers WHERE CustomerNo = '1';
BEGIN
   OPEN curCustomers;
```

```
    FETCH curCustomers INTO varCustomerName, varCustomerNo, varContactNo;
END;
/
```

Output:

```
PL/SQL procedure successfully completed.
```

The **FETCH** command can be placed inside a **LOOP ... END LOOP** construct, which fetches the data into the memory variables and processes it until all the rows in the Active Data Set are processed.

Write a program using PL/SQL that:

- Retrieves customer name, customer number, and contact number.
- Displays the same as:
  ```
  Customer Name ____________________
  Customer ID ______________________
  Contact Number ___________________
  ```

Solution:

```
SET SERVEROUTPUT ON
DECLARE
  varCustomerName Customers.CustomerName%TYPE;
  varCustomerNo Customers.CustomerNo%TYPE;
  varContactNo Customers.ContactNo%TYPE;
/* Declaring a cursor to hold customer details */
  CURSOR curCustomers IS SELECT CustomerName, CustomerNo, ContactNo
      FROM Customers;
BEGIN
/* Opening cursor */
  OPEN curCustomers;
/* Traversing throught the cursor */
  LOOP
  /* Fetching cursor data into memory variables */
      FETCH curCustomers INTO varCustomerName, varCustomerNo, varContactNo;
  /* Exit the loop when there are no more rows, as indicated by the Boolean
  variable NOTFOUND (= true when there are no more rows) */
      EXIT WHEN curCustomers%NOTFOUND;
  /* Displaying customer details */
      DBMS_OUTPUT.PUT_LINE('Customer Name ' || varCustomerName);
      DBMS_OUTPUT.PUT_LINE('Customer ID ' || varCustomerNo);
      DBMS_OUTPUT.PUT_LINE('Contact Number ' || varContactNo);
  END LOOP;
END;
/
```

Output:

```
Customer Name Sharanam Chaitanya Shah
```

```
Customer ID 21
Contact Number 91-022-24440094
Customer Name Vaishali Sharanam Shah
Customer ID 22
Contact Number 91-022-27740094
Customer Name Anil Mayekar
Customer ID 23
Contact Number
Customer Name Hansel
Customer ID 24
Contact Number 91-022-34340094
Customer Name Chaitanya Kantilal Shah
Customer ID 25
Contact Number 91-022-37640094
Customer Name Shravan Ashwin Benegal
Customer ID 26
Contact Number 91-022-40940094
Customer Name Prakash K Chouduary
Customer ID 27
Contact Number 91-022-47540094
Customer Name Stuti Kapil Khanna
Customer ID 28
Contact Number 91-022-54140094
Customer Name Deepika Anil Bakshi
Customer ID 29
Contact Number 91-022-57440094
Customer Name Manali Narendra Naik
Customer ID 30
Contact Number 91-022-60740094
Customer Name Amit Paul
Customer ID 31
Contact Number
PL/SQL procedure successfully completed.
```

Closing Cursor

After the data is fetched from the Active Date Set, the cursor needs to be closed. The **CLOSE** command achieves it by releasing the memory occupied by the cursor and its Active Data Set:

```
CLOSE <CursorName>;
```

After a cursor is closed, it can be reopened using the **OPEN** command.

Solution:

```
SET SERVEROUTPUT ON
DECLARE
   varCustomerName Customers.CustomerName%TYPE;
   varCustomerNo Customers.CustomerNo%TYPE;
   varContactNo Customers.ContactNo%TYPE;
   CURSOR curCustomers IS SELECT CustomerName, CustomerNo, ContactNo
```

```
        FROM Customers;
BEGIN
    OPEN curCustomers;
    LOOP
        FETCH curCustomers INTO varCustomerName, varCustomerNo, varContactNo;
        EXIT WHEN curCustomers%NOTFOUND;
        DBMS_OUTPUT.PUT_LINE('Customer Name ' || varCustomerName);
        DBMS_OUTPUT.PUT_LINE('Customer ID ' || varCustomerNo);
        DBMS_OUTPUT.PUT_LINE('Contact No ' || varContactNo);
    END LOOP;
    CLOSE curCustomers;
END;
/
```

Output:

```
Customer Name Sharanam Chaitanya Shah
Customer ID 21
Contact Number 91-022-24440094
Customer Name Vaishali Sharanam Shah
Customer ID 22
Contact Number 91-022-27740094
Customer Name Anil Mayekar
Customer ID 23
Contact Number
Customer Name Hansel
Customer ID 24
Contact Number 91-022-34340094
Customer Name Chaitanya Kantilal Shah
Customer ID 25
Contact Number 91-022-37640094
Customer Name Shravan Ashwin Benegal
Customer ID 26
Contact Number 91-022-40940094
Customer Name Prakash K Chouduary
Customer ID 27
Contact Number 91-022-47540094
Customer Name Stuti Kapil Khanna
Customer ID 28
Contact Number 91-022-54140094
Customer Name Deepika Anil Bakshi
Customer ID 29
Contact Number 91-022-57440094
Customer Name Manali Narendra Naik
Customer ID 30
Contact Number 91-022-60740094
Customer Name Amit Paul
Customer ID 31
Contact Number

PL/SQL procedure successfully completed.
```

Loop...End Loop

The company has decided to issue usernames and passwords to all existing employees. Here's a program using PL/SQL that:

- Fetches employee records in memory.
- Generates a username and password for each fetched employee.
- Updates the username and password columns of the Employees table with the generated values.

The username should be formed as:

FirstName	LastName	EmployeeNo	Username
Sharan**am**	**Sh**ah	**1**	**AMSH1**

The password should be formed as:

FirstName	LastName	Salary	Password
Sharanam	**Sh**ah	352**32**	SHSH**32**

Solution:

```
SET SERVEROUTPUT ON
DECLARE
/* Cursor Declaration. */
  CURSOR curEmployees IS
      SELECT EmployeeNo, FirstName, LastName, Salary FROM Employees;
/* Memory variables to hold the data fetched. */
  varEmployeeNo Employees.EmployeeNo%TYPE;
  varFirstName Employees.FirstName%TYPE;
  varLastName Employees.LastName%TYPE;
  varSalary Employees.Salary%TYPE;
/* Memory variables to hold the username and password. */
  varUsername Employees.Username%TYPE;
  varPassword Employees.Password%TYPE;
BEGIN
/* Opening cursor. */
  OPEN curEmployees;
/* If the cursor is open continue with the data processing else display
an appropriate error message. */
  IF curEmployees%ISOPEN THEN
      LOOP
          FETCH curEmployees
              INTO varEmployeeNo, varFirstName, varLastName, varSalary;
      /* Exiting the loop if no records are available. */
          EXIT WHEN curEmployees%NOTFOUND;
          IF curEmployees%FOUND THEN
          /* Generating Usernames and Passwords. */
              varUsername := SUBSTR(varFirstName, -2, 2)
```

```
                || SUBSTR(varLastName, 1, 2) || varEmployeeNo;
            varPassword := SUBSTR(varFirstName, 1, 2)
                || SUBSTR(varLastName, 1, 2)
                    || SUBSTR(TO_CHAR(varSalary), -2, 2);
        /* Updating Employees table with the generated values. */
            UPDATE Employees SET Username = varUsername,
                Password = varPassword WHERE EmployeeNo = varEmployeeNo;
        END IF;
    END LOOP;
  /* Making the changes permanent. */
    COMMIT;
  ELSE
    DBMS_OUTPUT.PUT_LINE('No records found in the Employees table');
  END IF;
/* Closing the cursor. */
  CLOSE curEmployees;
END;
/
```

In this example, an explicit cursor is declared to retrieve the EmployeeNo, FirstName, LastName, and Salary from the Employees table. Since the query retrieves multiple values, the following memory variables are declared to hold them:

```
varEmployeeNo Employees.EmployeeNo%TYPE;
varFirstName Employees.FirstName%TYPE;
varLastName Employees.LastName%TYPE;
varSalary Employees.Salary%TYPE;
```

As the query returns multiple rows, a LOOP is used to traverse through the records returned. In each iteration, the LOOP performs the following steps:

1. Fetches the data retrieved by the cursor into the memory variables.
2. Checks if the data was retrieved using FETCH:
    - Generates the Username and Password.
    - Updates the Employees table with the generated username and password for an employee.

These steps are repeated for all the records in the Active Data Set. Finally, a COMMIT is executed to make the changes permanent.

Output:

```
PL/SQL procedure successfully completed.
```

Querying Employees Table:

```
SELECT EmployeeNo, FirstName, LastName, Salary, Username, Password
  FROM Employees;
```

Output:

```
EMPLOYEENO FIRSTNAME     LASTNAME     SALARY   USERNAME PASSWORD
---------- ------------- ------------ -------- -------- --------
1          Sharanam      Shah         82500    amSh1    ShSh00
```

2	Vaishali	Shah	55000	**liSh2**	**VaSh00**
3	Keyur	Kapoor	22000	**urKa3**	**KeKa00**
4	Amit	Haria	22000	**itHa4**	**AmHa00**
5	Abhishek	Benegal	13334.2	**ekBe5**	**AbBe.2**
6	Chetan	Dedhia	13553.1	**anDe6**	**ChDe.1**
7	Narendra	Dodhia	13578.4	**raDo7**	**NaDo.4**
8	Meenal	Doshi	49500	**alDo8**	**MeDo00**
9	Anil	Mayekar	2750	**ilMa9**	**AnMa50**
10	Chaitanya	Kapoor	1320	**yaKa10**	**ChKa20**
11	Amit	Paul	31207	**itPa11**	**AmPa07**

11 rows selected.

While Loop

Using the same example as shown in the **Loop...End Loop** section.

```
DECLARE
/* Cursor Declaration. */
  CURSOR curEmployees IS
      SELECT EmployeeNo, FirstName, LastName, Salary FROM Employees;
/* Memory variables to hold the data fetched. */
  varEmployeeNo Employees.EmployeeNo%TYPE;
  varFirstName Employees.FirstName%TYPE;
  varLastName Employees.LastName%TYPE;
  varSalary Employees.Salary%TYPE;
/* Memory variables to hold the username and password. */
  varUsername Employees.Username%TYPE;
  varPassword Employees.Password%TYPE;
BEGIN
/* Opening cursor. */
  OPEN curEmployees;
/* If the cursor is open continue with the data processing else display
an appropriate error message. */
  IF curEmployees%ISOPEN THEN
      FETCH curEmployees
          INTO varEmployeeNo, varFirstName, varLastName, varSalary;
      WHILE curEmployees%FOUND
      LOOP
      /* Exiting the loop if no records are available. */
          EXIT WHEN curEmployees%NOTFOUND;
          IF curEmployees%FOUND THEN
          /* Generating Usernames and Passwords. */
              varUsername := SUBSTR(varFirstName, -2, 2)
                  || SUBSTR(varLastName, 1, 2) || varEmployeeNo;
              varPassword := SUBSTR(varFirstName, 1, 2)
                  || SUBSTR(varLastName, 1, 2)
                      || SUBSTR(TO_CHAR(varSalary), -2, 2);
          /* Updating Employees table with the generated values. */
              UPDATE Employees SET Username = varUsername,
                  Password = varPassword WHERE EmployeeNo = varEmployeeNo;
```

```
            FETCH curEmployees
                INTO varEmployeeNo, varFirstName, varLastName, varSalary;
            END IF;
        END LOOP;
    /* Making the changes permanent. */
        COMMIT;
    ELSE
        DBMS_OUTPUT.PUT_LINE('No records found in the Employees table');
    END IF;
/* Closing cursor. */
    CLOSE curEmployees;
END;
/
```

Explanation:

```
FETCH curEmployees INTO varEmployeeNo, varFirstName, varLastName, varSalary;
```

In this statement, the data is fetched twice. This is required for the following to work:

```
WHILE curEmployees%FOUND
```

The %FOUND attribute will only function if the data is fetched.

After the data is fetched, the WHILE loop runs till it finds no more records in the cursor.

Output:

```
PL/SQL procedure successfully completed.
```

Querying Employees Table:

```
SELECT EmployeeNo, FirstName, LastName, Salary, Username, Password
    FROM Employees;
```

Output:

```
EMPLOYEENO FIRSTNAME    LASTNAME     SALARY   USERNAME PASSWORD
---------- ------------ ------------ -------- -------- --------
1          Sharanam     Shah         82500    amSh1    ShSh00
2          Vaishali     Shah         55000    liSh2    VaSh00
3          Keyur        Kapoor       22000    urKa3    KeKa00
4          Amit         Haria        22000    itHa4    AmHa00
5          Abhishek     Benegal      13334.2  ekBe5    AbBe.2
6          Chetan       Dedhia       13553.1  anDe6    ChDe.1
7          Narendra     Dodhia       13578.4  raDo7    NaDo.4
8          Meenal       Doshi        49500    alDo8    MeDo00
9          Anil         Mayekar      2750     ilMa9    AnMa50
10         Chaitanya    Kapoor       1320     yaKa10   ChKa20
11         Amit         Paul         31207    itPa11   AmPa07

11 rows selected.
```

To modify the program to generate and allot usernames and passwords only for the first 5 employees, you can add a counter to track the number of processed employees and exit the loop after processing the fifth employee. Here's the updated program:

```
SET SERVEROUTPUT ON
DECLARE
/* Cursor Declaration. */
  CURSOR curEmployees IS
     SELECT EmployeeNo, FirstName, LastName, Salary FROM Employees;
/* Memory variables to hold the data fetched. */
  varEmployeeNo Employees.EmployeeNo%TYPE;
  varFirstName Employees.FirstName%TYPE;
  varLastName Employees.LastName%TYPE;
  varSalary Employees.Salary%TYPE;
/* Memory variables to hold the username and password. */
  varUsername Employees.Username%TYPE;
  varPassword Employees.Password%TYPE;
BEGIN
/* Opening cursor. */
  OPEN curEmployees;
/* If the cursor is open continue with the data processing else display
an appropriate error message. */
  IF curEmployees%ISOPEN THEN
     LOOP
        FETCH curEmployees
           INTO varEmployeeNo, varFirstName, varLastName, varSalary;
     /* Exiting the loop if the first five records are retrieved or no
     records are available whichever happens first. */
     EXIT WHEN (curEmployees%ROWCOUNT - 1) = 5
        OR curEmployees%NOTFOUND;
        IF curEmployees%FOUND THEN
        /* Generating Usernames and Passwords. */
           varUsername := SUBSTR(varFirstName, -2, 2)
              || SUBSTR(varLastName, 1, 2) || varEmployeeNo;
           varPassword := SUBSTR(varFirstName, 1, 2)
              || SUBSTR(varLastName, 1, 2)
                 || SUBSTR(TO_CHAR(varSalary), -2, 2);
        /* Updating Employees table with the generated values. */
           UPDATE Employees SET Username = varUsername,
              Password = varPassword WHERE EmployeeNo = varEmployeeNo;
        END IF;
     END LOOP;
  /* Making the changes permanent. */
     COMMIT;
  ELSE
     DBMS_OUTPUT.PUT_LINE('No records found in the Employees table');
  END IF;
/* Closing cursor. */
  CLOSE curEmployees;
END;
```

```
/
```

Since only the first five employees are to be considered, the EXIT command is written as:

```
EXIT WHEN (curEmployees%ROWCOUNT - 1) = 5
```

This indicates that the loop will continue:

- Until the number of records retrieved becomes 5:
  i.e. **(curEmployees%ROWCOUNT - 1) = 5**

OR

- The data retrieval process completes:
  i.e. **curEmployees%NOTFOUND**

whichever happens first.

Output:

```
PL/SQL procedure successfully completed.
```

Querying Employees Table:

```
SELECT EmployeeNo, FirstName, LastName, Salary, Username, Password
  FROM Employees;
```

Output:

```
EMPLOYEENO FIRSTNAME     LASTNAME     SALARY   USERNAME PASSWORD
---------- ------------- ------------ -------- -------- --------
1          Sharanam      Shah         82500    amSh1    ShSh00
2          Vaishali      Shah         55000    liSh2    VaSh00
3          Keyur         Kapoor       22000    urKa3    KeKa00
4          Amit          Haria        22000    itHa4    AmHa00
5          Abhishek      Benegal      13334.2  ekBe5    AbBe.2
6          Chetan        Dedhia       13553.1
7          Narendra      Dodhia       13578.4
8          Meenal        Doshi        49500
9          Anil          Mayekar      2750
10         Chaitanya     Kapoor       1320
11         Amit          Paul         31207

11 rows selected.
```

FOR Loop

A cursor allows using a FOR Loop to process multiple records. A FOR Loop:

- Implicitly declares a %ROWTYPE variable and uses it as the LOOP index.
- Opens a cursor.
- Read records.
- Closes the cursor automatically when all records have been processed.

Therefore, commands such as OPEN, FETCH, and CLOSE are not required here.

Syntax:

```
FOR <Variable> IN <CursorName>
```

Each record in the opened cursor is assigned to the memory variable of the **%ROWTYPE**.

> A cursor can also be closed using an **EXIT** or **GOTO** command to leave the loop prematurely or if an **exception** is raised inside the loop.

Using the same example as shown in the **Loop...End Loop** section:

```
DECLARE
/* Cursor Declaration. */
  CURSOR curEmployees IS
      SELECT EmployeeNo, FirstName, LastName, Salary FROM Employees;
/* Memory variables to hold the username and password. */
  varUsername Employees.Username%TYPE;
  varPassword Employees.Password%TYPE;
BEGIN
/* Using a For Loop. */
  FOR typEmployees IN curEmployees
  LOOP
  /* Generating Usernames and Passwords. */
      varUsername := SUBSTR(typEmployees.FirstName, -2, 2)
          || SUBSTR(typEmployees.LastName, 1, 2) || typEmployees.EmployeeNo;
      varPassword := SUBSTR(typEmployees.FirstName, 1, 2)
          || SUBSTR(typEmployees.LastName, 1, 2)
          || SUBSTR(TO_CHAR(typEmployees.Salary), -2, 2);
  /* Updating Employees table with the generated values. */
      UPDATE Employees SET Username = varUsername, Password = varPassword
          WHERE EmployeeNo = typEmployees.EmployeeNo;
  END LOOP;
/* Making the changes permanent. */
  COMMIT;
END;
/
```

Since a FOR loop is used, there is no need to declare any memory variable to hold cursor values. The **FOR typEmployees IN curEmployees** implicitly declares memory variables, as a **%ROWTYPE** record.

The FOR loop:

1. Automatically fetches the data retrieved by the cursor into the **typEmployees** record set.
2. For every iteration, the FOR loop checks if the data exists. If it does:
   - Generates the Username and Password.
   - Updates the Employees table with the generated username and password for an employee.

3. Closes the cursor when all the records in the cursor have been processed.

Finally, a COMMIT is executed to make the changes permanent.

Output:

```
PL/SQL procedure successfully completed.
```

Querying Employees Table:

```
SELECT EmployeeNo, FirstName, LastName, Salary, Username, Password
  FROM Employees;
```

Output:

```
EMPLOYEENO FIRSTNAME     LASTNAME     SALARY   USERNAME PASSWORD
---------- ------------- ------------ -------- -------- --------
1          Sharanam      Shah         82500    amSh1    ShSh00
2          Vaishali      Shah         55000    liSh2    VaSh00
3          Keyur         Kapoor       22000    urKa3    KeKa00
4          Amit          Haria        22000    itHa4    AmHa00
5          Abhishek      Benegal      13334.2  ekBe5    AbBe.2
6          Chetan        Dedhia       13553.1  anDe6    ChDe.1
7          Narendra      Dodhia       13578.4  raDo7    NaDo.4
8          Meenal        Doshi        49500    alDo8    MeDo00
9          Anil          Mayekar      2750     ilMa9    AnMa50
10         Chaitanya     Kapoor       1320     yaKa10   ChKa20
11         Amit          Paul         31207    itPa11   AmPa07

11 rows selected.
```

Defining An Inline Cursor

The FOR loop allows defining an inline cursor. An **inline cursor** is a cursor that is not declared in the DECLARE section but instead, the cursor definition is included directly in the FOR loop.

This example demonstrates using **an inline cursor:**

```
DECLARE
/* Memory variables to hold the username and password. */
  varUsername Employees.Username%TYPE;
  varPassword Employees.Password%TYPE;
BEGIN
/* Using a For Loop. */
  FOR typEmployees
     IN (SELECT EmployeeNo, FirstName, LastName, Salary FROM Employees)
  LOOP
  /* Generating Usernames and Passwords. */
     varUsername := SUBSTR(typEmployees.FirstName, -2, 2)
        || SUBSTR(typEmployees.LastName, 1, 2) || typEmployees.EmployeeNo;
     varPassword := SUBSTR(typEmployees.FirstName, 1, 2)
        || SUBSTR(typEmployees.LastName, 1, 2)
```

```
            || SUBSTR(TO_CHAR(typEmployees.Salary), -2, 2);
  /* Updating Employees table with the generated values. */
      UPDATE Employees SET Username = varUsername, Password = varPassword
            WHERE EmployeeNo = typEmployees.EmployeeNo;
  END LOOP;
/* Making the changes permanent. */
  COMMIT;
END;
/
```

Output:

```
PL/SQL procedure successfully completed.
```

Querying Employees Table:

```
SELECT EmployeeNo, FirstName, LastName, Salary, Username, Password
  FROM Employees;
```

Output:

```
EMPLOYEENO FIRSTNAME     LASTNAME     SALARY   USERNAME PASSWORD
---------- ------------- ------------ -------- -------- --------
1          Sharanam      Shah         82500    amSh1    ShSh00
2          Vaishali      Shah         55000    liSh2    VaSh00
3          Keyur         Kapoor       22000    urKa3    KeKa00
4          Amit          Haria        22000    itHa4    AmHa00
5          Abhishek      Benegal      13334.2  ekBe5    AbBe.2
6          Chetan        Dedhia       13553.1  anDe6    ChDe.1
7          Narendra      Dodhia       13578.4  raDo7    NaDo.4
8          Meenal        Doshi        49500    alDo8    MeDo00
9          Anil          Mayekar      2750     ilMa9    AnMa50
10         Chaitanya     Kapoor       1320     yaKa10   ChKa20
11         Amit          Paul         31207    itPa11   AmPa07

11 rows selected.
```

Defining a cursor inline has the advantage of self-documenting the cursor in the code. Instead of going back to the DECLARE section to determine the cursor definition, the programmer can see the definition directly in the code that calls it.

However, if the cursor is used multiple times in the same code block, it will have to be defined inline in multiple locations, reducing code maintainability. Another disadvantage with defining the cursor inline is that it will have no defined name, so cursor attributes cannot be accessed. This can be an issue if an exception is raised inside the cursor that causes it to jump out of the loop.

Passing Parameters To Cursors

Often, it is necessary to have a generic SQL query that retrieves data based on a parameter it receives. SQL queries accomplish this using a WHERE clause. Similarly, a cursor that uses an SQL query to retrieve the required data can be passed a parameter, which can then be used in the WHERE condition of the actual query.

A cursor that accepts parameters is called a **parameterized cursor**. The contents of such a cursor change depending on the value passed to its parameter.

Declaring Cursor

Syntax:

```
CURSOR <CursorName> (<VariableName> <Datatype>) IS
  <SELECT statement . . .>
```

Solution:

```
DECLARE
  CURSOR curEmployees (varLastName Employees.LastName%TYPE)
      IS SELECT EmployeeNo, FirstName, LastName, Salary FROM Employees
          WHERE LastName = varLastName;
BEGIN
END;
```

Opening Cursor

Syntax:

```
OPEN <CursorName> (<Value> | <Variable> | <Expression>)
```

```
FOR <VariableName> IN <CursorName> (<Value> | <Variable> | <Expression>)
```

Solution:

```
DECLARE
  CURSOR curEmployees (varLastName Employees.LastName%TYPE)
      IS SELECT EmployeeNo, FirstName, LastName, Salary FROM Employees
          WHERE LastName = varLastName;
BEGIN
  OPEN curEmployees('&LastName');
END;
```

Using the same example as shown in the **Loop...End Loop** section. In addition, this program also accepts a LastName:

```
SET SERVEROUTPUT ON
```

```
DECLARE
/* Cursor Declaration. */
  CURSOR curEmployees (varLastName Employees.LastName%TYPE)
      IS SELECT EmployeeNo, FirstName, LastName, Salary FROM Employees
          WHERE LastName = varLastName;
/* Memory variables to hold the data fetched. */
  varEmployeeNo Employees.EmployeeNo%TYPE;
  varFirstName Employees.FirstName%TYPE;
  varLastName Employees.LastName%TYPE;
  varSalary Employees.Salary%TYPE;
/* Memory variables to hold the username and password. */
  varUsername Employees.Username%TYPE;
  varPassword Employees.Password%TYPE;
BEGIN
/* Opening cursor. */
  OPEN curEmployees('&LastName');
/* If the cursor is open continue with the data processing else display
an appropriate error message. */
  IF curEmployees%ISOPEN THEN
      LOOP
          FETCH curEmployees
              INTO varEmployeeNo, varFirstName, varLastName, varSalary;
      /* Exiting the loop if no records are available. */
          EXIT WHEN curEmployees%NOTFOUND;
          IF curEmployees%FOUND THEN
          /* Generating Usernames and Passwords. */
              varUsername := SUBSTR(varFirstName, -2, 2)
                  || SUBSTR(varLastName, 1, 2) || varEmployeeNo;
              varPassword := SUBSTR(varFirstName, 1, 2)
                  || SUBSTR(varLastName, 1, 2)
                      || SUBSTR(TO_CHAR(varSalary), -2, 2);
          /* Updating Employees table with the generated values. */
              UPDATE Employees SET Username = varUsername,
                  Password = varPassword WHERE EmployeeNo = varEmployeeNo;
          END IF;
      END LOOP;
  /* Making the changes permanent. */
      COMMIT;
  ELSE
      DBMS_OUTPUT.PUT_LINE('No records found in the Employees table');
  END IF;
/* Closing cursor. */
  CLOSE curEmployees;
END;
/
```

Here, since the cursor **curEmployees** accepts a parameter, it will hold a restricted set of records based on the parameter received.

Output:

```
Enter value for lastname: Shah
old  19:        OPEN curEmployees('&LastName');
new  19:        OPEN curEmployees('Shah');

PL/SQL procedure successfully completed.
```

Querying Employees Table:

```
SELECT EmployeeNo, FirstName, LastName, Salary, Username, Password
  FROM Employees;
```

Output:

```
EMPLOYEENO FIRSTNAME     LASTNAME     SALARY   USERNAME PASSWORD
---------- ------------- ------------ -------- -------- --------
1          Sharanam      Shah         82500    amSh1    ShSh00
2          Vaishali      Shah         55000    liSh2    VaSh00
3          Keyur         Kapoor       22000
4          Amit          Haria        22000
5          Abhishek      Benegal      13334.2
6          Chetan        Dedhia       13553.1
7          Narendra      Dodhia       13578.4
8          Meenal        Doshi        49500
9          Anil          Mayekar      2750
10         Chaitanya     Kapoor       1320
11         Amit          Paul         31207

11 rows selected.
```

Cursor Within Cursor

The company holds employees and departments details in master tables called Employees and Departments. For reporting purposes, it is required to store the information from these tables in a de-normalized table, EmployeesDept. Write a program using PL/SQL that:

- Fetches departments from the Departments table.
- For every department, fetches employees belonging to that department from the Employees table.
- Adds all the information from both the tables to the EmployeesDept table.

Solution:

```
DECLARE
  /* First cursor */
     CURSOR curDepartments IS SELECT * FROM Departments;
  /* Second cursor */
     CURSOR curEmployees(varDeptNo Departments.DeptNo%TYPE)
        IS SELECT * FROM Employees WHERE DeptNo = varDeptNo;
  BEGIN
  /* Defining a For loop for first cursor */
     FOR typDepartments IN curDepartments
```

```
        LOOP
        /* Defining a For loop for second cursor */
            FOR typEmployees IN curEmployees (typDepartments.DeptNo)
            LOOP
            /* Inserting data from both the cursor */
                INSERT INTO EmployeesDept (EmployeeNo, FirstName, LastName,
                    DateOfBirth, ContactNo, Salary, Designation, ManagerNo, DeptNo,
                    DepartmentName, UserName, Password)
                        VALUES (typEmployees.EmployeeNo, typEmployees.FirstName,
                        typEmployees.LastName, typEmployees.DateOfBirth,
                        typEmployees.ContactNo, typEmployees.Salary,
                        typEmployees.Designation, typEmployees.ManagerNo,
                        typDepartments.DeptNo, typDepartments.DepartmentName,
                        typEmployees.UserName, typEmployees.Password);
            END LOOP;
        END LOOP;
    /* Make the changes permanent. */
        COMMIT;
END;
/
```

In this program, two cursors are declared. The first cursor, named **curDepartments**, holds records from the Departments table. The second cursor, named **curEmployees**, holds records from the Employees table. This is a parameterized cursor that accepts DeptNo as a parameter and retrieves only the employees who belong to that department.

The outer FOR loop is used to traverse through the records held by the first cursor, curDepartments. This FOR loop, in turn, contains another FOR loop that is used to traverse through the records held by the second cursor, curEmployees.

The first cursor holds department details. For each row it retrieves in the FOR loop, the DeptNo is extracted and passed as a parameter to the second cursor, curEmployees. This cursor then fetches only those employees who belong to that department.

After the data is fetched from both cursors, it is inserted in the de-normalized table EmployeesDept.

Output:

```
PL/SQL procedure successfully completed.
```

Locking Cursor Data

When a SELECT query is fired to retrieve data, no locks are placed on the selected rows. However, it is often necessary to lock a set of records before applying changes using a PL/SQL program.

Oracle provides the **FOR UPDATE** clause, which can be used with a SELECT statement to perform this locking.

If the FOR UPDATE clause is used with a SELECT query, Oracle obtains an exclusive row-level lock on all the rows identified by the SELECT statement. By applying an exclusive lock, no one else will be able to change any of these records until a ROLLBACK or COMMIT is executed.

Let's use the same example as shown in the **Loop...End Loop** section to ensure that while the Employees table is being updated, no one else updates the same table simultaneously:

```
SET SERVEROUTPUT ON
DECLARE
/* Cursor Declaration. */
   CURSOR curEmployees IS
       SELECT EmployeeNo, FirstName, LastName, Salary
           FROM Employees FOR UPDATE;
/* Memory variables to hold the data fetched. */
   varEmployeeNo Employees.EmployeeNo%TYPE;
   varFirstName Employees.FirstName%TYPE;
   varLastName Employees.LastName%TYPE;
   varSalary Employees.Salary%TYPE;
/* Memory variables to hold the username and password. */
   varUsername Employees.Username%TYPE;
   varPassword Employees.Password%TYPE;
BEGIN
/* Opening cursor. */
   OPEN curEmployees;
/* If the cursor is open continue with the data processing else display
an appropriate error message. */
   IF curEmployees%ISOPEN THEN
       LOOP
           FETCH curEmployees
               INTO varEmployeeNo, varFirstName, varLastName, varSalary;
       /* Exiting the loop if no records are available. */
           EXIT WHEN curEmployees%NOTFOUND;
           IF curEmployees%FOUND THEN
           /* Generating Usernames and Passwords. */
               varUsername := SUBSTR(varFirstName, -2, 2)
                   || SUBSTR(varLastName, 1, 2) || varEmployeeNo;
               varPassword := SUBSTR(varFirstName, 1, 2)
                   || SUBSTR(varLastName, 1, 2)
                       || SUBSTR(TO_CHAR(varSalary), -2, 2);
           /* Updating Employees table with the generated values. */
               UPDATE Employees SET Username = varUsername,
                   Password = varPassword WHERE EmployeeNo = varEmployeeNo;
           END IF;
       END LOOP;
   /* Making the changes permanent. */
```

```
        COMMIT;
    ELSE
        DBMS_OUTPUT.PUT_LINE('No records found in the Employees table');
    END IF;
/* Closing cursor. */
    CLOSE curEmployees;
END;
/
```

As soon as the cursor curEmployees is opened, all rows retrieved by that query are locked and remain locked until a COMMIT is issued to make the changes (if any) permanent, or a ROLLBACK is issued to cancel changes (if any). When either of these commands is issued, the locks on the rows are released.

Output:

```
PL/SQL procedure successfully completed.
```

Update/Delete Via Cursors

The records referenced using a SELECT query with FOR UPDATE clause can be updated or deleted using the **WHERE CURRENT OF** statement.

Syntax:

```
UPDATE <TableName> SET <Clause> WHERE CURRENT OF <CursorName>;
DELETE FROM <TableName> WHERE CURRENT OF <CursorName>;
```

The WHERE CURRENT OF statement allows updating or deleting the record that was last fetched by the cursor.

The company has decided to:

- Change the designation of all employees who are Peons to Office Boys.
- Remove the employees who are designated as Designers, as the company has changed its line of business and no longer requires designers.

Write a program using PL/SQL that:

- Fetches employee records into memory.
- Updates the designation from Peon to Office Boy.
- Deletes the employees with the designation of Designer.

Ensure that while the Employees table is being updated, no one else updates the same table simultaneously:

```
DECLARE
/* Cursor Declaration. */
    CURSOR curEmployees IS
```

```
      SELECT * FROM Employees FOR UPDATE;
BEGIN
   FOR typEmployees IN curEmployees
   LOOP
      IF typEmployees.Designation = 'Peon' THEN
      /* Updating Employees table. */
         UPDATE Employees SET Designation = 'Office Boy'
            WHERE CURRENT OF curEmployees;
      ELSIF typEmployees.Designation = 'Designers' THEN
      /* Deleting from Employees table. */
         DELETE FROM Employees WHERE CURRENT OF curEmployees;
      END IF;
   END LOOP;
END;
/
```

Output:

```
PL/SQL procedure successfully completed.
```

Query the employee table to view the records changed:

```
SELECT EmployeeNo, FirstName, LastName, Designation FROM Employees;
```

Output:

```
EMPLOYEENO FIRSTNAME    LASTNAME         DESIGNATION
---------- ------------ ---------------- -----------------
         1 Sharanam     Shah             Technical Writing
         2 Vaishali     Shah             Database Management
         3 Keyur        Kapoor           Testing
         4 Amit         Haria            Programming
         5 Abhishek     Benegal          Sales
         6 Chetan       Dedhia           HR
         7 Narendra     Dodhia           Accounts
         8 Meenal       Doshi            Auditing
         9 Anil         Mayekar          Office Boy
        10 Chaitanya    Kapoor           Office Boy
        11 Amit         Paul             Office Boy

11 rows selected.
```

The cursor is declared using the FOR UPDATE clause, which allows obtaining an exclusive lock on all the employee records. Using IF/THEN statements, the designation of the current employee in the cursor loop is determined.

Based on the value held in the designation column, either UPDATE or DELETE command is executed. The UPDATE ... WHERE CURRENT OF clause automatically updates the row that the cursor is currently using at that time. Since the update SQL does not need to relocate the row to update, it is very fast.

All the rows selected by the cursor remain locked, including the changed rows.

The transaction stays open, and the locks are held until a ROLLBACK or COMMIT is issued, making the changes permanent:

```
/* Making the changes permanent. */
  COMMIT;
```

Chapter

29

SECTION V: PL/SQL

Procedures And Functions

PL/SQL enables the creation of ***subprograms,*** which are named blocks of code consisting of logically grouped SQL and PL/SQL statements that perform specific tasks.

Benefits of Subprograms:

- Allow writing PL/SQL programs to meet various requirements.
- Facilitate breaking down PL/SQL programs into manageable modules.
- Promote code reusability, thereby enhancing code maintainability.
- Enforce security by granting appropriate permissions on procedures or functions that query specific tables to users.
- Boost database performance as no compilation is required during execution of procedures or functions.

Types of Subprograms:

- Procedures
- Functions

Procedures and Functions can be invoked by any PL/SQL code block within an application. Before being stored, the Oracle engine **parses** and **compiles** the procedure or function.

These subprograms are compiled and stored in the Oracle database as **Stored Programs**. Since these programs are stored in a **compiled form**, only execution occurs when they are invoked, saving time otherwise spent on compilation. Additionally, executing a procedure or function on the Oracle database server helps reduce network traffic.

Sections Of Procedures And Functions

Every subprogram, i.e., procedures and functions, is made up of the following sections:

Declarative Section

The declarative section usually holds the declarations of:

- Cursors
- Constants
- Variables
- Exceptions
- Subprograms

These declarations are local to the subprogram and become invalid once the subprogram (i.e., procedure or function) exits.

Executable Section

The executable section holds SQL and PL/SQL statements that help achieve the purpose for which the procedure or function is written. It includes code that:

- Assigns values to variables.
- Controls execution.
- Manipulates table data.
- Returns data to the calling environment after completing processing the code.

The variables declared in the declarative section are used within this code block.

Exception Handling Section

The exception handling section holds exceptions (if any) that may be raised during the execution of the code block in the **executable** section.

> Control cannot be shifted from the **Exception Handling** section to the Executable part.

Procedures V/s Functions

Procedure	Function
Return Value	
A procedure may return one or more values **through parameters** or may not return values at all.	A function always returns a value using the return statement.
Multiple Return Values	
By defining multiple OUT parameters, a procedure can pass/return multiple values to the caller. The OUT variable being global by nature, its value is accessible by any PL/SQL code block, **including** the one from which it was called.	A function can return only one value to the calling PL/SQL code block.
SQL SELECT queries	
A SELECT SQL query can call a function.	A SELECT SQL query cannot call a procedure.
DML queries	
DML statements can be used in procedures.	DML statements cannot be used in functions.
When To Create	
Example: If it is desired to update product prices, a procedure is preferred.	Example: If it is desired to retrieve the employee number (code) for a particular employee, a function is preferred.

Procedures

Procedure specification begins with **CREATE** and ends with the procedure name or arguments list. Procedures that do not take parameters are written without parentheses. The body of the procedure starts after the keyword **IS** or **AS** and ends with the keyword **END**.

Syntax:

```
CREATE OR REPLACE PROCEDURE [<Schema>.]<ProcedureName>
  (<Argument> {IN, OUT, IN OUT} <DataType>, ...) {IS, AS}
  <Variable Declarations>;
  <Constant Declarations>;
  BEGIN
     <Body code block>;
  EXCEPTION
     <Exception code block>;
  END;
```

Where,

- ***REPLACE:*** Recreates the procedure (if it already exists). This option allows changing the definition of an existing procedure without dropping, recreating, and re-granting object privileges previously granted on it. If a procedure is redefined, Oracle recompiles it.
- ***Schema:*** The schema that holds the procedure being created.
- ***Procedure:*** The name of the procedure being created.
- ***Argument:*** The name of arguments to the procedure. To make a procedure dynamic, arguments/parameters can be passed before execution. A procedure can then change its behavior depending on the parameters passed prior to its execution. An argument can be:
  - *IN:* A parameter whose value is passed into a procedure. The value of an IN parameter is a constant. It cannot be changed or reassigned within the module. It is the default mode.
  - *OUT:* A parameter whose value is passed out of the stored procedure back to the calling PL/SQL block. An OUT parameter is a variable, not a constant. A default value cannot be assigned to an OUT parameter.
  - *IN OUT:* A parameter that functions as both an IN and OUT parameter. The value of the IN/OUT parameter is passed into the stored procedure, and a new value can be assigned to the parameter and passed out of the procedure. An IN/OUT parameter is a variable, not a constant.

  Arguments can be assigned a default value using the **assignment operator (:=)** or the **DEFAULT** keyword. An argument with a default value need not be included in the procedure call:

```
<Argument1> IN Varchar2 := 'Sharanam';
<Argument2> IN Varchar2 DEFAULT 'Sharanam';
```

TIP: Parentheses can be omitted if no arguments are present.

  Arguments are declared with data types but **without data type length or precision**. This means that a parameter may be declared as:

```
Varchar2
```

  But not with a length component like:

```
Varchar2(30)
```

- ***DataType:*** The data type of the argument. Any data type supported by PL/SQL can be specified here.
- ***Body code block:*** The procedure definition consisting of PL/SQL statements.
- ***Exception code block:*** The section that holds defined exceptions.

> The user needs to have the CREATE PROCEDURE system privilege to create a procedure in the schema.

Employee attendance is stored in the EmployeeMuster table. The Attendance column of this table holds values like 'Present', 'Absent', or 'Sick Leave'. Let's write a procedure that:

- Accepts employee number as a parameter.
- Calculates the number of leaves from the data available in the EmployeeMuster table.
- Provides the updated number of leaves as a value.

Solution:

```
CREATE OR REPLACE PROCEDURE CalculateEmpLeaves(
   varEmployeeNo IN Varchar2, varLeaves OUT Number) IS
   BEGIN
   /* Retrieving the number of leaves from EmployeeMuster. */
      SELECT COUNT(*) INTO varLeaves FROM EmployeeMuster
         WHERE EmployeeNo = varEmployeeNo AND Attendance <> 'Present';
   END;
/
```

Output:

```
Procedure created.
```

Test the procedure using SQL as:

```
VARIABLE varNoOfLeaves Number;
EXEC CalculateEmpLeaves(4, :varNoOfLeaves);
PRINT varNoOfLeaves;
```

In order to call a procedure from the SQL*Plus, it is necessary to first define a variable to which the return value can be assigned. The variable named must be preceded by a colon (:).

Output:

```
VARNOOFLEAVES
-------------
            2
```

Test the procedure using PL/SQL program as:

```
SET SERVEROUTPUT ON
DECLARE
   varNoOfLeaves Number;
   varEmpNo Number;
BEGIN
   varEmpNo := &EmployeeNumber;
   CalculateEmpLeaves(varEmpNo, varNoOfLeaves);
   DBMS_OUTPUT.PUT_LINE('Employee No: ' || varEmpNo || ' has taken '
      || varNoOfLeaves || ' leaves till date.');
END;
```

```
/
```

Output:

```
Enter value for employeenumber: 4
old   5:        varEmpNo := &EmployeeNumber;
new   5:        varEmpNo := 4;
Employee No: 4 has taken 2 leaves till date.
PL/SQL procedure successfully completed.
```

> When calling a procedure from a PL/SQL block, the keyword **EXECUTE** is omitted.

The Accounts table holds a column called CurrentBalance, which is regularly updated with credits or debits. Let's write a procedure that:

- Accepts the account number and the amount to be credited.
- Updates the CurrentBalance column value in the Accounts table.
- Adds a new account in the Accounts table if the specified account number is not found.

Solution:

```
CREATE PROCEDURE AccountCredit (varAccountNo Number,
      varCreditAmount Number) AS
  varBalance Number;
  varUpdatedBalance Number;
  BEGIN
  /* Defining SQL query to retrieve the current balance */
      SELECT CurrentBalance INTO varBalance FROM Accounts
          WHERE AccountNo = varAccountNo FOR UPDATE OF CurrentBalance;
  /* Calculating the new balance */
      varUpdatedBalance := varBalance + varCreditAmount;
  /* Updating current balance in the Accounts table */
      UPDATE Accounts SET CurrentBalance = varUpdatedBalance
          WHERE AccountNo = varAccountNo;
  /* Making the changes permanent */
      COMMIT;
      EXCEPTION
      /* Defining an exception to handle new account opening */
          WHEN NO_DATA_FOUND THEN INSERT INTO Accounts (AccountNo,
              CurrentBalance) VALUES(varAccountNo, varCreditAmount);
      /* Defining an exception to handle other errors */
          WHEN OTHERS THEN
              ROLLBACK;
  END AccountCredit;
/
```

Output:

```
Procedure created.
```

Query the data before executing the procedure:

```
SELECT * FROM Accounts;
```

Output:

```
ACCOUNTNO ACCOUNTHOLDERNAME ACCOUNTOPENINGDATE ACCOUNTTYPE CURRENTBALANCE
--------- ----------------- ------------------ ----------- --------------
1         Sharanam          23-MAY-07          SB          13358.9
2         Vaishali          05-FEB-05          SB          5000
3         Gita              08-JUN-06          SB          2375.89
6         Michel            29-MAR-08          CA          3000
5         Micheal           20-OCT-03          SB          4000
4         Geeta             01-JAN-05          CA          46892.08
12        Puja              20-FEB-05          SB          4500
11        Pooja             07-JUL-03          CA          123890
10        Dipa              23-MAY-07          SB          1245
9         Deepa             08-JUN-06          SB          1000
8         Sita              20-OCT-03          SB          1234
7         Seeta             07-JUL-03          SB          3000

12 rows selected.
```

Execute the procedure:

```
EXEC AccountCredit(2, 2000);
EXEC AccountCredit(15, 10000);
```

Output (For each procedure executed):

```
PL/SQL procedure successfully completed.
```

Query the data after executing the procedure:

```
SELECT * FROM Accounts;
```

Output:

```
ACCOUNTNO ACCOUNTHOLDERNAME ACCOUNTOPENINGDATE ACCOUNTTYPE CURRENTBALANCE
--------- ----------------- ------------------ ----------- --------------
1         Sharanam          23-MAY-07          SB          13358.9
2         Vaishali          05-FEB-05          SB          7000
15                                                         10000
3         Gita              08-JUN-06          SB          2375.89
6         Michel            29-MAR-08          CA          3000
5         Micheal           20-OCT-03          SB          4000
4         Geeta             01-JAN-05          CA          46892.08
12        Puja              20-FEB-05          SB          4500
11        Pooja             07-JUL-03          CA          123890
10        Dipa              23-MAY-07          SB          1245
9         Deepa             08-JUN-06          SB          1000
8         Sita              20-OCT-03          SB          1234
7         Seeta             07-JUL-03          SB          3000

13 rows selected.
```

Write a procedure that:

- Accepts a department number and the percentage of raise in salary.

- Updates the salary of all employees in that department.

Solution:

```
CREATE OR REPLACE PROCEDURE IncrementDeptSal(
  varDeptNo Number, varIncrement Number DEFAULT 1.10) IS
/* Defining a cursor to hold salary of all employees in a particular
department */
  CURSOR curEmployees (varDeptNo Number) IS
      SELECT Salary FROM Employees WHERE DeptNo = varDeptNo
          FOR UPDATE OF Salary;
  BEGIN
  /* Defining a For loop */
      FOR typEmployees IN curEmployees(varDeptNo)
  /* Traversing through the loop */
      LOOP
      /* Updating salary of the current employee in the loop */
          UPDATE Employees
              SET Salary = typEmployees.Salary *((100 + varIncrement)/100)
                  WHERE CURRENT OF curEmployees;
      END LOOP;
  /* Making the changes permanent */
      COMMIT;
  END IncrementDeptSal;
/
```

Output:

```
Procedure created.
```

Query the data before executing the procedure:

```
SELECT EmployeeNo, DeptNo, Salary FROM Employees;
```

Output:

```
EMPLOYEENO     DEPTNO     SALARY
---------- ---------- ----------
         1          4      82500
         2          2      55000
         3          4      22000
         4          2      22000
         5          1    13334.2
         6          3    13553.1
         7          3    13578.4
         8          7      49500
         9          3       2750
        10          5       1320
        11                 31207

11 rows selected.
```

Execute the procedure:

```
EXEC IncrementDeptSal(3);
```

```
EXEC IncrementDeptSal(1, 5);
```

If the procedure is called only with the parameter 3, the default value 1.10 is assumed as specified in the list of parameters in the procedure definition.

Output (For each procedure executed):

```
PL/SQL procedure successfully completed.
```

Query the data after executing the procedure:

```
SELECT EmployeeNo, DeptNo, Salary FROM Employees;
```

Output:

```
EMPLOYEENO     DEPTNO     SALARY
---------- ---------- ----------
         1          4      82500
         2          2      55000
         3          4      22000
         4          2      22000
         5          1   14000.91
         6          3   13702.18
         7          3   13727.76
         8          7      49500
         9          3    2780.25
        10          5       1320
        11                 31207

11 rows selected.
```

Functions

Function specification begins with **CREATE** and ends with the function name or arguments list. The value to be returned by the function is indicated using the **RETURN** keyword. The body of the function starts after the keyword **IS** or **AS** and ends with the keyword **END**.

Syntax:

```
CREATE OR REPLACE FUNCTION [<Schema>.]<FunctionName>
  (<Argument> {IN, OUT, IN OUT} <DataType>, ...)
  RETURN <DataType> {IS, AS}
  <Variable Declarations>;
  <Constant Declarations>;
BEGIN
  <PL/SQL Sub Program Body code block>;
EXCEPTION
  <Exception PL/SQL code block>;
END;
```

Where,

- *REPLACE:* Recreates the function (if it already exists). This option allows changing the definition of an existing function without dropping, recreating, and re-granting object privileges previously granted on it. If a function is redefined, Oracle recompiles it.
- *Schema:* The schema that holds the function being created.
- *Function:* The name of the function being created.
- *Argument:* The name of arguments to the function. To make a function dynamic, arguments/parameters can be passed before execution. A function then changes its behavior depending upon the parameters passed prior to its execution. An argument can be:
  - *IN:* A parameter whose value is passed into a function. The value of an IN parameter is a constant. It cannot be changed or reassigned within the module. It is the default mode.
  - *OUT:* A parameter whose value is passed out of the function back to the calling PL/SQL block. An OUT parameter is a variable, not a constant. A default value cannot be assigned to an OUT parameter.
  - *IN OUT:* A parameter that functions as both an IN and OUT parameter. The value of the IN/OUT parameter is passed into the function, and a new value can be assigned to the parameter and passed out of the function. An IN/OUT parameter is a variable, not a constant.

  Arguments can be assigned a default value using the **assignment operator (:=)** or the **DEFAULT** keyword. An argument with a default value need not be included in the function call:

```
<Argument1> IN Varchar2 := 'Sharanam';
<Argument2> IN Varchar2 DEFAULT 'Sharanam';
```

> TIP: Parentheses can be omitted if no arguments are present.

  Arguments are declared with data types but **without data type length or precision**. This means that a parameter may be declared as:

```
Varchar2
```

  But not with a length component like:

```
Varchar2(30)
```

- *DataType:* The data type of the argument.
- *RETURN data type:* The data type of the function's return value. Since every function must return a value, this clause is required. Any data type supported by PL/SQL can be specified here.

- ***PL/SQL Sub Program Body code block:*** The function definition consisting of PL/SQL statements.
- ***Exception PL/SQL code block:*** The section that holds defined exceptions.

> The user needs to have the CREATE FUNCTION system privilege to create a function in the schema.

Let's write a function that accepts an account number and retursn its current balance:

```
CREATE FUNCTION FetchAccountBal(varAccountNo IN Number)
  RETURN NUMBER IS
  varCurrentBalance Number(12, 2);
  BEGIN
  /* Retrieving the current balance */
     SELECT CurrentBalance INTO varCurrentBalance FROM Accounts
        WHERE AccountNo = varAccountNo;
     RETURN(varCurrentBalance);
  END;
/
```

Output:

```
Function created.
```

Test the function FetchAccountBal by executing the following query:

```
SELECT FetchAccountBal(2) FROM DUAL;
```

Output:

```
FETCHACCOUNTBAL(2)
------------------
              5000
```

Write a function that accepts a department number and returns the total salaries of all employees in that department:

```
CREATE FUNCTION SalOfDept(varDeptNo Number) RETURN NUMBER IS
  varTotalSal Number;
  BEGIN
     varTotalSal := 0;
  /* Defining a For loop with an inline cursor */
     FOR typSal IN (SELECT Salary FROM Employees
        WHERE DeptNO = varDeptNo)
     LOOP
     /* Calculating total salary */
        varTotalSal := varTotalSal + typSal.Salary;
     END LOOP;
     RETURN varTotalSal;
  END SalOfDept;
```

```
/
```

Output:

```
Function created.
```

Test the function SalOfDept by executing the following query:

```
SELECT SalOfDept(2) FROM DUAL;
```

Output:

```
SALOFDEPT(2)
------------
       77000
```

Debugging Procedures And Functions

Let's introduce a compilation error into a previously declared procedure:

```
CREATE OR REPLACE PROCEDURE AccountCredit (
  varAccountNo NUMBER, varCreditAmount NUMBER) AS
  varBalance NUMBER;
  varUpdatedBalance NUMBER;
  BEGIN
      SELECT CurrentBalance INTO varBalance FROM Accounts
          WHERE AccountNo = varAccountNo FOR UPDATE OF CurrentBalance;
      varUpdatedBalancee := varBalance + varCreditAmount;
      UPDATE Accounts SET CurrentBalance = varUpdatedBalance
          WHERE AccountNo = varAccountNo;
      COMMIT;
      EXCEPTION
          WHEN NO_DATA_FOUND THEN
              INSERT INTO Accounts (AccountNo, CurrentBalance)
                  VALUES(varAccountNo, varCreditAmount);
      WHEN OTHERS THEN
          ROLLBACK;
  END AccountCredit;
/
```

The procedure is compiled and saved on the database. However, SQL*Plus warns about some compilation errors:

```
Warning: Procedure created with compilation errors.
```

To view the compilation errors, issue the following command:

```
SHOW ERRORS PROCEDURE AccountCredit;
```

Output:

```
LINE/COL ERROR
-------- -----------------------------------------------------------------
8/3      PL/SQL: Statement ignored
8/3      PLS-00201: identifier 'VARUPDATEDBALANCEE' must be declared
```

Getting Information About Procedures Or Functions

Information about the procedures and functions can be fetched from the **USER_PROCEDURES** view:

```
SELECT Object_Name, Aggregate, Parallel FROM USER_PROCEDURES;
```

Output:

```
OBJECT_NAME        AGGREGATE PARALLEL
------------------ --------- --------
SALOFDEPT          NO        NO
FETCHACCOUNTBAL    NO        NO
INCREMENTDEPTSAL   NO        NO
CALCULATEEMPLEAVES NO        NO

4 rows selected.
```

Destroying Procedures or Functions

A procedure or function can be deleted using the **DROP** command.

Solution: (Destroying Procedure)

```
DROP PROCEDURE CalculateEmpLeaves;
```

Output:

```
Procedure dropped.
```

Solution: (Destroying Function)

```
DROP FUNCTION SalOfDept;
```

Output:

```
Function dropped.
```

Chapter

30

SECTION V: PL/SQL

Packages

In application development, it is standard practice to group related code blocks, such as procedures and functions, into modules. Each module is accessed via an interface by application programmers to utilize its functionality. Similarly, Oracle allows grouping stored procedures, functions, variables, constants, cursors, and exceptions into **packages**. A package consists of:

Package Specification

The package specification acts as an interface to the package. It defines the **interface** visible to application programmers and lists the available procedures, functions, types, and objects. The specification does not contain the actual code. A package specification can be created using the **CREATE PACKAGE** statement:

```
CREATE [OR REPLACE] PACKAGE <PackageName> {IS | AS}
  <PackageSpecification>
END <PackageName>;
```

Where,

- *PackageName* is the name of the package.

- *PackageSpecification* lists the public procedures, functions, types, and objects.
- The ***OR REPLACE*** clause indicates the recreation of the package specification without losing existing grants.

Package Body

The package body holds the actual implementation code of the package specification. Any objects in the body not listed in the specification are private to the package. Private items can only be used inside the package body. A package body can be created using the **CREATE PACKAGE BODY** statement:

```
CREATE [OR REPLACE] PACKAGE BODY <PackageName> {IS | AS}
  <PackageBody>
END <PackageName>;
```

Where,

- ***PackageName*** is the name of the package, matching the package name in the specification.
- ***PackageBody*** holds the procedures and functions code.
- The ***OR REPLACE*** clause indicates the recreation of the package body without losing existing grants.

> **TIP** It is advisable to use a combination of public and private objects while building a package to hide complexity from the outside world.

A package, once written, is compiled and stored in the Oracle database. Only users with Execute permissions on the package can use it.

Benefits of Packages:

- ***Encapsulate Related Functionality:*** Group related functions into a single unit.
- ***Modularize PL/SQL Code:*** Build reusable code libraries, reducing redundant coding.
- ***Enable Overloading:*** Allow overloading of procedures and functions.
- ***Improve Performance:*** Load multiple objects/subprograms into memory at once, reducing subsequent I/O calls.

> **TIP** Any objects declared within the package's specification are visible outside the package. This allows PL/SQL code outside the package to reference objects using **dot notation**. These objects are called **Public**.

Oracle provides several useful packages, such as:

- ***UTL_FILE:*** For reading and writing files from PL/SQL programs.
- ***DBMS_JOB:*** For job scheduling.

- ***DBMS_SQL:*** To generate SQL statements dynamically during program execution, commonly used to create and delete tables within PL/SQL programs.
- ***DBMS_OUTPUT:*** To generate output.

Each package holds a set of useful procedures and function. For example, the common procedures provided by DBMS_OUTPUT include:

Procedure name	Description
DBMS_OUTPUT.ENABLE	Enables output.
DBMS_OUTPUT.DISABLE	Disables output.
DBMS_OUTPUT.PUT(`<String>`)	Appends (displays) `<String>` to output buffer.
DBMS_OUTPUT.PUT_LINE(`<String>`)	Appends `<String>` to the output buffer and adds a new-line marker.
DBMS_OUTPUT.NEW_LINE	Displays a new-line marker.

Creating Packages

Create a package named ShahLib. This package will hold the following:

- Procedures
- FetchAccountBal
- IncrementDeptSal
- Functions
- AccountCredit
- CalculateEmpLeaves
- SalOfDept

Solution:

```
CREATE OR REPLACE PACKAGE ShahLib AS
Author Varchar2(25) := 'Sharanam Shah';
Version Varchar2(5) := '1.0';
  PROCEDURE CalculateEmpLeaves(
      varEmployeeNo IN Varchar2, varLeaves OUT Number);
  PROCEDURE AccountCredit(
      varAccountNo Number, varCreditAmount Number);
  PROCEDURE IncrementDeptSal(
      varDeptNo Number, varIncrement Number DEFAULT 1.10);
  FUNCTION FetchAccountBal(varAccountNo IN Number) RETURN Number;
  FUNCTION SalOfDept(varDeptNo Number) RETURN Number;
END ShahLib;
/
```

Output:

```
Package created.
```

After the specification is created, the body of the package needs to be created.

> Subprograms written in the package body are accessible outside the package only if their specifications are included in the package specifications.

The package body can also contain private declarations. These private objects are usually declared for use in the internal processing of the package and are local in scope, hence cannot be accessed by external PL/SQL code blocks.

Solution:

```
CREATE OR REPLACE PACKAGE BODY ShahLib AS
   PROCEDURE CalculateEmpLeaves(
      varEmployeeNo IN Varchar2, varLeaves OUT Number) IS
   BEGIN
   /* Retrieving the number of leaves from EmployeeMuster. */
      SELECT COUNT(*) INTO varLeaves FROM EmployeeMuster
         WHERE EmployeeNo = varEmployeeNo AND Attendance <> 'Present';
   END;
   PROCEDURE AccountCredit(varAccountNo Number, varCreditAmount Number) AS
      varBalance Number;
      varUpdatedBalance Number;
   BEGIN
   /* Defining SQL query to retrieve the current balance */
      SELECT CurrentBalance INTO varBalance FROM Accounts
         WHERE AccountNo = varAccountNo FOR UPDATE OF CurrentBalance;
   /* Calculating the new balance */
      varUpdatedBalance := varBalance + varCreditAmount;
   /* Updating current balance in the Accounts table */
      UPDATE Accounts SET CurrentBalance = varUpdatedBalance
         WHERE AccountNo = varAccountNo;
   /* Making the changes permanent */
      COMMIT;
      EXCEPTION
      /* Defining an exception to handle new account opening */
         WHEN NO_DATA_FOUND THEN
            INSERT INTO Accounts (AccountNo, CurrentBalance)
               VALUES(varAccountNo, varCreditAmount);
      /* Defining an exception to handle other errors */
         WHEN OTHERS THEN
            ROLLBACK;
      END AccountCredit;
   PROCEDURE IncrementDeptSal(
      varDeptNo Number, varIncrement Number DEFAULT 1.10) IS
   /* Defining a cursor to hold salary of all employees in a particular
   department */
   CURSOR curEmployees (varDeptNo Number) IS
      SELECT Salary FROM Employees WHERE DeptNo = varDeptNo
         FOR UPDATE OF Salary;
   BEGIN
   /* Defining a For loop */
```

```
        FOR typEmployees IN curEmployees(varDeptNo)
    /* Traversing through the loop */
        LOOP
        /* Updating salary of the current employee in the loop */
            UPDATE Employees
                SET Salary = typEmployees.Salary *((100 + varIncrement)/100)
                    WHERE CURRENT OF curEmployees;
        END LOOP;
    /* Making the changes permanent */
        COMMIT;
    END IncrementDeptSal;
    FUNCTION FetchAccountBal(varAccountNo IN Number) RETURN Number IS
        varCurrentBalance Number(12, 2);
    BEGIN
    /* Retrieving the current balance */
        SELECT CurrentBalance INTO varCurrentBalance FROM Accounts
            WHERE AccountNo = varAccountNo;
        RETURN(varCurrentBalance);
    END;
    FUNCTION SalOfDept(varDeptNo Number) RETURN Number IS varTotalSal Number;
    BEGIN
        varTotalSal := 0;
    /* Defining a For loop with an inline cursor */
        FOR typSal IN (SELECT Salary FROM Employees
            WHERE DeptNO = varDeptNo)
        LOOP
        /* Calculating total salary */
            varTotalSal := varTotalSal + typSal.Salary;
        END LOOP;
        RETURN varTotalSal;
    END SalOfDept;
END ShahLib;
/
```

Output:

```
Package body created.
```

Invoking A Package

A procedure or function implemented in a package can be invoked from other procedures and functions using the following syntax:

- *TypeName* is the name of a user-defined type, such as record.

```
<PackageName>.<TypeName>
```

- *ObjectName* is the name of a constant or variable declared by the user.

```
<PackageName>.<ObjectName>
```

- *SubProgram* is the name of the procedure or function contained in the package body.

```
<PackageName>.<SubProgram>[(<List Of Parameters>)]
```

To call a procedure from SQL*Plus, use the EXEC command:

```
EXEC <PackageName>.<SubProgram>[(<List Of Parameters>)]
```

The following code prints the values held by the variables in the packages:

```
SET SERVEROUTPUT ON
BEGIN
  DBMS_OUTPUT.PUT_LINE('Author: ' || ShahLib.Author);
  DBMS_OUTPUT.PUT_LINE('Version: ' || ShahLib.Version);
END;
/
```

Output:

```
Author: Sharanam Shah
Version: 1.0
PL/SQL procedure successfully completed.
```

The following code invokes the procedure named CalculateEmpLeaves in the package:

```
SET SERVEROUTPUT ON
DECLARE
  varLeaves Number;
BEGIN
  ShahLib.CalculateEmpLeaves(4, varLeaves);
  DBMS_OUTPUT.PUT_LINE('Leaves: ' || varLeaves);
END;
/
```

Output:

```
Leaves: 2
PL/SQL procedure successfully completed.
```

TIP: When a subprogram within the package is invoked, Oracle creates an implicit save point. If the subprogram fails with an unhandled exception, Oracle rolls back to that save point and undoes changes made by the subprogram before returning to the host environment.

Recompiling Existing Packages

The **ALTER PACKAGE** command with the **COMPILE** keyword can be used to recompile a package.

```
ALTER PACKAGE <PackageName> COMPILE PACKAGE;
```

Recompiling a package recompiles all objects defined within the package but does not change the definition of the package or any of its objects.

To recompile the body of the ShahLib package:

```
ALTER PACKAGE ShahLib COMPILE BODY;
```

Output:

```
Package body altered.
```

Dropping a Package

An already existing package can be dropped using the **DROP PACKAGE** command.

To drop the ShahLib package:

```
DROP PACKAGE ShahLib;
```

Output:

```
Package dropped.
```

Overloading Procedures And Functions

Just like in other programming languages, PL/SQL allows overloading its subprograms (procedures and functions). This means more than one subprogram can be created with the same name within a package but with different parameters. Oracle makes extensive use of overloading. For example, TO_CHAR is an overloaded function that allows converting both numbers and dates to character format.

For example:

```
TO_CHAR(SYSDATE, 'DD/MM/YY');
TO_CHAR(10000, '$099,999');
```

Overloading greatly simplifies the processing logic of a program by eliminating multiple IF constructs or CASE constructs that would check the parameters passed and perform appropriate operations.

TIP: Standalone programs **cannot** be overloaded, nor can two independent modules be created with the same name but different parameter lists. If an attempt is made to overload an already existing procedure, the second attempt to create the procedure fails.

Solution: (First, attempt to create the IncrementDeptSal procedure)

```
CREATE PROCEDURE IncrementDeptSal(
```

```
    varDeptNo Number, varIncrement Number DEFAULT 1.10) IS
    CURSOR curEmployees (varDeptNo Number) IS
        SELECT Salary FROM Employees WHERE DeptNo = varDeptNo
            FOR UPDATE OF Salary;
    BEGIN
    . . .
    . . .
    END IncrementDeptSal;
/
```

Output:

```
Procedure created.
```

Solution: (Now, attempt to create another procedure with the same name)

```
CREATE PROCEDURE IncrementDeptSal(
    varDeptNo Number, varIncrement Number DEFAULT 1.10) IS
    CURSOR curEmployees (varDeptNo Number) IS
        SELECT Salary FROM Employees WHERE DeptNo = varDeptNo
            FOR UPDATE OF Salary;
    BEGIN
    . . .
    . . .
    END IncrementDeptSal;
/
```

Output:

```
CREATE PROCEDURE IncrementDeptSal(
                 *
ERROR at line 1:
ORA-00955: name is already used by an existing object
```

This error occurs because a procedure with the same name already exists. Therefore, to overload a subprogram, a package needs to be used.

Restrictions On Overloading

When overloading functions or procedures, the following points need to be considered:

- ***Parameter Data Types:*** The data type of at least one of the parameter in the overloaded function or procedure **must differ**. For example, the following is not allowed:

```
PROCEDURE MyProc(varStr1 IN Char, varStr2 OUT Char)
PROCEDURE MyProc(varStr1 IN Varchar2, varStr2 OUT Varchar2)
```

  Here, the overloaded procedure are distinguished by parameters with Varchar2 and Char data types, which is not allowed.

- ***Parameter List Differences:*** The parameter list of overloaded functions **must differ** by more than the name or parameter mode. For example, the following is not allowed:

```
FUNCTION MyProc(varDate1 IN Date) RETURN Boolean
```

```
FUNCTION MyProc(varDate2 IN Date) RETURN Boolean
```

Here, only the parameter names differ, which is not allowed. The PL/SQL interpreter cannot distinguish objects by name since the parameter name is replaced by the values sent to the objects when the package is called.

- *Parameter Modes:* Similarly, if the parameter in the first version of the overloaded subprogram is IN and the same parameter is IN OUT in the second version, the PL/SQL interpreter **cannot** distinguish using the package call. For example, the following is not allowed:

```
FUNCTION MyProc(varDate IN Date) RETURN Boolean
FUNCTION MyProc(varDate IN OUT Date) RETURN Boolean
```

The overloading attempts will result in the following error messages:

```
PLS-00307: too many declarations of 'value_check' match this call.
```

- *Return Data Type:* Overloaded functions **must differ** by more than their return data type. For example, the following is not allowed:

```
FUNCTION MyProc(varDate IN Date) RETURN Boolean IS
FUNCTION MyProc(varDate IN Date) RETURN Number IS
```

At the time the overloaded function is called, the PL/SQL interpreter does not know what type of data the function will return. Therefore, the interpreter cannot distinguish between different overloaded functions based on the return data type.

Create a package that holds two overloaded procedures named IncrementDeptSal. This procedure accepts:

- **DeptNo** and percentage increase in salary.

OR

- **DeptName** and percentage increase in salary.

and increments the salary of all the employees in the specified department.

Solution:

```
CREATE OR REPLACE PACKAGE EmpLib IS
   PROCEDURE IncrementDeptSal(
       varDeptName Varchar2, varIncrement Number DEFAULT 1.10);
   PROCEDURE IncrementDeptSal(
       varDeptNo Number, varIncrement Number DEFAULT 1.10);
END;
/
```

Output:

```
Package created.
```

Solution:

```
CREATE OR REPLACE PACKAGE BODY EmpLib IS
   PROCEDURE IncrementDeptSal(
       varDeptName Varchar2, varIncrement Number DEFAULT 1.10) IS
```

```
/* Defining parameterized cursor to hold salary of all employees in a
particular */
    CURSOR curEmployees (varDeptName Varchar2) IS
        SELECT Salary FROM Employees WHERE DeptNo = (SELECT DeptNo
            FROM Departments WHERE DepartmentName = varDeptName)
                FOR UPDATE OF Salary;
    BEGIN
    /* Defining a For loop */
        FOR typEmployees IN curEmployees(varDeptName)
    /* Traversing through cursor */
        LOOP
        /* Updating salary of the current employee in the loop */
            UPDATE Employees
                SET Salary = typEmployees.Salary *((100 + varIncrement)/100)
                    WHERE CURRENT OF curEmployees;
        END LOOP;
        COMMIT;
    END IncrementDeptSal;
PROCEDURE IncrementDeptSal(
    varDeptNo Number, varIncrement Number DEFAULT 1.10) IS
/* Defining parameterized cursor to hold salary of all employees in a
particular */
    CURSOR curEmployees (varDeptNo Number) IS
        SELECT Salary FROM Employees WHERE DeptNo = varDeptNo
            FOR UPDATE OF Salary;
    BEGIN
    /* Defining a For loop */
        FOR typEmployees IN curEmployees(varDeptNo)
    /* Traversing through cursor */
        LOOP
        /* Updating salary of the current employee in the loop */
            UPDATE Employees
                SET Salary = typEmployees.Salary *((100 + varIncrement)/100)
                    WHERE CURRENT OF curEmployees;
        END LOOP;
        COMMIT;
    END IncrementDeptSal;
END;
/
```

Output:

```
Package body created.
```

TIP: When a subprogram is invoked, Oracle chooses the procedure or function whose number of parameters and data type matches the values passed by the caller.

Query the data before executing the procedure:

```
SELECT EmployeeNo, DeptNo, Salary FROM Employees;
```

Output:

```
EMPLOYEENO     DEPTNO     SALARY
---------- ---------- ----------
         1          4      82500
         2          2      55000
         3          4      22000
         4          2      22000
         5          1    13334.2
         6          3    13553.1
         7          3    13578.4
         8          7      49500
         9          3       2750
        10          5       1320
        11                 31207

11 rows selected.
```

Execute the procedure:

```
EXEC EmpLib.IncrementDeptSal(3, 5);
EXEC EmpLib.IncrementDeptSal('HR Department', 3);
```

Output (For each procedure executed):

```
PL/SQL procedure successfully completed.
```

Query the data after executing the procedure:

```
SELECT EmployeeNo, DeptNo, Salary FROM Employees;
```

Output:

```
EMPLOYEENO     DEPTNO     SALARY
---------- ---------- ----------
         1          4      82500
         2          2      56650
         3          4      22000
         4          2      22660
         5          1    13334.2
         6          3   14230.76
         7          3   14257.32
         8          7      49500
         9          3     2887.5
        10          5       1320
        11                 31207

11 rows selected.
```

Write a function that accepts:

- ❑ DeptNo
  and returns:
- ❑ Total salaries of all the employees in that department

OR

- ❑ DeptNo and H

and returns:

- ❑ Highest paid salary in that department

OR

- ❑ DeptNo and L
  and returns:
- ❑ Lowest paid salary in that department

Solution:

```
CREATE OR REPLACE PACKAGE NewEmpLib IS
   FUNCTION SalOfDept(varDeptNo Number) RETURN Number;
   FUNCTION SalOfDept(varDeptNo Number, varType Varchar2)
        RETURN Number;
END;
/
```

Output:

```
Package created.
```

Solution:

```
CREATE OR REPLACE PACKAGE BODY NewEmpLib IS
   FUNCTION SalOfDept(varDeptNo Number) RETURN Number IS
        varTotalSal Number;
        BEGIN
             varTotalSal := 0;
        /* Defining a For loop with an inline cursor */
             FOR typSal IN (SELECT Salary FROM Employees
                  WHERE DeptNO = varDeptNo)
             LOOP
             /* Calculating total salary */
                  varTotalSal := varTotalSal + typSal.Salary;
             END LOOP;
             RETURN varTotalSal;
        END SalOfDept;
   FUNCTION SalOfDept(varDeptNo Number, varType Varchar2) RETURN Number IS
        varSal Number;
        BEGIN
             varSal := 0;
             IF varType = 'H' THEN
                  SELECT MAX(Salary) INTO varSal FROM Employees
                       WHERE DeptNO = varDeptNo;
             ELSE
                  SELECT MIN(Salary) INTO varSal FROM Employees
                       WHERE DeptNO = varDeptNo;
             END IF;
             RETURN varSal;
        END SalOfDept;
   END;
/
```

Output:

```
Package body created.
```

Test the function SalOfDept as:
Execute the following query:

```
SELECT NewEmpLib.SalOfDept(2) FROM DUAL;
```

Output:

```
NEWEMPLIB.SALOFDEPT(2)
----------------------
                 77000
```

Execute the following query:

```
SELECT NewEmpLib.SalOfDept(2, 'H') FROM DUAL;
```

Output:

```
NEWEMPLIB.SALOFDEPT(2,'H')
--------------------------
                     55000
```

Execute the following query:

```
SELECT NewEmpLib.SalOfDept(2, 'L') FROM DUAL;
```

Output:

```
NEWEMPLIB.SALOFDEPT(2,'L')
--------------------------
                     22000
```

Chapter 31

SECTION V: PL/SQL

Triggers

A **Trigger** is a widely used database object. It is a piece of code that runs automatically before or after a database table is modified.

A trigger can be defined on:

- ***Tables/Views:*** DML (INSERT, UPDATE ,DELETE).
- ***Schema:*** DDL triggers and Logon/Logoff event triggers.
- ***Database:*** System event triggers (Startup/Shutdown).

Common uses of triggers include:

- Generating running numbers before inserting new rows.
- Preventing invalid transactions.
- Permitting DML statements against a table only if issued during regular business hours or on predetermined weekdays.
- Keeping an audit trail of a table (i.e., storing modified and deleted records along with the operation performed and the time it was performed).
- Ensuring that an appropriate column is populated with default information to generate running numbers before inserting new rows.

- Ensuring a rollback if the information being added or modified in the database table is found to be inconsistent.
- Populating some other columns based on the new or old column values.

The trigger code defines ***the action the database needs to perform whenever some database manipulation, such as INSERT, UPDATE, and DELETE takes place using SQL commands.***

Differences between triggers and stored procedures/functions:

- Stored procedures and functions have to be called explicitly, while database triggers are invoked implicitly whenever a table is affected by any DML operations.
- Stored procedures and functions accept parameters, while triggers do not accept parameters.

TIP: Oracle does not place a limit on the number of triggers that can be created.

Parts Of Trigger

A trigger has three basic parts:

Triggering Statement

A **triggering event**, also called a **triggering statement**, is a SQL statement, database event, or user event that causes a trigger to fire.

The trigger fires automatically when any of the following events occur:

- An INSERT, UPDATE, or DELETE statement on a specific table or view.
- A CREATE, ALTER, or DROP statement on any schema object.
- A specific error message or any error message.
- A database startup or instance shutdown.
- A user logon or logoff.

Trigger Restriction

A trigger constraint specifies a Boolean expression that must be **TRUE** for the trigger to fire. It allows conditional control over the execution of a trigger. A **trigger restriction** is specified using a WHEN clause.

Trigger Action

The **trigger action** is a PL/SQL Procedure that contains the code to be executed when the trigger fires. The PL/SQL code block can hold SQL and PL/SQL statements, define PL/SQL language constructs, and call stored procedures.

If the trigger is a row trigger, the statements in a trigger action have access to the column values of the row being processed by the trigger. Correlation names provide access to the old and new values of each column.

Types of Triggers

The following are the different types of triggers:

Row Triggers

Row triggers are used when some processing is required every time a triggering statement affects a single row in a table. A row trigger is fired each time a row in the table is affected by the triggering statement. It uses the **FOR EACH ROW** clause. For example, if a DELETE command deletes multiple rows of a table, a row trigger is fired once for each row that is deleted. If the triggering statement affects no rows, the trigger is not executed at all.

Statement Triggers

A statement trigger is fired once on behalf of the triggering statement, independent of the number of rows the triggering statement affects (even if no rows are affected). Statement triggers should be used when a triggering statement affects rows in a table, but the processing required is completely independent of the number of rows affected.

Timed Triggers

When defining a trigger, it is necessary to specify the trigger timing, i.e., specifying whether to perform the trigger action BEFORE or AFTER the triggering statement. BEFORE and AFTER apply to both row and statement triggers.

Before Triggers

These triggers are fired before the INSERT, UPDATE, or DELETE operations occur on the table. They are generally used when the trigger action determines whether the triggering statement should be allowed to complete.

Using a **BEFORE trigger** for this purpose can eliminate unnecessary processing of the triggering statement and its eventual rollback in case an exception is raised in the trigger action.

After Triggers

These triggers are fired after the INSERT, UPDATE, or DELETE operations occur on the table. An **AFTER trigger** is generally used to perform different actions on the same triggering statement if a BEFORE trigger is already present. AFTER triggers are very useful when creating audit trails for database tables.

By using AFTER triggers, auditing information is recorded after the triggering statement is subjected to applicable integrity constraints, thereby preventing cases where audit processing is carried out unnecessarily for statements that generate exceptions to integrity constraints.

Timed Triggers Combined With Row And Statements

BEFORE and AFTER options apply to both statement and row triggers. Hence, by using the BEFORE and AFTER options, the following four types of row and statement triggers can be created:

- ***BEFORE Statement Trigger:*** The trigger action is executed BEFORE the triggering statement is executed.
- ***BEFORE Row Trigger:*** The trigger action is executed FOR EACH ROW BEFORE the triggering statement is executed.
- ***AFTER Statement Trigger:*** The trigger action is executed AFTER the triggering statement is executed.
- ***AFTER Row Trigger:*** The trigger action is executed FOR EACH ROW AFTER the triggering statement is executed.

INSTEAD OF Triggers

An **INSTEAD OF trigger** (normally defined on complex views) provides a transparent way of modifying a view that cannot be directly modified through DML (Data Manipulation Language) statements such as INSERT, UPDATE, and DELETE.

An INSTEAD OF trigger defined on a view is fired when an INSERT, UPDATE, or DELETE statement is executed against the view. When fired, the INSTEAD OF trigger modifies the underlying tables appropriately. An INSTEAD OF trigger defined on a view is always a row trigger, i.e., the trigger is fired for each modified row of the view. INSTEAD OF triggers can be designed only for views and not for tables. The BEFORE and AFTER options cannot be used with INSTEAD OF triggers.

Compound Triggers

COMPOUND triggers (introduced in Oracle Database 11g) allow defining more than one type of trigger in a single trigger.

DDL Triggers

A **DDL trigger** is a database trigger whose triggering event is a **D**ata **D**efinition **L**anguage (DDL) statement, i.e., a DDL trigger fires when a DDL statement (such as a CREATE, ALTER, or DROP statement) is executed in the database or a particular schema. A DDL trigger can be created either at the database level or schema level. The BEFORE or AFTER options can also be specified for defining the timing of the trigger.

- *BEFORE CREATE or AFTER CREATE Trigger:* This trigger is executed when a schema object is **created**.
- *BEFORE or AFTER ALTER Trigger:* This trigger is executed when a schema object is **altered**.
- *BEFORE or AFTER DROP Trigger:* This trigger is executed when a schema object is **dropped**.

System Event Trigger

A **system event trigger** is a **database trigger** defined on a system event. A system event trigger fires when a system event such as startup, shutdown, logon, logoff, or error occurs.

Database triggers on system events can be defined at the database or schema level. A database trigger defined on a database fires for each event for all users. However, a database trigger defined on a schema fires for each event for that particular user. For example, a trigger on database startup or shutdown can be defined only at the database level. However, a trigger on user logon or logoff can be defined at either the database level or schema level.

Database triggers can be created on the following system events:

- *SERVERERROR:* Causes the Oracle server to fire the trigger whenever a server error message is logged. The trigger on a SERVERERROR event can only be an **AFTER** trigger.
- *LOGON:* Causes the Oracle server to fire the trigger whenever a user logs on to the database. The trigger on a LOGON event can only be an **AFTER** trigger.
- *LOGOFF:* Causes the Oracle server to fire the trigger whenever a user logs off the database. The trigger on a LOGOFF event can only be a **BEFORE** trigger.
- *STARTUP:* Causes the Oracle server to fire the trigger whenever the database is opened. The trigger on a STARTUP event can only be an **AFTER** trigger.

- *SHUTDOWN:* Causes the Oracle server to fire the trigger whenever the database is shut down. The trigger on a SHUTDOWN event can only be a **BEFORE** trigger.

Sequence Of Trigger Firing

When two or more triggers are defined on the table, they are fired in following order:

1. All **BEFORE statement** triggers.
2. All **BEFORE row** triggers.
3. All **AFTER row** triggers.
4. All **AFTER statement** triggers.

Multiple triggers of the same type can be defined on the same table. For example, three BEFORE INSERT triggers can be defined on the same table. If multiple triggers are of the same type, they follow the above order, but there is no guarantee which one will be executed first unless it is created with the **FOLLOWS** clause.

Triggers, as well as declarative integrity constraints, can be used to constrain data input.

Creating Trigger

A trigger is created using **CREATE OR REPLACE TRIGGER** command:

```
CREATE OR REPLACE TRIGGER [<Schema>.] <TriggerName>
  {BEFORE, AFTER}
  {DELETE, INSERT, UPDATE [OF <Column>, ...]}        } Triggering Statement
ON [<Schema>.] <tableName>
  [ REFERENCING { OLD AS old, NEW AS new }]
  [ FOR EACH ROW [ WHEN <Condition>] ]               } Trigger Constraint
DECLARE
  <Variable Declarations>;
  <Constant Declarations>;
BEGIN
  <PL/SQL Subprogram Body>;
EXCEPTION                                            } Trigger Body
  <Exception PL/SQL block>;
END;
```

Where,

- *OR REPLACE:* Recreates the trigger if it already exists. This option can be used to change the definition of an existing trigger without requiring the user to drop the trigger first.
- *Schema:* Specifies the schema that contains the trigger.
- *TriggerName:* The name of the trigger to be created.

- *BEFORE:* Indicates that the Oracle engine fires the trigger before executing the triggering statement.
- *AFTER:* Indicates that the Oracle engine fires the trigger after executing the triggering statement.
- *DELETE:* Indicates that the Oracle engine fires the trigger whenever a DELETE statement removes a row from the table.
- *INSERT:* Indicates that the Oracle engine fires the trigger whenever an INSERT statement adds a row to table.
- *UPDATE:* Indicates that the Oracle engine fires the trigger whenever an UPDATE statement changes a value in one of the columns specified in the **OF** clause. If the OF clause is omitted, the Oracle engine fires the trigger whenever an UPDATE statement changes a value in any column of the table.
- *ON:* Specifies the schema and name of the table on which the trigger is to be created. If schema is omitted, the Oracle engine assumes the table is in the user's own schema. A trigger cannot be created on a table in the schema SYS.
- *REFERENCING:* Specifies correlation names. Correlation names can be used in the PL/SQL block and WHEN clause of a row trigger to refer specifically to old and new values of the current row. The default correlation names are **OLD** and **NEW**. If the row trigger is associated with a table named OLD or NEW, this clause can be used to specify different correlation names to avoid confusion between table name and the correlation name.
- *FOR EACH ROW:* Designates the trigger to be a row trigger. The Oracle engine fires a row trigger once for each row that is affected by the triggering statement and meets the optional trigger constraint defined in the WHEN clause. If this clause is omitted, the trigger is a statement trigger.
- *WHEN:* Specifies the trigger restriction. The trigger restriction contains a SQL condition that must be satisfied for the Oracle engine to fire the trigger. This condition must contain correlation names and cannot contain a query. Trigger restriction can be specified only for the row triggers. Oracle evaluates this condition for each row affected by the triggering statement.
- ***PL/SQL block:*** The PL/SQL block that the Oracle engine executes when the trigger is fired.

Write a trigger that fires every time the salary of an employee in the Employees table is updated. This trigger should print the old, new and the difference in the salary after the modification as:

Employee No:	1	**New Salary:**	75000
Old Salary:	50000	**Difference:**	25000

Solution:

```
CREATE OR REPLACE TRIGGER DisplayChangesInSalary
```

```
  BEFORE
      UPDATE ON Employees                          } Triggering Statement

  FOR EACH ROW WHEN (NEW.EmployeeNo > 0)           } Trigger Constraint

  DECLARE
      varDifference Number;
  BEGIN
      varDifference := :NEW.Salary  - :OLD.salary;
      DBMS_OUTPUT.PUT_LINE('Employee No: '
                                      || :NEW.EmployeeNo);
      DBMS_OUTPUT.PUT_LINE('Old salary: ' || :OLD.Salary);        } Trigger Body
      DBMS_OUTPUT.PUT_LINE('New Salary: ' || :NEW.Salary);
      DBMS_OUTPUT.PUT_LINE('Difference: ' || varDifference);
END;
/
```

Output:

```
Trigger created.
```

Oracle implicitly invokes this trigger every time an UPDATE command is fired on the Employees table:

- Indicates that this trigger will be fired before an update command executed by the user:

```
BEFORE UPDATE ON Employees
```

- Indicates that this trigger will be fired only if the EmployeeNo is a valid number greater than 0. Oracle evaluates this condition for each row affected by the triggering statement:

```
WHEN (NEW.EmployeeNo > 0)
```

- Since the BEFORE keyword is used, the trigger body can access the new values before they are updated in the database table:

```
varDifference := :NEW.Salary  - :OLD.salary;
```

- Indicates that this trigger will be executed multiple times while updating salaries of multiple employees:

```
FOR EACH ROW
```

To test the trigger, issue the following commands:

```
SET SERVEROUTPUT ON
UPDATE Employees SET Salary = Salary * 1.10 WHERE DeptNo = 1;
```

This command updates the salaries of all the employees who belong to department number 1. Since the trigger is set to run before every update, the output will be:

```
Employee No: 5
Old salary: 13334.2
New Salary: 14667.62
Difference: 1333.42
1 row updated.
```

Mutating Table Error

The **Mutating table error** is a well-known problem encountered in development environment:

```
ORA-04091: table <tablename> is mutating,
    trigger/function may not see it
```

The basic reason for this error is the way Oracle manages a read-consistent view of data. The error is encountered when a row-level trigger accesses the same table on which it is based, while executing. The table is said to be **mutating**. Mutation will not occur if a single record is inserted in the table (using the VALUES clause). If bulk insertion is done or data is inserted from another table, mutation will occur. The mutating error is not only encountered during queries but also for insert, updates, and deletes present in the trigger.

The following table explains various transactions scenarios that involve a trigger and whether it is prone to generate the mutating error:

Operation	Type	Mutating	
Insert	Before/statement-level	No	
Insert	After/statement-level	No	
Update	Before/statement-level	No	
Update	After/statement-level	No	
Delete	Before/statement-level	No	
Delete	After/statement-level	No	
Insert	Before/row-level	**Single row:** No	**Multi row:** Yes
Insert	After/row-level	Yes	
Update	Before/row-level	Yes	
Update	After/row-level	Yes	
Delete	Before/row-level	Yes	
Delete	After/row-level	Yes	

Write a trigger that fires every time the salary of an employee in the Employees table is updated either due to an insert, update, or delete. This trigger should print the total salary of the available employees after the modification:

```
CREATE OR REPLACE TRIGGER DisplayTotalSalary
  AFTER INSERT OR UPDATE OR DELETE ON Employees
  FOR EACH ROW WHEN (NEW.EmployeeNo > 0)
  DECLARE
      varTotalSal Number;
  BEGIN
      SELECT SUM(Salary) INTO varTotalSal FROM Employees;
      DBMS_OUTPUT.PUT('Total Salary: ' || varTotalSal);
  END;
/
```

Output:

```
Trigger created.
```

Oracle implicitly invokes this trigger every time an INSERT, UPDATE, OR DELETE command is fired on the Employees table.

Since the sum of salaries after such an update is required, the AFTER Trigger is used:

```
AFTER UPDATE ON Employees
```

To test the trigger, issue the following commands:

```
SET SERVEROUTPUT ON
INSERT INTO EMPLOYEES (EmployeeNo, FirstName, LastName)
  VALUES (12, 'Dhiraj', 'Kapoor');
```

Output:

```
INSERT INTO EMPLOYEES (EmployeeNo, FirstName, LastName)
*
ERROR at line 1:
ORA-00001: unique constraint (VAISHALI.EMPLOYEES_PK) violated on table
VAISHALI.EMPLOYEES columns (EMPLOYEENO)
ORA-03301: (ORA-00001 details) row with column values (EMPLOYEENO:12) already exists
Help: https://docs.oracle.com/error-help/db/ora-00001/
```

To test the trigger, issue the following commands:

```
SET SERVEROUTPUT ON
DELETE FROM Employees WHERE EmployeeNo = 11;
```

Output:

```
1 row deleted.
```

To test the trigger, issue the following commands:

```
SET SERVEROUTPUT ON
UPDATE Employees SET Salary = Salary * 1.10 WHERE DeptNo = 4;
```

Output:

```
UPDATE Employees SET Salary = Salary * 1.10 WHERE DeptNo = 4
       *
ERROR at line 1:
ORA-04091: table VAISHALI.EMPLOYEES is mutating, trigger/function may not see it
ORA-06512: at "VAISHALI.DISPLAYTOTALSALARY", line 4
ORA-04088: error during execution of trigger 'VAISHALI.DISPLAYTOTALSALARY'
Help: https://docs.oracle.com/error-help/db/ora-04091/
```

In the above example, as the Employees table is being queried in the trigger named DisplayTotalSalary that is based on the same table, a mutating error is received.

It is also possible for ORA-4091 to be encountered when querying a table other than the table on which the trigger is based. This usually happens when a foreign key reference is present with an ON DELETE CASCADE option.

A row-level trigger on the master table mutates if the detail table is being referred to in the trigger for a delete transaction. This will only happen if the foreign key on the detail table is created with the ON DELETE CASCADE option. No mutation occurs if the master table is being referred to in a trigger on the detail table.

Maintaining a consistent view of the data is an important feature of Oracle. The mutating error conflicts with maintaining a consistent view, therefore, care should be taken to write proper code and avoid such triggers. It is for developers to write proper logic so that such complications do not arise.

To avoid mutating table errors:

- A row-level trigger must not query or modify a mutating table. However, correlation names such as NEW and OLD can be accessed by the trigger.
- A statement-level trigger must not query or modify a mutating table if the trigger is fired as the result of a CASCADE delete.

Correlation Names

The data in the last SQL statement can be classified as new values and old values. When a user executes an INSERT statement, the values of the columns included in the insert statement can be read or set using **:NEW.columnname**.

Similarly, if the user updates a record, the value before the modification can be read using **:OLD.columnname**. The new values set using an update statement can be referenced using **:NEW.columnname**.

Write a trigger that fires every time the attendance is registered or updated in the EmployeeMuster table. This trigger should ensure that the MusterDate column does not hold a Sunday. If it does, the transaction should not go through:

```
CREATE OR REPLACE TRIGGER PreventSundays
  BEFORE INSERT OR UPDATE ON EmployeeMuster
  FOR EACH ROW WHEN (NEW.EmployeeNo > 0)
  BEGIN
     IF TO_CHAR(:NEW.MusterDate, 'DY') = 'SUN' THEN
        RAISE_APPLICATION_ERROR(-20000,'The MusterDate cannot hold
           Sunday.');
     END IF;
  END;
/
```

This line determines if the date being entered is a Sunday. If it is, then an exception is raised:

```
IF TO_CHAR(:NEW.MusterDate, 'DY') = 'SUN' THEN
```

RAISE_APPLICATION_ERROR is a procedure provided by Oracle that allows programmers to issue user-defined error messages:

```
RAISE_APPLICATION_ERROR(<ErrorNumber>, <Message>);
```

Where,

- ***ErrorNumber:*** A negative integer in the range **-20000 to -20999**.
- ***Message:*** A character string up to 2048 bytes in length.

RAISE_APPLICATION_ERROR can only be called in a stored subprogram such as stored procedures, functions, and database triggers. It is most commonly used in database triggers.

RAISE_APPLICATION_ERROR when called:

- Terminates the subprogram.
- Rolls back any database changes it made.
- Returns a user-defined error number and message to the application.

Output:

```
Trigger created.
```

To test the trigger, issue the following command:

```
UPDATE EmployeeMuster SET MusterDate = '06-Apr-2008' WHERE EmployeeNo = 1
      AND TO_CHAR(MusterDate, 'DD-MM-YYYY') = '29-04-2008';
```

Since the trigger is set to run before every update, the output will be:

```
UPDATE EmployeeMuster SET MusterDate = '06-Apr-2008'
       *
ERROR at line 1:
ORA-20000: The MusterDate cannot hold Sunday.
ORA-06512: at "VAISHALI.PREVENTSUNDAYS", line 3
ORA-04088: error during execution of trigger 'VAISHALI.PREVENTSUNDAYS'
```

To test the trigger, issue the following command:

```
INSERT INTO EmployeeMuster (EmployeeNo, MusterDate, Attendance)
  VALUES(21, '06-Apr-2008', 'Absent');
```

Output:

```
INSERT INTO EmployeeMuster (EmployeeNo, MusterDate, Attendance)
            *
ERROR at line 1:
ORA-20000: The MusterDate cannot hold Sunday.
ORA-06512: at "VAISHALI.PREVENTSUNDAYS", line 3
ORA-04088: error during execution of trigger 'VAISHALI.PREVENTSUNDAYS'
```

To test the trigger, issue the following command:

```
INSERT INTO EmployeeMuster (EmployeeNo, MusterDate, Attendance)
   VALUES(21, '07-Apr-2008', 'Absent');
```

Output:

```
1 row created.
```

The bank desires to maintain an audit trail of the accounts being registered in the Accounts table. Write a trigger that keeps track of the records being deleted or updated. The trigger should populate the AccountsAuditTrail table on every update and delete operation fired on the Accounts table. The AccountsAuditTrail table holds all the columns that the Accounts table holds, along with three additional columns to indicate:

- The user who performed the operation.
- The date on which the operation was performed.
- The kind of operation (Update or Delete) being performed.

Solution:

```
CREATE OR REPLACE TRIGGER AccountsAudit
   AFTER UPDATE OR DELETE ON Accounts
      FOR EACH ROW
   DECLARE
      varKindOfOperation Varchar2(8);
      varOperationDate Date;
      varUser Varchar2(8);
   BEGIN
      varOperationDate := SYSDATE;
      varUser := USER;
      IF UPDATING THEN
         varKindOfOperation := 'Update';
      ELSIF DELETING THEN
         varKindOfOperation := 'Delete';
      END IF;
   INSERT INTO AccountsAuditTrail VALUES (:OLD.AccountNo,
      :OLD.AccountHolderName,:OLD.AccountOpeningDate, :OLD.AccountType,
      :OLD.CurrentBalance,   varUser, varOperationDate, varKindOfOperation);
   END;
/
```

This trigger is fired when an UPDATE or DELETE operation is performed on the Accounts table. The trigger checks the operation being performed on the table using:

```
IF UPDATING THEN

ELSIF DELETING THEN
```

Depending on the kind of operation being performed, a memory variable is populated.

All the current values (old values before update or delete) available in the Accounts table for the row being updated or deleted are populated in the AccountsAuditTrail table.

In addition to the old values, the trigger also populates:

- The kind of operation being carried out.
- The date on which the operation was carried out.
- The user who carried out the operation.

Output:

```
Trigger created.
```

To test the trigger, issue the following commands:

1. Update a record in the Accounts table:

```
UPDATE Accounts SET AccountType = 'CA' WHERE AccountNo = 2;
```

Output:

```
1 row updated.
```

Query the AccountsAuditTrail table:

```
SELECT * FROM AccountsAuditTrail;
```

Output:

```
ACCOUNTNO ACCOUTHOLDERNAME ACCOUNTOP AC CURRENTBALANCE OPERATOR OPERATION OPERATIONTYPE
---------- --------------- --------- -- -------------- -------- --------- -------------
         2 Vaishali        05-FEB-05 SB           5000 VAISHALI 09-JAN-25 Update
```

2. **Delete a record from the Accounts table:**

```
DELETE FROM Accounts WHERE AccountNo = 12;
```

Output:

```
1 row deleted.
```

Query the AccountsAuditTrail table:

```
SELECT * FROM AccountsAuditTrail;
```

Output:

```
ACCOUNTNO ACCOUTHOLDERNAME ACCOUNTOP AC CURRENTBALANCE OPERATOR OPERATION OPERATIONTYPE
---------- --------------- --------- -- -------------- -------- --------- -------------
         2 Vaishali        05-FEB-05 SB           5000 VAISHALI 09-JAN-25 Update
        12 Puja            20-FEB-05 SB           4500 VAISHALI 09-JAN-25 Delete
```

The bank wants to ensure that a transaction recorded in the transactions table is completely valid. A transaction is valid if:

- The account number for which the transaction is being performed is a valid account number.
- The Transaction amount is not zero and is a positive number.
- The amount being withdrawn does not exceed the current balance for that account number.

Write a trigger on the Transactions table that helps achieve this.

Solution:

```
CREATE OR REPLACE TRIGGER ValidateTransaction
  BEFORE INSERT ON Transactions FOR EACH ROW
  DECLARE
      varAccountNo Varchar2(10) := 0;
      varCurrentBalance Number(10);
  BEGIN
  /* Checking if the account number is a valid account number. */
      SELECT COUNT(AccountNo) INTO varAccountNo FROM Accounts
          WHERE AccountNo = :NEW.AccountNo;
      IF varAccountNo = 0 THEN
          RAISE_APPLICATION_ERROR(-20000,'The Account number is invalid.');
      END IF;
  /* Checking if the transaction amount is a positive number. */
      IF :NEW.Amount <= 0 THEN
          RAISE_APPLICATION_ERROR(-20001,'The Transaction amount cannot
              be negative or zero.');
      END IF;
  /* Checking if the transaction amount exceeds the current balance in
  case of withdrawals. */
      SELECT CurrentBalance INTO varCurrentBalance FROM Accounts
          WHERE AccountNo = :NEW.AccountNo;
      IF varCurrentBalance < :NEW.Amount
          AND :NEW.TransactionType = 'Dr' THEN
          RAISE_APPLICATION_ERROR(-20002,'The amount of withdrawal
              cannot exceed the balance held in the account.');
      END IF;
  END;
/
```

Output:

```
Trigger created.
```

To test the trigger, issue the following commands:

1. **Negative Transaction amount:**

```
INSERT INTO Transactions VALUES(100, 1, '30-DEC-2008', 'Withdrawals', 'Dr', -500);
```

Output:

```
INSERT INTO Transactions VALUES(100, 1, '30-DEC-2008', 'Withdrawals', 'Dr', -500)
            *
ERROR at line 1:
ORA-20001: The Transaction amount cannot be negative or zero.
ORA-06512: at "VAISHALI.VALIDATETRANSACTION", line 13
ORA-04088: error during execution of trigger 'VAISHALI.VALIDATETRANSACTION'
```

2. **Invalid account number:**

```
INSERT INTO Transactions VALUES(100, 3, '30-DEC-2008', 'Withdrawals', 'Dr', 500);
```

Output:

```
1 row created.
```

3. **Short of funds:**

```
INSERT INTO Transactions VALUES(100, 1, '30-DEC-2008', 'Withdrawals', 'Dr', 25000);
```

Output:

```
INSERT INTO Transactions VALUES(100, 1, '30-DEC-2008', 'Withdrawals', 'Dr', 25000)
            *
ERROR at line 1:
ORA-20002: The amount of withdrawal cannot exceed the balance held in the account.
ORA-06512: at "VAISHALI.VALIDATETRANSACTION", line 21
ORA-04088: error during execution of trigger 'VAISHALI.VALIDATETRANSACTION'
```

The DBA desires to keep track of the user and the date on which objects are created or dropped in the database. Write a DDL trigger that inserts a record in the DDLAuditTrail table. This table holds:

- EventName
- ObjectOwner
- ObjectName
- ObjectType
- Operator
- OperationDate

Solution:

```
CREATE OR REPLACE TRIGGER DDLAudit
  BEFORE CREATE OR DROP ON SCHEMA
  BEGIN
     INSERT INTO DDLAuditTrail (SELECT Ora_Sysevent, Ora_Dict_Obj_Owner,
          Ora_Dict_Obj_Name, Ora_Dict_Obj_Type, USER, SYSDATE FROM DUAL);
  END DDLAudit;
/
```

This trigger fires every time an object, such as a table or view, is created or dropped. This trigger inserts a record in the DDLAuditTrail table to keep track of which objects were created or dropped, by whom, and when.

Output:

```
Trigger created.
```

To test the trigger, create and drop a few objects:

```
CREATE TABLE MyTable (MyColumn1 Varchar2(10), MyColumn2 Varchar2(10));
CREATE VIEW vwMyTable AS SELECT * FROM MyTABLE;
CREATE INDEX idxMyTable ON MyTable (MyColumn1);
DROP INDEX idxMyTable;
DROP TABLE MyTable;
DROP VIEW vwMyTable;
```

Query the DDLAuditTrail table:

```
SELECT * FROM DDLAuditTrail;
```

Output:

```
EVENTNAME OBJECTOWNER OBJECTNAME OBJECTTYPE OPERATOR OPERATION
--------- ----------- ---------- ---------- -------- ---------
CREATE    VAISHALI    IDXMYTABLE INDEX      VAISHALI 09-JAN-25
DROP      VAISHALI    IDXMYTABLE INDEX      VAISHALI 09-JAN-25
DROP      VAISHALI    MYTABLE    TABLE      VAISHALI 09-JAN-25
CREATE    VAISHALI    MYTABLE    TABLE      VAISHALI 09-JAN-25
CREATE    VAISHALI    VWMYTABLE  VIEW       VAISHALI 09-JAN-25
DROP      VAISHALI    VWMYTABLE  VIEW       VAISHALI 09-JAN-25

6 rows selected.
```

A view named EmpDept is made up of the following columns:

- EmployeeNo
- FirstName
- LastName
- Salary
- DeptNo
- DeptName

Solution:

```
CREATE VIEW vwEmpDept AS
   SELECT EmployeeNo, FirstName, LastName, Salary, Departments.DeptNo,
      DepartmentName FROM Employees, Departments
         WHERE Employees.DeptNo = Departments.DeptNo;
```

Output:

```
View created.
```

Since this is a complex view, i.e., it holds columns from two tables using a JOIN, data manipulation is not possible. Write a trigger that will help achieve this.

Solution:

```
CREATE OR REPLACE TRIGGER UpdateEmpForView
   INSTEAD OF INSERT ON vwEmpDept FOR EACH ROW
   DECLARE
      varEmployees Number;
      varDepartments Number;
   BEGIN
      SELECT COUNT(*) INTO varEmployees FROM Employees
```

```
        WHERE Employees.EmployeeNo = :NEW.EmployeeNo;
  /* Checking if employee does not exists */
      IF varEmployees = 0 THEN
          INSERT INTO Employees (EmployeeNo, FirstName, LastName, Salary)
              VALUES(:NEW.EmployeeNo, :NEW.FirstName, :NEW.LastName,
                  :NEW.Salary);
      ELSE
          UPDATE Employees SET Employees.FirstName = :NEW.FirstName,
              Employees.LastName = :NEW.LastName,
              Employees.Salary = :NEW.Salary, Employees.DeptNo = :NEW.DeptNo
                  WHERE Employees.EmployeeNo = :NEW.EmployeeNo;
      END IF;
      SELECT COUNT(*) INTO varDepartments FROM Departments
          WHERE Departments.DeptNo = :NEW.DeptNo;
  /* Checking if department does not exists */
      IF varDepartments = 0 THEN
          INSERT INTO Departments (DeptNo, DepartmentName)
              VALUES(:NEW.DeptNo, :NEW.DepartmentName);
      ELSE
          UPDATE Departments
              SET Departments.DepartmentName = :NEW.DepartmentName
                  WHERE Departments.DeptNo = :NEW.DeptNo;
      END IF;
  END;
/
```

- Indicates that this trigger will be fired when a record is being inserted via the view vwEmpDept:

```
INSTEAD OF INSERT ON vwEmpDept
```

- Determines if the employee number being inserted in the view is already available in the Employees table:

```
SELECT COUNT(*) INTO varEmployees FROM Employees
  WHERE Employees.EmployeeNo = :NEW.EmployeeNo;
IF varEmployees = 0 THEN
```

- Determines if the department number being inserted in the view is already available in the Departments table:

```
SELECT COUNT(*) INTO varDepartments FROM Departments
  WHERE Departments.DeptNo = :NEW.DeptNo;
IF varDepartments = 0 THEN
```

The trigger determines if the record being inserted or updated already exists in the base tables. If it does, then an UPDATE is fired, otherwise, an INSERT is fired.

Output:

```
Trigger created.
```

To test the trigger, issue the following commands:

1. **Query the base tables to view the data held before updates:**

```
SELECT EmployeeNo, FirstName, LastName, Salary, DeptNo FROM Employees;
SELECT * FROM Departments;
```

Output: (Employees table)

```
EMPLOYEENO FIRSTNAME   LASTNAME   SALARY     DEPTNO
---------- ----------- ---------- ---------- ------
1          Sharanam    Shah       82500      4
2          Vaishali    Shah       55000      2
3          Keyur       Kapoor     22000      4
4          Amit        Haria      22000      2
5          Abhishek    Benegal    13334.2    1
6          Chetan      Dedhia     13553.1    3
7          Narendra    Dodhia     13578.4    3
8          Meenal      Doshi      49500      7
9          Anil        Mayekar    2750       3
10         Chaitanya   Kapoor     1320       5
11         Amit        Paul       31207

11 rows selected.
```

Output: (Departments table)

```
    DEPTNO DEPARTMENTNAME                CAPACITY
---------- ------------------------- ----------
         7 IT Department                     20
         1 Sales Department                  15
         2 HR Department                      5
         3 Technical Department              25
         4 Purchase Department               15
         5 Customer Care Department          40
         6 Helpline Department               30
         9 Accounts

8 rows selected.
```

2. **Insert an already existing record:**

```
INSERT INTO vwEmpDept VALUES(11, 'Kajal', 'Shah', 10000, 2, 'HR Department');
```

3. **Insert a record that does not exists:**

```
INSERT INTO vwEmpDept VALUES(12, 'Tanvi', 'Shah', 5000, 8, 'Design Department');
```

Output: (For both the INSERT statements)

```
1 row created.
```

4. **Query the base tables to view the data held after updates:**

```
SELECT EmployeeNo, FirstName, LastName, Salary, DeptNo FROM Employees;
SELECT * FROM Departments;
```

Output: (Employees table)

```
EMPLOYEENO FIRSTNAME  LASTNAME     SALARY     DEPTNO
---------- ---------- ------------ ---------- ----------
        12 Tanvi      Shah               5000
         1 Sharanam   Shah              82500          4
         2 Vaishali   Shah              55000          2
         3 Keyur      Kapoor            22000          4
         4 Amit       Haria             22000          2
         5 Abhishek   Benegal         13334.2          1
         6 Chetan     Dedhia          13553.1          3
         7 Narendra   Dodhia          13578.4          3
         8 Meenal     Doshi             49500          7
         9 Anil       Mayekar            2750          3
        10 Chaitanya  Kapoor             1320          5
        11 Kajal      Shah              10000

12 rows selected.
```

Output: (Departments table)

```
    DEPTNO DEPARTMENTNAME            CAPACITY
---------- ------------------------- ----------
         8 Design Department
         7 IT Department                     20
         1 Sales Department                  15
         2 Design Department                  5
         3 Technical Department              25
         4 Purchase Department               15
         5 Customer Care Department          40
         6 Helpline Department               30
         9 Accounts

9 rows selected.
```

Similarly to allow deletes via view vwEmpDept, use the following trigger:

```
CREATE OR REPLACE TRIGGER DeleteEmpForView
  INSTEAD OF DELETE ON vwEmpDept
  FOR EACH ROW
  DECLARE
     varEmployees Number;
  BEGIN
     DELETE FROM Employees WHERE EmployeeNo = :OLD.EmployeeNo;
     SELECT COUNT(*) INTO varEmployees FROM Employees
        WHERE Employees.DeptNo = :OLD.DeptNo;
  /* Checking if no employee exists in a particular department */
     IF varEmployees = 0 THEN
        DELETE FROM Departments WHERE DeptNo = :OLD.DeptNo;
     END IF;
  END;
/
```

This trigger deletes the department only if no employee belongs to that department. This is checked using:

```
SELECT COUNT(*) INTO varEmployees FROM Employees
```

```
  WHERE Employees.DeptNo = :OLD.DeptNo;
IF varEmployees = 0 THEN
```

This trigger also deletes the employee from the Employees table when a delete is fired on the view vwEmpDept.

Output:

```
Trigger created.
```

To test the trigger, issue the following commands:

1. **Query the base tables to view the data held before updates:**

```
SELECT EmployeeNo, FirstName, LastName, Salary, DeptNo FROM Employees;
SELECT * FROM Departments;
```

Output: (Employees table)

```
EMPLOYEENO FIRSTNAME   LASTNAME   SALARY     DEPTNO
---------- ----------- ---------- ---------- ------
1          Sharanam    Shah       82500      4
2          Vaishali    Shah       55000      2
3          Keyur       Kapoor     22000      4
4          Amit        Haria      22000      2
5          Abhishek    Benegal    13334.2    1
6          Chetan      Dedhia     13553.1    3
7          Narendra    Dodhia     13578.4    3
8          Meenal      Doshi      49500      7
9          Anil        Mayekar    2750       3
10         Chaitanya   Kapoor     1320       5
11         Amit        Paul       31207      9

11 rows selected.
```

Output: (Departments table)

```
    DEPTNO DEPARTMENTNAME             CAPACITY
---------- ------------------------- ----------
         7 IT Department                     20
         1 Sales Department                  15
         2 HR Department                      5
         3 Technical Department              25
         4 Purchase Department               15
         5 Customer Care Department          40
         6 Helpline Department               30
         9 Accounts

8 rows selected.
```

2. **Delete an already existing record:**

```
DELETE FROM vwEmpDept WHERE EmployeeNo = 11;
```

Output:

```
1 row deleted.
```

3. Query the base tables to view the data held after updates:

```
SELECT EmployeeNo, FirstName, LastName, Salary, DeptNo FROM Employees;
SELECT * FROM Departments;
```

Output: (Employees table)

```
EMPLOYEENO FIRSTNAME   LASTNAME   SALARY     DEPTNO
---------- ----------- ---------- ---------- ------
1          Sharanam    Shah       82500      4
2          Vaishali    Shah       55000      2
3          Keyur       Kapoor     22000      4
4          Amit        Haria      22000      2
5          Abhishek    Benegal    13334.2    1
6          Chetan      Dedhia     13553.1    3
7          Narendra    Dodhia     13578.4    3
8          Meenal      Doshi      49500      7
9          Anil        Mayekar    2750       3
10         Chaitanya   Kapoor     1320       5

10 rows selected.
```

Output: (Departments table)

```
    DEPTNO DEPARTMENTNAME            CAPACITY
---------- ------------------------- ----------
         8 Design Department
         7 IT Department                     20
         1 Sales Department                  15
         2 HR Department                      5
         3 Technical Department              25
         4 Purchase Department               15
         5 Customer Care Department          40
         6 Helpline Department               30

9 rows selected.
```

Since after the deletion of the employee, the department has no more employees left, the trigger deletes the department as well.

The bank desires to maintain an audit trail of the accounts being registered in the Accounts table. Write a trigger that keeps a track of the records that are being deleted or updated. The trigger should populate the table AccountsAuditTrail on every update and delete fired on the Accounts table. The **same trigger should also be capable** of generating a new customer number and add the account holder as the new customer in the Customers table. The AccountsAuditTrial table holds all the columns that Accounts table holds along with three additional columns to indicate:

- The user who performed such operation.
- The date on which the operation was performed.
- The kind of operation [Update or Delete] being performed.

Solution:

```
CREATE OR REPLACE TRIGGER AccountsAudit
  FOR INSERT OR UPDATE OR DELETE ON Accounts
  COMPOUND TRIGGER
      varKindOfOperation Varchar2(8);
      varOperationDate Date;
      varUser Varchar2(8);
      maxCustomerNo Number(10);
  AFTER EACH ROW IS
  BEGIN
      varOperationDate := SYSDATE;
      varUser := USER;
      IF UPDATING THEN
          varKindOfOperation := 'Update';
      ELSIF DELETING THEN
          varKindOfOperation := 'Delete';
      END IF;
      INSERT INTO AccountsAuditTrail
          VALUES (:OLD.AccountNo, :OLD.AccountHolderName,
              :OLD.AccountOpeningDate, :OLD.AccountType,:OLD.CurrentBalance,
              varUser, varOperationDate, varKindOfOperation);
  END AFTER EACH ROW;
  BEFORE EACH ROW IS
  BEGIN
      IF INSERTING THEN
          SELECT NVL(MAX(CustomerNo), 0) + 1 INTO maxCustomerNo
              FROM Customers;
          INSERT INTO Customers (CustomerNo, CustomerName)
              VALUES(maxCustomerNo, :NEW.AccountHolderName);
      END IF;
  END BEFORE EACH ROW;
END;
/
```

This is a compound trigger that fires:

- When an UPDATE or DELETE operation is performed on the Accounts table
  - Makes an entry in the AccountsAuditTrial table.
- When an INSERT operation is performed on the Accounts table
  - Generates a new account number.

The first trigger:

```
AFTER EACH ROW IS
BEGIN
```

The trigger checks the operation being performed on the table using:

```
IF UPDATING THEN

ELSIF DELETING THEN
```

Depending on the kind of operation being performed, a memory variable is populated. All the current values [old values before update or delete] available in the Accounts table for the row being updated or deleted are populated in the AccountsAuditTrail table.

In addition to the old values, the trigger also populates:

- The kind of operation being carried out.
- The date on which the operation was carried out.
- The user who carried out the operation.

The second trigger:

```
BEFORE EACH ROW IS
```

Uses the MAX function to determine the highest value in the CustomerNo column:

```
MAX(CustomerNo)
```

If the Customer table holds no records, then, the MAX function returns NULL. This means the first CustomerNo will have to begin with 1.

To achieve this, NVL function is applied which returns 0, if the MAX function returns NULL:

```
NVL(MAX(CustomerNo), 0)
```

The value that is returned by **NVL()**, is assigned to the memory variable with 1 added to it.

Hence,

- If the highest CustomerNo was 3 then the next value will be 4.
- If there were no customers at all, then the next value will be 1.

Once the next value is formed, the value is assigned to the CustomerNo column using in the INSERT INTO statement:

```
INSERT INTO Customers (CustomerNo, CustomerName)
  VALUES(maxCustomerNo, :NEW.AccountHolderName);
```

Output:

```
Trigger created.
```

To test the trigger, issue the following commands:

1. **Update a record in the Accounts table:**

```
UPDATE Accounts SET AccountType = 'CA' WHERE AccountNo = 2;
```

Output:

```
1 row updated.
```

2. **Query the AccountsAuditTrail table:**

```
SELECT * FROM AccountsAuditTrail;
```

Output:

```
ACCOUNTNO ACCOUTHOLDERNAME ACCOUNTOP AC CURRENTBALANCE OPERATOR OPERATION OPERATIONTYPE
---------- --------------- --------- -- -------------- -------- --------- -------------
         2 Vaishali        05-FEB-05 CA           5000 VAISHALI 09-JAN-25 Update
```

3. Delete a record from the Accounts table:

```
DELETE FROM Accounts WHERE AccountNo = 12;
```

Output:

```
1 row deleted.
```

4. Query the AccountsAuditTrail table:

```
SELECT * FROM AccountsAuditTrail;
```

Output:

```
ACCOUNTNO ACCOUTHOLDERNAME ACCOUNTOP AC CURRENTBALANCE OPERATOR OPERATION OPERATIONTYPE
---------- --------------- --------- -- -------------- -------- --------- -------------
         2 Vaishali        05-FEB-05 CA           5000 VAISHALI 09-JAN-25 Update
        12 Puja            20-FEB-05 SB           4500 VAISHALI 09-JAN-25 Delete
```

5. Add a record:

```
INSERT INTO Accounts VALUES (13, 'Stuti', '23-Jun-2007', 'SB', 20000);
```

Output:

```
1 row created.
```

6. Query the Accounts table as:

```
SELECT * FROM Accounts;
```

Output:

```
ACCOUNTNO ACCOUNTHOLDERNAME         ACCOUNTOP AC CURRENTBALANCE
---------- ------------------------- --------- -- --------------
         1 Sharanam                  23-MAY-07 SB        13358.9
         2 Vaishali                  05-FEB-05 CA           5000
        13 Stuti                     23-JUN-07 SB          20000
         3 Gita                      08-JUN-06 SB        2375.89
         6 Michel                    29-MAR-08 CA           3000
         5 Micheal                   20-OCT-03 SB           4000
         4 Geeta                     01-JAN-05 CA       46892.08
        11 Pooja                     07-JUL-03 CA         123890
        10 Dipa                      23-MAY-07 SB           1245
         9 Deepa                     08-JUN-06 SB           1000
         8 Sita                      20-OCT-03 SB           1234
         7 Seeta                     07-JUL-03 SB           3000

12 rows selected.
```

7. **Query the Customers table as:**

```
SELECT CustomerNo, CustomerName FROM Customers;
```

Output:

```
CUSTOMERNO CUSTOMERNAME
---------- -------------------------
        32 Stuti
        21 Sharanam Chaitanya Shah
        22 Vaishali Sharanam Shah
        23 Anil Mayekar
        24 Hansel
        25 Chaitanya Kantilal Shah
        26 Shravan Ashwin Benegal
        27 Prakash K Chouduary
        28 Stuti Kapil Khanna
        29 Deepika Anil Bakshi
        30 Manali Narendra Naik
        31 Amit Paul

12 rows selected.
```

Compound triggers allow combining more than one trigger with different triggering timings into a single compound trigger. This is the biggest advantage of compound trigger as it allows modular programming with less cumbersome code.

Compound trigger contains declaration section and more than one section for each timing points such as before each row, after each row, after statement, and so on. The individual timing points share a single global declaration section, whose state is maintained for the lifetime of the statement. Once a statement ends, due to successful completion or an error, the trigger state is cleaned up.

In the previous releases of the Oracle database, this type of functionality was only possible by defining multiple triggers whose code spec and global variables were defined in a separate package, but the compound trigger allows for a much tidier solution.

Destroying An Existing Trigger

Syntax:

```
DROP TRIGGER <TriggerName>;
```

Where, ***TriggerName*** is the name of the trigger to be dropped.

Drop the trigger named DBAudit:

```
DROP TRIGGER DBAudit;
```

Output:

```
Trigger dropped.
```

Chapter

32

SECTION VI: CHAT WITH YOUR DATABASE USING SELECT AI

Diving Into Oracle Autonomous Database

What Is Oracle Autonomous Database?

Imagine a database that manages itself. That's the core idea behind **Oracle Autonomous Database**. It's a cloud-based database service that automates many of the traditional database administration tasks, freeing you up to focus on what matters most: using your data to drive insights and innovation. Think of it as having a highly skilled database expert working behind the scenes 24/7, handling everything from backups and security to performance tuning and patching.

Why Is It Useful?

Traditional database management can be complex and time-consuming.

Autonomous Database takes away the pain by:

- *Automating:* It handles tasks like patching, upgrading, backing up, and tuning automatically. This reduces manual effort and minimizes the risk of human error.
- *Saving Money:* By automating tasks, it lowers operational costs and frees up IT resources. You pay only for what you use.
- *Improving Security:* Built-in security features and automated patching help protect your data from threats.
- *Boosting Performance:* Autonomous Database continuously monitors and optimizes performance, ensuring your applications run smoothly.
- *Simplifying Development:* It makes it easier for developers to build and deploy data-driven applications.

The following are the key features of Autonomous Database:

- *Self-Driving:* Automates database administration tasks.
- *Self-Scaling:* Automatically adjusts resources (CPU, memory, storage) to meet the demands of your applications.
- *Self-Repairing:* Detects and fixes issues automatically, minimizing downtime.
- *Cloud-Based:* Accessible and scalable through **O**racle **C**loud **I**nfrastructure (OCI).

AI Capabilities: The Game Changer

Oracle Autonomous Database isn't just about automation; it's also about intelligence. It integrates AI and machine learning to provide powerful data insights and enhance database operations. A key highlight in Oracle 23 is Select AI.

Select AI: Unleashing The Power Of Natural Language

Select AI is a revolutionary feature that allows you to query your database using natural language. Instead of writing complex SQL queries, you can simply ask questions in plain English.

For example, instead of:

```
SELECT AVG(Sales) FROM Orders WHERE State = 'Maharashtra';
```

You can say:

```
What is the average sales in the Maharashtra state?
```

Select AI understands your natural language query and translates it into the appropriate SQL, retrieving the results for you. This makes data access much easier and more accessible to everyone, regardless of their SQL skills.

Practical Uses Of Select AI

- *Business Users:* Empower business users to get the data they need without relying on IT.
- *Data Analysts:* Accelerate data exploration and analysis.
- *Developers:* Simplify database interactions during application development.
- *Reporting:* Generate reports using natural language queries.

AI Vector Search: Finding Meaning In Unstructured Data

AI Vector Search revolutionizes how you search and analyze unstructured data like text, images, audio, and video. It uses AI to convert this data into numerical representations called **vectors**. These vectors capture the semantic meaning of the data, allowing you to find similar content based on meaning rather than just keywords.

How AI Vector Search Works?

1. *Embedding Creation:* AI models analyze the unstructured data and create vector embeddings that represent its meaning.
2. *Vector Storage:* These embeddings are stored in the database.
3. *Similarity Search:* When you search, the search query is also converted into a vector. The database then finds the stored vectors that are most similar to the query vector.
4. *Result Retrieval:* The results corresponding to the most similar vectors are returned.

Practical Uses Of AI Vector Search

- *Semantic Search:* Find documents or images that are conceptually related, even if they don't contain the exact same keywords.
- *Recommendation Engines:* Recommend products, articles, or videos based on user preferences and past behavior.
- *Fraud Detection:* Identify suspicious patterns in financial transactions.
- *Image and Video Search:* Search for images or videos based on their content.

Use Cases Of Autonomous Database

- *Data Warehousing:* Building and managing large data warehouses for business intelligence and analytics.
- *Transaction Processing:* Supporting high-volume, mission-critical applications.
- *Data Science:* Providing a platform for data scientists to train and deploy machine learning models.
- *Application Development:* Simplifying database management for application developers.

- *IoT (Internet of Things):* Ingesting and analyzing data from connected devices.

Example Use Case: Retail Analytics

Imagine a retail company using Autonomous Database. They can use Select AI to ask questions like:

```
"What were our top-selling products last month?"
"Which state had the highest sales growth?"
"What is the average customer spend?"
```

The database will understand these natural language queries and provide the answers, enabling the company to make data-driven decisions about inventory, marketing, and sales strategies.

Oracle Autonomous Database represents a major leap forward in database technology. Its combination of automation and AI, particularly with Select AI, makes it easier than ever to manage data, gain insights, and build intelligent applications. It empowers users of all technical levels to work with data more effectively, paving the way for innovation and business growth. In the following chapters, we'll delve deeper into the Select AI capabilities of Autonomous Database and explore how you can setup the required Autonomous Database on the **O**racle **C**loud **I**nfrastructure (OCI).

Chapter 33

SECTION VI: CHAT WITH YOUR DATABASE USING SELECT AI

Setting Up Autonomous Database Instance

This chapter will guide you through setting up a cloud database using **O**racle **C**loud **I**nfrastructure (OCI) and connecting it to the Cohere AI platform.

What Is Oracle Cloud Infrastructure (OCI)?

OCI is a cloud computing service that provides on-demand access to computer resources, like servers, storage, and databases, over the internet. Think of it as renting computing power instead of owning it. OCI offers a "Free Tier" allowing you to experiment with many services without charge, ideal for learning and small projects.

Signing Up For Oracle Cloud Free Tier

1. Visit the **Oracle Cloud website** (www.oracle.com/cloud).
2. Look for a "**Free Trial**", "**Sign Up for Free**", or "**Start for Free**" button.

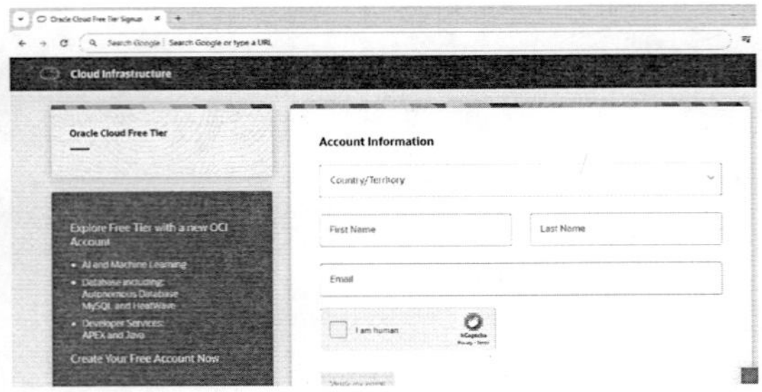

3. Provide your name, email address, and a password. You may be asked for a credit card for verification. As per Oracle, you won't be charged for "**Always Free**" services unless you upgrade.

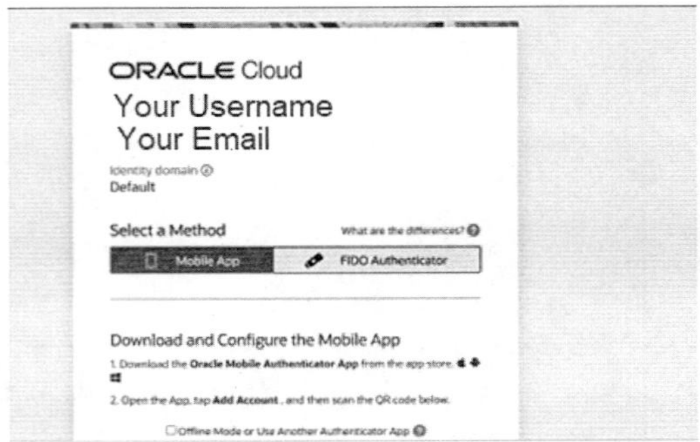

4. Wait for account setup. Verify your identity via phone or email. Click "**Done**" to finalize registration.

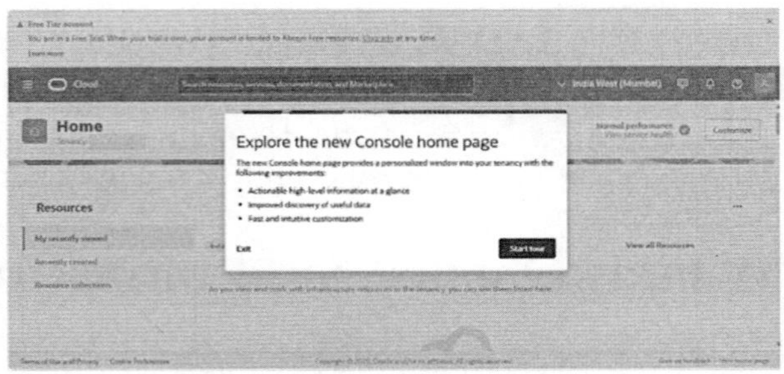

5. Log in to the **OCI console**. This is your control panel for managing cloud resources.

Configuring An Always-Free Oracle Autonomous Database Instance

1. After logging into Oracle Cloud, click the **Menu** icon, select **Oracle Database**, then **Autonomous Database**.

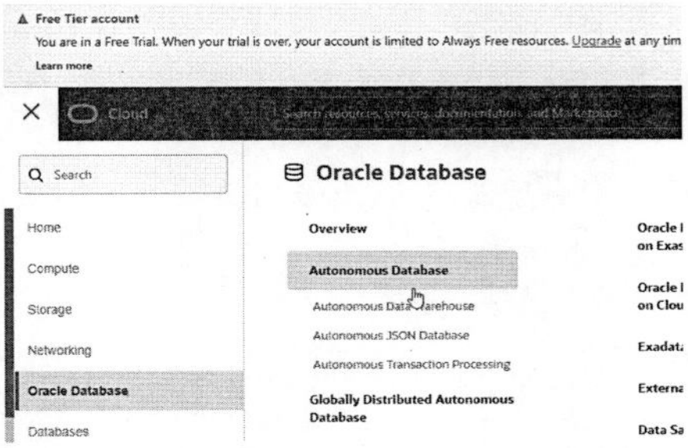

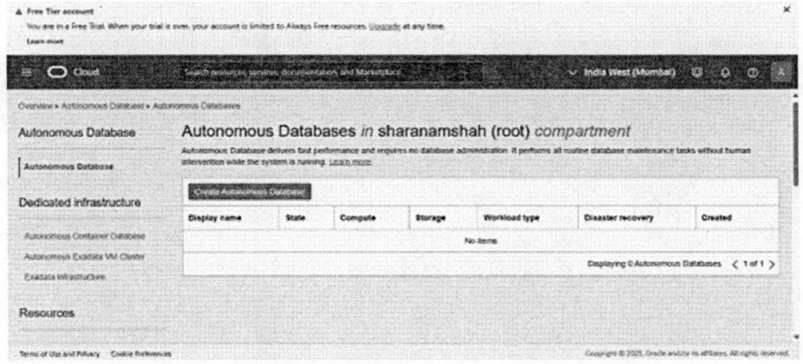

2. On the Autonomous Database page, click **Create Autonomous Database**.

3. Fill out the database information:
   a. Provide a display name and database name.
   b. Choose a **compartment** (a logical container for resources).
   c. Select **Transaction Processing** as the workload type (or another appropriate type).
   d. Choose **Serverless** as the deployment type (Exadata is not available for Always Free instances).
   e. Select your database version (e.g., Oracle 23ai). Ensure the **Always Free** slider is enabled.
   f. Create a strong password for the database admin user.

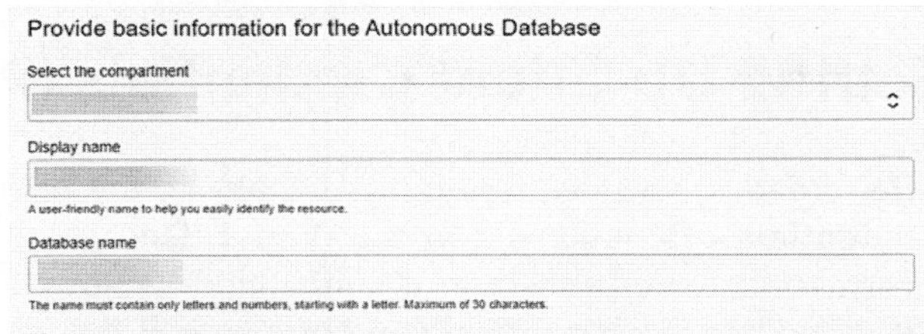

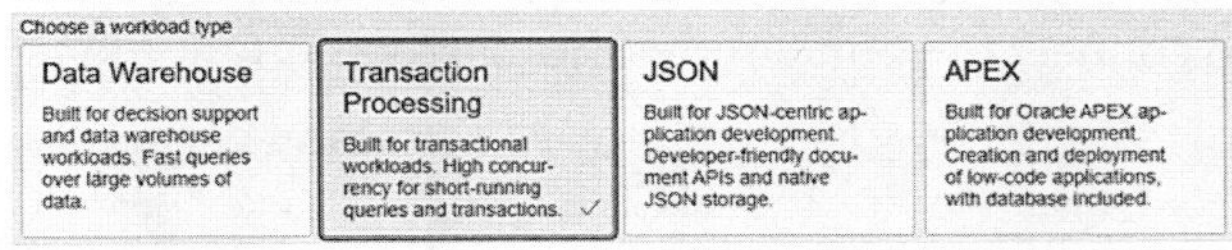

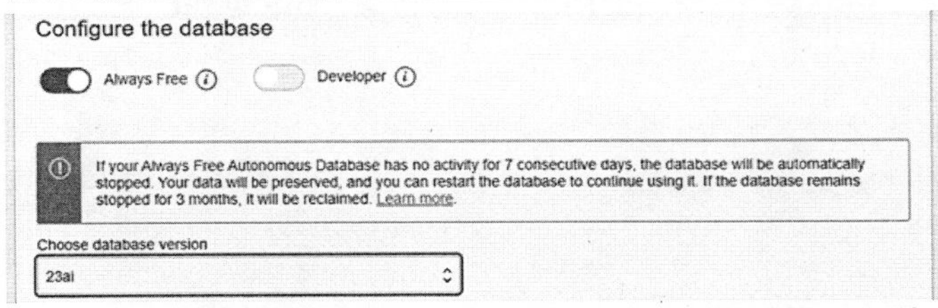

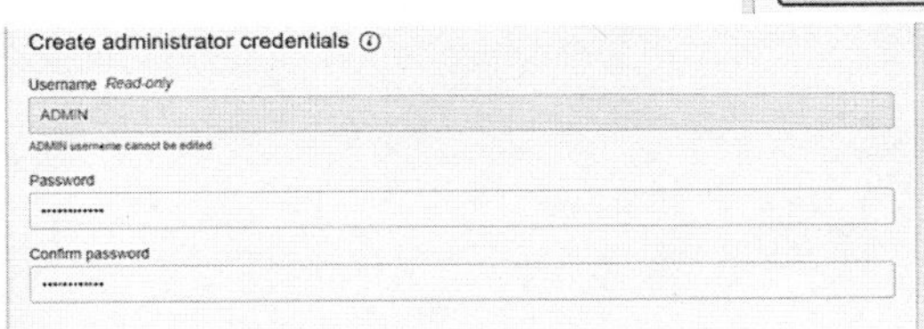

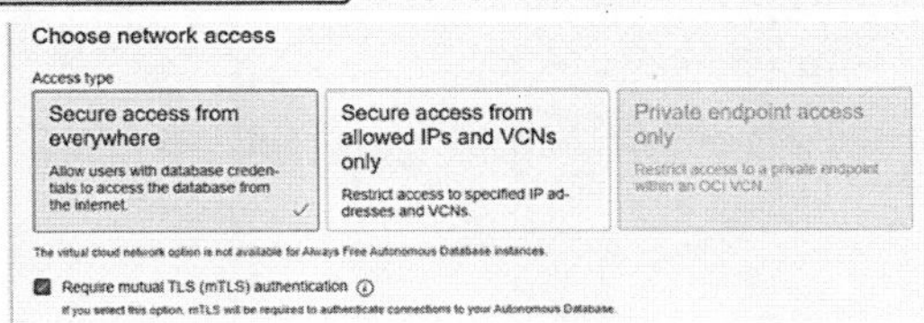

   g. Configure network access. **Secure access from allowed IPs and VCNs only** is recommended. Click **Add my IP address** for added security.

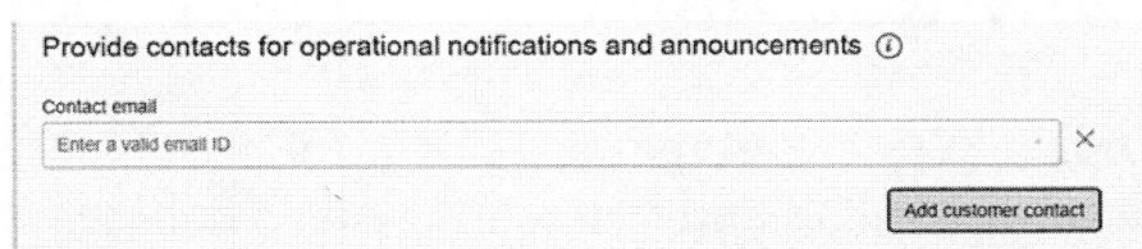

You can also enable mutual TLS (mTLS) authentication, which requires an Oracle wallet (downloaded after database creation). **Note:** We used **Secure access from everywhere**, but this is generally less secure.

h. Provide an operational email address.

4. Click **Create Autonomous Database**.
5. Your database will be created in moments. Access it from the **Autonomous Database** page.

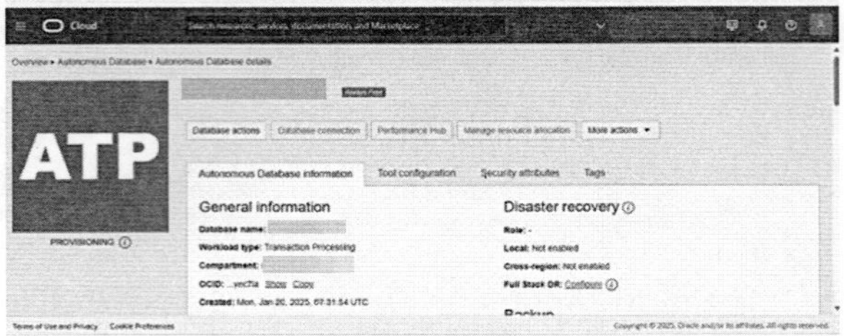

Setting Up Client Credentials (Wallet)

After creating your Autonomous Database, the next crucial step is downloading the **Client Credentials**, often referred to as a **Wallet**. This wallet file is essential, containing the necessary information for establishing a connection to your database. It's like a digital key, enabling authorized access. Specifically, when using SQL Developer, this wallet is required for the tool to connect to your cloud-based Oracle Autonomous Database.

1. Navigate to your **Autonomous Database** in the OCI console. Click **Database Connection**.

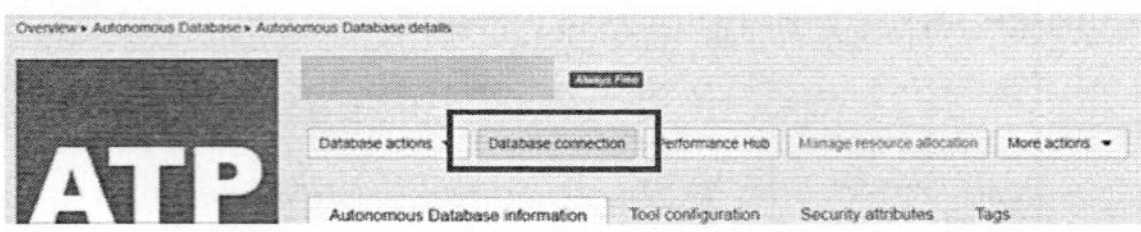

2. Scroll to the wallet section and click **Download Wallet**.
3. Enter a password for the wallet. The wallet zip file will download. Extract it to a secure location.

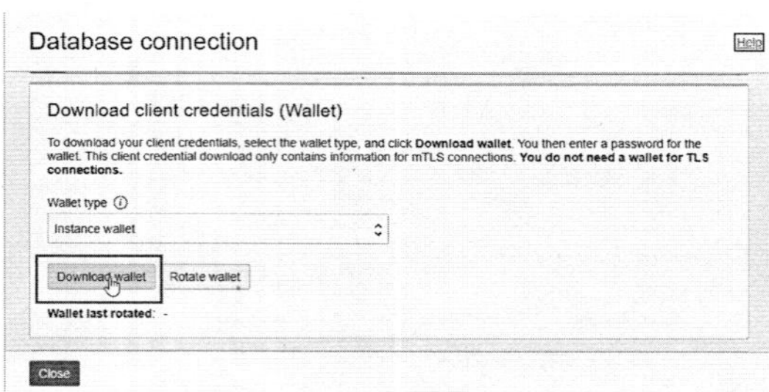

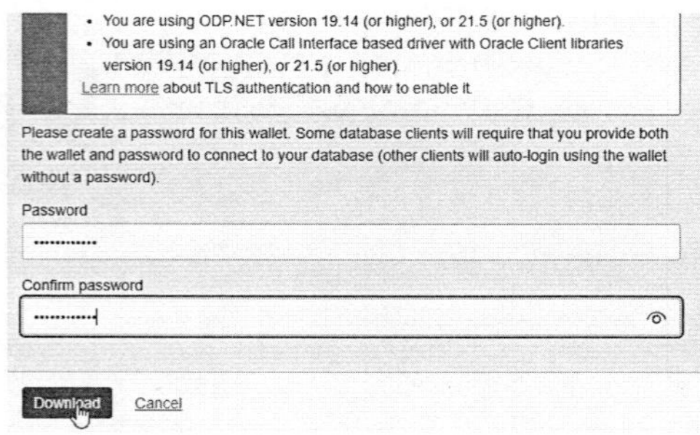

Downloading SQL Developer

Oracle SQL Developer is a powerful, free tool provided by Oracle that simplifies the process of connecting to and managing your database. It's our recommended tool for interacting with your Autonomous Database throughout this book.

This section will guide you through downloading and setting up SQL Developer.

1. Visit the Oracle SQL Developer download page.

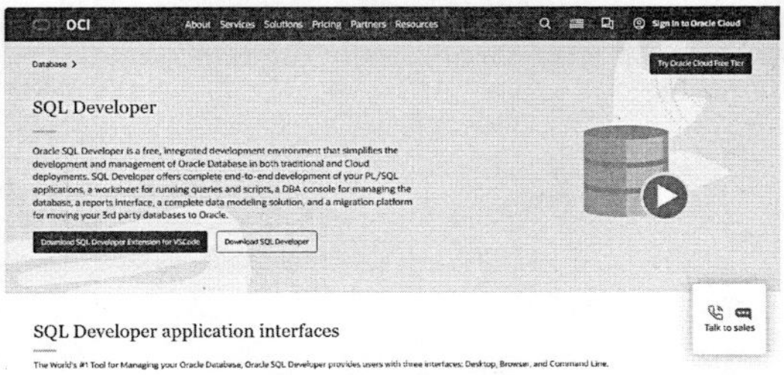

2. Once on the download page, you'll see various **versions** of SQL Developer available. It's crucial to select the correct version for your operating system. Oracle typically offers versions for Windows, macOS, and Linux. Select your operating system.

3. For ease of setup, we strongly recommend downloading the version of SQL Developer that **includes** a **Java Development Kit (JDK)**. This eliminates the need to install and configure Java separately. The download page usually clearly indicates which versions include a JDK. Download the zip file and extract it.

> At the time of writing this book, SQL Developer version 24.3.1 (windows 64-bit with JDK 17 included) was downloaded and unzipped.

Connecting To Your Autonomous Database Using Oracle SQL Developer

Now that you have SQL Developer installed and your Client Credentials (Wallet) downloaded, you're ready to connect to your Autonomous Database. This section provides a step-by-step guide.

1. Locate the SQL Developer executable (e.g., sqldeveloper.exe on Windows, or the corresponding executable on your operating system) within the directory where you extracted the SQL Developer ZIP file. Double-click the executable to launch the application.

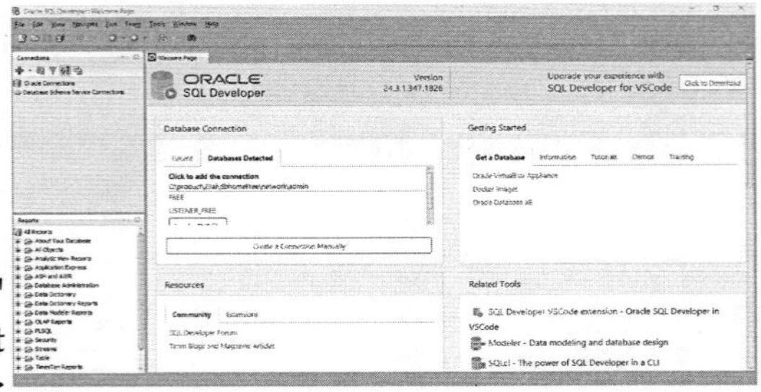

2. SQL Developer will present a "**Connections**" **pane** (usually on the left side). If it's not visible, you can open it via **View** > **Connections**.

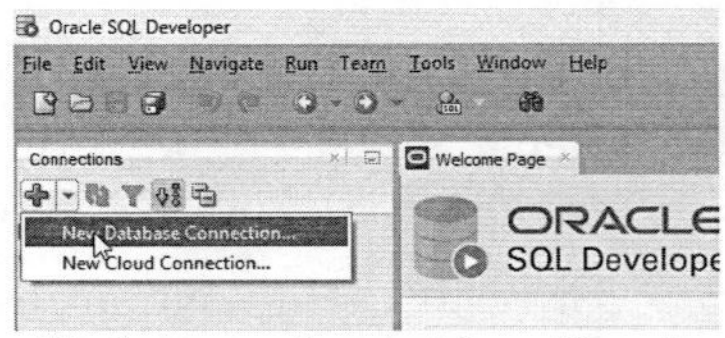

3. Create a **new database connection:**
   a. Click the green plus icon (+) labeled **New Database Connection...** to open the **New/Edit Database Connection** dialog.
   b. Provide a descriptive name for your connection (e.g., "MyAutonomousDB," "ProductionDB"). This name will be used to identify the connection in SQL Developer.

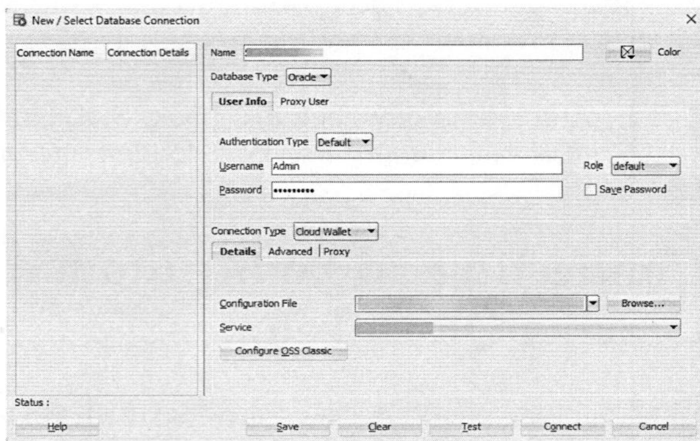

   c. Select "**Cloud Wallet**" as the connection type. This tells SQL Developer to use the wallet file for authentication.
   d. Enter the database administrator username. For Autonomous Databases, this is typically **ADMIN**.
   e. Enter the password you set for the ADMIN user during the database creation process.
   f. Click the **Browse...** button next to the **Configuration File** field. Navigate to the directory where you downloaded and extracted the Client Credentials (Wallet) ZIP file. Select the .**zip file** containing the wallet files, **not** an individual file within the .**zip file**.
   g. After selecting the wallet directory, a dropdown menu labeled **Service Name** will populate with the available database services within that wallet. Choose the appropriate service name. This name identifies the specific database instance you want to connect to. Often, there's a default service name.
   h. Before finalizing the connection, click the **Test** button. This will verify that SQL Developer can successfully communicate with your Autonomous Database using the provided credentials and wallet information. A **Success** message indicates everything is configured correctly. If you encounter errors, double-check your username, password, wallet location, and service name.

i. If the test is successful, click **Save**. SQL Developer saves your connection details. The next time you open SQL Developer, you can simply double-click the connection name in the **Connections** pane to connect to your database.

j. Click **Connect**. SQL Developer will now establish a connection to your Autonomous Database. The new connection will appear in the **Connections** pane, and you can begin working with your database.

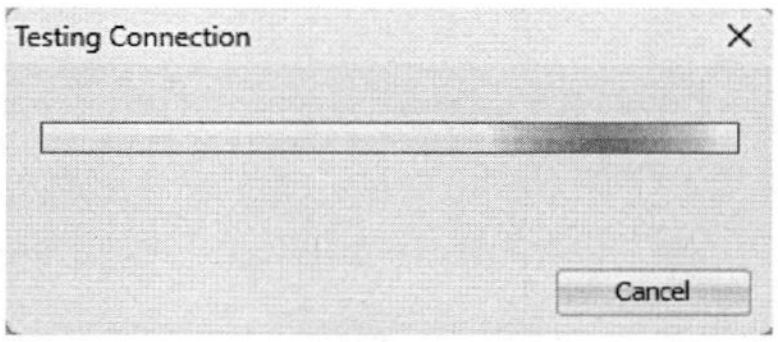

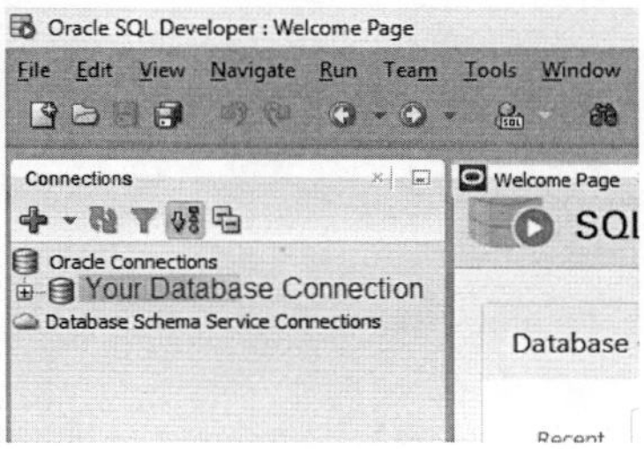

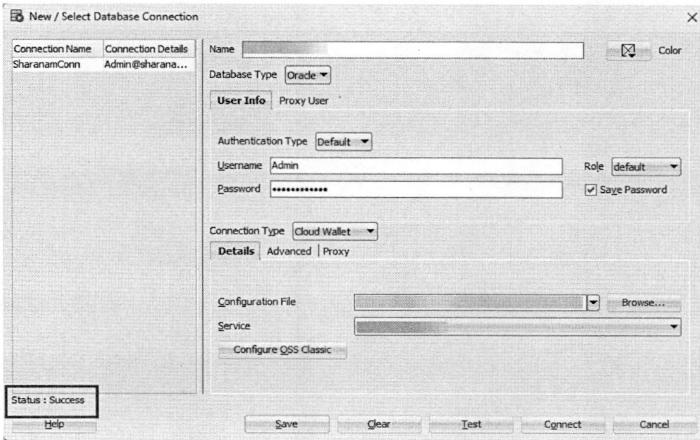

Chapter

34

SECTION VI: CHAT WITH YOUR DATABASE USING SELECT AI

Integrating GenAI With Autonomous Database

Generative **AI** (GenAI) is revolutionizing how we interact with data, enabling the creation of diverse content from text and images to code and music. Its potential for automating content creation, generating insights, and enhancing user experiences is vast. Oracle Autonomous Database, with its self-driving, self-securing, and self-repairing capabilities, provides an ideal platform for integrating and leveraging the power of GenAI.

This chapter explores the integration of GenAI with Oracle Autonomous Database, focusing on using Cohere as the AI provider. We will demonstrate how Oracle's Select AI feature can interact with Cohere's **L**arge **L**anguage **M**odels (LLMs) to generate SQL queries from natural language prompts. While Oracle Autonomous Database supports various AI providers, including Oracle OCI Generative AI, OpenAI, Azure OpenAI Service, Google Gemini, Anthropic Claude, and Hugging Face, this chapter concentrates on Cohere for a focused and in-depth exploration.

Before We Begin: Setting Up Sample Tables

Before we begin, let's create a few sample database tables. We will use these tables as a sample database to try out Select AI commands. To create these tables, use SQL Developer, connect to the database as the Admin user, and execute the following SQL commands.

To create these tables with sample data, you can also use the SQL script file named **SQLOracleForBeginnersAI.sql**, available at:
www.sharanamshah.com/books/oracleforbeginners/bookcodesAI.zip.

```
CREATE TABLE "Specialties" (
   "SpecialtyNo" NUMBER(10,0) NOT NULL ENABLE,
   "Specialty" VARCHAR2(15),
   CONSTRAINT "SPECIALTIES_PK" PRIMARY KEY ("SpecialtyNo") ENABLE);

CREATE TABLE "Authors" (
   "AuthorNo" NUMBER(10,0) NOT NULL ENABLE,
   "AuthorName" VARCHAR2(25),
   "ContactNo" NUMBER(15,0),
   "SpecialtyNo" NUMBER(10,0),
   CONSTRAINT "AUTHORS_PK" PRIMARY KEY ("AuthorNo") ENABLE,
   CONSTRAINT "AUTHORS_SPECIALTIES_FK1" FOREIGN KEY ("SpecialtyNo")
      REFERENCES "Specialties" ("SpecialtyNo") ENABLE);

CREATE TABLE "Publishers" (
   "PublisherNo" NUMBER(10,0) NOT NULL ENABLE,
   "PublisherName" VARCHAR2(25),
   "Address" VARCHAR2(50),
   CONSTRAINT "PUBLISHERS_PK" PRIMARY KEY ("PublisherNo") ENABLE);

CREATE TABLE "Books" (
   "ISBN" VARCHAR2(20) NOT NULL ENABLE,
   "AuthorNo" NUMBER(10,0),
   "BookName" VARCHAR2(50),
   "Cost" NUMBER(12,2),
   "NoOfPages" NUMBER(4,0),
   "NoOfChapters" NUMBER(2,0),
   "PublisherNo" NUMBER(10,0),
   "Category" VARCHAR2(25),
   CONSTRAINT "BOOKS_PK" PRIMARY KEY ("ISBN") ENABLE,
   CONSTRAINT "BOOKS_AUTHORS_FK1" FOREIGN KEY ("AuthorNo")
      REFERENCES "Authors" ("AuthorNo") ENABLE,
   CONSTRAINT "BOOKS_PUBLISHERS_FK1" FOREIGN KEY ("PublisherNo")
      REFERENCES "Publishers" ("PublisherNo") ENABLE);

INSERT INTO Specialties (SpecialtyNo,Specialty) VALUES (1,'Oracle');
INSERT INTO Specialties (SpecialtyNo,Specialty) VALUES (2,'Ajax');
INSERT INTO Specialties (SpecialtyNo,Specialty) VALUES (3,'PHP');
INSERT INTO Specialties (SpecialtyNo,Specialty) VALUES (4,'MySQL');
```

```
INSERT INTO Authors (AuthorNo,AuthorName,ContactNo,SpecialtyNo)
  VALUES (1,'Sharanam Shah',27385653,1);
INSERT INTO Authors (AuthorNo,AuthorName,ContactNo,SpecialtyNo)
  VALUES (2,'Hansel Colaco',74321547,3);
INSERT INTO Authors (AuthorNo,AuthorName,ContactNo,SpecialtyNo)
  VALUES (3,'Vaishali Shah',22356753,4);
INSERT INTO Authors (AuthorNo,AuthorName,ContactNo,SpecialtyNo)
  VALUES (4,'Chaitanya Naik',21324764,2);
INSERT INTO Authors (AuthorNo,AuthorName,ContactNo,SpecialtyNo)
  VALUES (5,'Ashwini Kolapure',27341939,2);
INSERT INTO Authors (AuthorNo,AuthorName,ContactNo,SpecialtyNo)
  VALUES (6,'Daniel Joshua',35793857,1);
INSERT INTO Authors (AuthorNo,AuthorName,ContactNo,SpecialtyNo)
  VALUES (7,'Anil Vaidya',98758362,1);

INSERT INTO Publishers (PublisherNo,PublisherName,Address)
  VALUES (1,'Apress','Berkeley, CA 94710');
INSERT INTO Publishers (PublisherNo,PublisherName,Address)
  VALUES (2,'Wrox','Indianapolis, IN 46256');
INSERT INTO Publishers (PublisherNo,PublisherName,Address)
  VALUES (3,'SPD','Vashi, Mumbai 287502');
INSERT INTO Publishers (PublisherNo,PublisherName,Address)
  VALUES (4,'BpB','Darya Gunj, Delhi 73945');
INSERT INTO Publishers (PublisherNo,PublisherName,Address)
  VALUES (5,'Prentice Hall','Boston, MA 02116');

INSERT INTO Books (ISBN,AuthorNo,BookName,Cost,NoOfPages,NoOfChapters,
  PublisherNo,Category) VALUES ('808-97365-80',6,'Oracle SQL and SQL*Plus',650,1200,
  17,1,'Database');
INSERT INTO Books (ISBN,AuthorNo,BookName,Cost,NoOfPages,NoOfChapters,
  PublisherNo,Category) VALUES ('978-34-13394-1',3,'Professional MySQL',550,900,
  16,4,'Database');
INSERT INTO Books (ISBN,AuthorNo,BookName,Cost,NoOfPages,NoOfChapters,
  PublisherNo,Category) VALUES ('21-783592-1',4,'PHP Tips And Tricks',600,700,
  10,3,'Server Side Scripting');
INSERT INTO Books (ISBN,AuthorNo,BookName,Cost,NoOfPages,NoOfChapters,
  PublisherNo,Category) VALUES ('1-34523-880',2,'Ajax With JSF',750,550,8,2,
  'Server Side Scripting');
INSERT INTO Books (ISBN,AuthorNo,BookName,Cost,NoOfPages,NoOfChapters,
  PublisherNo,Category) VALUES ('783-983242-23',1,'Oracle For Professionals',450,890,
  43,3,'Database');
INSERT INTO Books (ISBN,AuthorNo,BookName,Cost,NoOfPages,NoOfChapters,
  PublisherNo,Category) VALUES ('234-82911-1',1,'Oracle and Data Warehouse and Data
  Mining',250,450,12,3,'Database');
INSERT INTO Books (ISBN,AuthorNo,BookName,Cost,NoOfPages,NoOfChapters,
  PublisherNo,Category) VALUES ('90-987532-234',1,'Professional Projects On PHP And
  Oracle',400,800,19,1,'Project');
INSERT INTO Books (ISBN,AuthorNo,BookName,Cost,NoOfPages,NoOfChapters,
  PublisherNo,Category) VALUES ('2364-90452',3,'Database Concepts',300,600,  27,2,
  'Database');
INSERT INTO Books (ISBN,AuthorNo,BookName,Cost,NoOfPages,NoOfChapters,
  PublisherNo,Category) VALUES ('978-0-470-13394-1',5,'Mastering phpMyAdmin',700,
  1100,13,5,'Database');
```

Output:

```
Table "Specialties" created.
Table "Authors" created.
Table "Publishers" created.
Table "Books" created.
```

Output: (For every Insert statements)

```
1 row inserted.
```

Understanding Select AI And Cohere Integration

Oracle's Select AI simplifies interaction with LLMs for database tasks. It acts as a bridge, allowing users to express their database needs in natural language. Select AI then translates these requests into executable SQL queries using the chosen LLM, in this case, **Cohere**. This integration empowers users of all SQL expertise levels to query and manipulate data within the Autonomous Database.

Cohere provides powerful LLMs well-suited for understanding and generating human-like text, making them ideal for tasks like SQL generation. Integrating Select AI with Cohere allows us to:

- ❑ *Generate SQL:* Convert natural language descriptions of desired data into functional SQL queries.
- ❑ *Explain SQL:* Receive explanations of existing SQL queries in plain English, improving understanding and maintainability.
- ❑ *Chat with the LLM:* Engage in conversational interactions with the LLM to refine queries or explore data.

Using Select AI With Cohere

This section demonstrates how to use Cohere with Select AI to generate SQL statements from natural language prompts. The process involves:

1. *Setting up Cohere Credentials:* Obtain an **API key** from Cohere and configure Select AI to use it. This involves creating an **AI profile** within the **OCI environment** and specifying the Cohere API key.
2. *Creating an AI Profile:* Within OCI, create an AI profile specifically for Cohere. This profile stores the API key and other relevant configuration details.
3. *Using Select AI:* Once the profile is configured, use Select AI through various interfaces, such as SQL Developer Web or a command-line interface, to interact with Cohere.

Setting Up Cohere Credentials

1. Visit **Cohere's website** (www.cohere.ai). Look for a "Sign Up" or "Get Started" button. Cohere typically offers a free trial.

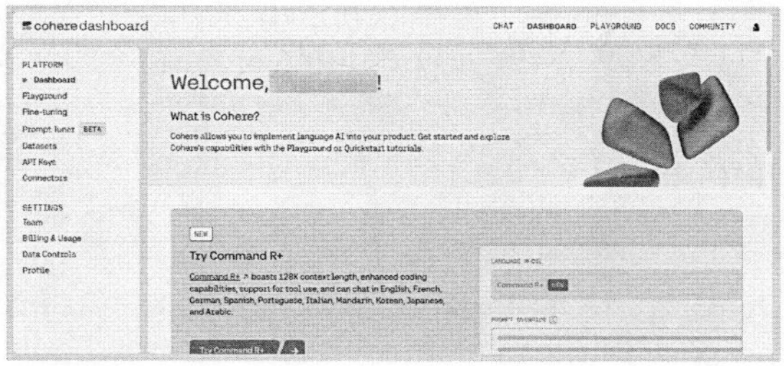

2. Provide the required information and create a **Cohere account**.
3. Once logged in, locate your API key (often found in the **Trial keys** or a similar section). This key is crucial for connecting to Cohere's services. Keep it secure!

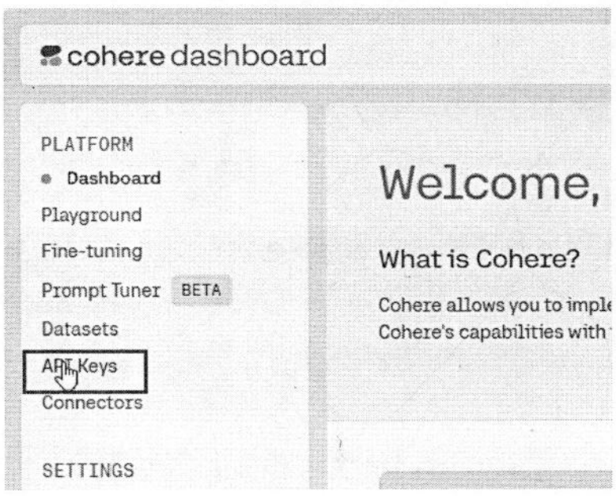

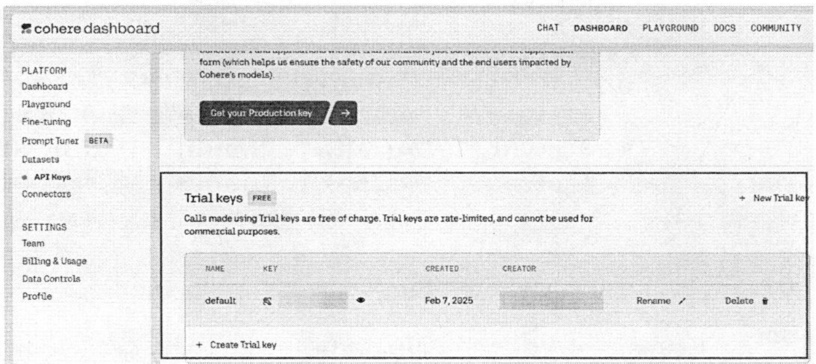

Creating an AI Profile

To leverage the power of Cohere's Large Language Models (LLMs) within your Oracle Autonomous Database using Select AI, you need to create an **AI profile**. This profile securely stores your Cohere API key and grants access to the necessary database tables. Follow these steps using SQL Developer.

Creating a Credential for Cohere: A **credential** in Oracle securely stores your Cohere API key (obtained during signup). This allows Oracle to access your Cohere credentials without exposing the API key directly in your code. Execute the following PL/SQL block in SQL Developer:

```
BEGIN
  DBMS_CLOUD.CREATE_CREDENTIAL(
     CREDENTIAL_NAME => '<A descriptive name (e.g., 'Cohere_CRED'>',
```

```
    username => '<Your Cohere username (typically your email)>',
    password => '<Your Cohere API Key>');
END;
/
```

Replace <A descriptive name>, <Your Cohere Username', and<'Your Cohere API Key> with your actual values. Keep your API key secure.

Output:

```
PL/SQL procedure successfully completed.
```

Creating the AI Profile: Next, create the AI profile, linking it to the credential you just created and specifying the tables (e.g., Authors, Books, Publishers, Specialties) that the AI will have access to. Execute the following PL/SQL block:

```
BEGIN
  DBMS_CLOUD_AI.CREATE_PROFILE(
    profile_name => '<A descriptive name (e.g., 'Cohere_Profile')>',
    attributes => '{"provider": "cohere",
      "credential_name": "< Your Credential Name>",
      "object_list": [{"owner": "ADMIN", "name": "AUTHORS"},
        {"owner": "ADMIN", "name": "BOOKS"},
        {"owner": "ADMIN", "name": "PUBLISHERS"},
        {"owner": "ADMIN", "name": "SPECIALITIES"}]
    }');
END;
/
```

Replace <A descriptive name> with a descriptive name. Ensure that <Your Credential Name> matches the name you used in the previous step. The **object_list** specifies the database tables the AI profile has access to. Adjust this list as needed. You can update the list later by updating the profile. Refer to *Managing AI Profiles And Credentials* chapter for more details. The **owner** is typically ADMIN for Autonomous Databases.

Output:

```
PL/SQL procedure successfully completed.
```

Finally, set the **current database session** to use the newly created AI profile. This activates the profile and allows you to use Select AI with Cohere. Execute the following:

```
EXEC DBMS_CLOUD_AI.SET_PROFILE('<Your AI Profile Name>');
```

Output:

```
PL/SQL procedure successfully completed.
```

Replace <Your AI Profile Name> with the name of the AI profile you created.

With the AI profile configured, you can now use natural language prompts within your SQL queries to interact with your data through Select AI. For example, you can use natural language to generate SQL queries, explain data, and perform other AI-powered tasks directly within your Oracle Autonomous Database.

Testing Select AI with Cohere: A First Example

With your AI profile configured, let's dive into a practical example of using Select AI with Cohere. We'll use a simple query against a hypothetical Authors table to illustrate the process.

Imagine you have an Authors table with columns like AuthorNo, AuthorName, and ContactNo. You want to find the names and contact numbers of authors whose contact numbers start with the digit '9'. Instead of writing a complex SQL query directly, you can use a natural language prompt like this:

```
SELECT AI Find the name and contact number of authors whose contact number
starts with 9
```

In SQL Developer, you would typically type or paste the above SELECT AI ... statement directly into the **SQL Worksheet** and run it. SQL Developer would then handle the interaction with Cohere and the database execution, showing you the final result set.

How it Works:

1. ***Prompt Submission:*** You enter this natural language prompt into SQL Developer.
2. ***Cohere Processing:*** Select AI sends this prompt to Cohere's LLM.
3. ***SQL Generation:*** Cohere interprets the natural language and generates the equivalent SQL query. In this case, it might produce something like:

```
SELECT AuthorName, ContactNo FROM Authors WHERE ContactNo LIKE '9%';
```

4. ***Query Execution:*** Select AI then executes this generated SQL query against your Oracle Autonomous Database.
5. ***Results Display:*** The results of the query (the author names and contact numbers matching the criteria) are displayed in SQL Developer, just as if you had written the SQL query yourself.

This simple example demonstrates the core concept. Select AI and Cohere can handle much more complex scenarios. You can use longer, more descriptive natural language prompts to generate more sophisticated SQL queries involving joins, aggregations, filtering, and other database operations.

This makes interacting with your data more intuitive, especially for those less familiar with SQL syntax. The real power of Select AI lies in its ability to translate your natural language requests into the precise SQL needed to retrieve the information you're looking for.

Chapter

35

SECTION VI: CHAT WITH YOUR DATABASE USING SELECT AI

Using Select AI For Natural Language Interaction With The Database

Oracle Database 23ai introduces **Select AI** - a **powerful tool** that enables you to interact with your data using natural language prompts. Instead of writing SQL queries manually, you can simply ask questions or provide commands in plain language, and Select AI translates them into SQL. This chapter explains the key concepts, supported actions, use cases, and practical examples using your database schema.

Overview Of Oracle 23ai And Select AI

Oracle 23ai brings **artificial intelligence** directly into the database. **Select AI** is one of these capabilities, designed to simplify data querying and application development. With Select AI, you can:

- Generate and run SQL from natural language prompts.
- See the generated SQL (using the "showsql" action).

- Get natural language explanations of your queries (using "narrate" and "explainsql").
- Engage in a conversational mode (using "chat") to explore your data interactively.
- Augment responses with domain-specific information via **R**etrieval **A**ugmented **G**eneration (RAG).
- Generate synthetic data for testing and development.

These features help both developers and nontechnical users work directly with data in a more intuitive way

Natural Language Prompts And The AI Keyword

At the heart of Select AI is the ability to use natural language in your SQL statements. By including the keyword **AI** in your SELECT statements, you tell Oracle that you are providing a prompt to be interpreted by LLM. This allows you to bypass traditional SQL syntax in favor of plain language requests. For example, instead of writing complex SQL code, you might write:

```
SELECT AI How many books are available
```

and the system will translate your prompt into a valid SQL query:

```
SELECT COUNT(*) FROM Books;
```

Examples Using The Provided Tables

Let's consider the sample tables (Authors, Books, Publishers, Specialties) created in the earlier chapter.

Querying Data From Natural Language

One of the primary uses of SELECT AI is to retrieve data from the database. Developers can quickly get **"starter" queries** generated by simply describing what they need.

For example, you want the total number of authors:

```
SELECT AI How many authors are listed
```

	AUTHORCOUNT
1	7

and the system converts it to a SQL query that counts the authors in the Authors table.

Non-technical users can interact with the database using plain language. Instead of writing SQL, they ask questions like:

```
SELECT AI List the names of the publishers along with their addresses
```

	PUBLISHERNAME	ADDRESS
1	Apress	Berkeley, CA 94710
2	Wrox	Indianapolis, IN 46256
3	SPD	Vashi, Mumbai 287502
4	BpB	Darya Gunj, Delhi 73945
5	Prentice Hall	Boston, MA 02116

and receive data without needing to know SQL syntax.

Data Analysis

SELECT AI can assist in performing **data analysis**. For instance, if you want to know the average cost of books published by a specific publisher, just ask:

```
SELECT AI What is the average cost of books published by SPD
```

SELECT AI Translation:

```
SELECT AVG(Cost) FROM Books
  WHERE PublisherNo = (SELECT PublisherNo FROM Publishers
      WHERE PublisherName = 'SPD');
```

By using natural language, you can significantly reduce the complexity of data analysis and make it more accessible to a wider audience. This allows you to focus on gaining insights from your data rather than struggling with SQL syntax.

Data Aggregation

Select AI simplifies **data aggregation**, allowing you to perform calculations on groups of data using natural language. Instead of writing complex SQL with GROUP BY and aggregate functions, you can express your aggregation requirements in plain English.

Let's say you want to determine the number of books written by each author. Using Select AI, you can ask:

```
SELECT AI How many books has each author written
```

SELECT AI Translation:

```
SELECT AuthorName, COUNT(BookName) FROM Authors
  JOIN Books ON (Authors.AuthorNo = Books.AuthorNo) GROUP BY AuthorName;
```

Filtering and Sorting

Select AI makes **filtering and sorting data** incredibly straightforward using natural language. You can express your filtering and sorting criteria in plain English, and Select AI will translate them into the corresponding SQL.

SELECT AI allows you to filter and sort results easily. Let's say you want to retrieve all books that have more than 1000 pages and sort the results by their cost:

```
SELECT AI Show me all the books with more than 1000 pages, sorted by cost
```

SELECT AI Translation:

```
SELECT BookName, Cost FROM Books WHERE NoOfPages > 1000
  ORDER BY Cost;
```

Joining Tables

Select AI dramatically simplifies the process of **joining tables** in your database. Instead of writing complex SQL JOIN statements, you can express the join relationship in natural language, making it much easier to retrieve data from multiple related tables. Let's say you have two tables: Authors and Specialties. You want to retrieve a list of author names along with their respective specialties. With Select AI, you can simply ask:

```
SELECT AI Show me the names of authors and their respective specialties
```

SELECT AI Translation:

```
SELECT AuthorName, Specialty FROM Authors
  JOIN Specialties ON Authors.SpecialtyNo = Specialties.SpecialtyNo;
```

Multi-Table Queries

You can perform **complex queries involving multiple tables**. Let's say you want to retrieve a list of author names, the titles of their books, and the names of the publishers who published those books. With Select AI, you can ask:

```
SELECT AI List the names of authors with their books and publishers
```

SELECT AI Translation:

```
SELECT Authors.AuthorName, Books.BookName, Publishers.PublisherName
  FROM Authors JOIN Books ON Authors.AuthorNo = Books.AuthorNo
  JOIN Publishers ON Books.PublisherNo = Publishers.PublisherNo;
```

Generating And Running A Query

The **default** behavior of Select AI, known as the **runsql** action, is to seamlessly translate your natural language requests into SQL queries and execute them directly against your database. This allows you to get results quickly and easily without needing to write any SQL yourself.

Here's how to use it within SQL Developer:

1. Open a SQL Worksheet:

In SQL Developer, open a new SQL Worksheet. You can do this by going to **File > New > SQL Worksheet** or by right-clicking on a connection in the Connections pane and selecting "Open SQL Worksheet."

2. Enter Your Natural Language Query:

In the SQL Worksheet, type or paste your natural language query, making sure to begin it with SELECT AI. For example:

```
SELECT AI How many books are there
```

Click the "Run Script" button (the green play icon) or press F5.

SQL Developer will send your natural language query to Select AI, which will:

1. Translate it into an SQL query (e.g., SELECT COUNT(*) FROM Books;).
2. **Automatically** execute the generated SQL query against your connected database.
3. Display the results directly in the "Script Output" tab of the SQL Worksheet. You'll see the count of books returned, just as if you had written and run the SQL query yourself.

Important Considerations:

- *Database Connection:* Ensure you have a valid database connection established in SQL Developer before running the query. Select AI needs this connection to execute the generated SQL.
- *Schema Awareness:* Select AI relies on the database schema to correctly translate your natural language into SQL. If your schema is complex or ambiguous, you might need to provide more context in your natural language query.
- *Error Handling:* If Select AI cannot understand your natural language or if there's an issue with the database connection or schema, you'll see an error message in the Script Output tab.

By following these steps, you can easily use Select AI's **runsql** action within SQL Developer to query your database using natural language, making data retrieval and analysis much more efficient and accessible.

Displaying The Generated SQL

While the runsql action automatically executes the generated SQL, sometimes you want to see the SQL query that Select AI creates from your natural language prompt. This is where the **showsql** action comes in. It allows you to inspect the generated SQL before it's executed, which is particularly helpful for learning SQL, understanding how Select AI works, and debugging complex queries.

Let's say you want to see the SQL generated for the following natural language request:

```
SELECT AI showsql list all authors with their books
```

This might produce:

	RESPONSE
1	SELECT a."AUTHORNAME" , b."BOOKNAME" FROM ADMIN."AUTHORS" a JOIN ADMIN."BOOKS" b ON a."AUTHORNO" = b."AUTHORNO"

Instead of executing the query, Select AI displays the generated SQL in the output area of SQL Developer (typically the "**Script Output**" **tab**). You can then examine the SQL, copy it, modify it, or execute it manually if you wish.

This is also useful for **Debugging**. If a query doesn't produce the expected results, showsql allows you to inspect the generated SQL and identify potential issues. You can then modify the SQL and run it manually.

Getting A Narrative Explanation

The **narrate** action in Select AI provides a natural language explanation or summary of the **results** of a query, rather than the query itself. This is incredibly useful for quickly understanding the meaning of query results, especially for complex queries or when sharing results with non-technical users.

Let's say you want to know how many publishers are in your database and want the answer explained in plain English. You can use the narrate action like this:

```
SELECT AI narrate how many publishers are in the database
```

The system response:

```
RESPONSE
There are five publishers in the database. This means that five different
publisher records are stored in the table "PUBLISHERS".
```

The narrate action makes it easy to understand the meaning of query results without having to interpret raw data. You can easily share query results with non-technical users by providing the natural language narrative.

Conversational Querying

The **chat** action in Select AI enables a conversational, interactive approach to data exploration. It allows you to ask follow-up questions, request clarifications, and refine your queries in a back-and-forth manner, much like a conversation with a data expert.

Let's start with a simple question:

```
SELECT AI chat What is the capital of India
```

This facilitates an interactive, step-by-step approach to data exploration:

```
RESPONSE
The capital of India is New Delhi. New Delhi is a city located in the
northern part of the Indian subcontinent. It was officially declared the
capital of India in 1931 and has a rich history and cultural heritage.
New Delhi is known for its historical monuments, museums, and cultural
attractions, making it a popular tourist destination...
```

Explaining SQL Behind A Query

The **explainsql** action in Select AI provides a plain-language explanation of a generated SQL query, breaking down each part of the query for clarity. This is invaluable for understanding how Select AI translates your natural language requests into SQL, learning SQL syntax, and debugging complex queries.

Let's say you want to understand the SQL generated for the following natural language request:

```
SELECT AI explainsql how many books are available with 'Oracle' as its name
```

The system returns:

```
SELECT COUNT(*) num_books_with_oracle_name FROM ADMIN.Books
  WHERE BookName LIKE '%Oracle%';
```

Instead of executing the query, Select AI provides a step-by-step explanation of the generated SQL in plain language. For the example above, the explanation might be:

```
1. The SQL query retrieves the count of books with names containing the
phrase "Oracle" using the 'COUNT(*)' function...
2. The 'FROM' clause specifies the source table, which is the 'BOOKS'
table in the 'ADMIN' schema...
3. In the 'WHERE' clause, the condition 'BOOKNAME LIKE '%Oracle%''
filters the rows...
```

The explainsql action is excellent for learning SQL syntax and how natural language maps to SQL concepts. It allows you to see how Select AI interprets your requests and generates SQL. If a query doesn't produce the expected results, the explainsql action can help you identify potential issues in the generated SQL.

Synthetic Data Generation

Select AI provides the capability to generate synthetic data that mirrors the structure and statistical properties of your real data. This is incredibly useful for testing, development, demonstrations, and training purposes, especially when working with sensitive information. By using synthetic data, you can protect confidential data while still having realistic datasets for experimentation.

Select AI leverages functions like those found within the DBMS_CLOUD_AI package to generate synthetic rows that conform to your existing database schema.

To generate synthetic records for the Authors table, execute the following PL/SQL block in SQL Developer:

```
BEGIN
```

```
    DBMS_CLOUD_AI.GENERATE_SYNTHETIC_DATA(
        profile_name => '<Your AI Profile>',
        object_name  => 'Authors',
        record_count => 10
);
END;
/
```

Replace <Your AI Profile> with the actual name of the AI profile you created earlier. This profile should have access to the Authors table.

This PL/SQL block will generate 10 synthetic author records. These records will have the same columns (e.g., AuthorNo, AuthorName, ContactNo, etc.) as your real Authors table, and the data within those columns will be generated to resemble the distribution and characteristics of your actual author data.

You can use the same **DBMS_CLOUD_AI.GENERATE_SYNTHETIC_DATA** function to generate synthetic data for other tables, such as Books, Publishers, and Specialties. Simply change the **object_name** parameter to the name of the table you want to generate synthetic data for.

Using the GENERATE_SYNTHETIC_DATA function you can protect sensitive real data by using synthetic data for development, testing, and demonstrations. You can test your applications and queries with data that resembles your production data, ensuring realistic performance and behavior. Experiment with new queries and data transformations without risking your real data. You can easily share synthetic datasets with others without compromising sensitive information.

RAG For Enhanced Responses

Retrieval-**A**ugmented **G**eneration (RAG) is a powerful technique employed by Select AI to provide more accurate, relevant, and comprehensive answers to your natural language queries. It combines the strengths of information retrieval from your database with the generative capabilities of **L**arge **L**anguage **M**odels (LLMs). This approach significantly reduces the risk of "**hallucinations**" (where LLMs generate incorrect or fabricated information) by grounding the LLM's response in your actual data.

Here's how RAG works within Select AI:

1. ***Embedding Generation:*** When you provide a natural language prompt, Select AI first generates vector embeddings for your prompt. These embeddings are numerical representations capturing the semantic meaning of your query.

2. ***Semantic Similarity Search:*** Select AI uses these embeddings to perform a semantic similarity search against a pre-built vector index. This index stores vector embeddings of your data (e.g., chunks of text from documents, structured data from tables, etc.). The search identifies the most relevant data or documents based on their semantic similarity to your prompt.
3. ***Information Retrieval:*** The search retrieves the most relevant data or documents from your database. This ensures that the LLM has access to the specific context needed to answer your query accurately.
4. ***Contextualized Prompt:*** Select AI combines the retrieved contextual information (the relevant data) with your original natural language prompt. This enriched prompt is then sent to the LLM.
5. ***Response Generation:*** The LLM generates a response based on both your prompt and the retrieved context. Because the LLM is grounded in your actual data, the response is much more likely to be accurate and relevant.

Let's say you ask:

```
SELECT AI Tell me the names of authors who specialize in Oracle and the titles of
their books
```

Without RAG, the LLM might give you a generic list of Oracle authors and books, potentially making up authors or titles. With RAG, Select AI does the following:

1. ***Embeddings:*** Creates embeddings for "Tell me the names of authors who specialize in Oracle and the titles of their books."
2. ***Similarity Search:*** Searches the vector index for data related to "Oracle", "authors", and "books".
3. ***Retrieval:*** Retrieves relevant data. This could involve retrieving the results of the following SQL query (or similar, depending on vectorization and indexing strategy):

```
SELECT a.AuthorName, b.BookName FROM Authors a
  JOIN Specialties s ON a.SpecialtyNo = s.SpecialtyNo
  JOIN Books b ON a.AuthorNo = b.AuthorNo
     WHERE UPPER(s.Specialty) = UPPER('Oracle')
```

4. ***Contextualized Prompt:*** Combines the original prompt with the retrieved data (the results of the query).
5. ***Response:*** The LLM, now grounded in the specific data from your database, generates a response like:

Authors specializing in Oracle and their books include:

	AUTHORNAME	BOOKNAME
1	Sharanam Shah	Mastering Oracle SQL
2	Daniel Joshua	Big Data and Analytics
3	Anil Vaidya	Cybersecurity Essentials
4	Daniel Joshua	Oracle SQL and SQL*Plus

... (and other authors and books from your database)

By using RAG, Select AI provides more accurate and reliable responses because the LLM's knowledge is augmented with your specific data. This is especially important when dealing with domain-specific information or when accuracy is critical. It bridges the gap between the general knowledge of LLMs and the specific data within your database, ensuring responses are relevant to your data.

Data Manipulation with Select AI: Indirect Approach

While Oracle 23's Select AI feature excels at querying data using natural language, it does *not* directly support **D**ata **M**anipulation **L**anguage (DML) commands like INSERT, UPDATE, and DELETE.

Select AI's primary focus is on data retrieval, analysis, summarization, and insight generation through natural language interaction.

However, Select AI can still play a crucial role in data manipulation by providing the information and insights needed to construct separate DML statements within your application logic. Think of Select AI as your intelligent assistant for **understanding** what data needs to be changed, while you handle the **how** of the changes using standard SQL.

Here's a breakdown of how you can use Select AI for data manipulation, using the provided table schema:

1. **No Direct DML:** Select AI itself does not have built-in commands for directly inserting, updating, or deleting rows. It's designed for querying, not modifying, data.
2. **Generate Insights and Information:** Leverage Select AI to analyze your data and identify what needs to be changed. Use natural language prompts to generate summaries, discover relevant data patterns, or extract specific information. For example:
   a. This could help identify authors whose books might need updating (e.g., new editions).

```
SELECT AI List all authors who specialize in 'Oracle' and their no of pages are less than 500
```

   b. This could inform decisions about which publishers to work with.

```
SELECT AI Show me the top 5 publishers by the average cost of books they publish
```

   c. This could be used to identify books that need price adjustments or other updates.

```
SELECT AI Which books have a 'Database' category and were published by 'SPD'
```

3. **Create Separate SQL Statements:** Based on the insights and information retrieved using Select AI, construct standard SQL INSERT, UPDATE, or DELETE statements **within your application code**.

For example: Updating the "Category" of books based on Select AI insights (conceptual)

a. Use Select AI to get the ISBNs of books needing category updates:

```
let booksToUpdate = execute "SELECT AI Which books have a 'Database' category
and were published by 'SPD'"
```

b. Loop through the results and construct UPDATE statements:

```
for each book in booksToUpdate {
  execute 'UPDATE Books SET Category = 'Oracle Database'
      WHERE ISBN = '${book.ISBN}';'
}
```

Select AI helps you **determine** what changes need to be made, but you implement those changes using standard SQL. The actual INSERT, UPDATE, and DELETE statements are written and executed within your application's logic, ***not*** directly through Select AI.

This chapter has equipped you with the knowledge and practical skills to harness the transformative power of Oracle Database 23's Select AI. From understanding the fundamental concepts to mastering advanced techniques like RAG and synthetic data generation, you've explored how natural language can bridge the gap between human intention and database interaction.

As you move forward, remember that Select AI is more than just a tool; it's a paradigm shift in how we approach data. By embracing conversational querying, leveraging schema metadata, and combining Select AI with traditional SQL, you can unlock new levels of efficiency, accessibility, and insight. The future of data interaction is intelligent, intuitive, and collaborative, and with Select AI in your toolkit, you're ready to shape that future.

Chapter

36

SECTION VI: CHAT WITH YOUR DATABASE USING SELECT AI

Managing AI Profiles And Credentials

Oracle Database 23 integrates powerful **A**rtificial **I**ntelligence (AI) capabilities directly into the database, enabling natural language interactions through **Select AI** queries. Two key components are essential for effectively utilizing this functionality:

- ***Credentials:*** These securely store the **API keys** or other authentication details required for accessing external cloud services, including the LLM provider. Credentials act as the secure passwords that allow Select AI to connect to the external services.
- ***AI Profiles:*** These define the connection details to external LLM providers and specify the database objects (tables, views, etc.) that the LLM can use to generate SQL queries. Think of an AI profile as the configuration that tells Select AI **how** to interact with the LLM and **what** data it can access.

This chapter provides a comprehensive guide to creating, viewing, updating, and managing AI profiles and credentials, ensuring you can effectively leverage the power of Select AI.

Managing Credentials For AI Access

Credentials securely store API keys and authentication details required for communicating with external AI providers. They act as the **passwords** that allow Select AI to access these services. Credentials are managed using the DBMS_CLOUD package.

Creating a Credential

Use the **DBMS_CLOUD.CREATE_CREDENTIAL** procedure to create a new credential:

```
BEGIN
  DBMS_CLOUD.CREATE_CREDENTIAL(
      credential_name => '<Your Credential Name>',
      username => '<Username used while siging up AI>',
      password => '<Password>'
  );
END;
/
```

> Replace the placeholder values with your actual credential name, username, and API key. Keep your API keys secure.

This procedure encrypts and stores the credential within the database. You'll reference this credential by name in your AI profile.

Viewing Existing Credentials

To view existing credentials, query the ALL_CREDENTIALS view:

```
SELECT credential_name, username, comments FROM all_credentials;
```

Deleting A Credential

If your API token changes, or if you want to remove an outdated credential, use the corresponding procedures such as **DBMS_CLOUD.DROP_CREDENTIAL:**

```
BEGIN
  DBMS_CLOUD.DROP_CREDENTIAL('<Credential Name to be Deleted>');
END;
/
```

What Are AI Profiles?

An **AI profile** in Oracle 23 is a **JSON-formatted configuration** that instructs the database on how to translate natural language prompts into SQL queries. It acts as the **bridge** between your natural language requests and the structured data in your database.

Key components of an AI profile include:

- ***Provider Information:*** Specifies the LLM provider to use (e.g., *"provider": "cohere"*). This tells Select AI which LLM service to connect to.
- ***Credential Reference:*** Indicates the name of the credential containing the API key or other authentication details (e.g., *"credential_name": "COHEREAI_CRED"*). This links the profile to the secure credentials required for authentication.
- ***Object List:*** A JSON array that lists the database objects (tables, views) that the LLM can access when generating SQL queries. This controls the scope of data that the LLM can use. For example:

```
"object_list": [
   {"owner": "ADMIN", "name": "Authors"},
   {"owner": "ADMIN", "name": "Books"},
   {"owner": "ADMIN", "name": "Publishers"}
]
```

- ***Additional Parameters (Optional):*** May include parameters such as token limits, model-specific attributes, or other settings specific to the LLM provider.

Using the DBMS_CLOUD_AI package, you can create, update, and enable these profiles. Once an AI profile is set for a database session, you can use natural language commands (with the SELECT AI syntax) to generate SQL queries that utilize the profile's metadata. This allows you to interact with your data using natural language, simplifying complex database interactions.

Creating And Enabling An AI Profile

AI profiles are created using the **DBMS_CLOUD_AI.CREATE_PROFILE** procedure.

For example, suppose you want to create a profile named cohereAI that uses the Cohere provider and exposes four objects from schema ADMIN:

```
BEGIN
   DBMS_CLOUD_AI.CREATE_PROFILE(
        profile_name => 'cohereAI',
        attributes => '{
             "provider": "cohere",
             "credential_name": "cohereAI_CRED",
```

```
            "object_list": [
                {"owner": "ADMIN", "name": "Specialties"},
                {"owner": "ADMIN", "name": "Authors"},
                {"owner": "ADMIN", "name": "Publishers"},
                {"owner": "ADMIN", "name": "Books"}
            ]
        }',
        status => 'enabled',
        description => 'AI profile to generate SQL using Cohere'
    );
END;
/
```

In this example:

- The **attributes** parameter contains a JSON string that defines the LLM provider (cohere), the credential name (cohereAI_CRED), and the list of database objects (tables) that the LLM can access. *The credential cohereAI_CRED must have already been created.*
- The **status** is set to enabled, making the profile active immediately.
- The **description** provides a helpful description of the profile.

Enabling the Profile for Your Session

After creating the profile, you **must** enable it for your current session using the following command:

```
EXEC DBMS_CLOUD_AI.SET_PROFILE('cohereAI');
```

This step is required for each new session where you want to use the profile.

Updating AI Profiles: Modifying the Object List

Your database schema might evolve over time. To keep your AI profile up-to-date, you can modify its attributes, especially the object_list, using the **DBMS_CLOUD_AI.SET_ATTRIBUTE** procedure. For example, to add a new table named KnowledgeBase:

```
BEGIN
  DBMS_CLOUD_AI.SET_ATTRIBUTE(
      profile_name => 'cohereAI',
      attribute_name => 'object_list',
      attribute_value => '[
              {"owner": "ADMIN", "name": "Specialties"},
              {"owner": "ADMIN", "name": "Authors"},
              {"owner": "ADMIN", "name": "Publishers"},
              {"owner": "ADMIN", "name": "Books"},
              {"owner": "ADMIN", "name": "KnowledgeBase"}
```

```
        ]'
   );
END;
/
```

This command **replaces** the entire object_list. If you need to add to the existing list, you should first retrieve the current list (using dictionary views, as described below), modify it, and then use SET_ATTRIBUTE to update the profile.

Viewing Existing AI Profiles

To view existing AI profiles, query the **USER_CLOUD_AI_PROFILES** view:

```
SELECT profile_name, status, description FROM user_cloud_ai_profiles;
```

This query returns the names, statuses, and descriptions of all AI profiles in your schema.

You can view the active profile attributes (including the object list) by querying views such as *USER_CLOUD_AI_PROFILE_ATTRIBUTES* or *DBA_CLOUD_AI_PROFILE_ATTRIBUTES* (depending on your privileges).

Deleting AI Profiles

To delete an AI profile, use the **DBMS_CLOUD_AI.DROP_PROFILE** procedure.

Example:

```
BEGIN
   DBMS_CLOUD_AI.DROP_PROFILE(profile_name => '<Your AI Profile Name>');
END;
/
```

If the profile does not exist, this command will raise an error. To suppress this error and force the deletion, set the force parameter to **TRUE:**

```
BEGIN
   DBMS_CLOUD_AI.DROP_PROFILE(
        profile_name => '<Your AI Profile Name>',
        force => TRUE);
END;
/
```

Using Select AI With Updated Profiles

After creating or updating your AI profile and ensuring the necessary credentials are in place, you can use Select AI. Remember to set the active profile for your session:

```
EXEC DBMS_CLOUD_AI.SET_PROFILE('cohereAI');
```

Then, you can use natural language queries:

```
SELECT AI How many urls are there in the knowledgebase
```

AI profiles and credentials work together to enable natural language querying with Select AI. By effectively managing these components, you ensure that Select AI uses the most current metadata and credentials, facilitating efficient and accurate natural language interaction with your database.

Index

U